THE TRIUMPH OF IMPERFECTION

THE TRIUMPH OF IMPERFECTION

The Silver Age of Sociocultural Moderation in Europe, 1815–1848

VIRGIL NEMOIANU

UNIVERSITY OF SOUTH CAROLINA PRESS

© 2006 University of South Carolina

Published in Columbia, South Carolina,
by the University of South Carolina Press

Manufactured in the United States of America

10 09 08 07 06   5 4 3 2 1

Library of Congress Cataloging-in-Publication Data

Nemoianu, Virgil.
  The triumph of imperfection : the silver age of sociocultural moderation in Europe, 1815–1848 / Virgil Nemoianu.
    p. cm.
  Includes bibliographical references and index.
  ISBN 1-57003-593-8 (cloth : alk. paper)
  1. European literature—19th century—History and criticism. 2. Romanticism—Europe. 3. Europe—Intellectual life—19th century. I. Title.
  PN751.N453 2005
  809'.9145—dc22

                                                        2005020247

A short article comprising sections from chapters 1 and 7 was published in Romania as "Displaced Images," *Synthesis* 19 (1993): 3–10. Chapters 2 and 3 were originally published in *Interpreting Goethe's Faust Today*, ed. Jane Brown et al. (Columbia, S.C.: Camden House, 1994), 1–16, and *Modern Language Studies* 31, no. 1 (Spring 2001): 45–58, respectively. Versions of chapter 5 were published in Germany as "The Dialectics of Diversity," *Arcadia* 31 (1996): 127–45, and in South Africa as "Relativising Cultural Relativism," *Journal of Literary Studies* 11 (December 1995): 3–4, 19–42. Brief fragments of chapters 6 and 11 originally appeared in *Romantic Non-Fictional Prose*, ed. Steven Sondrup and Virgil Nemoianu (Amsterdam: John Benjamins, 2003). A version of what is now chapter 9 appeared originally in Angela Esterhammer, ed., *Romantic Poetry* (Amsterdam: John Benjamins, 2002), 249–55. Chapter 10 appeared in slightly different form in Germany as *Festschrift für Horst Mellen*, ed. Michael Gassenmeier et al. (Heidelberg: Carl Winter, 1998), 223–39, and in the United States as *Romanticism across the Disciplines*, ed. Larry Peer (Lanham, Md.: University Press of America), 187–205. Chapter 8 was originally published in Holland in *Cultural Participation*, ed. Ann Rigney and Douwe Fokkema (Amsterdam: John Benjamins, 1993), 79–97. A few paragraphs of chapter 5 were first used in "Globalism, Multiculturalism, and Comparative Literature," *CNL World Report* (1996): 43–73.

For Martin and Martina, with love

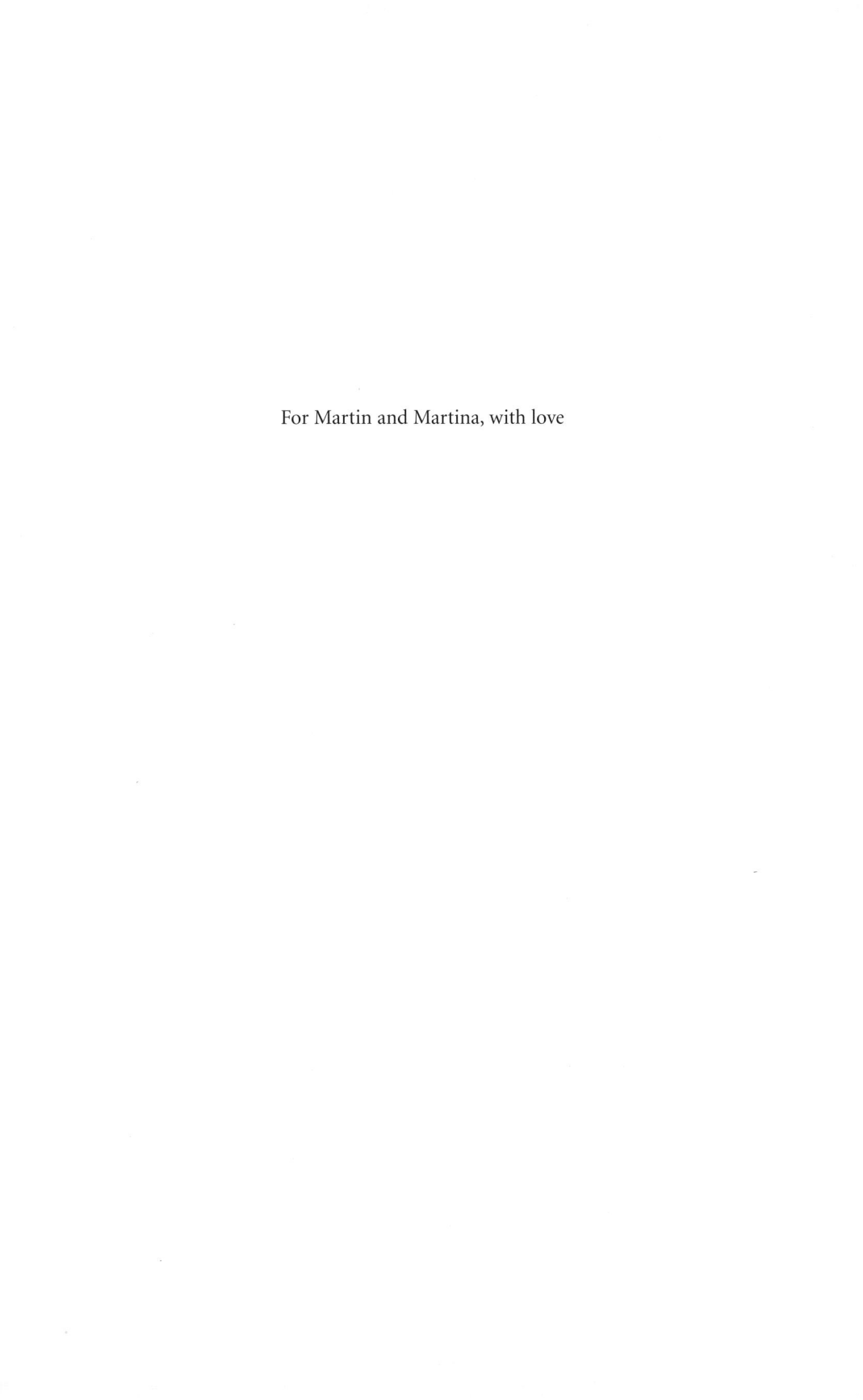

CONTENTS

Preface *ix*
Acknowledgments *xiii*

PART I Center, Margin, Absence

1 The Absent Center of Romantic Prose: Chateaubriand and His Peers *3*

PART II History: From Politics to Religion

2 Absorbing Modernization: The Dilemmas of Progress in Goethe's *Faust II* *37*
3 From Goethe to Guizot: The Conservative Contexts of Goethe's *Wilhelm Meisters Wanderjahre* *53*
4 From Historical Narrative to Fiction and Back: A Dialectical Game *64*
5 J. F. Cooper and Eastern European and African American Intellectuals: Borders and Depths of Multiculturalism *85*
6 Sacrality and Aesthetics in the Early Nineteenth Century: A Network Approach *111*

PART III Information: The Moderating Force

7 The Informative Narration: From Cultural Packaging to Psychological Geography *135*
8 Learning over Class: The Case of the Central-European Ethos *175*
9 National Poets in the Romantic Age: Emergence and Importance *203*
10 The Conservatism of Voracious Reading: The Case of Robert Southey's *The Doctor* *212*

PART IV Conclusions?

11 Romanticism: Beginnings, Explosion, Epidemic *231*

Index *253*

Preface

In 1985 I published a book titled *The Taming of Romanticism: European Literature and the Age of Biedermeier,* which received the Harry Levin Award from the American Comparative Literature Association and numerous favorable reviews. That book was devoted almost exclusively to literature proper (with some philosophical and morpho-cultural elements). In it I set out to show that most of what we usually call romanticism actually consists of poetic realism, or toned-down romanticism (often called in central Europe "Biedermeier"), for the simple reason that a pure and consistent romanticism could not be sustained for longer periods of time, as overwhelming ideals and absolute claims tend to self-destruct. In fact, it would not be wrong to say that the book's chief contribution was to establish and/or reinforce the distinction between high romanticism and low romanticism. The former refers chiefly to the period 1790–1815, the latter to the years 1815–1848. In the book I described high romanticism as nothing short of a revolutionary attempt to regenerate the human race, with the utopian goal of reestablishing an alleged original unity between reason and emotion, nature and civilization, the warring social classes, God and humanity, and the inner and the outer layers of the person. Low romanticism (or *Biedermeier*) I described as a period in which thinkers and writers tended to renounce such lofty or cosmic aims and to propose instead partial solutions (such as individual perfectioning, the "paradise" of hearth and family, social and/or national improvements), or even ironized high romantic accomplishments.

The present volume deals with discourses placed at the margins of literature proper: travel literature, historiography, religious writings, education, political topics, multicultural concerns. They all belong to the same (Biedermeier) period. The perspective put forward in this book deals with a value judgment of romanticism in its dialectic with tradition. I now believe—and I am not sure whether this was entirely clear from the *Taming of Romanticism*—that in the best romantic writing we recognize a certain complementarity with "traditional" literature. In fact the best and most durable romantics are in just such a relation of complementarity, rather than one of adversity and total difference, with earlier literature. That is the reason why Goethe, Schiller, Humboldt, Chateaubriand, Scott, Keats, and even Hölderlin and Novalis can be called romantic at all. Mario Praz brilliantly outlines the features of a romanticism devoid of such dialectic ties—of a romanticism, therefore, that concentrates almost exclusively on its differences with prior literary traditions. By contrast, even some very eloquent or pugnacious romantics (including the Schlegel brothers, for instance) sought complements in their predecessors, and specifically proposed alternative canons that would include Dante, Shakespeare, Cervantes, and similar luminaries. What low romanticism does after 1815 is to emphasize (with a vengeance!) the much more limited aims of a romanticism that does not want to abandon its own identity yet rejects equally deconstruction, relativism, or a total break with the past, in favor of a creative continuity.

As a consequence, my main dissident suggestion is that in my earlier book I chose, unlike most cultural historians who approach the decades after 1815 as an age of upheaval, revolution, and agitation, to deal with the opposite issue: why were these turbulent decades so peaceful, serene, and quiet? My answer was that throughout this period we discover a tremendous proliferation of moderating discourses and dialectics of consensus. To organize this answer, I resort in the present book to concepts experimented with in earlier works. Thus, the concept of literature suggested in my *Theory of the Secondary* (1989) is here applied in a much more concrete way. In that book I suggested that literature is a domain of human knowledge and activity in which defeat and imperfection are examined and studied. There is no question in my mind that the first part of the nineteenth century (and in a different way the second part as well) were pervaded by a feeling, and, if not, by a fear of defeat. The moderating impulses I talk about are precisely the lucid and resolute attempts to deal with defeat and to make imperfection acceptable.

Modernity, alienation, and the middle classes find themselves in an uneasy balance between already implemented revolutions and innovations (technological, political, in the mentalities), with their irreversible consequences on the one hand, and on the other hand the desire to preserve or restore a vast fund of mental structures, artistic and social forms and attitudes, values and conventions, as traditionally accumulated. The present volume deals with the manner in which the years in question managed to generate counterbalancing energies, foster compromise, and channel progress in a peaceful and beneficial fashion. The questions I ask are: What categories were devised? What intellectual vehicles were constructed? What intertextualities of discourse were resorted to in order to accomplish mediation? What structural means counteracted purely adversarial and conflicting power plays?

Together these converging discourses constituted a kind of safety net—a mode of dealing with the onslaught of modernity. The methods and discourses discussed in the present volume are not simply conservative braking devices; they also provide an occasion for coming to terms with a new, and often frightening or painful, human condition and social state that included, among other things, an undermining of Otherness and deepened tensions of ethnicity, class, and gender. The period I discuss is not one of boredom and peace: on the contrary, it is one of agitation of varying intensity. The way in which literary complements, or bridges, were devised is for me a subject of admiration and surprise. This appeasement was not perfect in nature nor did it even seek perfection. It made do with imperfection, turned it into a relatively satisfactory substitute for coherence and organicity. It is this relativity that calls to us now, at the beginning of the twenty-first century. It provides the model of a moderating imperfection that is both interesting and pragmatic.

Among the common features of these moderating discourses were the ability and willingness to use the beautiful as an epistemological vehicle and literary rhetorics as procedures for compressing and packaging knowledge; the stubborn remembrance of history and of the traditions it had engendered; the deft use of substitutive intertextuality and the techniques of analogy for the absorption of change; the vindication of interiority and subjectivity as enhancers of action and cognition; the utilitarian justification of emotional faculties; the preservation of value by the translation of tradition into new idioms; and the mutual relativization, imperfection, and limitation.

This very pragmatic and direct manner of engaging the need of value transfer, to refashion and displace idioms in radically and rapidly changing societies, continued to be used and perfected in successive generations and is still highly relevant today. It may offer, I hope, suggestions to some readers for intellectual solutions to our own contemporary problems. Not surprisingly, among the central figures of the volume are Chateaubriand, Goethe, and Scott. The first chapter depicts Chateaubriand as the "absent center," because in circle after circle of his broad and deep works the viscount sketches out the issues that I regard important: the moderating discourses of politics, nature, religion, the role of America, travel, and education. Surveying his work is thus a prelude for what is to follow in the present volume.

There is, however, a second way in which the present book engages modernity. Almost every chapter implies a certain critique of the harder principles of political correctness. Thus class, gender, and race are shown to have been often treated in a more judicious and a more appropriate way by the authors of earliest modernization than by those of the turn of the millennium. One chapter (chapter 5) dismantles the current banalities about multiculturalism and indicates a deeper way of thinking about it; another (chapter 8) shows that what is called class is far from being the fundamental or unique factor in the system of historical motivations of human societies. It is my hope that this procedure will encourage a deeper reflection on these matters, which appear to be of great importance for contemporary society.

Acknowledgments

I am sincerely grateful to Gerhart Hoffmeister, Theodore Ziolkowski, Gerald Gillespie, Marshall and Jane Brown, Larry Peer, Douwe Fokkema, Michael Ferber, Mihály Szegedy-Maszák, Manfred Engel, Mircea Anghelescu, John Neubauer, Michael Gassenmeier, Steven Sondrup, Angela Esterhammer, Clark Muenzer, Ann Rigney, Ina Gräbe, Sorin Antohi, and two anonymous evaluators for different forms of encouragement, support, and advice. For their valuable support in bringing this book to publication I wish to thank Barry Blose, Scott Evan Burgess, Anca Nemoianu, Jonathan Haupt, Mary Rakow, Susan Harris, and Daniel O'Connell. My particular gratitude goes to Ernest Suarez and George Garvey for their prompt and generous help.

I

CENTER, MARGIN, ABSENCE

CHAPTER I

The Absent Center of Romantic Prose
Chateaubriand and His Peers

TOWARD THE MIDDLE of Chateaubriand's masterpiece, his memoirs, the reader comes across one of the most breathtaking gestures of proud egotism and self-affirmation ever imagined. When the narrative reaches 1814, the narrator stops, switches gears, and, without batting an eyelash, begins a long section on the life and career of the most important historical-political figure contemporary with him, the heir of the French Revolution and conqueror of Europe, Napoleon Bonaparte.[1] The ostensible reason is to offer a suitable transition to the latter part of Chateaubriand's literary career and the beginning of his public, political career (*Mémoires*, 1:664–68) and thus to provide a background for a better understanding of the change. Since historical biography is the main discourse available to him, Chateaubriand will naturally fall back upon this age-hallowed vehicle and employ it, we are asked to believe. The reader will immediately see through this transparent pretext (Porter 1978, 65–79). What we have here is inspired by the writing modes of Greek antiquity; it is nothing short of an engagement with Plutarch's rhetorical history: an example of the parallel lives of illustrious figures. Chateaubriand proposes himself as the counterpart of the central figure of the age, as the alternative to the general and statesman who reshaped the map and the constitutions of Europe at the very moment when it was crossing the threshold into modernity.

The claim is enormous and unexpected, but a closer look shows that it is quite justified, indeed that Chateaubriand may stand more accurately as an emblem for the age of transition than the Corsican adventurer. Bonaparte is, many historians will agree, both misleading and apt as the entry door leading into a new world. In some ways he did represent, for better or worse, new tendencies. Streamlined and rationalistic legislative reforms inspired by his regime swept away the organic localist quilts of privilege and concession in which the arbitrary and concrete judgments of an older age were still at work. The ruthless mobilization of millions and their displacement over huge spaces were a harbinger of things to come in the nineteenth and, particularly, in the twentieth century. Radical acceleration of upward socioeconomic mobility, as well as its almost sarcastic cloaking in traditional forms, remain closely identified with the name of Napoleon: they point to the spread and triumph of alienated property structures, as well as to attempts to cushion the growth of purely utilitarian patterns of existence. In other ways Bonaparte seems almost like a throwback to earlier ages: a *condottiere*, an individualist iterating the gestures and the thinking of the past, a ruler with only a vague grasp of the economic mechanisms of society, a politician saddled with psychological immaturity and archaic naiveté.

Unquestionably, in his very contradictions and ambiguities, Napoleon heralds attitudes that were to mark and shape the whole of nineteenth-century civilization, with its uneasy, hesitant, and piquant mixture of revolutionary intention, traditionalist checks and balances, and simplifying pressures. Nevertheless, the greater complexity of Chateaubriand, his keen and often painful grasp of historical evolution, the more numerous sides and facets of his mind, as well as the fascinating (jittery and zigzagging) dialectic of consistency and discontinuity in his ideology give him an edge as a symbol of his time. But there is more. Chateaubriand's repeated failure to exert a significant impact upon the political events contemporary with him, no less than the ways in which he eluded commitments to either literary groups or political parties endow him with a quality of absence that, as I will show immediately, colors the whole of the Biedermeier age in Europe. Let me try to explain this statement in more detail, before returning to Chateaubriand and to his different contemporaries.

My premise is that the terms "period" in general, and "romanticism" in particular, can still be used in pragmatically meaningful ways, despite major opposition. I understand by "period-oriented literary history" a history that seeks to divide the literary field into areas ordered by the common denominator of time, usually cutting across the strict borders of linguistic and ethnic separation. This approach has encountered many objections and adversities. Some of these were purely nominalist and empirical: let us not touch the absolute autonomy of individual text or author. Others balked at the attempts to accord too much substantiality and content to periods and their representatives: "Baroque man" and similar constructs. Still others pointed an accusing finger at the imperfections of definition or of agreement on the object of study: Who belongs to what period? When does a period begin or end?—and the like.

The intellectual responses are numerous and eloquent, although they could barely put a dent in the ideological passion of their adversaries. For instance, why is it the case that when networks of homologies based on materialist determination are outlined (see Raymond Williams or Lucien Goldmann), "period" miraculously and suddenly becomes a more acceptable proposition? Likewise, why is it the case that heuristic groupings that borrow their categories from other fields (the Victorian era, feudalism, the Newtonian age, Revolution and Reaction, the age of discovery) are more acceptable than periodizations that assume some literary autonomy?

On a more serious level, literary scholars engaged in period studies have tried to meet their critics halfway and to refine the use of their concept. Thus, for instance, many scholars (from Benno von Wiese to Claudio Guillén) were ready to admit that "period" was just an instrumental, and not an ontological category. Others talked about literary periods as just one factor in a multicausal, plurisystemic explanatory complex. Others yet (Marshall Brown, Jeffrey Barnouw) chose to speak about the commonalities of "period" at the level of shared intentionality, or effort, or endeavor, that is to say, at the level of an attempt to respond creatively to the challenges of a given historical situation; "period" is thus placed not at the level of the answers, but of the common questionings of a given time. Such efforts were of little avail because they encountered the determined opposition and anguish of all those resolved to break up literature into a smattering of small and unrelated effects of a coherent external causal system. If teachers and students continue to speak about, say, romanticism at all, it is often for very practical reasons. They notice the epistemological weakness of the category and relish it: it provides a more convenient, a more tolerant form for the discussion of various authors than an economic, ideological, or religious frame. At the same time, readers, specialized or not, find it difficult to give a satisfactory account of Hölderlin or Shelley without referring to the complex relationship that engaged them with the values, affects, and aspirations they perceived as romantic. Linking literature with its whole cultural context (from politics and philosophy to the arts and music) would be much more difficult in the absence of some connecting bridge such as romanticism.

Let us assume however that the critiques of the period concept are largely justified and that under close scrutiny "period" turns out to be an absence, an ontological gap, a meaningless and inchoate area (from a literary point of view), and let us see what happens in that case to romanticism.[2]

Surprisingly enough we notice immediately that whether romanticism is regarded as a coherent age or not makes little difference for either the critic or for the age itself: the fact is that the actors themselves behaved as if the absence of romanticism was an event of overwhelming centrality, organizing capacity, and referential merit. Even a short demonstration happens to be sufficient.

The most common and probable understanding of romantic poetry is one that finds a burning desire and hope for regeneration and renewal of the whole human race at the very core of romantic activity: in thinking, in cultural creativity, in political action, perhaps even in some scientific pursuits, and certainly in the style of religiosity. This regeneration is based upon completeness and unification: overcoming class divisions and achieving full humanity, overcoming the separation of the faculties, and fusing reason with imagination. Wordsworth, Coleridge, and Blake, Hölderlin, Novalis, and Schelling each worked in this direction. Key efforts in the

French Revolution, as well as in other movements (radical, esoteric, universalist, and many others) were developed toward a regeneration not only of human society but of the human race and the human person as well. The initial paradisial point to be regained could be placed variously in medieval Europe or ancient Greece, in the biblical patriarchate, or in the Tahitian natural innocence, or in Eden itself. The future, by contrast, had to be rooted in the present, indeed it had to be its seamless expansion. All these things are known and usually accepted—irrespective of whether we regard them as ideological effluvia of a socioeconomic base, or whether we are inclined to credit them with a small or larger extent of autonomy.

The question that, curiously enough, is seldom asked is that regarding the reality principle in romanticism. Was the regeneration to be only a product of the imagination, or was an actual rebirth of society and of each or many human beings to occur in actuality? Or, at another level, can we point to a text that embodies and thus instantiates romanticism to the fullest? Is there a prototypical romantic canon?

It is easy to look at romanticism from the outside toward its inner core, as I did once myself (Nemoianu 1984). One notices and describes the margins of romanticism. There are the geographical margins: echoes and transformations of the romantic ideal in Hungary and Romania, in Spain and in transatlantic America. They are different from romanticism proper because they are farther away. Then there are the historical margins: the 1840s, the 1830s, the 1820s—in Restoration France and Biedermeier Germany. The works produced then and there are different from romanticism proper because they are farther off in time or because they incorporate a taming and a disappointment, melancholy withdrawal and shyness.

But let us step closer, looking at those who are specifically and undoubtedly core romantic: Wordsworth and Coleridge for instance. Where is their romanticism? In the case of Wordsworth surely not in the early *Evening Walk* and *Descriptive Sketches,* nor in the late *Ecclesiastical Sonnets,* nor indeed in almost any of the poems subsequent to 1815. This narrows down the field considerably, but an even closer look will show that even then it remains too broad. *The Prelude, Tintern Abbey,* and *Intimations of Immortality* would surely be considered to be the very core of Wordsworthian romanticism. Yet is the romantic integrity captured in them? *Tintern Abbey* and the *Intimations* ode are complaints about its loss, and *The Prelude* is a series of attempts to recapture it, successful, if that is what we want to call them in a few "spots of time." The same design—concentric circles with diminishing diameters—can be traced in the case of Coleridge. His romanticism is discovered to be hiding in a few paragraphs of the *Biographia,* a few fragments of the *Magnum Opus,* and a handful of poems (*The Rime of the Ancient Mariner, Kubla-Khan, Christabel,* and perhaps a very few others). Here again, as in the case of Wordsworth, a really close look can reveal that romantic integration, expansion, or regeneration are an illusion on a pragmatic and textual level. The poetic narrator in *Kubla-Khan* wants to recapture through melody and memory a fleeting though sublime moment of the past.

The *Ancient Mariner* similarly recounts an adventure of the past—by no means a happy one—with the purpose of impressing and frightening his audience, perhaps thus creating a short-range moral improvement (like Wordsworth's daffodils or impressions of the landscape near Tintern Abbey). Similarly discouraging conclusions can be drawn from a look at the writings of Hölderlin, at the philosophy of Schelling, or at the events of the French Revolution. To take up the French Revolution for a second: in what sense can it be said to have lived up to the highest expectations? Its more remote effects included military dictatorship, continental wars, colonialism, and nationalism. Its core (Jacobin) period is characterized by persecutions augmented to terror, economic anarchy, and ludicrously pompous public shows. Likewise, the philosophies of history corresponding to core romanticism tend to talk around some primary and crucial "event," its historical circumstances, the conditions of its occurrence, the regret for its failure to appear, its use as a measuring standard, and the like.

Therefore it is no exaggeration at all to state that any serious literary and historical investigation will show that at the center of romanticism there is an absence, a wide ontological gap. This sense of absence becomes overwhelming if we think for a minute also about quantitative factors: the response of the audience, general public preferences, the almost secretive or confidential writing of many romantics, and the widespread hostilities toward them.

Does this mean, however, that romanticism is nonexistent? Is absence a kind of being, or not? The opinions of modern analytical philosophers seem to be divided in this respect between those who follow Meinong, for instance, answering the second question in the affirmative, and the much stricter and segregationist Russellians who would deny it. Although my personal inclinations or preferences would go with the former, I will not try to take sides on the substance of the question but will take one step toward the historical and pragmatic question: Is there any epistemological good or use in resorting to romanticism? And why was romanticism assumed to exist by some contemporaries and was and still is assumed by many in later generations?

Because indeed, stunning as the gaping void at the center of the romantic movement may seem, it is but of banal significance compared to the process that developed around it and derived from it. For many decades writers defined themselves and organized their writing in terms of a mysterious central event: the romantic regeneration. Some were hostile to it, others nostalgic about it; some were trying to curb its energies and diminish its scope, others were exploring their own feelings of melancholic inadequacy towards it. Others yet, realizing that romanticism should be defined as a reintegration with a remote origin, collapsed the two—that is, the paradisial source, and its sublime effort at recuperation—and created an even more powerful referent. The romantic play with romanticism could and often did withdraw into pure fantasy, glorification of the aesthetic and various forms of individualism (strong or weak). But on a scientific level it encouraged bold forays into comparative linguistics and anatomy, experiments with vast cognitive syntheses, speculative plunges into the psychology of the unconscious and the vitality of electromagnetic energies; more specifically, in the literary-historical field, it stimulated the definition of a whole tradition (alternative to the classical one) that would justify the writing of romantic prose, drama, and poetry—the tradition of Dante, Shakespeare, and Cervantes. On a vaster historical plane, this very absent romantic reintegration and regeneration was instrumental in fostering and articulating—in the best tradition of politics as the art of the possible—decisive movements of social reform, feminine assertion, national revival, and populist affirmation or demand. It nourished restoration and revolt alike. All this huge domain of human activity, progress, and reaction is centered around an absent romanticism and understands itself in terms of it: emulation and epigonism, justification or adversity, adaptation or continuity or imitation are only some of the attitudes engendered by it. And I am not even speaking here about the waves upon waves of neoromantic revivals that have, to this day, further enriched this new culture. Similarly I cannot refer to the genuine social thickness of this culture that not only shaped in depth the attitudes of the middle class but probed even deeper into the levels of population: through linguistic-stylistic structures, patterns of behavior in the face of love, death, family life, or war-making. If we take at all seriously the insights of semantics, we cannot but acknowledge the power of such an empire of signs on the realities of social existence.

As in the case of classicism, but even more clearly than there, we are faced with a huge event devoid of a center, engendered perhaps by multiple and aleatory causes, a loose federation of values, facts, and impulses and yet itself of unmistakable size, mass, and substance. If the romantic mass preserves its own identity, then it is due precisely to the absence of a center. The positive location of a center would have limited the range and the possibilities of further expansion. True, the very configuration and organization of the romantic culture retrospectively began to shape the absence at its core, and many of us (partly as a kind of shorthand, partly out of sheer forgetfulness, partly out of negligence or wishful thinking) speak about it more positively and burden romanticism with more reality than it deserves or can carry. But I would argue that these are tiny failings indeed when measured against the heuristic advantages inherent in speaking about romanticism (as well as using other period terms) and against the dangers we incur when we acquiesce in the absence of these absences.

Not the least of the advantages of so thinking is that the historical colonialism of the 1980s and 1990s is thus averted: the conviction of readers that they possess a kind of superior understanding of past realities that must allow them (indeed obliges them) to impose that understanding upon history for its own benefit.[3] Be that as it may, the object of research in learned journals and of teaching in college classrooms is, realistically speaking, always a package: the author's texts plus the sum of reading perceptions that have accrued to it over the ages. Romanticism does not at bottom differ from other critical objects—its ur-text is small or elusive, while agglutinated semiotic materials keep growing and surrounding it.

I have referred so far chiefly to romantic poetry and philosophy, but what I have said applies much more obviously and clearly to all this fragmented and heterogeneous romantic prose, a true "realm of dissimilitude." Romantic prose is rich in disorder and in contradictory discourses, forms, and texts. It is, I believe, impossible to turn it even into a flexible polysystem, let alone into a pure system of any coherence at all. The absence of a center is even more strikingly obvious in romantic prose than in romantic poetry. What we can notice and record instead are the intersections of discourses—instigatory and utopian, as well as moderating and defensive, but above all digressive and complicating. The truly representative figures of romantic prose, Goethe and Mme de Staël, Chateaubriand, Manzoni, Cooper, and Scott, incorporate and employ these discourses. These are all heroes of moderation—individuals who try to act as historical mediators and to set up middle-of-the-road positions. Their purpose seems to be an enactment of the process of emancipation and alienation unfolding before their eyes. This enactment is, clearly, not bereft of ulterior motivations: it is each time intended to capture violent change and to translate it into modes of intelligible accommodation. The common purpose of this period's most characteristic and influential authors is precisely to find a middle ground between continuity and discontinuity, indeed to show that discarding the past can well be rife with a kind of preservation of the past and prospection of the future. To achieve this purpose many prose writers of the age (early romantics, as well as later, Biedermeier, figures) had to engage in two different (and usually divergent) operations. The first was to seek an ideologically coherent framework in which the negotiations of value transfer could take place and their implications could be explored and exhibited. The second was to imitate the age's own maneuvers and gesticulations. This imitation could only express itself in centrifugal and digressive texts, in fragmentariness, uncertainty, ambiguous allusion, and formal openness—all substitutes for, or masks of, absence.

Goethe's *Faust*, taken as a whole, is an attempt to harmonize the uneasy coexistence of these divergent operations (as I will show in chapter 2). Likewise, I am convinced that the "flaws" of Walter Scott's novels, rediscovered every generation by eager critics, are nothing but the inevitable consequence of the same fluid decentralization: a state of aesthetic consciousness where the center is not actually missing but rather is floating, skipping around, impossible to pin down. This kind of awareness also explains the darker colors and the dropping *tonus* in the writings of Manzoni or Cooper. In turn, both Constant and Mme de Staël displace social or cosmic disorientations onto a psychological level (in their novels), while trying to devise (with notable success) versions of liberal harmoniousness in their theoretical works.

However, more than any of the above Chateaubriand embodies and illustrates the furies and the delights, the posturings and the aporias of this "great divide" separating what was still a natural or spontaneous state of the polity and of the human soul from one in which rationalist-voluntarist forces were ready to play the lead role. To begin with he is himself an admirable example of such a change.

There is no question that Chateaubriand was a product of the "old regime," by origin as well as by existential and ideological choice. His youthful options and decisions were somewhat unreflective. Traveling to America (January 1791–January 1792) was a significant way out when choosing between liberal preferences and revolutionary practices seemed too painful an act. Emigration (July 1792–May 1800) soon after his return was also an inevitable act, in which purposeful deliberation played a small role. Chateaubriand's life in England, with its periods of starvation and illness as well as with its intellectual accumulations, was just as reactive and spontaneous. His earliest important work, *Essai historique, politique et moral, sur les révolutions anciennes et modernes, considérées dans leurs rapports avec la Révolution française* (1796),[4] neatly mirrored the state of mind of one who, cavalierly enough, wanted at the same time to approve and to disapprove of his time's most visible event. The *Essai* is intellectually inconsistent and, one feels obliged to add, thereby a good example of organic dissipation and contradictoriness. It was at this point that Count Louis de Fontanes (1757–1821) intervened in Chateaubriand's life. The two had been acquainted since approximately 1790, but they resumed their relationship in 1798 when the future marquess stayed in London. Fontanes, in equal parts sophisticated man-of-taste and politically adroit infighter, had left France only in June 1797 (pursued for lack of republican conviction in his journalistic columns) and returned in April 1799. (He spent a mere six months in England, from January to June 1798.) To be sure Chateaubriand had already been influenced by the classicist critic La Harpe (formerly considered Voltaire's most talented epigone, but now a recent convert to Catholicism and royalism) and perhaps by Pierre-Simon Ballanche's brief *Du sentiment considéré dans ses rapports avec la littérature et les arts* (1801). However, it was the Napoleonic right that contrived with masterful tenacity and clockwork precision to trigger the production of a masterpiece serving its interests at the exactly required time: *Génie du christianisme* burst on the market just four days before the signature of the Concordat with the Vatican, the official reestablishment of religion in France, and the first Roman Catholic High Mass at Notre Dame Cathedral in Paris after almost nine years of interruption (April 1802). Fontanes was here the mastermind. He channeled the orientation of the *Génie* and established connections with the already gelling Napoleonic administration, of which he was soon to become a key player, as chairman of its legislative body (1804–1808) and president (*grand maître*) of Paris University (1808–1814). Joseph Joubert (1754–1824), a recent Catholic convert and cool mind, established a connection with Lucien Bonaparte and his circle, as did Pauline de Beaumont (1768–1803), who offered not only invaluable emotional support and a small quiet rented house at Savigny-sur-Orge (not far from Paris) but also her important connections in the administration. Others yet (all the way to a suspiciously relaxed and, indeed, almost complicitous censorship) contributed to the overpowering success (meticulously prepared in the media) of his book (*Génie,* 1585–1600). From this point on, and to the very end of his life, Chateaubriand was to be a major figure of European public life.

Chateaubriand was to use this prominence in remarkable ways in order to work out in writing and in practice the various possibilities open to one who wished at the same time to acknowledge lucidly and without reservation the passing of time (for him human progression toward a different state of individual emancipation and compulsive atomic equality) and yet preserve an intense affection for the past. He was convinced that the past with its values and achievements must continue to play an essential role in shaping historical advance. This type of position was widely shared by the most thoughtful intellectuals of Europe both at the beginning of the nineteenth century and later all the way to the middle of the twentieth century.

Indeed even the high modernists (Eliot, Joyce, Proust) were concerned with the issues implied in it, and their work was defined at crucial points by the dialectic of this questioning of historical movement. However, for the modernists this was a yearning to participate in a battle already fought. Even intellectuals of the late nineteenth century found themselves caught in an already institutionalized and normative structure—classical liberalism in the garb of the feudal tradition.[5] By contrast, for Chateaubriand and his contemporaries (at least for those who wanted to reach a compromise or a synthesis between two radically opposed idioms of social praxis) facing this great divide was a fresh and bewildering experience, frightening and stimulating by turns but almost always overwhelming. The political and ideological contortions of Chateaubriand, as I will describe them shortly, are personal but far from unique. Thus the historians of English and German romantics have duly noted the movement from radical to conservative in Wordsworth, Coleridge, and Southey; Marx speculated that Byron would have moved in the same direction but for his untimely death; in Schiller we can recognize the same direction from *Die Räuber* (1781) and *Don Carlos* (1787) to the unfinished *Demetrius* (1805) or even the *Briefe über die aesthetische Erziehung des Menschen* (1795); Friedrich Schlegel and others underwent similar changes.[6] Goethe searched earnestly, and in ever-renewed qualifications, for a broad middle ground of both acceptance and fair critical judgment of the new age. Walter Scott tried tenaciously, in novel after novel, to explore the dynamics of value transfer: how to preserve the spirit of tradition while its flesh, or letter, or garb, changes, and how other ages and other places managed historical change. Scott's popular success and his array of great followers (Manzoni, Pushkin, Fenimore Cooper, Balzac, Willibald Alexis, Alfred de Vigny) can be explained precisely by the way in which he struck a raw nerve. A desire to reconstruct conservatism out of liberal materials is what animated Edmund Burke, John Adams, and François Guizot alike, no less than their less-well-known eastern European colleagues (József Eötvös and Széchény in Hungary, Dinicu Golescu and Ion Ghica in the Romanian principalities).

Chateaubriand plunged into this boiling cauldron of thoughts and passions much earlier and more thoroughly than others. A good way to understand his motives is to look at his intellectual background. It has been said all too often that Chateaubriand descends from Rousseau. This is true, but only in the sense in which Marx descends from Hegel: as an acceptance and reversal at the same time. Like Rousseau, Chateaubriand wholeheartedly embraced and accepted nature as the framework and foundation of humanity. Unlike Rousseau, Chateaubriand did not set nature against history; on the contrary, he found in nature the most persuasive arguments in favor of historical, cultural, and religious tradition. Whereas Rousseau believed that social equality and sentimental autonomy were the inevitable consequences of a return to nature, Chateaubriand argued that, until the great social and existential sea changes of his own day, history, religion, and culture had been but faithful applications of natural principles and that it is precisely an anomic ideology of fraternity that interrupts and denies our communication with nature. At the same time, Chateaubriand picked up on a long tradition of French Catholic writing in praise of the harmonies of nature and society, not least represented by Malebranche's *Entretiens sur la métaphysique et sur la religion* or Fénelon's *Aventures de Télémaque*, a tradition of which Bernardin de Saint-Pierre had provided in his descriptions of nature merely a more pietistic, more popular and colorful version.

It is this search for harmony, I propose, that impelled Chateaubriand to try at first to absorb the revolutionary shock in the abovementioned *Essai*. There he argued that while many features of the French Revolution were unsavory, they did not differ entirely from those to be found in other revolutions and regimes. The young Chateaubriand, who had not read Vico, developed nevertheless a kind of theory somewhat similar to that of the Neapolitan philosopher: there is something inevitable in the decline of society and in the human hunger for experimentation and change. The corruption of a restrictive society leads to unfettered freedom, which in turn must engender tyranny (Clément 1987). Additionally we find already some recurring leitmotifs of Chateaubriand's thought, such as the need to choose the lesser yoke given the fact that every regime will prove oppressive in one way or another. Likewise he proclaimed the need for virtue, morality, and religion as the basis of any worthwhile society. This seminal youthful work was dedicated "To all parties" and expressed a distrust of social-political solutions. It was also of a piece with Chateaubriand's early reluctance to commit himself decisively to one side; he preferred the flight into nature (the voyage to America) and culture. As said, he was literally pushed into emigration and returned as soon as he had an opportunity. His later life was to unfold the rich and exciting uncertainties of the *Essai*.

Indeed in many ways Chateaubriand was a committed liberal. He was intransigent on the issue of the freedom of the press. He had prepared a thundering speech to be given in the upper house of the French Parliament upon the debate of a (subsequently withdrawn) bill for restricting freedom of the press (February and

March 1827); this thwarted piece of oratory was thereafter published as a separate pamphlet (July 1827). In 1827 he founded the organization "Amis de la liberté de la presse." He took as his role model the Milton of *Areopagitica;* he allied himself in the 1827 elections with the Left in defense of basic civil rights and against censorship; he supported, like Byron, the Greek struggle for decolonization; he resigned his ambassadorial position in France in 1830 when he was persuaded that the Polignac administration and King Charles X were engaged on a disastrous course towards repression. Chateaubriand became the object of incipient judicial action in 1816 and 1818, and on another occasion was briefly arrested for political reasons (May–June 1832). No less explicit had been Chateaubriand's stands during the Napoleonic administration. Upon his return from England, Chateaubriand eagerly joined a group of intellectuals of the moderate right, who were engaged in whatever means of legal opposition were available at the time against personal dictatorship and in favor of civil liberties (Sainte-Beuve). He publicly condemned the kidnaping and execution of the politically inactive Duke of Enghien (March 1804). In July 1807 he published an article in which a comparison between the Emperor and Nero was suggested, whereupon his permission to reside in Paris was promptly withdrawn. His reception speech at the Académie Française (April 1811) was heavily censored by Napoleon in person, and he relinquished forthwith the privilege to be seated in that august body.

We must add here the way in which in his old age Chateaubriand felt at least some twinges of sympathy for socialism and a republican regime. He was friends with Alexis Carrel, with the (later) leftist Lamennais, also with Béranger (Sainte-Beuve; *Mémoires,* 2:878–88, and elsewhere). (This heralds also the inclination of some Catholic thinkers or activists of the nineteenth and twentieth centuries to seek the salvation of solidarist and communitarian values against the alienating and atomizing liberalism and capitalism of modernity on the left if it could not be found on the right.) It is significant to note that Chateaubriand's chief argument for freedom of the press was quite paradoxical. It was that freedom of speech strengthens rather than weakens monarchy and tradition by counteracting the powers-that-be of the representative system (*Mémoires,* 2:392–93). Chateaubriand was convinced of the need for "ces lumières qui jaillissent de la contradiction" (those lights that arise from contradiction) and that "une erreur trop commune aux gouvernements, c'est de croire qu'ils augmentent leurs forces en augmentant leur pouvoir: une armure trop pésante rend immobile celui qui la porte" (Clément 1987, 239). [Governments make all too often the error of believing that they increase their power by increasing their privileges: an armor that is too heavy makes the wearer immobile.] On the contrary "La liberté de la presse est … le seul contrepoids des inconvénients du gouvernement représentatif" (Freedom of the press is … the only counterbalance to the disadvantages of a representative government; 244) and, one paragraph up: "Si cette liberté avait existé sous nos premières assemblées, Louis XVI n'aurait pas péri" (244).

This paradoxical rhetoric, or "argumentation by absence," is very typical of Chateaubriand. We can easily recognize it in his position toward the very issue of representativeness that he brings up in connection with freedom of the press. Unlike Burke and Scott, even unlike many French *monarchiens* (from Rivarol to Mallet du Pan, both of whom he admired), Chateaubriand is almost amusingly candid as to his motivations. All his instincts impel him toward a defense of the ancien régime. At the same time he is too lucid and too intelligent not to recognize the impossibility of an absolutist system as put forward by his friend Bonald and others. Hence the open admission that a set of concessions is necessary given the direction of the world. His major work of constitutional politics, *De la monarchie selon la charte* (1816), is probably the best apology of the Restoration. In it he argues forcefully and eloquently for the need of a mixed solution, one that would preserve the best from the past while preparing the future: a future that was inevitably republican, Chateaubriand believed all along.[7] Monarchy should be untouchable and divine but not endowed with effective powers. In turn, the potential excesses of representativeness can be curbed by abolishing "the general police," by unbridled freedom of the printed media (*l'opinion*), by an aristocracy channeled towards military duty (and enjoying some privileges as such), and finally by explicitly building the state institution on religious foundations. Monarchy should be a kind of validating absence, a guarantee of continuity.

In a sense the two Bourbon kings (and certainly Charles X) never lived up to this concept of lofty absence. It was precisely after 1830, under the Orléans branch, that a renewed constitution could approximate the contradictory (and mutually suspending) claims Chateaubriand made to political organization. However, once this regime was set up, Chateaubriand reacted violently to, and separated himself from it, and installed himself in the very area of absence that he had previously reserved for the legitimate monarch.

Looked at from a certain angle, Chateaubriand's position is not devoid of a certain comic surrealism. For him, Napoleon is the proletarian king (that is, the dictator seen as the substitute of the venerable institution in an era of mass democracy). Orleanism is rejected tortuously: "Républicain par nature, monarchiste par raison et Bourbonnien par honneur, je me serais beaucoup mieux arrangé d'une démocratie si je n'avais pu conserver la monarchie légitime, que de la monarchie bâtarde octroyée par je ne sais qui" (Clément 1987, 141). [A republican by instinct, a monarchist by rational judgement, pro-Bourbon by honor, would have felt more at home in a democracy had a constitutional monarchy proved impossible, rather than under the hybrid monarchy bequeathed to us by who-knows-whom.] In turn, the utter archaic desuetude and even the heartrendingly ridiculous aspects of the royal family in its Hradschin refuge do not escape him. Thus Chateaubriand ends up by evading any firm commitment, or rather by setting up such a complicated system of preconditions for acceptance that it amounts to circumscribing an empty place. This absence is further underlined by the repeated inroads into the world of "might-have-been": an imaginary reconstruction of the future from the point of view of an altered past. Thus he speculates what Napoleon would have been like had he been more like George Washington (*Mémoires*, 1:222–26), or how the fortunes of the exiled Bourbons could have changed with other advisers and with other tutors (specifically himself!) for the future Henry V (*Mémoires*, 2:750–53, 677–78, 668). (This is amazing in foresight for those who remember the events after 1871 and how the chances of a restored constitutional monarchy were frittered away by the Duke of Bordeaux; Chateaubriand was quite right.)[8] Chateaubriand knew well how to populate this area of political perplexity and absence. If there was no satisfying deep structure to politics then at least a surface structure could be set up. To erect such a surface structure, Chateaubriand used materials borrowed from a line of predecessors (not too remote ones) such as Turgot and Montesquieu.

There are few passages more revealing in the whole of Chateaubriand's oeuvre than his enthusiastic praise of Montesquieu. In one such passage he says,

> En nommant Montesquieu, nous rappelons le véritable grand homme du dix-huitième siècle. *L'Esprit des Lois* . . . vivront aussi longtemps que la langue dans laquelle ils sont écrits . . . dans le livre qui a placé Montesquieu au rang des hommes illustres il a magnifiquement réparé ses torts . . . son génie qui embrassait tous les temps, s'est appuyé sur la seule religion à qui tous les temps sont promis. (*Génie*, 870; Sainte-Beuve 1978, 2:132–35)

> [When we pronounce the name of Montesquieu, we do it knowing that this is the truly great man of the eighteenth century. *L'esprit des lois* . . . will live as long as the language in which it was written . . . in this book, which placed Montesquieu at the level illustrious men, he magnificently compensated for all his weaknesses . . . his genius embraces every historical age, it was founded on the only religion to which all ages belong.]

Chateaubriand tried to emulate Montesquieu's political equanimity and to reach a kind of "English fairness" in his judgments of political ethics. This is seen above all in the passages on the greatness and the failings of the early United States (*Mémoires*, 1:269–79). The same evenhandedness is seen in passages that try to adjudicate between past and present or conservation and change,[9] as well as in his discussion of the inherent contradictions in the Restoration "Charte," which he had otherwise praised so vocally (*Mémoires*, 2:701–6). In a word, Chateaubriand reveals himself surprisingly close to Tocqueville, the unimpeachable classical liberal (who, incidentally, was his close relative).[10]

Turgot, who is barely mentioned in the *Mémoires*, had already outlined many of the views for which Chateaubriand was to become later famous. Turgot was pointing to the religious sources of the Enlightenment. In his 1750 "Discours sur les avantages que l'établissement du christianisme a procurés au genre humain," Turgot underlines the merits of Christianity in preserving the values of antiquity, in boosting individual personality, and in fostering an ethical public order. He also praises the virtues of trade and the market in preserving peace, increasing prosperity, and a moderate progress.

Like Turgot, but with more dramatic flair, Chateaubriand kept repeating that freedom can only grow out of religious values, and preeminently, Christianity. "Je ne crois qu'á la vérité religieuse, dont la liberté est une forme" (*Mémoires*, 1:418). [I only believe in religious truth, of which freedom is one aspect], he kept repeating. This brings Chateaubriand close to Guizot (who in the last decades of his life was directly concerned with French Protestantism), as well as to the positions advocated by Mme de Staël after *De l'Allemagne,* and in particular after 1815. Nevertheless, his positions towards both (as well as, more predictably, toward Constant (*Mémoires*, 1:871–72) remained ambiguous. He had esteem for them but could not hide a certain jealousy; or at least he behaved as if he feared on the one hand that they expressed his views equally well, on the other that these differed from him in some hidden but essential ways.

All these hybrid positionings were perhaps somewhat theatrical or coquettish, as has been all too often charged. There is nevertheless in Chateaubriand's political writings and actions a deep seriousness, an earnest search for answers, a certain delight in the exploration of a suddenly expanded disponibility, and a sketchy plotting out of behaviors and attitudes that were to become much more common in the nineteenth century.

How organic the different parts of Chateaubriand's praxis (textual or actively social) were all along becomes obvious if we look at the way in which traveling and travel literature can be seen as his responses to bafflement and political aporias. As I said before, the expedition to America was the flight from a looming moral-political crisis, and so was the avoidance of further conflicts with the Napoleonic administration by means of a long Mediterranean journey. Whenever Chateaubriand's perception of a crumbling traditional structure of mentality and of social functioning became too painfully intense, he resorted not to rearguard battles but to a forward strategy. He found a way out by reaching toward expansion, roaming, accumulation, as if his rule had been that (incompletely quoted) Guizotian *enrichissez-vous* transferred on a spiritual-cognitive level. Chateaubriand thus set down the paradigm of the "progressive conservative," one that from Disraeli to Theodore Roosevelt, and deep into the twentieth century, was to be replicated: preserving tradition not by reactive mummifying or negative gestures but by suddenly opening up new areas and flying forward. Tradition and firm values are helped not by solidifying but, in a more creative way, by extending the line of their reach and action much further and thus validating these traditional values in their past and present also. Enhancement is achieved through extension and roving. The deliberate design of Chateaubriand is seen when we compare the flimsy and scant, albeit real, basis of his American journey and the imaginary construct he offered to his readers (and undoubtedly to himself).

Chateaubriand touched land on the Chesapeake Bay and disembarked in Baltimore on July 10, 1791, then spent some time in Philadelphia trying to see President Washington, to whom he had a letter of introduction. He narrates a brief visit with Washington, but most historians doubt the account, simply because of a note of September 5 to the Marquis de la Rouërie in which Washington informs his friend that he was indisposed and could not see the voyager. De la Rouërie was one of the military leaders of the French voluntaries fighting on the American side. (Better known as "le colonel Armand," the Marquis was then forty, close to Washington but also, as a fellow-Breton gentleman, close to the circle of Chateaubriand's friends.) It is not impossible that Chateaubriand should have met Washington subsequently.

Chateaubriand briefly visited New York and possibly the battlefield of Lexington and then wandered through upstate New York and Pennsylvania to Niagara Falls and Lake Erie (July–August 1791). Most interesting are the remaining three months (Chateaubriand left North America on December 10). He claimed to have toured the Appalachian Mountains and to have observed the Ohio and the Mississippi rivers, indeed to have pushed on as far as Alabama, Louisiana, and northern Florida.

The young author left three contradictory descriptions of these explorations, one in *Essai*, another in the material of *Les Natchez* (as used separately in *Atala* and in *René*—all written in the late 1790s), and the last in *Mémoires d'outre-tombe*. Chateaubriand's early accounts were immediately doubted and criticized on both sides of the Atlantic, most notably in the *American Quarterly Review* of December 1827, by René de Mersenne—pseudonym of Bins de Saint-Victor—in 1832 and 1835, and by Eugène Ney, the son of the executed imperial marshal, in the widely circulated *Revue des Deux-Mondes* of March 1, 1833.

They, as well as later critics (cf. Painter 1977, 1:135–222; Castries 1974, 60–76; Lebègue 1979, 32–124), missed the point. Chateaubriand was engaged in an enormous operation of rewriting reality. Experiential facts were placed where they could interact with vast numbers of travel accounts, poetic echoes (conspicuously Tasso and Virgil), imaginative sentimentalism, and the ideology of conservative primitivism. As I said before, a discourse that was prima facie Rousseauist (Dédéyan) conjures up an intertextual world of cultural choices, Homeric and biblical, as well as derived from Milton, Shakespeare, and "Ossian."

I will not insist too much on Chateaubriand's second great voyage, around the Mediterranean (July 1806–June 1807), because it is treated in another chapter of this book. Suffice it to say that there, also, straight factual reporting is pushed to the background and reconstructed as a journey through history. The temporal dimension displaces the spatial one: Chateaubriand reflects on the sources of European culture, that is, on the Eastern roots of Western Christendom. The main commonality between the two great journeys is their attempt to capture a global and non-Western vantage point for better comprehension of current (and future) Western stances. Thus both are acknowledgments (not least because they lack any kind of clear finality) of a radical absence inside European culture: that of internal self-explanation.

Even more emphatic (though carefully disguised) is the dialectic of absence in *Génie du christianisme,* Chateaubriand's chief work of Christian apologetics. It is true that throughout his life (perhaps excepting a few years in his youth) the viscount had professed a staunch Catholicism. It is, however, also true that in his private life he had shown considerable independence of church guidance, and in his public life he did not seem particularly inclined to enter into church alliances. He was in effect separated (though not formally divorced) from his wife for many decades, and even in his last years he had settled into the highly unusual triangular routine of which Mme Récamier was a part (for example, Ormesson 1982). His comments on the state of the Vatican in *Mémoires d'outre-tombe* are detached and cool (*Mémoires,* 1:497–502; 2:223–56), though not unfriendly, while his alliances during his fifteen to twenty years of political activity are by no means marked by "ultra-montanist" inclinations (Dru 1967).

True, his historical novel *Les martyrs,* the forerunner of numerous sentimental or melodramatic works of Christian history (Gingras 1995; a whole genre or sub-genre in the nineteenth and even the twentieth centuries) was intended as a kind of Christian modern epic, continuing Milton[11] and responding to Homer, as he himself often explained (*Génie,* 627–47; *Mémoires,* 1:636–37). However, *Génie du christianisme* is a much more ambiguous work. Nowhere therein is the divinity of Christ clearly and loudly proclaimed: foregrounding is reserved to the mundane sweetness and compassion of Jesus. The presentation and the knowledge of dogmatics and theology are vague and lacunar. What is truly stunning, as has been noted by Maurice Regard, is that in this book the appeal to God often seems an appeal to nothingness. Eternity is associated with darkness, silence, desert, flight, and death. Repeatedly we are told that God is a "profound secret," an ineffable, unknown, evasive entity; immensity, dispersal in creation, mystery, confusion, mere appearance—these are, as often as not, the features of Chateaubriand's Divine.[12] While it can be argued that part of this attitude can be identified with a pantheistic version of Christianity common among romantics (though not confined to them), we must also admit that Chateaubriand was renewing, less than wittingly, a long line of Patristic and mystical thinking that goes back all the way to Origen, Pseudo-Dionysus the Areopagite, and St. Maximus Confessor.

Above all, however, Chateaubriand was deliberately trying to remove the debate about Christianity from under the sovereignty of analytical rationalism. This decision is affirmed by Chateaubriand lucidly and without hesitation. "Il n'est rien de beau, de doux, de grand dans la vie que les choses mystérieuses" (In human life only mysteries can be beautiful, sweet, grand); and "Tout est caché, tout est inconnu dans l'univers" (In the universe everything is hidden, everything is unknown); or "les plaisirs de la pensée sont aussi des secrets" (The pleasures of reason are also secrets).[13] At the beginning of book 5, part 1, he declares: "Toujours fidèle à notre plan, nous écarterons des preuves de l'existence de Dieu et de l'immortalité de l'âme, les idées abstraites, pour n'employer que les raisons poétiques et les raisons de sentiment" *Génie,* 557). [Ever consistent with our project, we shall ignore from among the proofs of God's existence and of the soul's immortality any abstract ideas and confine ourselves to poetic and emotional reasons.]

Chateaubriand's mechanism of motivation and apology is more complex still. He boldly institutes a kind of supply-side defense of religion. In criticizing older forms of apologetics he argues: "Il fallait prendre la route contraire: passer de l'effet à la cause, ne pas prouver que le Christianisme est excellent, parce qu'il vient de Dieu; mais qu'il vient de Dieu, parce qu'il est excellent" (*Mémoires,* 1:1; *Génie,* 469). [The opposite route should be taken: passing from effect to cause, proving not that Christianity is excellent in that it comes from God; but that it comes from God because it is excellent.] This is a pragmatic, almost a utilitarian, kind of argument, similar to one that, among contemporary American thinkers, a George Gilder uses, in keeping with the biblical admonition, "By their fruits you shall know them."[14]

Thus the door is opened to Chateaubriand's central and most important argument. Of the essentials signaling divinity in its fullness, it is Beauty, at least as much as (and perhaps more than) Truth or Goodness, that is the most accessible and reliable. The preverbal forces of sense-impression and of emotional movement provide more convincing testimony to the nature of Creation and of God than rational debate and analysis. An important distinction has to be immediately and emphatically pointed out. It was said by many throughout the nineteenth century, but perhaps by none more eloquently than by Arthur Schopenhauer and Matthew Arnold, that poetry or art (embodiments of Beauty) can (perhaps *must*) act as replacements of religious experience. A good part of the public was indeed confident that the aesthetic had displaced the religious. Chateaubriand had proposed something different, but his views were also enthusiastically accepted by a wide public; similar positions were put forward by others in the early nineteenth century, and a recognizable line of thought continued during the later nineteenth century. This position was that sacrality and religiousness are still central to human existence, that they could not be displaced but that Beauty is the most certain sign for recognizing them, and they must be sought in artistic creation.

There is a clear distance not only between Chateaubriand and Schopenhauer but also between Chateaubriand and true and powerful restorationists such as Klement Maria Hofbauer and his circle of followers, or Jaime Balmes in Spain. When all is said and done, this difference comes down, as I pointed out, to Chateaubriand's acknowledgment of mystery, of absence, or of an ontological gap at the center of being. In typical fashion this absence is offset not merely by Beauty but also by the way in which Beauty is understood: diverse abundance and (we would say ecological or homeostatic) harmony. Book 5 of part 1, "Existence de Dieu prouvée par les merveilles de la nature," offers particularly impressive examples of this procedure. Chateaubriand praises the generosity of alligators and rattlesnakes and extols the merits of wetlands and swamps (pt. 1, bk. 5, ch. 10). Nothing is superfluous in the eyes of divinity: "Dieu n'agit pas comme nous d'une manière bornée; il se contente de dire: *Croissez et multipliez;* et l'infini est dans ces deux mots" (*Génie*, 587; pt. 1, bk. 5, ch. 10). [God does not act in a limited way, as we do; it suffices that He says "grow and multiply"; infinity is in these two words.] Portraits of waterfowl (ch. 7) are combined with considerations on the genius of nest-building in birds (ch. 6), with the admiration of migratory instincts (chs. 4, 7, 8), and with a continuous emphasis on the relevance of all these for human life (*Génie*, 571–74; 569–71).

Chateaubriand's leitmotif here is that of fertility and the abundance of the concrete. Equally striking, however, is his care to show the continuity and fraternity between nature and culture. For him, nature is full of examples and of support to human activity. Thus sea-birds are here to announce "tous les accidents des mers, les flux et les reflux, le calme et l'orage" (pt. 1, bk. 5, ch. 8), [all marine accidents, ebb and flow, calm and tempest], indeed they act exactly in the way Coleridge's albatross will act soon enough: "Compagnes des mariniers, elles suivent la course des navires, et prophètisent la tempête. Le matelot leur attribue quelque chose de sacré, et leur donne religieusement l'hospitalité" (*Génie*, 576–79). [companions of the mariners, they pursue the trail of ships and prophesy the tempest. The seaman attributes them a kind of sacredness, and religiously offers them hospitality.] Not only do birds and plants provide analogies to human behavior (ch. 11) and birds to social organization (*Génie*, 586–89; pt. 1, bk. 5, ch. 8), but Providence designed bird songs for the pleasure of our hearing (*Génie*, 575–79; pt. 1, bk. 5, ch. 5). Archetypal human existence as recorded in the Bible ("sous les tentes de Jacob ou de Booz" (*Génie*, 578; ch. 8) is, in turn, one guided not by abstract, and therefore uncertain calendars, but rather by signs culled from the natural world—an abundance of geese announced a long winter much as the first flight exercises of young larks exhorted the villager to begin harvesting.

The arguments for the truth and value of religion drawn from cultural achievements continue almost seamlessly those regarding nature. Indeed, the whole structure of the *Génie* is such that natural arguments and examples are sandwiched between theological/divine and literary/artistic ones, though the former tend then to crop up in later parts, such as is the case with the justly renowned chapters on ruins (*Génie*, 881–92; pt. 3, bk. 5, chs. 3–6) and tombs (*Génie*, 926–37; pt. 4, bk. 2, chs. 1–8. See also Dieguez 1965, 186–89). Chateaubriand pleads loudly in favor of monastic orders and their way of life precisely because of their closeness to nature and their impact on civilization's ability to interact with nature, economy, agriculture, and the sciences: "Le clergé a trouvé des terres incultes; il y a fait croître des moissons" (*Génie*, 1057; pt. 4, bk. 6, ch. 8) [The clergy found uncultivated land; and turned it into fertile land.], or "Le paysan apprit, dans le monastères, à retourner la glèbe, et à fertiliser le sillon. . . . Les moines furent donc réellement les pères de l'agriculture, et comme laboureurs eux-mêmes et comme les premiers maîtres de nos laboureurs" (pt. 4, bk. 6, ch. 7). [The peasant learned in the monasteries to work the land and to dig the furrow. . . . Therefore the monks were actually the parents of agriculture, both as land laborers and as teachers of laborers.][15]

Broader yet are the points made in connection with Jesus Christ.[16] Chateaubriand believes that we should speak about two successive acts of creation. The first is the one depicted in the biblical account in *Genesis;* it is the creation of physical nature. The second act of creation is the teaching of Jesus Christ, which had the same creative power in the psychological and moral order of things that the Father's creativity had had in the natural one:

> Avant Jesus Christ, l'âme de l'homme était un chaos; le Verbe se fit entendre, aussitôt tout se débrouilla dans le monde intellectuel, comme à la même Parole, tout s'était jadis arrangé dans le monde physique: ce fut la création morale de l'univers. (*Génie II*, 513–14; pt. 2, bk. 2, ch. 1)

> [Before Jesus Christ, the human soul had been a chaos; the verb rang out, immediately everything gained order in the intellectual world, much as the same verb had earlier ordered the physical world: we may call this the moral creation of the universe.]

In other words, there is a perfect correspondence between the cultural and the natural realms if we use religion as our avenue of access. We come across many smaller continuities and analogies between the physical and the cultural order in Chateaubriand's *Génie:* trinitarian structures are said to be the archetype of the universe (*Génie,* 475–77; pt. 1, bk. 1, ch. 3); eucharistic bread and wine do nothing but "retrace the pictures of agriculture" (*Génie,* 491–92; pt. 1, bk.1, ch. 7); and the natural and primitive are identified not with savagery, but with primary Christianity (*Génie,* 495–96; pt. 1, bk. 1, ch. 8).

Methodologically things are not otherwise. Along with Bonald, Chateaubriand can be considered one of the inventors of sociology, of an "aesthetic" sociology in his case.[17] The purpose of these conservatives was to control and limit historical disasters; by postulating the repetitiveness of history they banished or limited its dangers. Another view of history was renewed instead: the gestalt of a struggling humanity in the face of God could qualify and soften the impact of pure linearity and progress. The historical spectacle as "vanity of vanities" is but the theatrical scenery required by the beauty of absence:

> Partout ou se trouve beaucoup de mystère, de solitude, de contemplation, de silence, beaucoup de pensées de Dieu, beaucoup de choses vénérables dans les costumes, les usages et les moeurs, là se doit trouver une abondance de toutes les sortes de beautés. (*Génie,* 961–62; pt. 4, bk. 3, ch. 5)

> [Wherever we find much mystery, solitude, contemplation, silence, many divine thoughts, many venerable aspects of customs, habits, manners, we also inevitably find an abundance of all kinds of beauties.]

In turn, the modes of discourse exercised by Chateaubriand, his stylistic and aesthetic options, all present a number of rather stable features, irrespective of whether the author's purposes were history, travel, apology, polemics, or strict literature. What is more, this consistency points in the same direction as those highlighted above: a dialectical game of hide-and-seek with absence; the ability to engage in quick and ever-renewed substitutions; the constructive energy engaged around doubt and the void; a multitude of excellent values clustered about the mystery that is Jesus.

Most often this was noticed in Chateaubriand's virtuoso treatment of time, one that was to set the tone of prose and poetry for almost two hundred years—that is, to Proust and beyond. The viscount's conservative nostalgia no less than his passionate involvement in the affairs of the present were inextricably bound with switches from different phases of the past tense to the present of the writing self and the future of the reader: superimposed temporal strata. In the *Mémoires d'outre-tombe* these often include, as one critic explained, a moment in the past remembered at the time just reached by the narrative, the writer's own remembrance (in which existence and writing collapse), the moment of editing and correction, and often also the rememoration by writing of another moment of writing (Vial 1972, 53, 110–17). Things are sometimes further complicated by the "anticipated recollection" of the place where the author *will be writing* about a moment in the past. The proto-Brechtian awareness and transparency of this temporal complication are recognized in the preface of 1846, written, of course, after the memorialistic work was concluded:

> Les formes changeantes de ma vie sont entrées les unes dans les autres: il m'est arrivé que dans mes instants de prospérité j'ai eu à parler de mes temps de misère; dans mes jours de tribulation, à retracer mes jours de bonheur. Ma jeunesse pénétrant dans ma vieillesse, la gravité de mes années d'éxpérience attristant mes années légères, les rayons de mon soleil, depuis son aurore jusqu'à son couchant, se croisant et se confondant, ont produit dans mes récits une sorte d'unité indéfinissable; mon berceau a de ma tombe, ma tombe a de mon berceau.

> [The ever-changing forms of my life have been mutually combined. Thus in my moments of good fortune I had to speak about miserable events; during my days of tribulation, I had to sketch out my days of happiness. Since my young age merged with my senectitude, the gravity of my years of experience saddened my flightier years, the sun rays of my life, from sunrise to sunset crossed each other and identified with each other producing an undefinable unity; my cradle has reminders of my grave, my grave of my cradle.]

For the reader inclined toward comparison it is not difficult to place this writing mode: it belongs clearly in the company of Wordsworth (Richard 1928, 174–55, 169, and elsewhere; Sainte-Beuve 1978, 1:88), Hölderlin, Senancour, and Lamartine— the great authors of the internalized epic, the explorers of temporal subjectivity. It is in particular Wordsworth's "double vision" or "loss of vision" owing to the passage of time from childhood on that we find (independently) replicated in Chateaubriand's discourse. He says himself: "La majeure partie du génie se compose de cette espèce de souvenirs. Les plus belles choses qu'un auteur puisse mettre dans un livre sont les sentiments qui lui viennent, par réminiscence, des premiers jours de sa jeunesse" (*Génie*, 868–69; pt. 3, bk. 4, ch. 5). [The largest part of genius is composed of this kind of memory. The most beautiful things an author can put in a book are the feelings derived by remembrance from the first days of his youth], which is straight Wordsworthian doctrine. (The parallel was noted as early as 1848 by Sainte-Beuve 1978, 1:116.) Additionally Chateaubriand had the voluptuousness of writerly revision and of the critical correction of his earlier writings and self, something seen not only in the *Mémoires*, but also in the new 1826 edition of the *Essai sur les révolutions*. Perhaps the most celebrated, and most often quoted, interferences of the time is the one describing the episode with Charlotte Ives: it begins in the manner of Goethe's idyll at Sesenheim as depicted in *Dichtung und Wahrheit*, continues (still in an analogy with Goethe) with Wertherian outbursts of passion, and culminates over a quarter of a century later with the reappearance of a mature married lady (this time reminding us of some scene in the eerily eponymous Lotte of Thomas Mann's short novel *Lotte in Weimar; Mémoires,* 1:368–77).

Chateaubriand rereads, he tells us, manuscripts he had (after thirty years) completely forgotten (*Mémoires,* 1:663), and he engages in sophisticated time-games as soon as he becomes more clearly aware of the potentialities in his mode of writing. The earliest major (and still blunt) case is the passage interpolated after narrating his years in Combourg: how he spends his life as a mature man and French ambassador in Potsdam, at the Prussian court, in the early 1820s (*Mémoires,* 1:107–11). The dialog of the time-layers intensifies when Chateaubriand considers how, unbeknownst to him, later acquaintances or lovers must have shared similar experiences (*Mémoires,* 1:193–98, 360–61, 387; 2:69–70, 481–82). Eventually the author himself notices a kind of synthesis, or mutual embrace of perceptions, leading to a collapse of the time experience: "Ma mémoire oppose sans cesse mes voyages à mes voyages, montagnes à montagnes, fleuves à fleuves, forêts à forêts, et ma vie détruit ma vie. Même chose m'arrive à l'égard des societés et des hommes" (*Mémoires,* 2:585). [Ceaselessly my memory confronts my voyages, mountains to mountains, rivers to rivers, forests to forests, and my life destroys my life. The same happens to me in connection with societies and individuals.] (The latter statement confirmed of course by what we observed before regarding the invention of "sociology" during the Biedermeier age.) This comes as a kind of culmination in the narration of an Alpine trip in 1832 (*Mémoires,* 2:578–88).

In any case it cannot be denied that in the *Mémoires d'outre-tombe,* Chateaubriand's temporal modes become the object of conscious and metacritical judgment. When his youthful colleague Saint-Riveul perishes in a pre-Revolutionary political skirmish, he muses on memory, possibility, and the replaceability of destinies (*Mémoires* 1:165). On other occasions he goes from self-commentary and self-directed hermeneutics to an incipient theory of myth-making that one would place among contemporary critical approaches.[18]

These temporal voids or uncertainties are compensated (in genuinely Biedermeier fashion) by other things. Thus Chateaubriand is a master of intertextuality and palimpsestic practices—no mean competitor to modernists like Joyce or Eliot in this respect. I will confine myself rather briefly here to refer to Homer and Torquato Tasso, to Milton, Longus, and Fénelon, the Bible and Chateaubriand himself, abundantly used in *Les martyrs* and elsewhere. On other occasions—in the *Itinéraire,* and in *Génie* conspicuously, but (more seldom) even in the *Mémoires,* where the second half accumulates quotations, own letters and documents, and long passages from others—Chateaubriand reminds the reader of the baroque tradition of Burton and Browne, that is, the massing together of eccentric and delightful facts (*Mémoires,* 2:216ff., 819ff., and elsewhere).

Equally characteristic and plainly complementary are the "grand images," sudden vistas, or vistas of vast and breathtaking scope. The structure of such images was learned in the epic tradition of Homer and Milton, but it was also transferred to Baudelaire, Claudel, or the Flaubert of *Salammbô.* Thus says Chateaubriand (on Velasquez and Michelangelo):

> Ces fameux artistes passaient leurs jours dans des aventures et des fêtes; ils défendaient les villes et les châteaux; ils élévaient des églises, des palais et des remparts; ils donnaient et recevaient des grands coups d'épée, séduisaient des femmes, se réfugiaient dans les cloîtres, étaient absous par les papes et sauvés par les princes. (*Mémoires,* 2:240)

> [These famous artists filled their days with adventures and feasts; they defended cities and castles; they erected churches, palaces, and bastions; they gave and received mighty blows of the sword, seduced women, found refuge in monasteries, were absolved by popes and saved by princes.]

Or, as he says in the *Génie:*

> Voyez le néophyte debout au milieu des ondes du Jourdain: le solitaire du rocher verse l'eau lustrale sur sa tête; le fleuve des patriarches, les chameaux de ses rives, le temple de Jérusalem, les cèdres du Liban paraissent attentifs. (488)

> [Watch the neophyte standing amidst the waves of the River Jordan: the hermit of the rocks pours luminous water over his head; the stream of the patriarchs, the camels on its shores, the temple of Jerusalem, the cedars of Lebanon seem to pay attention.]

Such imagery can be seen diversifying into what amounts practically to small poems in prose or lyrical pieces; these are frequent particularly in the third part of the memoirs (for example, *Mémoires,* 2:347, 352; cf. Sainte-Beuve 2:16–17, 33). Nor should we ignore Chateaubriand's recurring imagistic obsessions—trees as columns, winds, leaves, and birds (Richard 1928, 48).

A further dialectic tying abundance with ontological void is unveiled when we look at the ways in which Chateaubriand's lucidity turns from commentary of self and others to sarcasm and self-irony. As far as I know there is no full-length study of this humorous and ironic side of Chateaubriand, one which further joins him to the body of Biedermeier literary practice. Actually the variety in the *Mémoires* and the *Itinéraire* is remarkable: from kind humor to "le fou rire" (the guffawing merriment in the face of grotesque absurdity), from gentlemanly mockery to wholesale deconstruction. However the underlying note is almost always one of sarcasm—predictably so, one might say, for one centrally preoccupied with the vanishing or unreliability of reality. Typical is this scene in the Restoration House of Peers:

> Un jour le premier rang des fauteuils, tout près de la tribune, était rempli de respectables pairs, plus sourds les uns que les autres, la tête penchée en avant et tenant à l'oreille un cornet dont l'embouchure était dirigée vers la tribune. Je les endormis, ce qui est bien naturel. Un d'eux laissa tomber son cornet; son voisin réveillé par la chute, voulut ramasser poliment le cornet de son confrère, il tomba.

> [One day the first row of seats, the one closest to the rostrum, was filled with respectable peers, one deafer than the other, their heads leaning forward, and with hearing horns at their ears, the openings of which were directed toward the speaker's stand. Predictably my speech made them fall asleep. One of them let his horn fall to the ground; his neighbor woke up, politely tried to pick up the hearing aid, and himself fell to the floor.][19]

Lafayette is the object of light chivalrous contempt (*Mémoires,* 2:875–78), while Louis-Philippe and his cohorts are the object of violent sarcasm, and Talleyrand of lethal malice (2:896–905). Some of the most terrible scenes ever penned by Chateaubriand are those depicting his visit to Bohemia—where at Hradschin Castle the exiled Bourbon family had withdrawn in gloomy and musty isolation—precisely because of their tragicomic register (2:663–700). Chateaubriand is as pitiless toward the monarchy as he was toward Marat or Danton, even if the undertone of moral disgust is missing (2:429–30, 504).

When, as often the case, this fascinating tension between plentitude and absence becomes too intense, Chateaubriand resorts to a variant of the fragmentary that is highly personal and yet well attuned to the romantic/Biedermeier style that was widely used by other European contemporaries. The "conversational essay" to which I refer here was of course a genre that was retrieved in England from the eighteenth century by all those later (or Biedermeier) romantics who wanted to moderate the ambitions of high romanticism without abandoning its paradigm:

Leigh Hunt certainly, but also Hazlitt and Lamb. In France some of the writings of Paul Louis Courier, as well as the general tone of Sainte-Beuve (not least when he comments on Chateaubriand himself), are among the relatively sparse examples of a genre that programmatically injected theoretical purpose with a deconstruction of philosophical generalization and with digressionary literary energy. But elsewhere in southern, central, and eastern Europe, the *costumbrismo* and the "physiognomies" of people and situations were doing much of what Chateaubriand felt obliged to do: wary of the general and the absolute, rein it in by modest and limited cases, in a playful yet melancholy manner. These short and pointed pieces sometimes carried a moral conclusion and sometimes implied it precisely by cutting it off.

About *Génie du christianisme,* Sainte-Beuve said that it is composed out of a "suite de *tableaux*" (1:231) and shrewdly connected this with a broader fictitious unity, one made out of bits and pieces, "une vraie marqueterie. Royaliste, républicain, pêle-mêle et tour à tour, il est féal et rebelle, champion de l'autel, champion du trône, aidant à le renverser, et quand il l'a mis à bas, lui demeurant fidèle . . . il avait tiré parti de brisures même et des irrégularités brusques" (1:237). [A motley picture. Royalist, republican, helter-skelter, and one after the other, he is loyal, faithful, and a rebel, a champion of the altar, champion of the throne. Helping to overthrow it, and once down, supportive of it . . . he knew how to take advantage of any crack and unexpected irregularity.]

Certainly the most famous such inserted pieces of self-contained musing and consideration in *Génie* must be the short one on bells (pt. 4, bk. 1, ch. 1), and the longer ones on ruins (pt. 3, bk. 5, chs. 3–5), and on tombs (pt. 4, bk. 2, chs. 1–8). These are all built on a counterpoint of historical information, typological description, and lyrical subjectivity.[20] The essay on tombs reviews burial institutions in a global fashion: China and Egypt, Islam and Rome, Tahiti and ancient Scotland are equally quoted with an emphasis on the futility of human endeavor and the restful sweetness of nonexistence. Christianity is, as usual for Chateaubriand, the crowning expression of tendencies that were already present in multiple human societies.

If such inserted pieces are less than surprising given the structure of *Génie,* it is highly confirmatory that they should also emerge with frequency in the *Mémoires.* On Rome, Chateaubriand writes with the fond benevolence and easy familiarity in which Lamb writes on London (*Mémoires,* 2:363–64). Venice becomes the subject of a lesson in cultural morphology (2:770–72) while not losing its descriptive specificity. "The French in Rome" is a feuilleton in itself (2:360–63). The description of the Escorial is halfway between the tourist handbook and the moral-symbolic landscape (1:760–61). Out of the blue, under the full sway of romanticism, we run into a diatribe against mountains, the purpose of which is, of course, to signal the author's doubts concerning the sublime (2:591–92).

The typological portraits develop into essays on individuals. Thus Chateaubriand is no less astute in investigating the "dandy" than will be later Barbey d'Aurevilly and Baudelaire (*Mémoires,* 2:77–78). He knows how to turn the fairy-tale into essay when he writes about Mme Récamier (2:158–61); his Fouché has (for the later reader) overtones of Vladimir Lenin (1:945–46); the portrait of Louis XVIII (1:940–41) is an essayistic "physiognomy," much as that of Czar Alexander (1:864–65). More generally speaking, Chateaubriand's art of the portrait introduces both stoppages and abundance in the narrative. To select some of these examples is not an easy task, but a number of feminine portraits come to mind: Mme De Lévis (1:942–43), Mme de Genlis (2:182), along with the (devastating) one of Cardinal Latil (2:679), the brilliant gallery of English portraits (2:84–86), or, above all these, the one of Mme de Staël and of her last lover in their last (dying) days: fearsome and comically sublime at the same time (2:214–15). One cannot help guessing whether the latter portrait is not successful (beyond Chateaubriand's ambiguity towards Mme de Staël, as well as Guizot—people similar but no less different from him) precisely because it touches upon a personality at the very moment of its decomposition.

Such a hypothesis seems confirmed if we look at the most successful "scenes" strewn along the narrative. The coronation of Pius VIII (surely a scene of triumph and fulfillment) begins with:

> Le jour s'affaiblissait: Les ombres envahissaient lentement les fresques de la chapelle et l'on n'apercevait plus que les grands traits du pinceau de Michel-Ange. Les cierges, tour à tour éteints, laissaient échapper de leur lumière étouffée une légère fumée blanche, image assez naturelle de la vie que l'Écriture compare à *une petite vapeur.*
>
> [Daylight was weakening. Shadows invaded slowly the frescoes in the chapel and the eye could barely distinguish the broad strokes of Michelangelo's brush. The candles, gradually extinguished, turned their smothered light into tight white smoke, the natural emblem of the life that is in the Scriptures compared to a light steam.]

It ends with the sentence: "C'est une belle chose que Rome pour tout oublier, mépriser tout et mourir" (2:340). [Rome is well fit for those who want to forget everything, to despise everything, and to die.] The same sepulchral atmosphere is encountered in several famous early scenes of the *Mémoires* such as "mon donjon," the description of family life at Combourg, or even the slightly grotesque afternoon of the author's grandmother at Plancouët with her old maid and old bachelor friends (1:79–85, 23–24).

This mixture of abundant concreteness against a background of dark dissolution into nothingness culminates with a suite of images of a perishing monarchy in Prague. Chateaubriand first describes the huge, dark room faintly lit in a corner by candles for a game of whist while dusk is invading through half-open windows: "La monarchie s'éteignait entre ces deux lueurs expirantes. Profond silence, hors le frôlement des cartes et quelques cris du Roi qui se fâchait". [Monarchy was fading out between these two expiring glimmers. Profound silence, except for the rustling of the cards and occasionally of the king when he got angry.] Upon the visitor's departure he says,

Je passai les salles désertes et sombres que j'avais traversées la veille, les mêmes escaliers, les mêmes cours, les mêmes gardes, et descendu des talus de la colline, je regagnai mon auberge en m'égarant dans les rues et dans la nuit. Charles X restait enfermé dans les masses noires que je quittais: rien ne peut peindre la tristesse de son abandon et de ses années. (2:683)

[I walked the deserted and somber halls I had crossed the day before, the same stairs, the same courtyards, I passed the same sentinels, and, having desceded the hill, I returned to my inn, losing my way in the streets and the night. Charles X remained imprisoned in the black masses I had left: nobody could depict the sadness of his abandonment and his old age.]

These examples may suffice to illustrate the general point of this chapter: why and how we are entitled to consider Chateaubriand's work as an exceptionally apt illustration of the literary and intellectual age 1815–1848 in Europe. Despite his remarkably wide appeal and his successful competition in different walks of life, he was never considered a leading or central figure, neither in his lifetime nor by later readers, except by some inspired loners such as Vladimir Nabokov or Charles de Gaulle. Chateaubriand *is* what he represents: an absence of center and the gleeful plentitude that follows from such an experience. He engages this state of things in a dialog that is as important as anything in human life. Let me briefly summarize the ways before outlining some conclusions.

On the national side, better than other younger contemporaries, Chateaubriand incorporated the dynamic, or evolution, of French romanticism: its complex touch-and-go dealings with the Revolution, friendship with Saint-Martin and Ballanche, an adventurous life, settling right in the middle of the complexities of the Biedermeier age, opposition to doctrinaire romanticism. At least as important was his cultural (or intellectual-spiritual) side, with its implications for Europe and the global changes being set in motion at the time. These include historicism, the ways in which Chateaubriand stands for Biedermeier romanticism, his scenarios and fears of global historical change, the substitutive impulse, and the instituting of subjectivity as objectivity. All these would become widely recognized "megatrends" in the early and later nineteenth century.

The overriding preoccupation with temporality is present everywhere, but it also crystallizes in more specific points. Among these I would count Chateaubriand's close ties with an emerging historicism. He refers several times in the *Mémoires* (for example, 1:411) and in his volume on English literature, to Walter Scott, with the kind of grudging appreciation reserved to those ideologically close to him (Mme Staël or Guizot). With Augustin Thierry, one of the leaders of the new school of historical writing he was on terms of close friendship.[21] Chateaubriand's own view of history was unabashedly Biedermeier in nature. His invidious comparison of George Washington with Bonaparte (written up in 1822 but conceived much earlier) spells out in detail the way in which revolutionary impulses ought to be captured and tamed (1:273, 222–25). Biedermeier features and mentalities abound in the *Mémoires*—attributed to Napoleon or to the duc d'Orléans,[22] culled from his own political documents, referred to, or seen through, cartoon characters, or seen through the eyes of sisterliness.[23] His descriptions of the landscapes near the Bavarian-Bohemian border match those of Adalbert Stifter (2:660–61), and his relaxed coupling of grandeur and intimacy points in the same direction.

Chateaubriand belongs in France and in Europe to the class of founding fathers of the modern age, those who knew each other and debated the scenarios for the future two centuries: Mme de Staël and Benjamin Constant, Guizot and Tocqueville, Lamennais and Sainte-Beuve, Hugo and Bonald, Fourier and Ballanche, Saint-Simon and Comte. He himself always returned to speculations on the future, which were frequently but not always pessimistic. A notation from 1833 neatly summarizes his awareness of historical change: "J'ai traversé le Rhin à deux heures de l'après-midi; au moment ou je passais, un bateau à vapeur remontait le fleuve. Qu'eût dit César s'il eût rencontré une pareille machine, lorsqui'il bâtissait son pont?" (2:740). [I crossed the Rhine at two in the afternoon; the moment I passed a steamship was floating upriver. What would Caesar have said upon encountering such a machine while he was building his bridge?] Throughout the *Mémoires* there are intimations of a totalitarian future, lucid but dark, including the birth of modern war with its very special kind of inhumanity (2:920–30).

Punctuating his career, his articles and essays preceding the *Mémoires,* convey the intense feeling that he is at a crossroads, that he is faced with the end of one world and the beginning of another.[24] Sometimes this is seen merely as a sociohistorical event, sometimes even as a religious one: the coming of a post-Christian age: "J'ai prié avec la foule chrétienne, qui représente la vieille société au milieu de la nouvelle" (2:734). [I prayed with the Christian crowd, which represents the old society in the midst of the new.] Nevertheless, Chateaubriand's conclusions, as they culminate in the last chapters of the *Mémoires,* are somewhat Tocquevillian. With the lucidity of an unprejudiced and disenchanted conservative (a stance he adopted with great consistency [2:59–60, 252–54]) Chateaubriand accepts the coming of a mass society based on the collapse of older religious-ethical values, a dynamic of agitation, growth of knowledge, instant (or accelerated) communication, obsolescence of human labor, abolition of borders, and centrifugal individualism. He does not deny entirely the possible advantages of a new state of affairs, but he openly proclaims his anxiety as to the consequences of an alienated, inorganic society (whether with a capitalist or a communitarian slant). His only solution is that of an evangelical Christianity. Precisely because the future seems inevitably democratic (whether in the guise of a republic or in that of a constitutional monarchy), it must also be Christian. Political values follow from the Gospels—Lamennais might have been their true spokesman had he not given up on the church, Chateaubriand laments. He sees a planetary unity emerging and suggests that we live on a "spaceship

Earth;" he foresees the automobile and electricity; and he understands society as a pluricultural construct (Richard 1928, 142, 147, 159). In his view it ensues necessarily that the broad sweep of a liberated Christianity must provide the spiritual dimension of such a globalized state of affairs, since it is the most compassionate and the most universal of all religions and philosophies (25). It is also, according to Chateaubriand, the only religion capable of a growth based on transfer of values: detaching values and tenets from the physical (or historical) environment in which they are embedded and carrying them over to other shapes in which their essence can remain constant.

There are three horizons that, like concentric circles, frame these positions. The first is the horizon of alienation and exile. For all his anxiety of the inorganic state, Chateaubriand is an author of exile and loneliness. His all-pervasive intertextuality is itself a kind of recovery and acceptance/refusal of alienation. (Goethe's *Faust* immediately comes to mind as another gesture of recuperation.) The author revels in the very individualism that he otherwise denounces.

This brings us to the second horizon. In the same way in which Chateaubriand institutes a dialectic of plenitude and absence, or in which the former grows out of the latter (Richard 1928, 29, 37), he also sets up one between subjectivity and objectivity. Subjectivity is emphasized to the degree that it is turned into a kind of solid and reliable substitute for objective reality. For Chateaubriand, reality is a probability of internal resources. Since everything is doubtful and a "vanity of vanities," why not reconstruct reality, starting not from (hard) arbitrary will but from the (soft) intuitions and feelings of the I?

Substitution is the key word here (and the third horizon), not only for Chateaubriand, but for his contemporaries and the whole of the Biedermeier age. This was an age of frantic agitation in the hope and search for stability and stasis. It was led by an attempt at consolidation and by the desire to accept yet absorb modernizing events. This could be done, many of the best minds of the time believed, by quickly scurrying and replacing one area with the other, or by filling in the gaps of the one with the materials of the other. From the aesthetic to the religious, from the religious to the political, from the political to the philosophical, from there to love and travel, and so forth, in an unceasing dance, they tried to convert historical dynamics into circular stability. This is, as we have seen, the formula of Chateaubriand's writing and thinking. Therefore Chateaubriand imposes himself on us as an apt emblem of an age in which the center is absent and yet ever-replenished.

Notes

1. *Memoires*, 1:667.

2. I adapt here, as well as in the previous and subsequent paragraphs, parts of my own article (Nemoianu, *Organizing Absence*, 1992).

3. The numerous theories on the "construction of meaning" and invention of literary "institutions" (mostly descending from Michel Foucault) are, in my opinion, transpositions

into the past of some of the sociocultural practices of the late twentieth century. See, somewhat along parallel lines, Siebers 1991.

4. Chateaubriand, *Génie*.

5. See Mayer 1981; see also, along the same lines, Girouard 1981, or even Schorske 1981.

6. Fleischmann 1988 gives an excellent survey of the amazing number of intellectuals hovering more or less consistently and intentionally in the same direction.

7. Cf. *Mémoires*, 2:663–90, 849–57, and, of course, the majestic conclusion, 916–41, to which I will revert several times. Even Barbéris 1974, 393, admits Chateaubriand's vacillation between two poles. The answer was *Le conservateur* (October 1818–March 1820), a kind of response to Benjamin Constant's *Minerve française*. Not only did Chateaubriand provide the first modern political use of the term "conservative," but he instituted a framework for a variety of voices, some illustrious, such as Lamennais, Bonald, and Castelbajac, others merely belonging to the highest aristocracy (Lévis, La Rochefoucauld, Polignac) or to important political figures (Custine, Villèle, Vitrolles). The journal began somewhat cautiously, on a two-week schedule with a run of three thousand but soon moved to a weekly (albeit irregular) basis and a circulation of six thousand to eight thousand five hundred (cf. Reboul 1973, 317–31; *Mémoires*, 2:17–20, 120–22). We might point to conservative-reformist comments in *Mémoires*, 2:66–67, 123, 152–53, 464–75, 477–82. It bears repeating that Chateaubriand constantly admired Montesquieu. Cf. also Sainte-Beuve 1978, 2:132–33.

8. Actually, soon after 1871, when the royalists had huge parliamentary majorities, France remained a republic because of the failure of legitimists and Orleanists to cooperate, but more specifically because of Henri's diehard refusal to accept the tricolore instead of the traditional Bourbon white flag as a national symbol.

9. A few examples are found in *Mémoires*, 1:181, 251, 442.

10. *Mémoires*, 1:576, 1066; 2:527, 746.

11. The topic of Chateaubriand's epic ambition was often studied with acknowledgment of his Christian variant: see Naylor 1930, 178ff., 192–211; Beall 1934; Hart 1928, 162–67; Smead 1924, 161–62; see also Chateaubriand himself in notes to *Les martyrs, Mémoires*, 2:800–11, 366, 371 (on Tasso), and elsewhere; also in *Génie* (pt. 2, bk. 1, ch. 1).

12. See Maurice Regard in *Génie*, 1602–5 (the accompanying study). It bears mentioning that Chateaubriand was otherwise perfectly aware that he was writing in a generic tradition of religious apologies. In his *Défense* (1803), usually attached to modern editions, he mentions Sannazaro, Lowth, Fleury, Bossuet, and others.

13. *Génie*, 472–74; pt. 10, bk. 1, ch. 2. This chapter and the following are good examples of what I would call "Christian humanism." All happens as if the later techniques of myth theorists (Frazer, Eliade, Campbell) were turned upside down before even being written. Arguments that would reduce Christianity to a fund of archetypal traditions become arguments favoring the idea that mythical and archetypal traditions are nothing else but preparations for the future advent of Christianity.

14. The whole of Calvinist-capitalist civilization is based upon the evangelical principle of knowing and judging others by the "fruits" of their labor; cf. Gilder 1981.

15. *Génie*, 1056. This corresponds exactly to the conclusions of recent scholars on the Medieval agricultural revolution.

16. *Génie*, 513–14; pt. 1, bk. 2, ch. 1; cf. the excellent parallel to Bernardin de Saint-Pierre in Sainte-Beuve 1:170.

17. Spaemann 1959, on Bonald; I merely propose and extend the analogy. See also, in a more simplistic way Barbéris 1974, 394, 404–6.
18. *Mémoires* 2:354–55, 793; *Mémoires,* 1:1008–9, among many other places.
19. *Mémoires,* 2:7; cf. 817–18, 519–31.
20. *Mémoires,* 2:184–94; this passage reminds one of *costumbrismo,* or of Addison and Steele. There is no space in this chapter to examine at any length passages of the kind in *Génie:* the pompous purity of Communion, the admiring gravity of the Last Rites, the rural marriage, the numerous animal portraits worthy of Buffon, natural scenes and mythical landscapes, the considerations on the pioneering role of monks, and the civilizational of the Church.
21. *Mémoires* 2:510, 574, and elsewhere. Also Sainte-Beuve 1978, 2:18–19. This must be connected with Chateaubriand's experience with British literature and with Scott in particular, *Mémoires,* 1:405–19, and elsewhere. See also Miller 1925.
22. *Mémoires,* 1:908–9, 947. In fact I do consider King Louis-Philippe a Biedermeier figure. See for instance Louis-Philippe 1977, 159, 136, 102–5, 48–50, 73, 17, 32–44, 14–15, 431–33, and in general the influence of Mme de Genlis on his early formative years.
23. *Mémoires,* 2:491. The episode on the Roman embassy is in its majority comprised of documents, (2:223–370). See also Steiner 1980, 12–17, 33–35, on "sisterliness" in the age. The example of the Wordsworths could be added.
24. For the whole preceding paragraph see *Mémoires,* 2:916–40, the brilliant and somber conclusion of the book.
25. For detailed analyses of the way in which Chateaubriand saw Christianity as the cornerstone of future progress and liberty see Clarac 1975, 15–44; Barbéris 1974, 453–55; Dupuis et al. 1967; *Memoires,* 2:581.

Bibliography

Barbéris, Pierre. 1974. *A la recherche d'une écriture. Chateaubriand.* Paris: Mame.
———. 1975. *Chateaubriand. Une réaction au monde moderne.* Paris: Larousse.
———. 1978. *Aux sources du réalisme. Aristocrates et bourgeois.* Paris: 10/18.
Beall, Chandler. 1934. *Chateaubriand et le Tasse.* Baltimore: Johns Hopkins University Press.
Castries, René de. 1974. *Chateaubriand ou la puissance du songe.* Paris: Perrin.
Chateaubriand, François-René, vicomte de. 1978. *Essai sur les révolutions.* Ed. Maurice Regard. Paris: Gallimard / Nouvelle Revue Française.
———. 1978. *Génie du christianisme.* Ed. Maurice Regard. Paris: Pléiade.
———. 1988. *Mémoires d'outre-tombe.* 2 vols. Ed. Maurice Levaillant and Georges Moulinier. Paris: Gallimard / Nouvelle Revue Française.
Clarac, Pierre. 1975. *A la recherche de Chateaubriand.* Paris: Nizet.
Clément, Jean-Raul, ed. 1987. *François-René de Chateaubriand. De l'ancien régime au nouveau monde. Ecrits politiques.* Paris: Hachette.
Dédéyan, Charles. 1973. *Chateaubriand et Rousseau.* Paris: Société d'Edition d'Enseignement.
Dieguez, Manuel de. 1965. *Essai sur l'avenir poétique de Dieu.* Paris: Plon.
Dru, Alexandre. 1967. *Erneuerung und Reaktion: Die Restauration in Frankreich 1800–1830.* Munich: Kösel.
Dupuis, Georges, Jean Georgel, Jacques Moreau, eds. 1967. *Politique de Chateaubriand.* Paris: Armand Colin.

Fleischmann, Kornelius. 1988. *Klemens Maria Hofbauer, sein Leben und seine Zeit.* Graz: Styria.

Gilder, George. 1981. *Wealth and Poverty.* New York: Basic Books.

Gingras, George. 1995. "Pop-Martyrdom: Nineteenth-Century Novels with a Message." *Living Light* 31, no. 4: 41–57.

Girouard, Mark. 1981. *The Return to Camelot: Chivalry and the English Gentleman.* New Haven: Yale University Press.

Hart, Richard. 1928. *Chateaubriand and Homer.* Baltimore: Johns Hopkins University Press.

Lebègue, Raymond. 1979. *Aspects de Chateaubriand. Vie, voyage en Amérique, oeuvres.* Paris: Nizet.

Lelièvre, Michel. 1983. *Chateaubriand polémiste.* Paris: Presses Universitaires de France.

Louis-Philippe. 1977. *Memoirs 1773–1793.* New York and London: Harcourt Brace Jovanovich. (Orig. pub. in French 1973).

Mayer, Arno. 1981. *The Persistence of the Old Regime.* New York: Pantheon.

Miller, Meta Helena. 1925. *Chateaubriand and English Literature.* Baltimore: Johns Hopkins University Press.

Naylor, Louis H. 1930. *Chateaubriand and Virgil.* Baltimore: Johns Hopkins University Press.

Nemoianu, Virgil. 1984. *The Taming of Romanticism: European Literature and the Age of Biedermeier.* Cambridge: Harvard University Press.

———. 1992. "Organizing Absence: The Usefulness of Romanticism as a Period Concept." *Comparatistica* 4: 54–64.

Ormesson, Jean d'. 1982. *Mon dernier rêve sera pour vous. Une biographie sentimentale de Chateaubriand.* Paris: J. C. Lattès.

Painter, George. 1977. *Chateaubriand: A Biography.* 2 vols. London and New York: Random House.

Porter, Charles. 1978. *Chateaubriand: Composition, Imagination and Poetry.* Stanford French and Italian Studies 9. Saratoga, Calif.: Anma Libri.

Reboul, Pierre. 1973. *Chateaubriand et le conservateur.* Lille: Editions Universitaires.

Richard, Jean-Pierre. 1967. *Paysage de Chateaubriand.* Paris: Seuil.

Saint-Beuve, C. A. 1978. *Chateaubriand et son groupe littérarire sous l'empire.* 2 vols. Ed. Maurice Allem. Paris: Classiques Garnier. (Orig. pub. 1848.)

Schorske, Carl. 1979. *Fin-de-siècle Vienna.* New York: Knopf.

Siebers, Tobin. 1991. "Cold War Criticism." *Common Sense* 1, no. 3: 60–90.

Smead, Jane Van Ness. 1924. *Chateaubriand et la Bible.* Paris: Presses Universitaires de France.

Spaemann, Robert. 1959. *Der Ursprung der Soziologie aus dem Geist der Restauration.* Munich: Kösel.

Steiner, George. 1980. *Antigones.* Oxford: Oxford University Press.

Vial, André. 1972. *Chateaubriand et le temps perdu. Devenir et conscience individuelle dans les "Mémoires d'outre-tombe."* Paris: 10/18. (Orig. pub. 1963.)

II

HISTORY

From Politics to Religion

CHAPTER 2

Absorbing Modernization
The Dilemmas of Progress in Goethe's Faust II

GOETHE CAN BE REGARDED, along with Chateaubriand and Scott, as the most representative figure at the turn of the nineteenth century. Additionally, all three are bridges that assure a smooth transition from high romanticism to the Biedermeier period. All three stand for the process of sociohistorical moderation that is, in my view, the most characteristic achievement of the early nineteenth century. It is therefore highly important to look at Goethe's weltanschauung in his fully mature works: *Faust* and *Wilhelm Meisters Wanderjahre*. Let us begin with the former, remaining in the comparative vein.

Any attempt to decode the political-historical implications of Goethe's *Faust* must begin with the reminder that Goethe's positions on contemporary politics, and on historical development in general, have been a subject of puzzlement for almost two centuries. Goethe's stands have been read as ambivalent, timid, opportunistic, slyly toadying, and even downright backsliding. Indeed his work (and *Faust* in particular) has been seen as open to reactionary and exclusionary exploitation. A comparable number of readings have highlighted progress, tolerance, and Enlightenment broadmindedness and tried to define these as the center of gravity in his work.[1]

Such debates reflect first Goethe's sociocultural influence as it continues well beyond the confines of his life and of his age; second, they embody the questionable enterprise of translating accurately and completely literary-aesthetic discourse into ideological-political formulations. In fact, confronting these two modes of discourse can be truly helpful only if their relation is envisaged not as the passive mimesis of one sphere by the other but rather as genuine intermeshing in which the literary-aesthetic rhetoric and utterance is a senior participant that can explain the historical text at least as much as it is explained by the latter.[2]

Each of the opposing positions on Goethe's sociohistorical role is marred by the unfortunate and deep-rooted prejudice that Goethe's Olympian stature somehow precludes indeterminacies ("Goethe knew"). It is closer to the truth to say that Goethe was struggling honestly with a phenomenon of enormous historical proportion, trying to enact it dramatically before articulating answers that in any case often proved unsatisfactory. Goethe was indeed trying to shape a synthesis by formulating a centrist and moderating answer, but he was simultaneously trying to make sense of an unfolding historical process. For better or for worse, such wrestling with the truth was considered at the time an essential part of being fully human, and Goethe certainly shared this view.

The debate on Goethe's role also foundered more than once on the fantastic-utopian categories of Hegelian-Marxist pedigree that obfuscate, sometimes hopelessly, historical readings.[3] The writers and thinkers who (like Goethe) were busy at the Enlightenment/romanticism intersection read history not in Hegelian or Marxist terms but, as it turns out, in terms much closer to those of Max Weber, Ralf Dahrendorf, Ernst Gellner, or W. W. Rostow—what is currently called "modernization theory."[4] In these terms the problem confronting the age can be summarized as a series of accelerated displacements from traditional, organic, biological modes of governance and social behavior to rationalist and transactional social structures; from rural to urban and industrialized existence and production; from tribal to individualist consciousness; from communitarian constraint to contractual and alienated modes of association; from stability and harmony to speed, homogeneity, and creativity; from eccentricity and tentativeness to streamlining and discipline. These broad tendencies had been gathering momentum since the Renaissance, but the Industrial Revolution in northwest Europe and the political upheavals in France, North America, and elsewhere rendered them painfully visible and forced conscious deliberation upon both intellectuals and society at large.

Goethe's political opinions per se are not especially acute or profound, perhaps just symptomatically interesting as the views of one intelligent individual at the time.[5] By contrast, in the enactments of his literary works Goethe puts forward sophisticated and nuanced responses to the historical situation of his time—to my mind, some of the most complex and satisfying ever put forward. The encodings and decodings of historical dilemmas and aporias, the enactments of tradition and progress, of transactional versus organic, of liberal versus conservative, that are incorporated in *Faust* are, to repeat for emphasis, all better described by taking a comparative approach in order to place Goethe more firmly inside his age, rather than the age inside Goethe.

A reference to Walter Scott is therefore in order. Scott is the closest literary counterpart of Edmund Burke. Scott lacked Burke's rhetorical energy, subtlety, and precision, but he made a rather similar case with the additional efficiency that the ambiguities of dramatized situations can provide. Reflection on the accelerated movement of history was forced upon him by the local example that he knew in great detail; for Scotland represents one of the first cases of violent colonial imposition of technological and economic advance with the concomitant political loosening of biologically rooted social forms. The tragic undecidabilities of historical progress were painfully immediate for Scott as he observed the century-long struggle between the Hanoverian regime and the archaic clan organization of the Scottish Highlands. In novel after novel such as *Waverley, Old Mortality, Rob Roy,* and *Redgauntlet,* Scott tried to assess the advantages and the drawbacks of the one civilizational model as opposed to another, and tried to delineate their value systems and their human costs. The answers become clear enough after perusing several of his novels: Scott wants us to accept the inevitability of the historical movement away from the organic bindings of blood and soil towards the society of unattached individuals whose rationally negotiated contracts shape their personal destinies.[6] At the same time, worried about the loss of values invested in the historical past, Scott declares the novelist's primary task to be salvaging these values by providing images of balance that would be fully human, rounded, and integrated. This can be done, he suggests, by detaching the values of an archaic, natural, and organic society from their previous material (physical and social) environment and transferring them into a new medium by finding new vehicles for them. (It goes without saying that even the mere contemplation of such an abstract exercise already places Scott in the imaginative world outlined by Adam Smith and Adam Ferguson.) These older values, once implanted in the minds and souls of younger people, could survive and perhaps even revive, albeit in new bodies and with entirely new meanings and languages.

Scott returned with amazing doggedness to this his favorite topic, looking at it from different angles and in different historical circumstances. Harking back to the etymological roots of "revolution,"[7] he often tried out on his readers combinations in which the "reactionary" and the truly "revolutionary" were allegories of each other or overlapped in different ways (*Old Mortality*). The enormous international impact of Scott's novels proves that his political philosophy responded to an acutely felt need. Major figures such as Manzoni, Victor Hugo, Pushkin (*Kapitanskaya Dochka*), and others in eastern and southern Europe immediately came up with their own versions of Scott's scenario. I also believe that Balzac was more deeply marked by the example of Scott (that is, well beyond his early and rather unsuccessful *Les Chouans*) than usually assumed. Perhaps Scott's most faithful and thoughtful follower was James Fenimore Cooper, who masterfully translated the opposition between the archaic, Highlands clan-based civilization and the modernizing, individual, and contractual civilization into the opposition of Native Americans versus settlers, with their opposing systems of values and alternative versions of paradise, in the Leatherstocking series and elsewhere (see chapter 5). Similarly the broadest acceptance of Scott's views of history may have been in the Old South of the United States, although with its own local distortions.[8]

Comparable attempts at an uneasy balance can be found, as indicated in the previous chapter, in the work of Chateaubriand, who once (trying to place himself inside the constitutional crisis of 1830) claimed that "Républicain par nature, monarchiste par raison et bourbonnien par honneur, je me serais beaucoup mieux arrangé d'une démocratie si je n'avais pu conserver la monarchie légitime, que de la monarchie bâtarde octroyée par je ne sais qui."[9] In a more disorderly and dispersed way, Chateaubriand, as explained in chapter 1, engaged in the same kinds of enactments as Scott; he elaborates the possibilities inherent in Scott's narrative model and assays them in unexpected ways. Throughout the *Mémoires d'outre-tombe*, for instance, we find the continuous suggestion that the writer is at a crossroads, witnessing the end of a world and negotiating with the dawning age of modernity. Pessimistic as it is, the final essay in the *Mémoires*, on the future of the twentieth century, summarizes, not much differently from Tocqueville, what Chateaubriand saw as the challenges of a natural humanity with its rich interiority abruptly confronted with artificial and manipulated social environments.

This tone of moderate (or liberal) conservatism, of reformist progress, of change and preservation, of orderly advancement, of continuity in transition, soon became diffused throughout Europe.[10] It can be illustrated sufficiently by examples from opposite ends of the continent. In Spain, the school of the *costumbristas* tried in its short essays to outline the dialectic of change and continuity, rather in the spirit of Jovellanos (the "Spanish Burke" and Goya's good friend), while in Hungary the "liberal romantics", as they have been called (István Széchény, József Eötvös, and others), took surprisingly analogous positions.[11]

Let me return to Walter Scott and the peculiar interconnections between him and his Weimar contemporary. Scott was an enthusiast of German literature and knew it well, though in somewhat disorderly fashion. Goethe was one of his early favorites, and Scott's first book-length publication was a translation of *Götz of Berlichingen* (1798; with the active support of "Monk Lewis"). Despite numerous (and hilarious) linguistic howlers (he admitted this himself in letters written in his old age; his German improved steadily over the years), the work was considered worthy of inclusion in the prestigious Bohn's Library (with due corrections) because of Scott's capacity to catch the flavor of Goethe's style (see also his translation of "Erlkönig," which is admirable despite Scott's belief that the action was placed in the "Black Forest of Thuringia"). *Götz* exerted a clear influence on Scott's *Lay of the Last Minstrel* and *Marmion*. (The titular hero of the latter work was patterned after Weislingen, the main female character of the former after Elisabeth.) Further Goethean influences have been detected in *Ivanhoe* (by as early a commentator as Lockhart) and in the play *The House of Aspen* (1799), a "remake" of an obscure play by one G. Wachter, as well as in other works. For example, Fenella in *Peveril of the Peak* is modeled on Mignon in the *Lehrjahre*, while the portrait of Louis XI in *Quentin Durward* seems to be indebted to the figure of Mephistopheles. Smaller borrowings have been noted in *The Antiquary* and the Leicester / Amy Robsart relationship in *Kenilworth* (after Egmont and Clara).

Scott kept abreast of Goethe's main publications. His son-in-law John Gibson Lockhart visited Goethe in Weimar and eventually the two exchanged long and highly complimentary letters (January 12, 1827, from Weimar and July 9, 1827, from Edinburgh); both correspondents were pleased and flattered by the other's letter. In 1832, just two weeks before his death, Goethe (responding to a letter from Italy from an already seriously ill Scott) invited the novelist to come to Weimar. In 1831, at Carlyle's initiative, fifteen distinguished Englishmen offered Goethe as an anniversary gift a golden seal inscribed with "Ohne Hast aber ohne Rast"; Scott was one of them.

Meanwhile Goethe had started reading massive amounts of Scott (his introduction was *Kenilworth* in 1821): not only novels (*Waverley, Ivanhoe, Rob Roy, The Black Dwarf, The Fair Maid of Perth*)—about which he was highly complimentary—but also other works such as *The Life of Napoleon* and *Letters on Demonology and Witchcraft*. Goethe also read and sometimes summarized articles from the *Edinburgh Review* and other Scottish and English journals. The reception of Helena by Faust (act 3, "Innerer Burghof") is indebted, it has been convincingly argued, to the reception of Elizabeth I by the Earl of Leicester as described in Scott's *Kenilworth*. It is also generally accepted that some of the material in act 4 of *Faust II* is indebted to Scott's *Letters on Demonology and Witchcraft* (which, in turn, contains precisely the materials on Nicolai that had stimulated Goethe's lampoon in the "Walpurgisnacht").[12]

There can be no doubt that we are faced with a close and intimate connection. The reflections of Scott and Goethe on the movement of history were remarkably similar primarily, I believe, because of parallels in their fundamental philosophical orientations. However, I do not exclude certain kinds of ideological reinforcement through direct influence. Goethe must have been heartened by the kinship he sensed in Scott's novels in the years when he was writing *Faust II*. For Scott, in turn, the ambiguous and tragic loneliness of Götz in the turbulence of historical progress, and Goethe's own vacillations with regard to progress in that play, may well have motivated his later (novelistic) treatments of the dilemmas of progress.

In any case, where do Goethe and *Faust* fit in this wider European scene? Above all Goethe is bound to these contemporaries by the shared view that imagination, beauty, and subjectivity, all symbolic and emotional resources, can and should be used as legitimate tools for cognition, human action, and historical praxis. This view was increasingly abandoned after 1850, but until then (in romantic historiography, in travel literature, and indeed, everywhere) one can observe many kinds of entwining of the fictional with the mimetic and reproductive. Practically this was a vindication of the past (in which sentimental and aesthetic factors were supposed to have been prevalent) by demonstrating its continued utility for the present and future. If a passing civilization could be boiled down to its interiority—rather than to its externals, which, as was almost unanimously admitted, could and must be discarded—then the issue would be to find an effective function for the faculties and values put in doubt by the advent of modernity. It is here that *Faust's* relevance to the progress/conservation debate must be sought.

For cultural history *Faust* is most usefully read as a kind of document in which the dialectics and possibilities of transition are outlined and worked out in systematic fashion. I will review a few aspects briefly and dwell upon others in more detail.

Faust has often been described as a summa of the past, a repository of genres and meters, and stylistic possibilities. In the same sense it can also be seen as a survey of modes of government, of sociopolitical frameworks, in the manner of both Montesquieu's *Esprit des lois* (typologically) and Fénelon's narrative unpacking of possibilities in *Aventures de Télémaque*. Fairly detailed presentations of the mechanisms of a medieval city-state are presented in *Faust I*, the functioning of baroque and/or enlightened absolutism (with its bureaucracies, financial dealings, internal power struggles, emphasis on spectacle and splendor) is seen in the first act of *Faust II*. Slightly more complicated (but also more stimulating) are the last two structures of governance presented in the play. The Faust/Helena monarchic experiment looks back to archaic clan organization; at the same time it depicts a modern alternative, in the guise of the Biedermeier *Kleinstaat*, to the imperialist macroeconomic frameworks that were emerging at the time. The same ambiguity obtains in the case of Faust's final governmental experiment. This is in some ways an egalitarian, democratic, state-socialist construct; but in other ways it is firmly dirigiste, directed by bureaucracies, realpolitik, and collectivist volition. Needless to say, this survey is also historical in its progress from the Middle Ages, through the centuries, to the near and predictable future.

The fact that *Faust* is a repository of the past can be considered a conservative side of the drama; nevertheless the very fact that this array of shapes (aesthetic as well as historical-cultural) is now in need of preservation marks a radical turning point, as the inception of a new and progressive age that is thus acknowledged and accepted.[13]

Like the contemporaries whose examples I briefly adduced at the beginning, Goethe is most anxious to identify elements of the past that can resist the sociohistorical rush of an accelerated and inevitable future, to identify what can resist time. The answer is certainly not clear, neither for Faust nor for Goethe nor for *Faust*. (We do not have, if I am not mistaken, a Bakhtinian reading of *Faust*, but it is not usually disputed that *Faust* is a work of plural voices and of thick layers of deliberate indeterminacy.) The answer is least clear for Faust himself, who is not very strong on memorizing. He has to be reminded of his social efficiency by the country people during his early bouts of dejection (981–1063). He relies thereafter increasingly on Mephistopheles as a repository of memory. Faust does not quite recognize Gretchen during the Walpurgisnacht orgy (4183–88), nor does he seem to recognize her, or understand her as an agent of his salvation in the final scene of *Faust II*. At least as typical are the repeated incidents of swooning and fainting, devices by which episodes are brought to an end but also illustrate Faust's general passivity and dreamlike state. The first of these episodes occurs even before the pact, when Mephistopheles easily escapes his power by inducing Faust's cataleptic sleep (1425–1525). Others occur at the conclusion of *Faust I* and the beginning of *Faust II*: the most significant of these discontinuities is the result of the grab for Helena ("Explosion. Faust liegt am Boden") commented on by Mephistopheles' exasperated-condescending,

> Hier lieg, Unseliger, verführt
> Zu schwergelöstem Liebesbande!
> Wen Helena paralysiert,
> Der kommt so leicht nicht zu Verstande. (6566–69)

This explosion leads to a longer paralysis but not to loss of memory, although it could be argued that the wanderings along the upper and lower Peneios show a rudderless and easily distracted individual. Finally, act 5 of *Faust II* gives no indications of continuity with previous experiences.[14] Faust is unable to reestablish contact with his former students and colleagues, and one may wonder whether any kind of actual growth process can be imagined as going on inside Faust. One could almost argue that the Lord is seriously mistaken in providing grace, salvation, and forgiveness to Faust on the basis of some putative *streben* (striving) and *bemühen* (endeavor), of which there is precious little evidence. In a curious way it is not Mephistopheles who represents a side of Faust, but rather Faust who could be seen as a variant of Mephistopheles; Faust's much-vaunted creativity is merely a *Verneinung* (negation) of a historical environment made available to him through no merit or effort of his own. (In this sense the acclamation of "Faustianism" by Spengler and others as the very center of Western culture/civilization appears as highly doubtful.)

Although Faust is thus a master of oblivion and of liberal discontinuity, *Faust* can be seen as a monument of the struggle with, and for, memory, and thus as a conservative work.[15]

The evolutionary continuity in *Faust* as a whole, and in *Faust II* in particular, must therefore be placed not at the level of the character's subjective consciousness but at that of Goethe's objective understanding of historical movement. Precisely because Faust has a weak and unreliable historical memory he is more fully engaged in each given historical situation and responds with a relative lack of inhibition to the given circumstances. Faust the character pays little attention to his own past; he integrates readily into the power configurations inside which he is placed and does what is required of him. Faust-in-the-context is what should be subjected to examination.

In act 1 ("Kaiserliche Pfalz"), power relations and governance are based on the overwhelming nominal privileges of the ruler. Mephistopheles describes these in unctuous superlatives in the passage beginning,

> Das bist du, Herr! weil jedes Element
> Die Majestät als unbedingt erkennt.
> Gehorsam Feuer hast du nun erprobt;
> Wirf dich ins Meer. (6003–6)

Mephistopheles ends with "Und, höchster Herr! / die Erde hast du schon." (line 6030; cf. also the flattery of the herald in 5072–76). In reality, however, the powers of the emperor seem limited not only by economic constraints but also by the assertive intervention of advisors ("Saal des Thrones"), all jealous of their privileges and speaking for powerful constituencies, not least the astrologer (4955–70, 5047–56), the equivalent of the modern-day social scientist and think-tank guru.[16] The people are heard from often; they have their own identity and opinions (often cynical or skeptical, [4885–89, or 4951–54]) and are implicitly taken into account in the decision-making process (4757–60, 5484–93, 5715–26, 5748–56). Indeed, there are complaints about the growth of individualism and "greedy self-interest" at the expense of common causes and of the central budget:

> Wohin man kommt, da hält ein Neuer Haus,
> Und unabhängig will er leben;
> Zusehen muss man, wie er's treibt.
> Wir haben so viel Rechte hingegeben,
> Dass uns auf nichts ein Recht mehr übrigbleibt.
> [...]
> Ein jeder kratzt und scharrt und sammelt,
> Und unsre Kassen bleiben leer. (4836–51).

In neat contrast to act 5, the cabinet-minister Mephistopheles advises the Emperor: "Nimm Hack' und Spaten, grabe selber! / Die Bauernarbeit macht dich gross" (5039–40), and the latter complies (5047) with meek fussiness ("Nur gleich, nur gleich! / Wie lange soll es währen!") in a gesture that would be quite out of character with the imperial/sociobureaucratic Faust of the final scenes.[17] At any rate, in act 1 Faust, whether as Plutus or as himself, is merely a minister and advisor, with no sovereign powers.

By contrast, in act 3 Faust enjoys sovereign autonomy over his small fief north of Sparta. His image (and self-image) is that of a benevolent, paternal ruler. The Vossian/Homeric meters, the constant reminders, in adages of pompous piety, of a power based on age and legitimacy (often with reference to biblical-patriarchal modes of governance as much as, or more than, to ancient Greek ones), the mild and benign behavior of both Helena and Faust all point to this image. In particular Faust's long tirade (9514–61) represents a veritable governmental program, since it comes just after the beginning of his reign.

Against this "progress" stand at least two elements. The first is the heart of darkness inside this benignity. The mode of governance is based upon ritual sacrifice, human destruction, slavery, and a notably more ruthless treatment of subjects than in act 1. Faust's and Helena's tolerance is just that, toleration, when in fact there is no constraint against the most ruthless behavior (8921–29). The second is the artificial nature of this governmental concoction. There are repeated references to the artificiality of Faust's little state. Faust himself asks, "Was bin ich nun? ... / ... meine Mauern / unsicher" (9264–66), and the anguished feminine chorus wonders:

> Alles deckte sich schon
> Rings mit Nebel umher.
> Sehen wir doch einander nicht!
> Was geschieht? gehen wir?
> Schweben wir nur
> Trippelnden Schrittes am Boden hin?
> [...]
> Ja auf einmal wird es düster,
> [...]
> Ist's ein Hof? ist's tiefe Grube?
> Schauerlich in jedem Falle! (9110–25)

The artificial and uncertain nature of this "nation" is analogous to the hybrid and historically contrived nature of much of Biedermeier and nineteenth-century statehood, with its veneer of chivalric-feudal externalities and its modernizing deep-structures.[18] In a word, the society outlined in act 3 is in its aims and even in its praxis more liberal than the empire of act 1; nevertheless, we notice that the power of the ruler (and/or of Faust personally) has been growing considerably, while the voice of the people or the participatory nature of the governance has been losing ground.

In act 5, a comparison with the third sociopolitical experience confirms this pattern. The ideals of this last society portrayed in *Faust* ("the end of history" as it were) come much closer to a modern socioliberal agenda, with its concerns for job-creation ("Arbeiter schaffe Meng' auf Menge, / Ermuntere durch Genuss und Strenge, / Bezahle, locke, presse bei!," [11552–54]), ecology ("die Erde mit sich selbst versöhnet," [11541]), civil rights and communitarian options ("viele Millionen," "paradiesisch Land," "Völkerschaft," "Gewimmel," [11563–79]) to the point that, as I said earlier, a number of readers were convinced that Goethe was projecting, wittingly or unwittingly, a socialist future. If not Goethe then at least Faust must have thought along these lines.

The transfer into practice of these high ideals looks different, and of course we see here the other, conservative side of the coin, or to be more precise, the kind of corrective that conservative skepticism and realism ought to bring, in Goethe's scenario, to the utopian pressures for progress exerted by the collectivist project. On the one hand Faust, immersed in the dynamics of his activist improvement efforts, forgets all about his own mortality and about how one can lose touch with reality; as Mephistopheles comments with a malice bordering upon pity: "Den letzten, schlechten, leeren Augenblick, / Der Arme wünscht ihn festzuhalten" (11589–90), when all along the construction activity consisted only of funeral preparations: "Man spricht, wie man mir Nachricht gab, / Von keinem Graben, doch vom Grab" (11557–58). On the other hand, Goethe pointedly identifies the human cost of a radical progress that all too easily succumbs to (imperialist and administrative) coercion as the best means to hasten the achievement of the social good and to implement lofty ideals. Three of the seven scenes of act 5 are devoted to Philemon and Baucis and their destruction. For Faust, the "Jeffersonian in a hurry," the possibility of imperfection or of an exception to collective goals is intolerable: "Dass sich das grösste Werk vollende, / Genügt *ein* Geist für tausend Hände" (11509–10). Individual traditions, even the least threatening, become unacceptable from the vantage point of the socially desirable: "Das Glöckchen läutet, und ich wüte!" (11258). Procedural shortcuts, streamlined judicial procedure are impatiently resorted to: "Dass man, zu tiefer, grimmiger Pein, / Ermüden muss, gerecht zu sein" (11271–72). Faust's subsequent regret, whether sincere or hypocritical, at the liquidation of conservative minorities is quickly dispelled by the renewed opportunity for creative work, much in the vein of a (blind) totalitarian ruler.

It would be wrong to read immediately into the Philemon und Baucis episode a full-scale condemnation of the liberal-globalist project: if nothing else, Faust's redemption in the last scene of the dramatic poem indicates the contrary. The most plausible and convincing reading is one that highlights the dilemma posed by the episode and the centrality of a dialectics of peril in it. Certainly a pattern can be recognized as we advance in the reading of *Faust II:* the ideal of a liberalized civilization gains ground, indeed seems to advance triumphant, while at the same time the possibilities for manipulation, control, and social engineering grow and are, as a matter of fact, implemented by Faust.

Another pattern of contradiction and uncertainty, while not identical with the one just described in the section above, nevertheless tends to reinforce it, and occasionally overlaps with it. I refer to the growth of abstraction, rationality, and artificiality as the sociopolitical experiences of *Faust II* unfold. There is, unquestionably, manipulation at work in the "Kaiserliche Pfalz": adornment, pretense, realpolitik, and outright lying. Nevertheless we also observe a certain ingenuousness and directness in the conversations between emperor and advisors, and, in any case, the very resort to allegory (the "Mummenschanz" in "Weitläufiger Saal") reaffirms belief in a one-to-one relationship between illusion and reality. At bottom, only the introduction of paper currency indicates a decisive orientation toward the artificial, abstract, and transactional. Of course this money literally undermines the foundation on which the empire rests.

This is not so north of Sparta. Crisp, apposite, to the point as usual, Phorkyas/Mephistopheles explains what the northern invaders are bringing new and different into Hellenic lands:

> Und seine Burg! Die solltet ihr mit Augen sehn!
> Das ist was anderes gegen plumpes Mauerwerk,
> Das eure Väter, mir nichts dir nichts, aufgewälzt,
> Zyklopisch wie Zyklopen, rohen Stein sogleich
> Auf rohe Steine stürzend; dort hingegen, dort
> Ist alles senk- und waagerecht und regelhaft.
> Von aussen schaut sie! himmelan sie strebt empor,
> So starr, so wohl in Fugen, spiegelglatt wie Stahl.
> Zu klettern hier—ja selbst der Gedanke gleitet ab.
> Und innen grosser Höfe Raumgelasse, rings
> Mit Baulichkeit umgeben, aller Art und Zweck. (9017–27)

The spirit of geometry takes over here as order, abstraction, logical linearity, and abstract shapes replace the natural agglutinations of the past. Similarly the companions of Faust, the "kühn Geschlecht / [. . .] dringend aus cimmerischer Nacht," (8999–9000) seem artificially bred in their "geregelter Zug" (9155) and are unattractive sexually to the otherwise bold and lusty female followers of Helena:

> Gern biss' ich hinein, doch ich schaudre davor;
> Denn in ähnlichem Fall, da erfüllte der Mund
> Sich, grässlich zu sagen! mit Asche. (9162–64)

The abstract and artificial atmosphere is further heightened precisely by the uncertainty of present reality: "Vielleicht auch irrt sie zweifelhaft im Labyrinth / Der wundersam aus vielen einsgewordnen Burg" (9145–46), in which everybody suspects the reality of everybody else and thick mists obliterate the surroundings.

Once Faust is no longer a feudal leader, but a modern one, he and Mephistopheles can shed all inhibitions; naturally derived modes are abandoned in favor of rational abstractions.[19] Mephistopheles's engineering helpers are mechanical and robot-like; their masterpiece is a "grosser, gradgeführter Kanal" ("Palast" [stage direction between lines 11142 and 11143]). Faust avows that "der Tüchtige" should abandon the search for ultimate truths and turn to pragmatic pursuits: "Was er erkennt, lässt sich ergreifen" (11448). The family—Faust himself had been notoriously luckless in raising one, whether in the test tube or otherwise—must give way to manipulated organizations. The clouds and mists of the Lacedemonian hills now are replaced by full blindness, the precondition of sterile rationality and arbitrary abstraction, ironically at the very moment that Faust clamors obsessively for visual control. Does not Lynkeus resemble a supervising guard on top of the wooden tower at the corner of a penal colony or prison camp? Does not Faust console himself for the misfortune of Philemon and Baucis by saying, "Doch sei der Lindenwuchs vernichtet / Zu halbverkohlter Stämme Graun, / Ein Luginsland ist bald errichtet, / Um ins Unendliche zu schaun" (11342–45)? On the whole, act 5 reminds us of the theories of Goux on the growth of abstraction as the foundation of modern societies.[20]

For Goethe, the increase in abstraction and replaceability as well as the decline of the sensorial and the concrete signal mankind's relentless modernization; he is deeply ambivalent about them. This is not to say that he is hostile: armies of readers (even in our own time a good majority, I would guess) have looked upon the progress outlined in *Faust II* with approval: the capitalist growth ("Nur mit zwei Schiffen ging es fort, / Mit zwanzig sind wir nun im Port" [11173–74]), the ensuing social sharing, the ceaseless advance ("Im Weiterschreiten find' er Qual und Glück," [11451]). Surely this means that there is enough semantic gesturing to offset any outright opposition by the author to radical progress and to demote opposition to mere doubt. Thus the pattern described here resembles the one described above, the modernization of structures of governance, even though the two are not identical.[21]

Despite the pattern of progress from act 1 to act 5, I am not too inclined to emphasize the historicity or chronology of these dramatic events, as many critics have done. Their arrangement is more a matter of communication and convenient rhetoric. In fact it is more rewarding to think of these episodes as contemporaneous, as a series of existential and historical options offered to the reader, or offered by the author to himself as part of his reflection on what was happening to the world and where human society was heading. We may also wonder whether the tragedy of Gretchen could not be interpreted, in a political vein, as a historical necessity—the break of history with a small, secure, and secluded environment, the break with the microharmony of modest personal happiness. In that case the tragedy would be precisely the inevitability of individual sacrifice.

Does *Faust II* offer any conclusions in the light of these considerations? Is Goethe pessimistic or optimistic about the direction in which the world is moving? I believe that the parallels with Tocqueville's considerations about American democracy are rather obvious.[22] The tone is amiable resignation, marked lack of enthusiasm, but therefore neither hostile opposition, nor, certainly, despair of human resilience and ingenuity to cope with radically modified historical environments or to preserve the features of humanity as Goethe understood them.

Two qualifiers, or accents, ought to be added here. First, the evolution of environments in social history as imagined by Goethe and some of his more lucid contemporaries (not least Scott and Chateaubriand) oddly resembles the vision widely accepted at the end of the twentieth century and derived from Durkheim and Max Weber, or Ernst Gellner and Karl Polanyi. (If further names are needed to flesh out what I have in mind they could be those of the neoclassical figures of Friedrich Hayek, Karl Popper, Louis Dumont, or even Dahrendorf and Andrew Janos).

Second, quite central to the whole project of Faust, I am convinced, and probably also dear to Goethe's heart, was the argument that there are only systemic problems, no systemic solutions. Solutions can only be provided in and through individual praxis. Faust is the individual who must learn the virtues of the individual; *Faust* is the ultimate anti-*Candide*. Each episode that concludes with Faust's "unhappiness" or alienation indicates that the main hero is unable or unwilling to adapt. It also indicates that a system or framework as such is unable to respond fully to real individual human needs. The semantic value of the religious element at the very end is precisely this: it is extrasystemic. This is not to say that we should overlook the superadded irony of a religious framework that is itself placed inside the mode of contractual negotiation and arbitrary sign-attribution it is supposed to supersede, but only that Goethe indicates that imperfection and tragic tension are too integral to "being-human" to be eradicated except by transcendence of the human, irrespective of the nature (or probability) of such a transcendence.

Once we accept these two qualifications it is easy to see how Goethe's attempt to use history as a universalizing idiom has much relevance for today. Goethe thinks that history cannot be made in a real sense by the human person; but this does not involve him in either antihistorical negation or the passive sufferance of a "whirlwind." He suggests in *Faust II* and elsewhere that history is or can be acceptable if it is responded to by moderating discourses of deflection and digression. This is Goethe's equivalent to romantic fragmentariness in the Schlegel-Nietzsche tradition. *Faust II* (or *Faust* as a whole) is itself such a deflective discourse, but it also contains instances of deflection, avoidance, and moderation, like many smaller laboratories inside a medical building. Even if we do not accept this conception, we can still admire, or at least understand, the strenuous honesty of its effort.[23]

The possibilities for the transfer of Faustian situations onto a global, turn-of-the-millennium scale are considerable. The transitional pressures experienced by German / northwest European areas first around 1800 (and not entirely mastered even now) have been generalized to the entire globe by the end of the twentieth century. Showing how these pressures were processed in *Faust* and other contemporary works clearly vindicates the continuing relevance of some humanistic/canonical areas. I am sure I do not make an exaggerated claim in saying that works like Faust are a kind of "cushioning" area that allows everyone to work out the asperities of transitions in a more compassionate way than pure political-economic decisions, no matter how well-intentioned or democratically well-crafted they may otherwise be.[24]

Notes

1. For a short discussion of Börne, Gregorovius, and others see Chiarini and Dietze 1981, 102–3. Cf. also Borchmeyer 1977, 303.

2. Druse (1985, 81–82) misses precisely this point in objecting to Heinz Schlaffer's interpretation of Goethe's readings on economics. Cf. also Cape 1991, 131, 141.

3. Thus my main objection to the (otherwise excellent) study by Schlaffer (1981) is that it weakens its own argument by resorting to Marxist arguments rather than, for example, to Karl Polanyi's tripartite sequence of reciprocity, redistribution, and market.

4. According to Tomlinson (1991, 142) Marx should also be included (along with Simmel, Durkheim, and Tönnies) in this group of classical sociologists. Tomlinson also argues against understanding capitalism as "the single principle behind cultural modernity," although it "inflects modernity in a particular way" (141).

5. Perhaps of all Goethe's statements on his political philosophy, the most famous and the most significant are those noting the acceleration of the means of communication and the commercial speed of paper money, as well as the Eckermann passage in which he placed himself halfway between revolution and "arbitrary rule." See the comments on these in Mommsen 1948, 276–77, 284, and Bergsträsser 1962, 90, 199–203.

6. Octavio Paz uses the phrase "condemned to modernity" (cf. Tomlinson 1991, 136, 141). Numerous commentators noticed the attitude expressed by this phrase in Goethe's case. Compare also Borchmeyer 1977, 307–8, and Wild 1991, 89, 95. See also Nemoianu 1984.

7. This was in fact still true about German usage at the time. See, for example, Saine 1988, 328.

8. On Goethe's knowledge of Scott and of Scotland, see, among others, Hennig 1987, 70–88; see also Staiger 1952, 3:414.

9. Clément 1987, 141. The phrase appears in an essay published in 1831 as a political pamphlet, "De la nouvelle proposition relative au bannissement de Charles X et de sa famille."

10. It is very difficult to dig out on the theoretical level a "conservative" position in the full and strong sense of the word during the *Goethezeit* and even before 1789. Thus none other than Prince Metternich thought of himself as just a pre-Revolutionary liberal. Cf. von Srbik 1987, 1:60–66, 227–28. Jacques Godechot in his fundamental work has difficulty finding pure ultraconservative doctrines, before as well as during the Revolution. The closest would be the handbook used for teaching politics to the future Louis XVI and his younger brothers, that is, the original short (and specifically commissioned) form of Jacques Nicolas Moreau's later enormously expanded *Principes de morale, de politique et du droit publique puisés dans l'histoire de notre monarchie* (cf. Godechot 1961, 18–20). I also tend to agree with more recent historical work that thinks of the revolutionary terror of the 1790s as a persecutory and paranoic ploy meant to cover up the despair of the victors at the absence of genuine opposition.

11. Gaspar Melchor de Jovellanos (1744–1811), unlike his English counterpart and although he was also twice in government, was deemed a dangerous liberal; he was banished from Madrid (1790–1797) and imprisoned in Majorca (1801–1808). See, among others, de la Cierva 1987. On the Hungarians, see Menczer in Kaltenbrunner 1978, 219–40, and on the Austrians see Nyíri 1968, 10–39. Actually, positions of varying similarity can be found in contemporary Romanian or Russian works.

12. For some full treatments, see Bulloch 1970, and particularly Needler 1950.

13. For an exploration of the separate issue of the ambivalent nature of creative originality, see Nemoianu 1984, 69–75.

14. These episodes are much in keeping with the depiction of Scott's main heroes in some of his Waverley novels (Edward in *Waverley*, Frank Osbaldistone in *Rob Roy*, Darsey Latimer in *Redgauntlet*, and others) who are similarly sleepwalking, manipulated individuals with only a sketchy grasp of what they are experiencing; dreamlike passivity rather than action likewise characterizes many of Chateaubriand's figures, as well as Renzo in *I Promessi Sposi*.

15. Of course, ultimately any true literary writing is about memory, as Czeslaw Milosz once remarked. I would add: it is thus conservative at heart, hence the determined struggle of the zeitgeist of each age, regarding itself as the embodiment of progressive values, against literature. See also Schlaffer 1981, 19–28, who uses the intelligent formula "Goethes Versuch, die Neuzeit zu hintergehen." All quotations are from Goethe, *Faust*.

16. Schlaffer 1981, 124.

17. Other parallels, usually not noticed by critics, are to be found in the parade of Graces, Fates, and Furies in "Weitläufiger Saal" (5300–5455) in opposition to "Mitternacht," and Faust's much more intense and dangerous involvement with similar figures, e.g. the "Vier graue Weiber" or, indirectly, "die drei gewaltigen Gesellen."

18. Cf. Girouard 1981.

19. This has been very well depicted by Schlaffer (1981, 130–34, 143, and elsewhere). Cf. also Wild 1991, 120–28. Eppelsheimer (1982, 386–417) argues more intemperately that the Faust of act 5 is an anti-Faust, alien from the ecologist, anticolonialist, and spiritualized figure of the rest of the drama.

20. Goux 1978.

21. As Schlaffer (1981, 54–55, 82–86) and others (e.g. Wild 1991, 8–9, 32–33, 40–41; Borchmeyer 1977, 171–73; Bergsträsser 1962, 301) have shown, Goethe's interest in and awareness of socioeconomic developments and trends was extensive, covering the whole range of options, from Adam Smith and his followers (Georg Sartorius in Germany) to Saint-Simon and utopian communism.

22. Bergsträsser 1962, 310–11; Mommsen 1948, 106–15, 198; Borchmeyer 1977, 255–87; Cape 1991, 14, 139; Wild 1991, 1–6; the influence of Möser was processed by Goethe in the same direction, cf. Mommsen 1948, 29–33; also Krippendorff 1988, 27; Borchmeyer 1977. Goethe, in fact, intuited Max Weber's basic insight as to the connection between Lutheran Reformation and modernity (Cape 1991, 138).

23. I am not saying that the quintessentially dialectical and antisystemic nature of both Goethe and Faust (and their insistence on the concept of imperfection) have gone unobserved. See Ortega y Gasset's essay of 1932, also Borchmeyer 1977, 200–207; Hamm 1978, 20–21, 159; Mommsen 1948, 205–75; Krippendorff 1988, 116, 118 (on lack of enthusiasm for history, see Schlaffer 1981, in Chiarini 1987, 12; even Staiger 1952, 3:456).

24. I am grateful to Jane Brown, Harry Redner, and Jeffrey Barnouw for suggestions on terminology and substance.

Bibliography

Bergsträsser, Arnold. 1962. *Goethe's Image of Man and Society.* Freiburg: Herder. (Orig. pub. 1949.)

Borchmeyer, Dieter. 1977. *Höfische Gesellschaft und französiche Revolution bei Goethe.* Kronberg: Athenäum.

Bulloch, J. M. 1970. *Scott and Goethe: German Influence on the Writings of Sir Walter Scott.* Port Washington: Kennikat Press. (Orig. pub. 1925.)

Cape, Ruth. 1991. *Das französiche Ungewitter: Goethes Bildersprache zur französichen Revolution.* Heidelberg: Carl Winter.

Chiarini, Paolo, ed. 1987. *Bausteine zu einem neuen Goethe.* Frankfurt am Main: Athenäum.

Chiarini, Paolo, and Walter Dietze, eds. 1981. *Deutsche Klassik und Revolution.* Rome: Edizioni dell'Ateneo.

Cierva, Ricardo de la. 1987. *La Derecha sin remedio.* Barcelona: Plaza y Janes.

Clément, Jean-Paul, ed. 1987. *Chateaubriand politique.* Paris: Hachette, Pluriel.

Druse, Jens. 1985. *Tanz der Zeichen: Poetische Struktur und Geschichte in Goethes "Faust II."* Königstein: Anton Hain.

Eppelsheimer, Rudolf. 1982. *Goethes "Faust": Das Drama im Doppelreich: Versuch einer Deutung im Geiste des Dichters.* Stuttgart: Verlag Freies Geistesleben.
Girouard, Mark. 1981. *The Return to Camelot: Chivalry and the English Gentleman.* New Haven and London: Yale University Press.
Godechot, Jacques. 1961. *La contre-révolution: Doctrine et action 1789–1904.* Paris: Presses Universitaires de France.
Goux, Jean-Joseph. 1978. *Les iconoclastes.* Paris: Seuil.
Hamm, Heinz. 1978. *Goethes "Faust": Werkgeschichte und Textanalyse.* Berlin: Volk und Wissen.
Hennig, John. 1987. *Goethes Europakunde.* Amsterdam: Rodopi.
Kaltenbrunner, Gerd-Klaus, ed. 1978. *Rekonstruktion des Konservatismus.* Bern and Stuttgart: Paul Haupt.
Krippendorff, Ekkehart. 1988. *"Wie die Grossen mit den Menschen spielen": Versuch über Goethes Politik.* Frankfurt/Main: Suhrkamp.
Mayer, Arno. 1981. *The Persistence of the Old Regime: Europe to the Great War.* New York: Pantheon.
Molnár, Miklós, and André Reszler, eds. 1989. *Le génie de l'Autriche-Hongrie.* Paris: Presses Universitaires de France.
Mommsen, Wilhelm. 1948. *Die politischen Anschauungen Goethes.* Stuttgart: Deutsche Verlags-Anstalt.
Needler, George H. 1950. *Goethe and Scott.* Oxford: Oxford University Press.
Nemoianu, Virgil. 1977. *Micro-Harmony: The Growth and Uses of the Idyllic Model in Literature.* Bern: Peter Lang.
Nemoianu, Virgil. 1985. *The Taming of Romanticism. European Literature and the Age of Biedermeier.* Cambridge, Mass.: Harvard University Press.
Nyíri, J. Christoph. 1968. *Am Rande Europas.* Budapest: Akadémiai Kiadó.
Polanyi, Karl. 1985. *The Great Transformation.* Boston: Beacon Press. (Orig. pub. 1944.)
Porter, Roy, and Mikulá's Teich, eds. 1988. *Romanticism in National Context.* Cambridge: Cambridge University Press.
Saine, Thomas P. 1988. *Black Bread–White Bread: German Intellectuals and the French Revolution.* Columbia S.C.: Camden House.
Schlaffer, Heinz. 1981. *"Faust Zweiter Teil": Die Allegorie des 19ten Jahrhunderts.* Stuttgart: Metzler.
Srbik, Heinrich von. 1987. *Metternich.* 2 vols. Munich: Bruckmann. (Orig. pub. 1925.)
Staiger, Emil. 1952. *Goethe.* 3 vols. Zurich: Atlantis.
Tomlinson, John. 1991. *Cultural Imperialism: A Critical Introduction.* Baltimore: Johns Hopkins University Press.
Wild, Gerhard. 1991. *Versöhnungsbilder: Eine geschichtsphilosophische Untersuchung zu Goethes späten Werken.* Stuttgart: Metzler.

CHAPTER 3

From Goethe to Guizot
The Conservative Contexts of Goethe's Wilhelm Meisters Wanderjahre

IN THIS CHAPTER I intend to go beyond what I said in chapter 2 and to outline briefly some general features of Goethe's political philosophy. I believe that the elusive nature of this philosophy, as discussed before, becomes clearer when placed in a more specific European context and when focused on one of his latest works. I will actually join the majority that regards Goethe as a conservative writer. However, the label itself is not very helpful unless thoroughly qualified: whether we look around us or toward the past, we notice immediately the multiplicity of conservative modes.

For the sake of clarity, I will begin by stating that in my opinion there are four separate contexts that ought to be taken into consideration, and these in turn will lead us to integrate Goethe in a broader European context that also contains figures such as Chateaubriand, Mme de Staël, Guizot, Burke, Adam Smith, Tocqueville, Scott, perhaps Southey or Cobbett also, Jaime Balmes, Rosmini, with unavoidable similarities and differences. To my knowledge this has been done rarely, if ever.

These four contexts of conservatism (or "conservatism") that I regard as the most useful in explaining Goethe's mode of thinking are: (1) the influence of Justus Möser; (2) the connection with and serving of his own Duke Karl-August; (3) the delicate and intricate dialectics of Goethe's rapport with Metternich and Metternich's Europe; (4) (and most important in my view) the way in which the elder Goethe found himself on the same wavelength with François Guizot, and through him with the vast network of abovementioned European intellectuals who, while accepting of the precipitated changes that became apparent around 1800, did so with some reluctance, hesitation, regret, or warning. They themselves saw this attitude as part of a search for moderation and "due process." Hence I would like to place Goethe under the name of "Goethe Cunctator."

I also believe that the very form of *Wilhelm Meisters Wanderjahre* (or the formlessness of which it was so often accused) expresses Goethe's struggle for a solution to the dilemmas of the new age and really makes it quite relevant for the twenty-first century (in the same way that *Faust II* is quite relevant). In some ways it is the focus and the answer to the whole matter.

Let me briefly describe successively each of these four modes. Justus Möser (1720–1794) influenced, as is well known,[1] the young Goethe, whose views had been marked by lability. While Herder also exerted some influence, it seems to me that some specific features of the political philosophy of the wise old man of Osnabrück set a mark on Goethe that was to remain indelible all the way into his own old age. Part of this was an early option for the "British political and historical mode of change" that Möser had understood much earlier than later (post-1789) converts. Let us remember that Osnabrück was in all respects close to English political and intellectual life: in some ways it had the status and ways of thinking of the American possessions. In fact several times Möser praised and offered as example the Pennsylvania Dutch community.[2] (Here Goethe's fascination with what we can call "the American solution" of his older age may have had its remote sources.) In any case, despite his "patriotic" gesturing Möser was closer to the English eighteenth-century intellectual environment than to the German (and "Frenchified," in the neoclassical version) one.

Additionally Goethe liked the "organicist" metaphor for history that Burke (a Whig to the end of his life) was soon to theorize and ultimately spread throughout Europe. Furthermore the emphasis of Möser was on decentralization, a kind of early form of the doctrine of "subsidiarity."[3] He struggled vigorously against centralizing leveling, expansion of taxes, division of the population into castes, rationalistic politics, and in favor of individual or, as he called it, "genuine" ownership. Möser defended the patchwork of legal rules and tiny privileges inherited from the Middle Ages as being more reliable and authentic defenses against tyranny than general laws and political dogmas. (Again I see in *Wilhelm Meisters Wanderjahre* with its microsocieties and its archipelagoes of property a remote echo of these theories.)

Finally, perhaps as a detail, I will refer to the much-debated "technical description" of textile home-production, which so many critics have regarded as a total aesthetic breakdown.[4] Two things must be said here. The first is that Goethe seems to be a forerunner: many novels in many languages during the nineteenth and twentieth centuries resort to the same narrative technique. Second, Möser was a thorough connoisseur and apologist of this kind of textile production. There can be no doubt that Goethe's careful description owes much to Möser's essays such as "Schreiben über die Kultur der Industrie,"[5] in which Möser points out that one can recognize the origin and texture of cloth on the basis of the senses and of the production philosophy of families and/or communities.

Let us now turn to the second issue, that of the long service of Goethe under Duke Karl-August. Increasingly we have come to recognize that Goethe took his administrative duties seriously and that he did contribute to political-managerial activities.[6] Without unduly expanding into biographical details let me just dwell on two points.

First, I should record my disagreement with the overemphasis on Goethe's servility and traditionalism. He was indeed a convinced monarchist, and he also was clearly in favor of law and order whether in the tiny principality where he was active or in the broader European society. By no stretch of the imagination can we say, however, that Goethe was a fanatic of any rigorous class division or of general stagnation. For every quotation in one direction one can easily adduce a quotation in a different direction.[7] Most specifically the conclusion of *Faust II*, along with *Wilhelm Meisters Wanderjahre* in its entirety, speak to a system of general prosperity, civil rights and freedoms, progress, and social mobility (horizontal certainly, but also vertically).[8] Second, I am increasingly opposed to the Marxist-Leninist terminology of "feudalism," "capitalism," and so forth, which I find hollow and meaningless.[9] In fact it is precisely the type of relationship between Goethe and Karl-August that proves my point: a relationship formally respectful and ceremonious, in reality egalitarian, even with an edge to Goethe.

The third contextual level (one that flows naturally out of the previous one) is the uneasy and delicate relationship between Goethe and Metternich's Europe (or even Prince Metternich personally). The two men met in person only twice (1818 and 1819, both times in Karlsbad), but Goethe maintained indirect contact with well-accredited representatives such as Gentz and others.[10] During the Age of Restoration, Goethe was, and this should not be hidden, cautiously but undoubtedly a foe of the revolutionary movements, and he was glad to notice a reestablishment of order. From here we do not have to jump immediately to the conclusion that he approved in all details the measures and structures of the reorganized society. We know very well that Goethe firmly kept a certain distance toward the powerful statesman, who would have gladly drawn him into his circle of adherents. We ought to underline that Goethe's influence and activity even inside Sachsen-Weimar-Eisenach diminished after 1815 and that he was much more of a private person than he had been earlier (Sengle 1993, 375–491).

There is another aspect here that, in my opinion, has not been sufficiently discussed. During the period of 1815–1848 (and even somewhat later), liberalism and nationalism went hand in hand in Germany, as well as in the rest of Europe. Nationalism (even racism) were the property of the Left: the argument went that equality and fraternity grew out of national commonalities and could thus beneficially overthrow long-standing and legally entrenched class separations. Following this train of thought, grim ethnic separations emerged quite easily later on, but this happened chiefly in the second half of the nineteenth century.

The extent to which Goethe rejected the radicalism of the students (as well as of other groups) was due largely, if not exclusively, to his disgust for their nationalism, which was categorically alien to Goethe's cosmopolitan humanism. Under these circumstances Metternich's way of thought and action was simply the lesser evil. Any full identification between Goethe and the Metternich political structuring of Europe would be extremely difficult to prove on a practical level. In fact it would be much easier to demonstrate substantial distinctions. Therefore, although I do not place myself in opposition to commentators who argue that Goethe approved of Restorationist Europe, I maintain that he felt less than comfortable when he observed some of its ruling methods.[11]

These distinctions become even more obvious when we approach what I describe as level four of Goethe's conservatism. At a certain point (actually in the very middle of the Metternichian Age) Goethe seems to have become aware of an alternative solution. This solution crystallized for him a kind of political middle of the road: in other words, a way of finding (in and between the extremes that he instinctively disliked) the outline of a framework compatible with his political philosophy.[12] This was at least the thinking (since Goethe was too old to experience the actual political practice) of François Guizot: at the very doors of Germany, and well integrated in the European world that Goethe had always tried to promote.[13]

A few words on Guizot are in order here. He belongs to the same family of ideological thought as Tocqueville (Broglie 1990, 410–13, 102) and (the kinship is here slightly more distant) Benjamin Constant, that is to say figures of impeccable liberal credentials, indeed one might say founders of classical liberalism. In a more speculative mood we may well describe Guizot as intellectually akin to Goethe's good friend Wilhelm von Humboldt. His library contained books or pictures of Leibniz (one of the fundamental spiritual roots of liberalist Enlightenment and a close philosophical relative of Goethe's), Mme de Staël, Chateaubriand, and similar figures (Broglie 1990, 403–4, 62). According to Guizot these all had argued in favor of "une révolution sans devenir révolutionaires" (Broglie 1990, 116).

Furthermore, Guizot can be defined as the equivalent of Sir Robert Peel in England. (As I have suggested before, the actual political influence and power of both Guizot and Peel came to the fore immediately after Goethe's demise.) Still this point remains important. The emergence in political Europe of a leftist conservatism, or rightist liberalism, to use some very approximate terms, was for Goethe a reason for rejoicing: he certainly approved of them and saw in them the vindication and the best formulation of his own combinative and ambiguous thinking.[14] Guizot described himself several times (particularly after 1830) as belonging to the "party of resistance"—that is, resistance against the radicalization of change and progress. Does this turn him somehow into the equivalent of Metternich? After all, both statesmen lost power as a result of the 1848 revolutionary movements. Nevertheless the proposition is doubtful and, to my knowledge, has never been put forward as a credible argument. True, Metternich was much less of a reactionary than he was thought at his time (and than he is described and thought of even nowadays). Nobody characterized the man better than Heinrich von Srbik, namely as a belated Enlightenment figure who tried (after romanticism and revolution) to introduce or maintain its values. Nevertheless, Metternich (and many of his equivalents in Russia, in the France of Louis XVIII, and particularly of Charles X), in the England of Canning, Wellington, Castlereagh, and elsewhere did not (I am firmly convinced) satisfy the desires of Goethe. Actually, despite his pretense of calm and indifference, Goethe was often in the claws of fear and of anger.[14] The enthusiastic reading of Guizot was a tremendous relief for him. Goethe found in Guizot's writings a political model that was theoretically much better structured than he had ever been able to articulate himself.[15]

It might be tempting to go into the complicated issue of how, when, and/or whether specifically *Wilhelm Meisters Wanderjahre* was influenced by the reading of Guizot or not; in any case there are significant parallels. Let me mention some of them. Guizot considered Peel (and this may well be seen as a self-description) as "un conservateur acquis aux changements et non … un libéral venu à la politique conservatrice" (Broglie 1990, 428, 343, 237) [a conservative devoted to change, not a liberal turned into a conservative], or, to quote Guizot directly, "Un bourgeois chargé de soumettre à des dures réformes une puissante et fière aristocratie, un libéral sensé et modéré, mais vraiment libéral, traînant a sa suite les vieux tories et les ultras protestants" (Broglie 1990, 426). [A bourgeois whose task was to subdue by tough reform a powerful and proud aristocracy, a moderate and commonsensical liberal, carrying in his wake old Tories and extremist Protestants.]

Like Scott, Guizot "est … le prophète de la montée en puissance politique de la bourgeoisie. Il a travaillé à lui donner une culture politique, à lui forger une mémoire, à la faire entrer dans l'âge politique" (the prophet of the powerful rise of the middle classes. He labored in order to give them a memory, to introduce them to political adulthood). He is a kind of "Lénine de la bourgeoisie" (Rosanvallon 1985, 185, 171). In a Biedermeier spirit, Guizot proceeds to solve (and this is what intensely preoccupied Goethe, particularly in *Wilhelm Meisters Wanderjahre,* but also elsewhere) "Comment rester attaché aux résultats généraux de la révolution sans être aucunement révolutionnaire?" (Rosanvallon 1985, 77). [How to preserve the gains of the revolution without being a revolutionary at all.] The opposition between revolution and tradition can be solved only if we understand the former as a kind of hidden, unachieved tradition; only revolution "condenses" tradition into history seen as both act and narration (Rosanvallon 1985, 287).

The issue for Scott, Goethe, and Guizot was that of "transfer of values"—preserving some essential spiritual principles and behaviors under categorically modified historical circumstances. This would allow progress of a constructive, not a destructive nature, a kind of building on solid and historically well-tested foundations. At the same time it would mean a certain deceleration. Guizot's "Enrichissez-vous!"[16] solution to political inequality would have allowed Goethe to maintain a class structure that he considered just, while modifying it at the same time.

One other important parallel should be mentioned here. While Goethe was struggling with the aporias of a comprehensive humanization, Europe after 1815 was witnessing a truly extraordinary religious revival, one of those massive changes that Catholicism (but not only Catholicism) seems to undergo once every couple of hundred of years. I say not only Catholicism because in the early nineteenth century we recognize such a change in various branches of Protestantism, to some extent in Eastern Orthodox Christianity, as well as in Judaism as developed inside Europe. A few short references will suffice as reminders. During much of the eighteenth century it seemed that the fate of Judeo-Christian belief (or beliefs) was sealed. The intellectual and educated layers had turned toward atheism or, at best, toward vague convictions of a deist or pantheist tinge. More fundamentalist believers sought refuge in mystical and esoteric systems, enthusiastic piety devoid of a rationalist backbone: Methodism, Hassidism, Pietism, let alone the traditions of Swedenborg or Jakob Boehme.

As I will develop in more detail in another chapter, if we are to choose one turning point (even though there had been several of the kind), it would have to be Chateaubriand's *Génie du christianisme* (1802), which, in a bold, even stunning, gesture declared that Christianity could find a rationally credible support in the Beautiful, as it had relied on the True and the Good in the past. Immediately thereafter, sometimes synchronically, we notice the work of Lamennais, the late Mme de Staël and the enormous impact of Hannah More on both sides of the Atlantic. To this must be added the huge polemical but also constructive systems of Rosmini and Balmes, the circle of German literary and philosophical stars around Archbishop Klemens Maria Hofbauer in Vienna, the Tractarians (Anglican, Anglo-Catholic, and Roman Catholic), and Alois Gügler in Switzerland. Guizot, who was born a Protestant, devoted the last part of his long life to the cause of ecumenicism and to the unification of churches. Goethe places himself in rhyme with most of these people, whether he knew them or not. This can be seen in *Wilhelm Meisters Wanderjahre* and in the ending of *Faust II*. From the very beginning of *Wilhelm Meisters Wanderjahre* intriguing intertextual analogies (immediately noticed by readers and critics) abound. The most famous is at the very beginning, in Meister's first letter to Natalie in connection with the "St. Joseph II" episode. It has been less often noticed that the "St. Joseph" location is similar to all those Californian centers that, religiously founded and named, became, in an ironic turnover, highly secular locations. Like them it is a former place of prayer and meditation that has been turned in a center of labor and production. But is this not exactly what Emperor Joseph II (the symmetrical opposite of St. Joseph and at the same time his corresponding rhyme, as the craftsman/technologist) had been doing in his domains? Had he not liquidated monasteries and religious activities that did not correspond to the practical/utilitarian duties of his empire? In a word, *Wilhelm Meisters Wanderjahre* begins as a work of secularization while maintaining heavy religious overtones. I regard this as Goethe's response to and integration in the religious revival network that he observed growing around him.

In the long run all these successive levels of conservative context to Goethe's work and activity have to be connected to the ferment of responses to "modernization" alluded to earlier: urbanization and alienation, communication and rationalization, transactional modes of contact, historical acceleration, and the prevalence of social and ethnic amalgamations. The self-consciousness of these changes, as emerging a few decades before and after 1800, led to an enormous number of interesting responses, many (perhaps, most) of which continue to be relevant and to shape our thinking and action, directly or indirectly.[18] In the *Wanderjahre* Goethe approaches the depth and the tortured effort to "absorb modernization" that we recognize more easily in *Faust*.[19]

Goethe, like many of his most brilliant contemporaries (political scientists, religious apologists, poets, and philosophers), was wrestling mightily with this process of socioeconomic (better: existential) modernization, which had been pressing the West for several centuries but was now becoming conscious for most people and was also expanding on a planetary scale.[20] His hero roams the world seeking (and finding) islands of normality and organic intelligence that still survive in a chaotic world.

In *Faust II* (no less than in *Faust I*) we recognize a gleaning gesture, an effort to save and redeem, to bring back together all the values of the past. But is this a mere conservative gesture and activity? My conviction is that it is not.

Why not? It seems to me that in choosing out of all the features of this modernization Goethe was preoccupied (at a more or less conscious level) with the issue of increased information: the accumulation of knowledge, the informational onrush that tended to break the dams of order, harmony, and predictability. This explains the peculiar stylistics of *Wilhelm Meisters Wanderjahre*.

Many characters there are preoccupied by the issue of emigration, of a new beginning as a replacement for revolution and utopia, in a way analogous to Chateaubriand and Tocqueville. (Let us not forget that Chateaubriand embarked upon his famous expedition to the newly independent United States at the very beginning of the French Revolution in order to evade his own ambiguous sentiments toward this historical event, and that Tocqueville went to the United States a generation later curious to find out what a democratic system in action, and likely to represent the future of his own homeland, might look like. Both were trying to explore alternatives to violent sociohistorical overthrow.) Here we have on the one hand the beginnings of an understanding of exile as a key condition of modernity; however in Goethe's typical moderating fashion it should be an exile that is freely chosen and freely assumed.

In a more specifically literary fashion the book has to acquire an "archival" and discontinuous style. The discontinuities of the plot are a faithful mirror of the historical discontinuities that Goethe was discovering with more than a little vexation. Far from being a sign of senility, the disjointed structure of the book announces things to come: one might even say, only partly tongue-in-cheek, that the book is one of the earliest postmodernist exercises in European prose.[21] Documentary and digressionary techniques were in any case to become more and more frequent in the nineteenth and, again, particularly the twentieth century. *Wilhelm Meisters Wanderjahre* constitutes a line of continuity between the "romances" of the sixteenth and seventeenth centuries and the stylistics of the novel in the twentieth century. Meister and his son travel (between deliberation and randomness) among islands of happiness and quiet prosperity: discontinuities of contentedness and peace that crystallized into social constructs rising over and beyond, I dare say, the actual "pedagogical province." In its turn the informational avalanche could be accommodated by the relative disorder or discordance of the plot stylistics. By choosing the special organization of *Wilhelm Meisters Wanderjahre*, Goethe argues for the multiplicity and pluralism of a future society. His main strategy in *Wilhelm Meisters Wanderjahre* remains, as in *Faust*, one of gleaning, of selecting and bringing together genres, modes, ideas, and themes. However, Goethe seems here much more convinced of the justification of disorder. The constitutional arrangements of the projected colony are part of a much more chaotic, but also exciting future.

The subtitle *Die Entsagenden* does not suggest to me primarily resignation, but rather restraint.[31] Goethe suggests not only a kind of slowing down as the "cunctator" that he was, but also methods of voluntary limitation and renunciation for the sake of happiness. The conflict between freedom and happiness (as formulated a century after *Wilhelm Meisters Wanderjahre* by Aldous Huxley) was to become crucial for the ideologies and policies of the nineteenth and particularly of the twentieth century. The renunciation or restraint in *Wilhelm Meisters Wanderjahre* is above all not an ethical nor even a political one, but an aesthetic one.[22] This brings us back to the archival organization of *Wilhelm Meisters Wanderjahre*.[23]

Notes

1. Goethe had read the *Patriotische Phantasien* (1775–1786) probably as soon as they came out and expressed enthusiasm for them. Cf. Claassen 1936, 182ff.; Kass 1909. Mommsen (1948, 29–34) thinks this influence is to be recognized particularly in *Götz von Berlichingen,* but I see it as much more pervasive.

2. See, for example, Möser 1944–1968, 3:20 or 1:31.

3. "Subsidiarity" is a term that was coined in Papal encyclicals (particularly in *Quadragesimo Anno,* 1931), where it meant that every social activity ought to be fulfilled at the lowest possible level: something that the family can take care of must not be assigned to the school or the city; in turn whatever may be accomplished by the neighborhood community or the county must not be taken over by the state government, and so on. The term soon began appearing in works of secular political theory and practice in Europe, particularly in the last two decades. However as Millon-Delsol shows in *L'état subsidiaire,* the concept, notably developed by the Calvinist administrator Johannes Althusius in his *Politica* (first published in 1603 and developed later in the 1610 and 1614 editions), had existed in one form or another for many centuries before the term was coined.

4. Walter Benjamin, Thomas Mann, Ed Spranger, and F. Gundolf, among others; earlier Burckhardt, Mundt, and Scherer. See, in a more specifically scholarly vein, Staiger 1952–1959, 3:181–87. Equally puzzling for some was Goethe's "synthesis" of the scientific and the literary. For a balanced treatment see Steer 1979.

5. Möser 1944–1968, 5:110–14. Corresponding passage in Goethe's *Wilhelm Meisters Wanderjahre* (1829, 3:5).

6. See Tümmler 1976, and esp. Cape 1991, 10–16, 36–46, 127–44.

7. For a nice general review see Gille 1971; see also Flitner 1947; Wergin 1980; Lukács 1947; Witte et al. 1996, 3:217–31. This stands in sharp contrast to most German romantics; among many conclusive anthologies see Beiser 1996.

8. See Zenker 1990, or Thielicke 1982; again, one is reminded of Möser's influence.

9. Even somebody as knowledgeable and objective as Friedrich Sengle uses *Spätfeudalismus* in the subtitle of his excellent book *Das Genie und sein Fürst*.

10. We can skip here the relationship between Goethe and Napoleon, although the motives were complex and even fascinating. Goethe's vanity was touched by Napoleon's attention, certain amounts of prudence and of anxiety in the face of a powerful dictator must also be assumed. Additionally, Goethe's well-known Francophilia undoubtedly played a certain role there.

11. Rothe 1998, 7–11, 49–61, 76–77, 92–107, 124–29, 134–89. Even earlier, Mommsen 1948, 7–18, 28–34, 108–16, 166–280.

12. In fact one could almost argue that the whole of Goethe's later career is concentrated on this issue and returns to it in a stubborn and melancholy way. This was noticed early on. See Wundt 1913, or (later) Bergsträsser 1962; or Schlechta 1982, 27–33, 47–53, 75–91, 228–35; also Karnick 1968, or Schwamborn 1997.

13. Guizot wrote his most important theoretical works in the 1820s, but exerted much more political influence in the 1830s and particularly the 1840s when he was almost without interruption a cabinet minister and the ideologue of King Louis-Philippe's regime.

14. See, for example, Goethe's conversations with Eckermann on February 17, April 2, 3, 6, 1829; cf. Broglie 1990, 102, 272.

15. I would argue, although this is probably not the place to do it, that Goethe's delighted reading of Walter Scott's early novels was due to equivalent sentiments. I say this because I know very well that Goethe's sophisticated aesthetic preferences would have made him reserved toward Scott. However here too the threads are tightly interwoven. French historians and critics (Mignet, Thierry, and in fact Guizot himself) correctly read Scott as an author of "histoire démocratique," "le romancier des peuples," a political novelist, etc. Cf. Rosanvallon 1985, 200.

16. This is his most famous but historically dubious sentence. See a detailed discussion in Broglie 1990, 333–35. See *Wanderjahre* (1829, 1:6). Cf. also Mommsen 1948, 264.

17. Let us also say that although in speaking about the nineteenth-century novel in Europe we think usually of Balzac and Flaubert, Tolstoy and Dostoyevsky, Austen, Dickens, and George Eliot, German contributions on a realistic level (Fontane), or on a sentimental one (Raabe and Storm), or on a philosophical one (Goethe in particular) do contribute to the intellectual debates of the century and to its processes of self-definition.

18. For a more detailed discussion see chapter 2 of this volume. A somewhat materialistic but rather accurate reading can be found in Jessing 1991. For an excellent and clear interpretation

of the literary thematization of the process of "modernization," see also Beller 1995. Mayer (1989) openly declares at the very beginning of his book that his thesis is that the novel provides us with "eine bislang kaum gewürdigte Antwort . . . auf die Frage nach der Existenzmöglichkeit von Kunst in einer von Ökonomie und Technik beherrschten Welt."

19. Following wiser and more competent thinkers, I have pointed this out in chapters 2 and 5 of this volumne. See also Witte et al. 1996, 3:15, 203. It is not absurd, although a little exaggerated in my view to draw parallels between *Wilhelm Meister II* and the view of the two Mills; the closest would be perhaps John Stuart Mill's *On Liberty*.

20. Scholarly arguments can be found in Brown 1975, and Bennett 1993.

21. For a meticulous discussion of the issue see Peschken 1968, 213–15. See also Bahr 1983, 161–75. Needless to add, I disagree entirely with the arguments in Degering (1982). For a brilliant alternative interpretation see Schlaffer 1980.

22. An interesting and, in my view, largely justified argument can be found in Fülleborn (1995, 146–48), which is bolstered by a whole chapter of preceding examples from Goethe's earlier poems to the conclusion of *Faust II*. For Fülleborn the wanderings of Meister are a mode of declining possession, whether material or even erotic.

23. Well after finishing this chapter I read the excellent essay of Engel, "Wertwandel und neue Subjektivität," which is on the same wavelength as my own ideas here, although it does not deal in comparatist matters.

Bibliography

Armin, Peter. 1987. *Goethe als Manager. Eine Führungslehre*. Hamburg: Steintor.

Bahr, Ehrhard. 1983. "Revolutionary Realism in Goethe's *Wanderjahre*." In *Goethe's Narrative Fiction*. Ed. W. J. Lylliman, 161–75. Berlin and New York.

Beiser, Frederick, ed. 1996. *Early German Romantic Political Writings*. Cambridge: Cambridge University Press.

Beller, Walter. 1995. *Goethes "Wilhelm Meister" Romane: Bildung für eine Moderne*. Hannover: Revonnah.

Bennett, Benjamin. 1993. *Beyond Theory: Eighteenth-Century German Literature and the Poetics of Irony*. Ithaca, N.Y.: Cornell University Press.

Bergsträsser, Arnold. 1962. *Goethe's Image of Man and Society*. Freiburg: Herder.

Broglie, Gabriel de. 1990. *Guizot*. Paris: Perrin.

Brown, Jane K. 1975. *Goethe's Cyclical Narratives: "Die Unterhaltungen deutscher Ausgewanderten" und "Wilhelm Meisters Wanderjahre."* Chapel Hill: University of North Carolina Press.

Cape, Ruth. 1991. *Das französische Ungewitter: Goethes Bildersprache zur französischen Revolution*. Heidelberg: Carl Winter.

Claassen, Peter. 1936. *Justus Möser*. Frankfurt: Suhrkamp.

Degering, Thomas. 1982. *Das Elend der Entsagung: "Wilhelm Meisters Wanderjahre."* Bonn: Bouvier.

Engel, Manfred. 2000. "Wertwandel und neue Subjektivität." *Erlanger Forschungen* 91: 87–111.

Flitner, Wilhelm. 1947. *Goethe im Spätwerk: Glauben, Weltbild und Ethos*. Hamburg: Claassen und Goverts.

Fülleborn, Ulrich. 1995. *Besitzen als besässe man nicht: Besitzdenken und seine Alternativen in der Literatur*. Frankfurt: Insel.

Gille, Klaus, ed. 1971. *Goethes "Wilhelm Meister": Zur Rezeptionsgeschichte der Lehr- und Wanderjahre.* Königstein: Athenäum.
Goethe, Johann Wolfgang von. 2000. *"Wilhelm Meisters Wanderjahre" in Hamburger Ausgabe.* Ed. Erich Trunz, 8:7–486. Munich: Deutscher Taschenbuch Verlag. (Orig. pub. 1948.)
Jessing, Benedikt. 1991. *Konstruktion und Eingedenken: Zur Vermittlung von gesellschaftlicher Praxis und literarischer Form in Goethes "Wilhelm Meisters Wanderjahre."* Wiesbaden: Deutscher Universitätsverlag.
Karnick, Manfred. 1968. *"Wilhelm Meisters Wanderjahre," oder die Kunst des Mittelbaren.* Munich: Wilhelm Fink.
Kass, Georg. 1909. *Möser und Goethe.* Berlin: B. Paul.
Lukács, György von. 1947. *Goethe und seine Zeit.* Bern: Francke.
Lylimann, W. J., ed. 1983. *Goethe's Narrative Fiction.* Berlin and New York: De bruyter.
Mayer, Mathias. 1989. *Selbstbewusste Illusion: Selbstreflexion und Legitimation der Dichtung im "Wilhelm Meister."* Heidelberg: Carl Winter.
Millon-Delsol, Chantal. 1992. *L'état subsidiaire: Ingérence et non-ingérence de l'état: Le principe de subsidiarité aux fondements de l'histoire européenne.* Paris: Presses Universitaires de France.
Mommsen, Wolfgang. 1948. *Die politischen Anschauungen Goethes.* Stuttgart: Deutsche Verlags-Anstalt.
Nemoianu, Virgil. 1996. "Globalism, Multiculturalism, and Comparative Literature." *Council of National Literatures World Report:* 43–73.
Peschken, Bernd. 1968. *Entsagung in "Wilhelm Meisters Wanderjahre."* Bonn: Bouvier.
Rosanvallon, Pierre. 1985. *Le moment Guizot.* Paris: Gallimard / Nouvelle Revue Française.
Rothe, Wolfgang. 1998. *Der politische Goethe: Dichter und Staatsdiener im deutschen Spätabsolutismus.* Göttingen: Vandenhoeck und Ruprecht.
Schlaffer, Hannelore. 1980. *Das Ende der Kunst und die Wiederkehr des Mythos.* Stuttgart: Metzler.
Schlechta, Karl. 1982. *Goethes "Wilhelm Meister."* Frankfurt: Vittorio Klostermann.
Schwamborn, Claudia. 1997. *Individualität in Goethes "Wanderjahre."* Paderborn: Schöningh.
Sengle, Friedrich. 1993. *Das Genie und sein Fürst: Die Geschichte der Lebensgemeinschaft Goethes mit dem Herzog Carl-August von Sachsen-Weimar-Eisenach. Ein Beitrag zum Spätfeudalismus und zu einem vernachlässigten Thema der Goetheforschung.* Stuttgart: Metzler.
Srbik, Heinrich von. 1925. *Metternich: Der Staatsman und Mensch.* 2 vols. Munich: Bruckmann.
Staiger, Emil. 1952–1959. *Goethe.* 3 vols. Zurich: Atlantis.
Steer, Alfred. 1979. *Goethe's Science in the Structure of the "Wanderjahre."* Athens: University of Georgia Press.
Thielicke, Helmut. 1982. *Goethe und das Christentum.* Munich: Piper.
Tümmler, Hans. 1976. *Goethe als Staatsmann.* Göttingen: Musterschmidt.
Wergin, Ulrich. 1980. *Einzelnes und Allgemeines: Die aesthetische Virulenz eines geschichtsphilosophischen Problems.* Heidelberg: Carl Winter.
Witte, Bernd et al., eds. 1996. *Goethe-Handbuch.* 4 vols. Stuttgart: Metzler.
Wundt, Max. 1913. *Goethes "Wilhelm Meister" und die Entwicklung des modernen Lebensideals.* Berlin und Leipzig: Goschen.
Zenker, Markus. 1990. *Zu Goethes Erzählweise versteckter Bezüge in "Wilhelm Meisters Wanderjahre; oder, die Entsagenden."* Würzburg: Königshausen und Neumann.

CHAPTER 4

From Historical Narrative to Fiction and Back
A Dialectical Game

AFTER A DISCUSSION of the "moderate conservatism" that played such a crucial role in the early nineteenth century and, grown in the soil of romanticism, managed to change it in decisive ways, it is time to cast a glance at the historical inclination that shaped the same age. Indeed, to the extent to which we can speak about a "relativism" of the age, this was, in its turn, mostly moderated and disguised in the garb of succession and evolution. A wave of interest in continuity or, to be more precise, in the dialectic between continuity and change, swept Europe and colored all fields of human endeavor and knowledge. Radical modification (of human societies and minds) or outright "reinvention" found themselves buffered by thick layers of continuity. Here also literature had intervened decisively, even though its almost symbiotic connection with history at the time (and for a while later) remained fascinating. Literature borrowed from history to the extent that it gave birth to the historical novel as a psychomachia, while the counterpart was the crystallization of a historiography bolstered decisively by literary techniques and effects.

The year 1815, when Walter Scott's *Waverley* was published anonymously but to unexpected acclaim and popular success (both in England and abroad), is conventionally taken as the year when a new genre (or subgenre) was born: the historical novel. Similarly we can say that what a British male had done was replicated, indeed with some chronological precedence, by a British woman: Mary Shelley launched the powerful and still ever-increasing field of science fiction with her *Frankenstein*. Neither of the two novels was devoid of a literary pedigree or emerged on an empty territory. In the case of *Waverley* we can think of eighteenth-century "Gothick" and /or horror novels, of diverse *Rittergeschichten,* even earlier of dramatic productions that clothed moral and psychological issues in historical garb (not least the neoclassical writings by Corneille, Racine, and their descendants throughout Europe; but then again this was a writing strategy to which already the Spanish *siglo de oro* had occasionally resorted).[1]

We shall focus, however, on the question of why the historical novel as revamped and reconstructed by Walter Scott was perceived as something genuinely innovative and why it was so eagerly imitated throughout Europe and North America, and soon even outside the confines of the Western world. Part of the answer, but, I hasten to say, not the only or the most important, was the lifeline that Scott had established to poetry. It has been said more than once that Scott switched over to the novel as a vehicle when and because he felt that the plot(s) of his narrative(s) could no longer be contained by the verse stories that he had practiced with some enthusiasm. I believe this is true, and, more broadly, this is the point of prominent commentators such as György von Lukács when they regarded the historical novel as the middle-class substitute for the agonizing epic. (The exercise in epic-writing was continued, although seldom and without a powerful echo, for example in *Olympischer Frühling,* by Carl Spitteler, inspired by ancient Greek mythology, or, even more typical, in *Das Kaiserbuch,* by Paul Ernst, which followed the pattern of medieval Persian historical chronicles in verse.)

I believe, however, that a more contextual examination can provide us with richer explanations, and I will refer briefly to three of these contexts. One is the age-old dispute between poetry and history, a matter that preoccupied such luminaries as Aristotle and Sir Philip Sidney. The second one is, as mentioned, the explosive emergence of history as a central discipline in the late eighteenth and early nineteenth centuries and the need and desire of many (perhaps most) other discourses to emulate it. Here, however, the process became dialectical, with history itself learning and borrowing from literature. The third is what some describe as ideological, though I for one prefer to call morphocultural: conveying a message of solution, of peaceful reconciliation, of "taming" of the radicalities of romanticism and revolution—this is, of course, the very theme of the present volume—or, in other words, producing real historical detente through the writerly discourse of historical detente. Let me dwell briefly on each of these and provide some examples.

At the end of the sixteenth century, Sir Philip Sidney defends poetry mostly against the arguments that imaginative literature must inevitably be inferior to realistic or factual narrative, insofar as the latter deals with truth and reality, whereas the former is merely a creature of invention. Sidney argues, to some extent ironically, in *A Defence of Poetry* that poetry (in the broadest sense of the word) reaches Truth in different ways, namely by focusing on the central ideas, the Platonic archetypes, and depicting them in ways in which history never could. The historian, "laden with old mouse-eaten records, authorizing himself (for the most part) upon other histories, whose greatest authorities are built upon the notable foundation of hearsay" (30), is more likely to be a liar. By contrast, poetry is the most ancient form of human learning, does not contain evil, and mixes delight and goodness (48). It is the least likely to contain lies since it does not affirm anything; it is profitable to memory, rich in morality, able to stir courage, to strengthen man, and is rightly praised by such luminaries as Saint Paul and Plato (48–60).

Although Sidney can be fairly described as a neo-Platonist, there is also an obvious continuity with Aristotelian thinking here. We remember that in the *Poetics* Aristotle had also argued that poetry is something more philosophic and of more serious import than history; for poetry tends to deal with the general while history is concerned with limited particular facts. An instance from his *Poetics* of the general (with which poetry undertakes to deal) is this: "What are the sorts of things which, according to the law of probability and necessity, various types of individuals tend to do and say? This is what poetry aims to make when it attaches names to characters. An instance of particular facts is: what did Alcibiades do, or what was done to him?" (18–19). Another instance is: "If the objection is raised: 'this is not true,' the answer is: perhaps the poet is portraying it *as it should be*" (58–59).

The main point to keep in mind for further demonstrations is that both these powerful classicist thinkers were keenly aware of a certain dialectic between history and fiction. They realized similarities and they tried to draw distinctions at the same time. Narrative and memory provided a common ground, yet at a certain point there was a branching out depending on the mode in which they were used and on the goals that were pursued. This is, in my opinion, the general background of aesthetic philosophy against which the historical novel eventually appeared.

I come now to my second point, namely to the fact that the sociocultural context emerging at the end of the eighteenth and the beginning of the nineteenth centuries was dominated by the "discovery" of history as a leading force in intellectual life. Why? Let me answer by developing the brief indications given in the first paragraph of this chapter. First, this is so precisely because there was an increasing sense of acceleration in society at all levels, a kind of revolutionary need to reform more and more radically not only the present and the future, but also the past. The latter is reformed in both senses: to make it compatible with the present and the future, but also to employ it as a kind of symmetrical counterbalance to them. The social and the natural sciences inscribed themselves immediately, vigorously, and enthusiastically in this comprehensive historicizing tendency. Thus paleontology sought a variety of explanations as to how the animal world had reached its current stage, and though the answers of Cuvier, Geoffroy de Saint-Hilaire, or Erasmus Darwin may have differed (until Charles Darwin's unifying but equally "historical" theory seemed to provide common explanational ground), they and others had one thing in common: they agreed on a kind of historical methodology for research. The questions asked were directed toward the process of development in nature.

In linguistics (to take a totally different example), although earlier (that is, eighteenth-century) questioning concentrated on the philosophy of language, changes were soon apparent, and throughout the nineteenth century, in fact until Saussure, Potebnya, and Baudoin de Courtenay, the respectable academic pursuit was that of the way in which language changed: how modern Romance and Germanic tongues grew out of Latin and "common Germanic," the latter together with Slavic, Celtic,

Sanskrit and others out of Indo-European ancestors. Admissible and recommended research also included dialectology, that is to say the branching out and the diversification of one common trunk into its regional or local variants, another historical process.

It has been argued that sociology also came out of historical curiosity: discovering the causal regularities that led to the construction of present-day interhuman worlds. (This was argued by Spaemann, for instance, with respect to Bonald, but François Guizot and his adversary Jaime Balmes had said similar things already in the 1820s and 1830s.) No less active was the history of law when it tried to establish continuities and pedigrees connecting Roman law or primitive Germanic law with the current legislation. As to the study of literature, it was, in academic institutions, until well after World War I primarily an examination of sources, manuscripts, the "ancientness," and thus the credibility and validity of texts. In fact the history of literature tended to stop short of contemporary vernaculars and to deal admiringly with dead literatures of different kinds.

Above all it is impossible to overlook the dramatic jump in the development of historical research itself of all kinds. Naturally this included the older philosophical approaches of Bossuet, Voltaire, and Herder. It also included, however, the passionate collecting of facts and details, of "monuments," the emergence of systematic museums, along with the analysis of shorter, more focused periods. Clearly some of this work had a political and ideological purpose. It was, for instance, a competitional agon between nations as to cultural achievements, moral perfection, antiquity of glory, victories of all kinds.[2] Or, alternatively, for nations that were struggling to establish their identity and to validate themselves, it could be an accumulation of justifying evidence of their admissibility in the company of the higher and most civilized nations. (This applies primarily to nonindependent nations such as the eastern European ones: Hungary, the Czech Republic, Romania, Poland, and numbers of others, but also to major and culturally insecure ones such as Russia or Italy.)

However, another and more general motivation ought to be considered. There was a widespread anxiety of continuity and of origin. As long as the religious and specifically biblical framework was still very solid the scrambling for historical validation could remain marginal: an antiquarian, dilettantish, innocuous pursuit. The moment this religious framework became uncertain or shaky, the fear of chaos, the anxiety of free-floating, suddenly lent an enormous seriousness to the historical work. In Freudian terms this is a search for the lost father: a theme that is incredibly frequent in literature throughout the nineteenth century. It seems very likely that the emergence of the historical novel is largely due to civic and not to merely aesthetic pursuits. The writers of historical novels and plays were subconsciously convinced that they could contribute in their own way and with their own methods to a common effort toward a worthy goal. Thus the historical novel is on the one hand a solution to the age-old tension between fiction and history, but it is also a mode to reach a wider audience than the one of the scientific historian. The historical novel is meant to popularize and to explain in a more gentle way continuities, breaks, or just causalities that had led to the present-day situation.

This brings us to the third contextual element. The historical novel is born as an actual and active mode of writing precisely at the time when Western society was grappling with the issue of moderating or taming its own revolutionary tendencies and handling them in an acceptable way. (Obviously "revolutionary" is not used here in its much narrower political sense but rather in the broadest possible one: it refers to mentalities, to ways of life, to values, orientations, and standards, and so forth.) As shown in other chapters, a great variety of vehicles and approaches were devised in order to serve the goal of such a reconciliation between the past and the rapidly arriving future, and in order to appease the looming conflicts. Collaborations with religious discourses, interweaving with travel literature, and a host of other generic techniques were resorted to, not to mention directly theoretical works. Inside this luxuriant vegetation of ingenious literary techniques the historical novel occupied a place of honor. As conceived by Walter Scott in his Waverley cycle, the historical novel was meant to dramatize the conflict between two great modes of life (socioeconomic systems, weltanschauung, systems of customs and of existence, philosophies of behavior), but above all to reach a reasonable synthesis between the two, to reestablish continuities, to reveal stabilities, to transfer values. In the novels of Walter Scott and of his followers we find always the argument that a certain reconciliation is possible between the past and the onrushing future. (It is gratifying to see that more and more readers, such as Burgess (2000, 190) or Duncan (1992, 8–9, 53), admit the idea of Scott's historical novel as a "teleological construct" even when they do not clearly define the subject matter of this teleology.)

Naturally such broad intentions can only be described as conservative. It would be futile to repeat here what was so often and so well explained: that Scott himself was a staunch conservative and in several ways, too, a conservative (see also Spearman 1987, 29ff.) of the Scottish identity, an adversary of the French Revolution, and clearly a Burkean (in fact in his understanding of the sublime also—not only in matters of political philosophy—an individual desirous to be included in the landed squirearchy of his time). It is also clear that the Lukácsian theory of translation of the ancient epic into the bourgeois prose of the historical novel will not be very helpful or take us very far. In my opinion Scott revealed again, and brilliantly, how a psychomachia, fictional though it may be, can have an eloquent influence on the audience. His theory of history is certainly not unique; as a matter of fact it may be regarded as utopian, at least in the sense that it is wishful thinking. Nevertheless it is not wrong. It moves in the direction of human or social progress. It takes into account losses over the years and centuries and it emphasizes adroitly the issue of transfer of values. Scott proposes solutions to issues that were at the time (and largely continue to be) of great moment for everybody. (Despite his attachment to the cloying neo-Marxist theorizing of yesteryear, Kaufmann [1995, 93–122] has shrewd and useful comments on the political economy of Scott's novels and on Scott's balancing act between Burke and Adam Smith.) We can thus explain the overwhelming success of the Waverley cycle, as well as other of Scott's novels, and we can account most convincingly for the legions of imitators in most countries. Perhaps the most successful and percipient among these was James Fenimore Cooper, who transferred in America the struggle between a modernizing English society and a traditional, localist, and diversitarian Scotland, this time at the even more terribly serious level of racial interaction: Amerindian against Euro-American, with even deeper chasms separating them—one might argue whether the Leatherstocking pentalogy is not perhaps the first great multiculturalist work (at least in North America, as I pointed out in chapter 5 of this volume). However, some early works by Balzac (*Les Chouans* for instance), Hugo's *Notre-Dame de Paris,* Vigny's only novel (*Cinq-Mars*), and some writings by Gil y Carrasco in Spain also follow Scott. Hugo's chief historical novel is particularly subtle and significant. Hugo sets up in *Notre-Dame de Paris* the opposition between cathedral and book: the former is supposed to represent the concreteness and the organicity of human handicraft, the latter the "mechanical reproduction of the work of art," the quantification, the numerization of existence. The French romantic, at least in his youngest creative years, presses this opposition into a kind of confrontational melodrama, with Quasimodo and other characters connected to the cathedral as deformed (a signal of defeat) even monstruous images. However, even as late as 1872, Hugo in his novel *Quatrevingt-treize* creates a character (Gauvain) who is equally the spiritual son of a liberal aristocrat and of a radical and pitiless revolutionary, much in the tradition of numerous Scottian figures. Balzac frankly and unabashedly imitates Scott, while Vigny projects (as Alexandre Dumas-Père was to do a little later) the opposition into the contrast between a waning feudalism of liberty and individuality versus the ordering and leveling power of centralized absolutism. (I will not even speak here about comparatively minor figures such as Barginet, Mortonval, or even Vitet, who were nevertheless widely read and discussed at the time.)[3] Gil y Carrasco in Spain proudly recognized himself as a descendant of Scott. Manzoni is more original, undoubtedly, and his thematics are somewhat different (he also in his later years tried to distance himself from the historical novel, unsuccessfully in my opinion), but it would be difficult to understand and even imagine him outside the horizon outlined by Scott, the same being true of Pushkin's *Captain's Daughter,* as well as of a considerable number of eastern European works, not least Mickiewicz's admirable *Pan Tadeusz.* In Germany, where the historical novel was highly important throughout the nineteenth century, one critic highlighted particularly four works (of which at least three closely followed Scott or were contemporary with him: Achim von Arnim's unfinished *Die Kronenwächter* (with its conspiratorial-fantastic shades) in 1817; *Lichtenstein* by Wilhelm Hauff, set in the early sixteenth century and based on tensions between local, rural, and monarchic forces; *Die Hosen des Herrn von Bredow,* as well as other novels by Willibald Alexis (in 1823 Alexis had already reviewed Scott); some works by Adalbert Stifter follow soon, but arguably the hybrid and ambiguous *Die Epigonen* by Karl Immermann could be included, though it misses the neater conclusions of the purely Scottian tradition (Hartkopf in Glaser 1980–1987, 4:134–51).

A special place is occupied here by the subgenre of Christian historical novels that enjoyed great popularity in the nineteenth and early twentieth centuries, beginning with Chateaubriand's *Les martyrs,* but soon learning from Scott, particularly in the matter of the antagonism between an old and decadent but aesthetically beautiful classical culture in its opposition to a grosser but vigorous and young Christian one. It may seem digressive but it is worth mentioning that any novel (or any narrative) is a historical novel. The most realistic (that is, topically contemporary) text is willy-nilly a few minutes behind the facts it purports to depict: simultaneity is the greatest illusion of them all. Moreover the contemporary soon pales and fades away, absorbed by the historical. Jane Austen and John Dos Passos are now read by most as historical novels, though nothing was farther from their authors' minds; early-twenty-first-century undergraduates see little difference in time frame between *Middlemarch* and *Romola.* We have often to fall back upon the much maligned authorial intention if we want to distinguish a true "historical novel" from its brethren.

Let me now revert to the original question, that of the borders (if any) between history and fiction, borders that were patently porous for the writers of the early nineteenth century. There is no better way to deal with this than by engaging Scott's novels not in their strict text but as whole packages, that is to say by including in our text-reading the prefaces and (in this specific case) the long final notes that are added to the Waverley novels in particular. Thus, for instance, in *Waverley* itself we find explanations and justifications regarding the personality and the conditions of the death of Colonel Gardiner (notes 3 and 19), geographical circumstances in the same novel (notes 7, 16, 17, and others), customs alluded to in the text (notes 5, 10, 11, and others), or else highly visible, historically attested figures like Prince Charles-Edward (long note 22). In *Redgauntlet* Scott not only resorts to a postscript by "Mr. Dryasdust," but also to justifying notes on the characters and the circumstances in the novel. Likewise, in *Rob Roy* we find at the end several documentary letters written by the chief and titular character. This goes on in novel after novel. Curiously enough, literary scholars have not thought that it is worth examining more seriously or extensively Scott's ample works of history and "antiquarianism" (Dryden, Swift, Napoleon, demonology and witchcraft, and early ethnology among other things), and we likewise miss in-depth discussions of his prefaces to the novels. For my purposes here, however, suffice it to say that Scott clearly had the ambition to evoke history by literary means, by expanding suddenly the angle of view, presenting scenes, exploring the psychological motivations, imagining the emotions of historical characters, and depicting backgrounds (habitual human beings and natural or urban scenery). The notes were supposed to bolster the narrative and offer convincing material as to the mimetic truth of the texts. In turn it should be added that the reading of Scott and others had at least some influence on the social imaginary across the Atlantic, and particularly in the South of the emerging United States (Fraser 1982, 7–18, 36–41, 52–53, 64–65, 74–75).

At the same time Scott and many other followers of his were convinced of the importance of details in ways in which earlier historians (for example, Bossuet or Voltaire) were not. It has often been observed that Scott established as a generic rule that the main and well-documented historical characters ought to function as secondary fictional characters in the background (or obliquely referred to), while secondary or outright invented historical figures are the ones who function as foregrounded fictional characters (Maignon 1970, 276–91). Novelists such as Scott thought of themselves as useful, perhaps indispensable, auxiliaries of historians, and they were often welcomed as such by historians, not least because of their freedom of dealing with these secondary or invented characters. (A full theory of this mode of history-writing came much later, by the end of the nineteenth century, with Dilthey and the concept of *Einfühlung*.) This double role of historian/novelist can also be recognized in the actual language used inside the texts. Formal, elegant, theoretical passages alternate easily with the dialectal idioms of specific locality in ways which had been rarely used in the past.

Perhaps it would have been interesting here to dwell a little more on prose that deals (critically or not, but in any case intentionally) with contemporary events in the manner of the historical novel, but neither space nor the direction of this study will allow us to work in this direction. Examples could be found not only in the writings of Balzac and of Stifter but also in a couple of Scott's novels or in the (unfinished) short story *Der arme Raimondin* by Brentano.

Important links between literature and historiography are provided by widespread societal topoi such as the "idyllic model" and particularly the idea of organicism. Idyllism emerged fully in the eighteenth century, mostly as the half-real, half-imagined portrait of a society (a macro-image) dominated by moderation and avoiding or refusing to acknowledge extremes: extremes in ethics (good or bad), in the depiction of society (the heights and the bottoms of society), in climate and in geography (the precipitous peaks and abysses, the deserts and the arctic areas, the cyclones, the unmeasurable oceanic expanses, the ferocious predators), in illness and violence—in a word in anything human or environmental, at all levels. This was used for a stretch of time as a desirable ideal, but later most of the romantics resorted to it mostly as a contrastive referential level or played around with it ironically, often in an openly derogatory fashion (Nemoianu 1977). Nevertheless, by the beginning of the nineteenth century and thereafter (in the later nineteenth and even in the twentieth century), idyllism came also to be seen as a serious option by sociologists and politologists: an ideal to be pursued institutionally. Obviously, this newly captured seriousness could sometimes reverberate in historical writings: it could be simply become part of the descriptive discourse on historical periods such as classical antiquity, the Middle Ages, the Elizabethan Age, or, for that matter for remote pre-Christian and non-Western cultures.

The ideal of organicism was perhaps even more important ideologically. It had been around for the longest time. We recognize it in Plutarch, perhaps even in Aristotle. It was cherished by many of the high scholastics. In those ages, and later as well, organicism was the short term for a balanced society, one based on solidarity, on the complementary links between the classes, groups, and individuals in society. In a sense, one might say that in all cultures that grew biologically, or naturally, a retroprojection on the communities and tribes out of which they had grown was to be expected. This was certainly true for thousands of years for societies such as the Indian and Chinese, both on a theoretical and practical level. This view was powerfully challenged by seventeenth-century rationalism and by the eighteenth-century Enlightenment/modernization project. Here a contractual mode was eloquently and unabashedly put forward (by Hobbes, Locke, Rousseau, and eventually the French Revolution). It was only natural that, challenged by the events between 1789 and 1815, the reaction of many should have been a kind of conservatism that picked organicism as a state theory. The most influential argument along these lines was the one proposed by Edmund Burke in his response to the French Revolution. He repeatedly castigated the French Revolutionaries for abandoning organic growth and an organic structuring of society, which should be in concordance with the natural and spiritual worlds. The German romantics adopted this view enthusiastically after Gentz had made it widely known (1793 translation) the more so as some of them had been inclined toward it to begin with (Novalis might be a prime example). Adam Müller was one of the staunchest followers of Burke (radicalizing him in the process and adding an aestheticist element). Friedrich Schlegel and Coleridge developed clearly theories of an organicist nature that rejected equally enlightened absolutism and revolutionary rationalism. Similar views had wide followings in eastern Europe, not least in societies imbued by Eastern Orthodox Christianity, where they were nourished by an age-old tradition of neo-Platonicism.

However, for us and for the purposes of this volume the truly interesting matter is not the sociopolitical impact of such topoi, but rather the manner in which they served as bridges between fictional and historical narratives. It is easy to see that in novels and other works of the kind organicism could be helpful: Immermann's *Oberhof* (his celebrated insert in *Die Epigonen* is a perfect example), or else Keats's unfinished *Eve of Saint Mark,* to give a completely different example, and certainly so the (later) works of Stifter, most conspicuously his *Nachsommer.* Examples could be multiplied: they all illustrated nostalgia, the beautifying afterglow of distance in time, or simply acted as implicit critiques of the present not to be otherwise taken too seriously (although the "seriousness" obviously varied from case to case).

It is in a way more surprising and certainly more significant to follow the way in which historians made use of these same images and frameworks. This is true particularly about those dealing with the Middle Ages (Schwering in Schanze 1994, 541–55). The German historian and writers in particular included in their historical narratives a somewhat idealized version of the Middle Ages, in which the organicist topos played a decisive role (for example, Salomon 1922; Göllwitzer 1964; Mahl 1965). They were not the only ones. Macaulay's "Whig" narrative of English history carries with it strong indications of a similar organicism with regard to the post-1688 period and (to a lesser extent) of the Elizabethan Age. These and other examples (see Silver's studies on Spanish history and literature with their emphasis on the reconstruction of the historical past by the romantics in *Ruin and Restitution*) indicate very well how the overlap of the historical and the fictional prose discourses came about.

Many legitimate historical authors, in particular French, were trying to do rather similar things: to provide a colorful, attractive picture system of historical situations. It is quite true that the early nineteenth century also hosted the beginnings of a positivist strain of history-writing: from Leopold von Ranke (1795–1886) to the later Theodor Mommsen (1817–1903), albeit that one can also in these cases find moral and philosophical implications and agendas, structures proximate to the lesson and to the sermon. German, French, and English historians, not least Savigny, Mignet, or Froude can be included here (Gooch 1962, 24–49, and elsewhere). Nevertheless, the dominant romantic school from one end of Europe to the other was generated in France. The most typical contrastive case is provided by Augustin Thierry in his *Récits des temps mérovingiens,* and to a great extent *Histoire de la conquête de l'Angleterre par les Normands.* Thierry divides historicity in two parts: critique and evocation. About two-fifths of his Merovingian book contain a kind of general theoretical judgment of prior authors, as well as an attempt to define the specificity of his research field (of what French history is or how it ought to be defined). The actual bulk of the text is composed of narratives, based on sources, to be sure, but freely extended and expanded on the basis of psychological probability, imaginative complements, and free formulation of "likely" speech. Balzacian characters appear and cross each other (actually Thierry freely admitted that he felt influenced by Scott) from one story to the other. The distinction between the two races—the barbarous, treacherous, and violent Frankish one, and the refined, thoughtful, and thorough Roman-Gallic one (much underlined by later commentators)—seems to me less interesting than Thierry's historical methodology and horizon. For him historicity seems to be the fact that there is no complete formal closure; instead we have characters, destiny, and colorful adventures but not exactly a termination or final points. The best proof as to Thierry's breakthrough was that he influenced the Right as well as the Left (not least Marx). In any case, the lessons of Thierry found analogies or else were solidly assimilated by other early-nineteenth-century historians in France and abroad (see also Gooch 1962, 163–65). Thierry was friends with Chateaubriand, and, after all, Chateaubriand may also be considered as part of the category of French romantic historians.

The multivolume *Histoire des ducs de Bourgogne* by Prosper de Barante mixes the naivety and directness of the medieval chronicles with a most conscious art and practised pictorial skill (again a case in which Scott's novel-writing, here specifically *Quentin Durward*, was influential as a trigger at least). Jules Michelet, the disciple of Vico and Herder, goes over and beyond Thierry in his literary-visionary discourse, ultimately including geology and cosmology in his depiction of history. (I refer here primarily to some of his works of the 1850s and 1860s such as *L'oiseau, La mer, La montagne* and others.) "Michelet provides tableaux rather than a record of events. He hurries across large tracts of territory and lingers over individuals and occurrences that strike his imagination" (Gooch 1962, 171). His account of the French Revolution is undoubtedly ideological but even more subjectively imaginative. (Orr [1976, 53] points out that Michelet trails in a contrarian manner Tocqueville's theorizing.) We might say that Michelet's colleague and disciple Edgar Quinet follows him in as far as he dabbles in vast syntheses of spirituality and visionary democracy and openly turns historiography into the ancilla of this kind of ideological program. Both historians can be placed in useful parallel with the cosmological poems of Victor Hugo. Villemain is the epitome of belletristic historiography. Even as sober-minded a figure as François Guizot followed the trend of the times in the kind of discourse he used when writing his *Histoire de la révolution d'Angleterre*. As to Lamartine, he regarded his own historical writings as frankly literary in nature and indeed his *Histoire des Girondins* is written with the verve and the color of a breathtaking historical novel (Orr 1976, 146; in fact Sainte-Beuve felt the need to criticize his literary excesses in *Causeries du lundi*, 4:296–307).

The eight volumes of Karamzin's history of Russia (perhaps the pioneering work of Russian historiography) is rich in memorable literary portraits of major figures such as Ivan the Terrible or Boris Godunov that in turn remained models and fixtures for later literature and for the collective imaginary of Europe in general. In Germany at the same time Friedrich von Raumer's multivolume *Geschichte der Hohenstaufen und ihrer Zeit* served as a treasurehouse for future literary adaptations and in fact was soon dramatized by Raupach into a cycle of sixteen performances, which enjoyed enormous success in Berlin, as shown by the way in which they were sold out. Even Barthold G. Niebuhr, perhaps the first solid source historian, was nourished as a child with knowledge of Homeric and Middle Eastern narrative literature, and he was convinced that the earliest historical chronicles drew from songs, funeral panegyrics, and the like (Gooch 1962, 15, 19). Jakob Grimm is a typical case of the deep involvement of historical and language sciences with the romantic literary imagination (Gooch 1962, 50–53, among many others).

The five-volume *Geschichte von Böhmen* by the Czech Frantisek Palacký and *Istoria românilor sub Mihai Vodă Viteazul* (printed only in 1878, but written before

1848) by the Romanian Nicolae Bălcescu are just two further examples of belletristic history. The former tends to demonstrate that the Czech nation is Janus-faced in as far as it was constructed out of the dialectic between a Slavic foundation and a Germanic/Romanic context. It also emphasized the importance of the Jan Hus historical episode for the awakening of Czech national consciousness (Gooch 1962, 398–99; Palacký, vols. 1 and 3). The latter chooses to turn a short episode of early Romanian history (ca. 1593–1601) into a model for what a revived nation could and ought to be: brave and unified, a respectable player on the European chessboard.

Nor can it be said that British history-writing falls outside this domain. Above all the figure of Thomas Carlyle stands out here. His justly famous *French Revolution* has often been said to be a model of the perfect combination of journalistic reporting, history, and literature. There is clearly a certain amount of ideological intentionality in it, not excluding nationalism (the English gradualist way is seen as preferable to the wild oscillation between extremes of French history: from absolutism to outright terror). Nevertheless, the literary principle of combining a kind of direct, eyewitness account with the psycho-moral portraying of individuals and scenes, and with an abundance of details (often culled from documents, but more than once invented or intuited) is what truly stands forward and justifies the contemporary success and the continuing influence of the work. On the other hand the cavalier way in which philosophers, poets, and literati of all kinds managed to write history is amazing: Goldsmith and Hume (in the eighteenth century), Scott and Southey (in the nineteenth) are just some names that come to mind, their number being swelled by those of figures like Schiller in Germany or Chateaubriand and Lamartine in France, among many others. Naturally these were not professional historians. However they encouraged and justified true historians like Thomas B. Macaulay in their specific writing. Not only is Macaulay's masterpiece, *The History of England,* a kind of novel and hymn of praise addressed to the Whig development of England, but his actual historical research alternates with pieces that are more purely literary, such as portraits of historical figures of sundry ages. (Gooch 1962, 281–82, among many others). Echoes of their influence can be recognized in the writings of later figures such as Henry Buckle, James Froude, and W. E. H. Lecky, all the way to Lord Acton, or even to G. K. Chesterton and H. Belloc, who all injected the imaginative in their historical writings.

Historical literature and art were openly encouraged by monarchs such as Ludwig I of Bavaria (Gottfried 1979) or Friedrich Wilhelm IV of Prussia (Barclay 1995, 30, 66), and many others. The period after 1815 can be truly called an age of museums, collections, and, more generally, a period of institutionalized historical recuperation—in all parts of Europe.

One further interesting observation that is highly indicative and symptomatic of the obsessive power of the historical imagination is the interest of writers, on the left as well as the right, in ideas such as immortality (secular, so to say, rather than in a religious-theological sense), communication with the dead, spiritism, revival, and so on. There are aspects of naive superstition here but also of a kind of early globalism that would like to include the forefathers in the community of the world and extend equality beyond life and death; there are also traces of an anthropomorphic expression of historicism in these views that we can find from Victor Hugo, George Sand, and Théophile Gautier to Bulwer-Lytton and even George Eliot (Underwood 2002; Muray 1984).

Between these extremes of discourse (if indeed extremes they may be called)—that is, in the space opened up between fictional prose and poetry and "scientific" historiography, a remarkable variety of writings placed themselves. I will briefly discuss three of these: the historical portrait, the abovementioned *tableau vivant*, and the writing of memoirs. Historical portraits were extremely popular and, one may assume, in great demand. Walter Savage Landor's "Imaginary Portraits" (of which we have no fewer than 152 printed between 1824 and 1853) are perhaps the most typical and the most sophisticated intellectually. What Landor was trying to do was to explore the motivations and the psychological and cultural mechanisms and contexts of the major and best historical figures that may or may not have met each other, but who in any case engage in almost Plato-like dialogs of intellectual self-justification. These are clearly works of fiction, but their purposes are also clearly those of research: reaching out toward zones that are inaccessible to the mere historian, who remains tied to strict rules of documentation and reference. The fact that they are meant to be "just" literary can be seen in the elegant and careless way in which the method was taken over by poets, above all Robert Browning, who composed literary monologs in verse, a kind of stream of consciousness of historical figures of varying importance. Many of the essays of Sainte-Beuve and of Macaulay (while much more craftsman-like) could be considered "imaginary portraits."

The *tableaux vivants* became by the end of the nineteenth century a kind of parlor game: reproduction of famous paintings for instance, or representation of great historical scenes; they were almost a kind of predecessors of cinema. However, at the time we are talking about (that is, the early nineteenth century) they were of interest primarily for painters and for authors. Historical painting may be said to have dominated the nineteenth century from Benjamin Haydon and Eugène Delacroix all the way to the impressionist revolution. My chief point here would be the matter of size: it is quite clear that the abundance of figures and the dimensions of the paintings were such that they implied a historical ambition, a substitute of the missing documentary. Similar efforts can be recognized on a literary level, although they are nowadays more often forgotten than the painterly ones. Prosper Mérimée scored a genuine public success with his 1828 *La jacquerie: Scènes féodales* in thirty-six scenes, and he prepared something similar for the history of Russia. George Sand composed *Une conspiration en 1537*, which is known to have influenced Musset's *Lorenzaccio*. Ludovic Vitet was particularly diligent with his *Les barricades, La mort de Henri III, Les états de Blois*, and numerous other parts of his masterpiece, *La ligue* that might be described anachronistically as the docudramas of the age: relatively short explanatory introductions followed by long dramatizations with dozens of characters. Lamartine's abovementioned *Histoire des Girondins* could also be included here. In any case whole books have been written not only about the literary aspects of historiography proper, but also about the poetic aspects of early endeavors and experiments in literary history, with the kind of emphasis on the fraternity between erudition and imagination that I discuss in the Southey chapter (chapter 10) of the present book (Holter 1989).

Finally, while the romantic and the Biedermeier ages were not the inventors of the memorialistic genre, they used it systematically as a vehicle for historical writing that should also be subjective, and these writings are as often as not included in surveys of literature, simply because they were read as literature by contemporaries and posterity. Celebrated examples are Chateaubriand's *Mémoires d'outre-tombe* and François Guizot's eight-volume *Mémoires pour servir à l'histoire de mon temps*, from 1858–1867 (the title indicates the prudence and the moderation of a Biedermeier statesman). I want to stop just a little more on this later essential but all-too-often forgotten work.

The reader of the works of this period will immediately notice that traditional conservatisms disappeared quickly, to the extent that they may have still existed even in the last decades before 1789. In any case, no sooner had the French Revolution begun than any significant reactionary opposition ceased. The very excesses of revolutionary terror, it may be convincingly argued, were due not so much to the bloodthirstiness of the new masters as to the supine acceptance of the aristocratic victims, who willingly acceded to their own persecution and demise. A dispassionate look at the European scene after 1815 (one that ignores the din of wooden, academic cliches) shows hardly any signs of return to the ways of the past. At most we notice some attempts at bridge-building with the Enlightenment (with its combination of liberal ideals and authoritarian methods). Metternich himself, the greatly demonized figure of the age, was nothing but an eighteenth-century liberal: he did not crave a reversal to feudal or medieval political patterns. Theocratically validated absolute monarchy had utterly disappeared, even in the case of the marginal Russian emperor Alexander I, who himself tried to combine in a visionary/eccentric manner the values of enlightened liberalism with the Byzantine/Czarist traditions descending from his predecessors Ivan III and Peter I.

The demise of a purely reactionary conservatism is provided by its supporters themselves; Joseph de Maistre understood perfectly that his only chance to convey his views was to forge a discourse of paradox and provocation, to reach out toward brilliant and puzzling arguments rather than rely on tradition and precedent, as the latter were crumbling.[4] Similar imaginative reinventors were Adam Müller, one of the first to resort openly to the aesthetic as a substitute instrument of politics (see, among others, Baxa 1929; Marquardt 1993; and particularly Koehler 1980). It might be discussed whether, in a more moderate way, some key British conservatives (Coleridge and Southey for instance) did not also draw maps of future conservative possibilities rather than trying to describe continuations of the past. Chateaubriand and Goethe we have already discussed, but we might briefly mention again that Donoso Cortés distanced himself from pure reactionarism (Nicomedes Pastór Diaz), choosing instead a different view of history: that Balmes was an early Christian-Democrat, that Jovellanos was by no means more right-wing than Burke, and that at least one of the causes of the defection of the Spanish South American colonies was clerical conservatism irate at the changes in the imperial metropolis. Eastern Europe (Hungary, Russia, and Romania, at least) was particularly rich in combinations of this kind, as were the United States, the equivalent of eastern Europe at the time (or for a while) as a margin of core Europe.

Before proceeding to conclusions I want to provide a foreshortened account of a single book that I consider particularly important and indeed exemplary for the period, as well as for the dynamic process of writing interactions discussed in this chapter: François Guizot, who was not only an untiringly active political activist but also an amazingly prolific author of a great variety of works, one of whose masterpieces deserves for several reasons to be highlighted here and brought to the attention of the reader. I refer to his eight-volume memoirs (see Guizot 1858–67). I am convinced that more than any of his German political contemporaries (and even his English colleagues, perhaps with the exception of Sir Robert Peel, as indicated in chapter 3) he was the Biedermeier political thinker par excellence. This opinion is to a good extent based on Guizot's self-understanding of his own ideas and actions as mirrored in the memoirs, a work that also combines, almost perfectly, the (para)literary and the historical. Thus he becomes a peerless champion of moderation, both through his mode of writing and through his thinking and action.

It is difficult to organize Guizot's stupendously large work according to strictly temporal principles. Nevertheless, we can say in a very rough manner that his best creations in the field of political philosophy belong to the 1820s and 1830s, that the acme of his political influence and power can be placed in the 1840s, and that the period of his old age was devoted to religious issues (albeit often to matters of ecclesiastical politics such as the organization of French Protestants and the possibilities of an approach between Protestants and Catholics). Once we have said this we can immediately recognize that throughout his life his literary interests remained a continuous preoccupation (whether as literary criticism and history or as translation, mostly from English; among the latter I particularly prize the Shakespeare prose translations, which are unfortunately less than well known, although they are among the best ever accomplished in the French language). We can also recognize that Guizot's fall from power after 1848 encouraged him to a much more reflective attitude and led him to write his exceptional memoirs in which the literary, the historical, and the theoretical were combined better than in any other of his writings.

Guizot had belonged, rightly or wrongly, to the vast majority of French intellectuals (including, for instance, Chateaubriand) who were convinced, at least in the 1820s and under the scepter of Charles X, that France was in real danger of falling (*Mémoires,* 2:173, and in fact the whole of volume 2) into the hands of absolutism. Ironically, in the 1840s, when he owned the keys of power, he was to suffer a similar fate: he was suspected of coveting a similar hunger for power. His memoirs are largely devoted to a patient and detailed explanation of his intentions and of his thinking during this period. Personal or intimate facts are rare in these volumes. On the other hand, the perspectives opened on the political life and on its main characters are spectacularly wide.

From the point of view of this chapter the most interesting thing is the imbrication of balances in the book. There is a balance between ideologies that brings together the conservative and the liberal horizons of the time; there is another one between the theoretical and the historical; and a third one between the artistically narrative and the dryly factual.

To begin with the third, it is expressed aesthetically above all by the gallery of admirable portraits of many leading figures of the two Restorations: Lafayette, Manuel, d'Argenson (*Mémoires,* 1:238–49); Chateaubriand (1:260–61, 267; in no way enthusiastic, but then we have already seen in the first chapter that there was no love lost between these two great men); the duc de Richelieu (1:211–12); Louis XVIII (1:85, 87, 149–50); Fouché (1:73–74); Martignac (1:131); General Soult, Guizot's close collaborator (2:359–60); the vivid description of Casimir Perrier's untimely illness and death (2:312–13, also 177–97, and in many other places in vol. 2); the atmosphere in the Paris of July 1830 (2:319–23); King Louis-Philippe as a Biedermeier figure (2:273, 258–59); the somewhat sour depiction of Benjamin Constant (2:143–45); Lafitte (2:44–45, 162–65); Thiers (2:164–65; he saw him as valid interlocutor despite the political differences among them 2:229); and the superb depiction of the different literary/intellectual/political coteries and salons in their genealogy from the 1780s to the 1830s (2:397–423). These examples will suffice, although they do not exhaust the abundant gallery. Besides, we can easily regard them as mere symptoms of the more theoretical views in which the same balancing act can be recognized (On Guizot's "middlingness," or centrism, see Crăiuţu 2003; del Corral 1956; Kahan 1992; and even to some extent Johnson 1963; Woodward 1930; Weintraub 1988; or Rosanvallon 1985).

By the time he wrote his memoirs, Guizot had largely detached himself of the views of Victor Cousin (who had influenced him so deeply in youth) and in a way of those of Royer-Collard who may be rightly described as the pioneer of the liberal "doctrinaires" (1:82, 142–44, 162, 201, 333) and their informal leader at he beginning of the 1820s. He now spoke in cautiously favorable tones of Prince Metternich (2:339, 290–91, 252–54). More important he did not hesitate to depict himself (tacitly or aloud) as a post-Burkean (1:27, 35, 61–62). Most specifically he did not lose any occasion to outline his resistance against the excesses of the French Revolution, or even of the (much more modest) ones of the 1830 actions (1:202–10; 3:26, 30; 2:157; "politique d'ordre et de résistance" as opposed to politics of "mouvement et laisser-aller," 2:75; 1:301–12; 2:201–7). In fact to the extent to which he himself defined as belonging to a party, it was neither liberal nor conservative nor anything else but the "resistance." Guizot tried whenever possible to highlight the balance and the compatibility between tradition and liberty (1:321; 2:217, 295–97; 3:14–15; note the typical and, in different formulations, recurring phrase "les principes . . . de liberté fortement constituée"; 1:183, 190–91); collaboration among classes (1:147); the need for force and success to be balanced by a respect for stable values and virtues (1:134); the need for decentralization and local initiative (1:51, 189–90; 3:12–14). He also lashed out against extremism (2:33–34, 108–9, 169–70, 226–27, 236; 1:47), and he suggested often the need to follow the models of English constitutionalism (3:18–23; 1:111; 2:260–61).

The narrative power of Guizot's memoirs comes out of its consistent game between explosion and containment: it is an admirable, comprehensive story illustrating the manner in which moderation controls rebellion. (For Guizot the "doctrinaires" were the rational alternative to the absolute rationalism of the revolution [1:157–59].) It should be added here that the memoirs of Guizot with their combination of the political and/or social with the personal/individual find a counterpart in one of Tocqueville's lesser known works, but are preceded by what is almost unanimously recognized as Chateaubriand's greatest achievement, his *Mémoires d'outre-tombe*. I discussed these in some detail in chapter 1; therefore I will simply repeat or reemphasize what I said there. Chateaubriand seeks to be simultaneously a historian and a fiction writer. His work is not overwhelmingly narrative in the mode of Goethe's *Dichtung und Wahrheit*. It does include highly significant personal and subjective elements, even intimate confessions. However these alternate (and sometimes intertwine) with purely historical materials. In turn, these may present either personal experience and reminiscences or they may be objectively historical narratives (the most striking example is of course the Napoleonic episode). In any case, Chateaubriand's work, at least as much as Guizot's, remains a major achievement of the kind discussed in this chapter: the collaboration between pure narrative fiction and historiography proper.

What we notice in examining this dialectic between historiography and historical fiction in the early nineteenth century is a kind of feedback and shuttling between two domains, an intertwining that is rarely equaled at other points in history. Twentieth-century history-writing can serve as a good contrastive example. Unquestionably both periods have in common the fact that history is presented in a biased way, that is to say from a certain point of view it is presented based on an ideological or philosophical agenda. Nevertheless I prefer the early-nineteenth-century approach. The reason is that in its case these preferences, value choices, and intentions are outlined in a much more honest and open way.

In twentieth-century historiography, ideology is more often than not hidden. Twentieth-century historiography claims to be objective, indeed almost absolute and definitive. A certain sneakiness and lack of sincerity is perceived unpleasantly by the reader. Obviously, ideological intentions always exist: the question is what the historian is doing with them. Does he lazily allow himself to float with them? Is he carried by them? Or is he on the contrary trying to limit such ideological purposes, keep them within bounds, create counterbalances, ultimately consciously deal with them?

The interesting thing in studying the historical writing of the early nineteenth century is that authors chose neither the first nor the second solution. They preferred this very special relationship between the subjective and objective. Almost a hundred years were to pass before a truly solid theoretical justification of this approach came about: I refer to the philosophy of history of Wilhelm Dilthey, with its formulation of empathy as an indispensable tool of the historians. Although it was not theorized, in actual practice this discursive procedure remained amply illustrated. The relationship between subjectivity and objectivity was understood not only in the early nineteenth century but even later as the instrumental and auxiliary use of subjectivity in order to penetrate more deeply and more efficiently inside the dynamics of historical unfolding. The historians and the novelists of early-nineteenth-century romanticism certainly regarded themselves as indispensable collaborators to the extent that they considered that the "writing of history requested *all* faculties: emotion, imagination, empathy, along with reason and empirical imagination." In fact subjectivity was seen as something indispensable, and the errors of past historians were attributed to their failure to make use more courageously of subjectivity. Victor Hugo formulated this even more bluntly (and, one might say, a little simplistically): "La Vendée ne peut être complètement expliquée que si la légende complète l'histoire; il faut l'histoire pour l'ensemble et la légende pour le détail" (232). The side-effect of such a *démarche* must be inevitably a marginalization of pure rationalism with its radicalism: the intervention of the aesthetic forges a moderating framework for the understanding of the past, and, by the same token but perhaps more relevantly, of the present and of the future. One last point in this respect: as I explained in previous chapters, later romanticism, the Biedermeier age, is generally founded on the substitutive mode—aesthetics and religion, geography and social (or national) physiognomy, hard and soft sciences, liberalism and conservatism, the arts and literature, sometimes the special uses of education, literature, and music, the line can continue, and it does, precisely with the history/fiction dichotomy, as outlined above.

Notes

1. See Rigney 2001, ch. 1.
2. Waldemar Zacharasiewicz, "The Rise of Cultural Nationalism in the New World: The Scottish Element and Example" in Drescher and Volkel 1989, 315–34. Kaufmann 1995,

93–137, offers a gross and simplistic reading of Scott's early novels; still he has the merit of understanding that the author had philosophical intentions and that he was on the same wavelength with Burke.

3. It should be noticed that I confine myself in this chapter to writings in prose. This is because my chosen topic is the relationship between historiography and fiction. However, the early nineteenth century was tremendously rich in historical drama and poetry: in poetry from Southey, Shelley, Scott, and Keats to Ludwig Uhland and Victor Hugo; in drama from Grabbe and Platen to (again) Victor Hugo, to name just a very few names. This historical dimension could be in subject matter or to echoes of style, and it did not exclude actual rewritings, as in the case of Brentano's "Italian" folktales and many others.

4. See the excellent essay by Cioran (1977) which demonstrates admirably the connection between the linguistic and the ideological in one case, but with wider implications.

Bibliography

Barbéris, Pierre. 1967. "La pensée de Balzac: Histoire et structures." *Revue d'Histoire de la Littérature Française* 1:18–55.

Barclay, David E. 1995. *Frederick William IV and the Prussian Monarchy 1840–1861* Oxford: Clarendon Press.

Barthes, Roland. 1987. *Michelet.* New York: Hill and Wang.

Barzun, Jacques. 1941. "Romantic Historiography as a Political Force in France." *Journal for the History of Ideas* 2: 318–29.

Baxa, Jakob. 1929. *Adam Müllers Philosophie, Asthetik und Staatswissenschaft.* Berlin: Junker und Dünnhaupt.

Burgess, Miranda. 2000. *British Fiction and the Production of Social Order: 1740–1830.* Cambridge: Cambridge University Press.

Burke, Edmund. 1793. *Betrachtungen über die französiche Revolution.* Trans. Friedrich von Gentz. Berlin: Friedrich Vieweg dem Älteren.

Burrow, J. W. 1982. *A Liberal Descent: Victorian Historians and the English Past.* Cambridge: Cambridge University Press.

Cioran, Emil M. 1977. *Essai sur la pensée réactionnaire: Á propos de Joseph de Maistre.* Saint-Clément-de-Rivière: Fata Morgana.

Crăiuțu, Aurelian. 2003. *Liberalism under Siege: The Political Thought of the French Doctrinaires.* Lanham, Md.: Rowman and Littlefield.

Crossley, Ceri. 1993. *French Historians: Thierry, Guizot, the Saint-Simoniens, Quinet, Michelet.* London: Routledge.

Díez del Corral, Luis. 1956. *El liberalismo doctrinario.* Madrid: Instituto de Estudios Politicos.

Drescher, Horst, and Hermann Volkel, eds. 1989. *Nationalism in Literature / Literarischer Nationalismus.* Frankfurt, Bern, New York, and Paris: Peter Lang.

Duncan, Ian. 1992. *Modern Romance and the Transformations of the Novel: The Gothic, Scott, Dickens.* New York and Cambridge: Cambridge University Press.

Epps, Preston, trans. 1972. *The Poetics of Aristotle.* Chapel Hill: University of North Carolina Press. (Orig. pub. 1942.)

Ermarth, Elizabeth. 1997. *The English Novel in History 1840–1895.* London: Routledge.

Fraser, John. 1982. *America and the Patterns of Chivalry.* Cambridge: Cambridge University Press.

Friedman, Geraldine. 1996. *The Insistence of History: Revolution in Burke, Wordsworth, Keats, and Baudelaire.* Stanford: Stanford University Press.

Glaser, Horst Albert, ed. 1980–1987. *Deutsche Literatur: Eine Sozialgeschichte.* 10 vols. Hamburg: Rohwohlt.

Göllwitzer, Heinz. 1964. *Europabild und Europagedanke: Beiträge zur deutschen Geistesgeschichte des 18. und 19. Jahrhunderts.* Munich: Beck.

Gooch, George Peabody. 1962. *History and Historians in the Nineteenth Century.* Boston: Beacon Press. (Orig. pub. 1913.)

Gottfried, Paul. 1979. *Conservative Millenarians: The Romantic Experience in Bavaria.* New York: Fordham University Press.

Grudzinska Gross, Irene. 1991. *The Scar of Revolution: Custine, Tocqueville, and the Romantic Imagination.* Berkeley: University of California Press.

Guizot, François. 1858–67. *Mémoires pour servir à l'histoire de mon temps.* 8 vols. Paris: Michel Lévy Frères.

Holter, Achim. 1989. *Ludwig Tieck: Literaturgeschichte als Poesie.* Heidelberg: Carl Winter.

Hugo, Victor. 1872. *Quatrevingt-treize.* Paris: Gallimard Folio Classique.

Johnson, Douglas. 1963. *Guizot: Aspects of French History 1787–1874.* London: Routledge and Kegan Paul.

Kahan, Alan. 1992. *Aristocratic Liberalism.* Oxford and New York: Oxford University Press.

Kaufmann, David. 1995. *The Business of Common Life: Novels and Classical Economics between Revolution and Reform.* Baltimore: Johns Hopkins University Press.

Koehler, Benedikt. 1980. *Ästhetik der Politik: Adam Müller und die politische Romantik.* Stuttgart: Klett-Cotta.

Lukács, György von. 1969. *The Historical Novel.* London: Harmondsworth/Penguin. (Orig. pub. 1955.)

Mahl, Hans Joachim. 1965. *Die Idee des goldenen Zeitalters im Werk des Novalis.* Heidelberg: Carl Winter.

Maignon, Louis. 1970. *Le roman historique à l'époque romantique.* Geneva: Slatkin. (Orig. pub. 1898.)

Marquardt, Jochen. 1993. *Vermittelnde Geschichte: Zum Verhältnis von ästhetischer Theorie und historischem Denken bei Adam Heinrich Müller.* Stuttgart: Hans-Dieter Heinz.

Marsch, Edgar, ed. 1993. *Über Literaturgeschichtsschreibung: Die historisierende Methode des 19ten Jahrhunderts in Program und Kritik.* Darmstadt: Wissenschaftliche Buchgesellschaft. (Orig. pub. 1975.)

Moreau, Pierre. 1957. *Le romantisme.* Paris: Del Duca.

Muray, Philippe. 1984. *Le 19e siècle à travers les âges.* Paris: Denoël.

Neff, Emery. 1947. *The Poetry of History: The Contributions of Literature and Literary Scholarship to the Writing of History since Voltaire.* New York: Columbia University Press.

Nemoianu, Virgil. 1977. *Micro-Harmony: The Growth and Uses of the Idyllic Model in Literature.* Bern: Peter Lang.

Orr, Linda. 1976. *Jules Michelet: Nature, History and Language.* Ithaca: Cornell University Press.

———. 1990. *Headless History: Nineteenth-Century French Historiography of the Revolution.* Ithaca: Cornell University Press.

Palacký, Frantiseck. 1968. *Geschichte von Böhmen.* 6 vols. Osnabrück: Otto Zeller. (Orig. pub. 1844–1867.)

Powers, Richard H. 1957. *Edgar Quinet: A Study in French Patriotism*. Dallas: Southern Methodist University Press.

Ricoeur, Paul. 1980. *The Contribution of French Historiography to the Theory of History*. Oxford: Clarendon Press.

Rigney, Ann. 2001. *Imperfect Histories: The Exclusive Past and the Legacy of Romantic Historicism*. Ithaca: Cornell University Press.

Rosanvallon, Pierre. 1985. *Le moment Guizot*. Paris: Gallimard.

Sainte-Beuve, Charles Augustin. 1853. *Causeries du lundi*. Paris: Garnier. (Orig. pub. 1851.)

Salomon, Gottfried. 1922. *Das Mittelalter als Ideal der Romantik*. Munich: Drei Masken Verlag.

Schanze, Helmut, ed. 1994. *Romantik-Handbuch*. Tübingen: Kröner.

Schlaffer, Hannelore und Heinz. 1975. *Studien zum ästhetischen Humanismus*. Frankfurt: Suhrkamp.

Seillère, Ernest. 1919. *Edgar Quinet et le mysticisme démocratique*. Paris: Société d'économie sociale.

Sidney, Sir Philip. 1966. *A Defence of Poetry*. Ed. Jan van Dorsten. Oxford: Oxford University Press.

Silver, Philip W. 1997. *Ruin and Restitution: Reinterpreting Romanticism in Spain*. Nashville, Tenn.: Vanderbilt University Press.

Spaemann, Robert. 1959. *Der Ursprung der Soziologie aus dem Geiste der Restauration: Studien aber L. G. A. de Bonald*. Munich: Kösel.

Spearman, Diane. 1987. "Walter Scott as a Conservative Thinker." *Salisbury Review* 5, no. 3 (April): 29–32.

Srbik, Heinrich von. 1951. *Geist und Geschichte: Vom deutschen Humanismus bis zur Gegenwart*. 2 vols. Munich: Bruckmann.

Underwood, Ted. 2002. "Historical Difference as Immortality in the Mid-Nineteenth-Century Novel." *Modern Language Quarterly* 63, no. 4 (December): 441–69.

Weintraub, Karl. 1988. *Visions of Culture*. Chicago: Chicago University Press.

Woodward, Ernst Llewellyn. 1930. *Three Studies in European Conservatism*. London: Constable.

CHAPTER 5

J. F. Cooper and Eastern European and African American Intellectuals
Borders and Depths of Multiculturalism

IF INDEED THE HISTORICAL MOLDS virtually the whole of the nineteenth century, then it seems appropriate to deal with the historical from another point of view. The historical (and, even more so, historicism) is a rather specific form of relativism, one that controls, orders, and moderates itself and, in the long run, relativizes itself. This implies not least that we can not and are not allowed to turn into a dogma the perception of separation between races and cultures. While differences between these are real enough, there also exist large areas of commonality, which turn words such as "mankind" and "human nature" into reasonably operative tools—epistemologically weak but by no means weaker than many others that we use all the time without compunction, such as "power," "gender," "society," "compassion," "environment," "peace," and many others. The second consequence is that we can actually point, albeit briefly, to a few of these commonalities that shrink cultural distances and tend to encourage a more positive view of a universal humanity. Among these are: (1) religious-ethical dimensions of human functioning; (2) the fact that, and the way in which, "modernization" created suffering and resentment among very different kinds of cultures; and (3) similarities in the dynamics of mediation in very different societies and cultures.

As the central helpful example I will choose the novels of J. F. Cooper, which, at the beginning of the nineteenth century (the period discussed in this book), embody a wrestling with the issue of multiculturalism. I find it interesting (in order to bolster this position, but also in order to provide a "control") to resort to two further and quite different examples: (1) the struggle of the Romanian intellectual community in the nineteenth and twentieth centuries with the issue of modernization; and (2) the dilemmas of the African American intellectual community when faced with the matter of its most desirable positioning toward the European American and North Atlantic culture surrounding and outnumbering it.

Obviously I am writing against the grain, but I do so intentionally. In North American cultural life a powerful system of cultural relativism has taken root, grounded in some local pragmatic traditions but also drawing from more recent western European theories of deconstruction and of left-oriented interpretations of the Nietzsche-Heidegger philosophical tradition. Separately taken these ingredients are far from being as dogmatic and unilateral as their combined outcome is. Thus American pragmatism as expounded by Peirce (and perhaps also by Dewey) seems fairly confident in its ability to predict results and provide guidelines for our functioning in the world, even if it eschews the metaphysical issues of ultimate realities. In turn, Heidegger, no less than Nietzsche or Schopenhauer, supported in no uncertain terms a number of values, both epistemological and axiological. Heidegger's relativism was accompanied by anxiety, not by exultance; Schopenhauer's by deep pessimism; and Nietzsche's explosions of joy are triggered not by discoveries of relativity but by the confidence in the affirmative force of subjective vitalism. Derrida and his followers seldom reach out toward extra-European categories and modes of thinking and always remain squarely rooted inside Western horizons, as do, of course, the Nietzscheans or the pragmatists, up to and including Richard Rorty.[1]

However, in their combination as understood and provided by its (mostly American) followers in literary criticism and in cultural studies, the new cultural relativism seems unyielding and mostly bent on undercutting Western certitudes, affirmations, and modes of behavior. (This is due, I am convinced, largely to a contamination with Marxist purposes and the substitution of epistemological intentions by sociopolitical aims and games.) Dogmatic nihilism in Europe and the United States thus inscribes itself in the family of leveling utopianisms. It is the heir or ally of doctrines that have produced and justified totalitarian and destructive regimes in the twentieth century. Nihilism, therefore, tends to diminish constructive productivity, as well as human difference, despite its claims to the contrary.

First, let me provide a reminder about Eurocentrism. This is a phenomenon much more limited in time and scope than is generally believed. Western society unfolded a confidence in its prophetic mission on the planet and its inherent superiority to all other races and societies, past and present, chiefly in the eighteenth and nineteenth centuries. Up to the ages of the Renaissance, exploration, and discovery, Europeans were relatively modest. Gapes of admiration saluted the narratives of wealth, power, and achievement of Eastern empires, even when their possessions were impotently coveted. To take one example among many, any reader of the *Chanson de Roland* understands that compared with the sophisticated, cosmopolitan, worldwide Arabic civilization of the eighth and ninth centuries A.D., European Christendom was not more than a local peasant culture, tenaciously clinging to its own identity. Additionally the Byzantine Empire of the same age was recognized as a more legitimate offspring of Greco-Roman civilization than the West.

Likewise, after 1950 and despite the imperial might of the United States, it was increasingly clear that, shorn of their erstwhile colonial empires, humbled by the disastrous outcome of the "European Civil Wars" (as the two World Wars were sometimes called), subject to the vigorous competition of the alternative civilizations of Russia and soon eastern Asia, and alert to the demographical imbalance (and gradually, also, the economic surge) of the Southern Hemisphere, the Europeans at least could no longer offer themselves as the guiding light of the world.

However, in the intervening centuries and, as I have said, particularly in the eighteenth and nineteenth centuries, such doubts and reservations were exceedingly rare. Hegel's philosophy of history, in which eastern and non-European cultures are described as just a prologue to the real history (that of the West), is but one example of what was generally taken for granted by authors ideologically as different as Bossuet and Gibbon, Dr. Johnson and Voltaire, and scores of others. The comic but deeply sincere exclamation of Montesquieu's Parisian gentleman—"Comment peut-on être Persan?"—neatly summarizes a whole state of mind, for which even eastern and southern Europe and even the confines of Scotland and Ireland, were areas of questionable reality (compare Nemoianu 1996).

In the eighteenth and nineteenth centuries the issue was joined (on an ideological level) between a conservative position and a liberal-progressive one. The former proposed as a basic attitude toward the outside world, a position of ironic indifference mixed with (occasional) careless brutality, a cruelly selfish but not programmatically colonialist policy. The Left by contrast proposed conquest as the framework of systematic modification: a benign reformation through educational means and an adaptation of the rest of the world to the modes of life and behavior of Western culture. It cannot be repeated often enough that, contrary to the views of Edward Said, Mary Louise Pratt, Marianna Torgovnick, and others, some of the worst forms of mental and physical oppression invented by the West were but a consequence of highminded progressive and utopian purposes. In one form or the other, these principles and attitudes are still operative in the early years of the twenty-first century. By contrast, zoologists, linguists, pioneers in the discipline of comparative myths and religions, and geographical travelers were not instruments of some evil master plan but usually sincere multiculturalists who tried to establish a balance between universalist frameworks and local truths.

It is interesting to note this even in some cases when the ostensible purpose is the opposite. I will repeat, from a different angle, something mentioned in the first chapter. At one point in his *Génie du christianisme* (1978) Chateaubriand offers a long list with the tables of commandments of some main religions. His intention is to show that the Ten Commandments received by Moses on Mount Sinai have considerably more emotional depth and subtlety than their equivalents in other religions. Ironically Chateaubriand manages to prove the opposite. The reader of today and most likely some of Chateaubriand's own contemporaries must have been struck by the close similarity between the tables of moral laws of Islam, Hinduism, Zoroastrism, ancient Greece and Rome, and others, with those of Christianity and Judaism. As a matter of fact, by the middle of the next century an unabashed apologist of Christianity such as C. S. Lewis was using similar comparisons in order to emphasize the common religious fund of humanity.

This is not an isolated example. In fact, appearances and voluble arguments to the contrary, religious discourses proved their value as mediations between cultures. When James Frazer (or others in the school of "Cambridge ritualists") painstakingly unearthed thematic similarities between Christian narratives and the body of extra-European myths and archetypes, they did not so much undercut the former (though this may have been their purpose) as legitimize the latter, by pointing to ties with common experiences of mankind.[2]

Moreover, a centuries-old theological line inside Christianity (much favored in the Renaissance and no less in the seventeenth and even eighteenth centuries) held that we must account for two forms (or waves) of divine revelation. Only the second of these found its expression through the Scriptures. The first was natural creation and, simultaneously, the establishment of "natural" religions. The latter, the more liberal theologians insisted, should not be regarded as enemies but rather as imperfect sketches of truths that the Scriptures could offer in a more complete and reliable version. Very often throughout the sixteenth to the eighteenth centuries missionary activities were accompanied by detailed studies of local cultures, and sometimes by attempts to devise genuine combinations between local traditions and the message of Christianity (North American and East Asian examples were often adduced). The most ambitious project of this kind ever designed must remain that of the Jesuit Matteo Ricci shortly before 1600, but there were other experiments of longer or shorter duration and scope.[3]

Such initiatives did not really go against the innermost tendencies of Christianity, although historically these had found themselves as often as not blocked by rigid and intolerant impulses. Part of the geohistorical success of Christianity over twenty centuries was undoubtedly its willingness to engage in enculturation, in multiple hybrid combinations with local cultures—in a word, in its willingness to change and adapt. Examples are numerous, from Coptic Christianity to the Chaldean and Armenian variants, from Mormons and Quakers to the Starobryadtsy.

In an even broader sense the same expansion was based on metamorphosis, cooption and adaptation. Within two centuries or so of its foundation, Christianity had changed from a small and somewhat cohesive branch of Judaism into a major, Mediterranean-wide and open kind of religion by absorbing and adapting to the prevalent Greco-Roman religious and ideological idioms, as well as by other accretions. Again, beginning around 800–900 A.D., Christianity began to seek tenaciously a symbiosis with the barbarian Germanic and Slavic tribes, and not only changed accordingly, but responded by generating new branches of itself, usually referred to as Eastern Orthodoxy and Protestantism. There are reasons to believe that, despite a certain sluggishness, something similar, establishing rapport with a new global situation, began around 1500–1600 A.D.

I will now move to my second argument: the way in which a great variety of communities and of individuals responded to the global process of modernization. Despite bouts of ostensible enthusiasm, this response habitually included hostility. In the best cases we notice attempts to mediate, to find idioms, images, cognitive and social tools, that would help people to effect the movement from a traditional and, as most thought, natural or biological system to the rationally controlled, transactive, and negotiative one, which was expressed by "alienation" (that is, a weakening or vanishing of community ties), to industrial urbanization, quantified and abstract values, intense self-consciousness, and scientific, technological, and economic achievement.[4]

True, this process began in northwestern Europe and from there spread throughout the world. It is not correct, however, to describe it exclusively as a process of Western pressure on the rest of the world. The reason is that for many centuries modernization (to use the habitual shorthand term) was challenged, critiqued, and even actively opposed in many parts of Europe, including the core area of Britain, France, the German-speaking lands, and northern Italy (as late as the early nineteenth century; see Johnson 1991, 280–82). We know that for several centuries Scotland violently opposed its colonial inclusion in the capitalist system. (What are Walter Scott's novels, but a belated dramatization of this recalcitrance?) Likewise, Ireland was an area that in some ways, even to this day, tried to oppose the very same modernization. Many of the vagaries and convulsions of French politics from the seventeenth to the nineteenth centuries, as well as part of the history of northern France and of Germany as a whole, can be read in the same fashion. In Bavaria and Austria the growth of streamlining was encountered by sullen and persistent disagreement (Gottfried 1979). Bitter resentment confronted the modernizing process in Provence, Bretagne, Sicily, not to mention eastern Europe. In fact, in the rural societies of southern and eastern Europe modernization had to take place primarily through imposition from above, by political-administrative means, rather than from below, through economic growth (Gerschenkron 1966). The southern states of the newly formed United States had to be subdued at the end of a bitterly fought and protracted war with much bloodshed.

Only after the defeat of these oppositions can we begin to speak in earnest of massive shaping actions directed toward non-European areas. For what was often claimed and believed to be their own good, India, Mexico, Egypt, Japan, and scores of other nations with a proud past found themselves involved in an accelerated, truly global evolution that was gaining a momentum beyond the intentions of its agents. This happened also because in European, as well as in non-European, areas social and intellectual forces were at work that were persuaded of the superior merits and beneficial attractiveness of the new "progressive" order of things, and which actually encouraged and promoted it. While admittedly there was usually little choice, we are not wrong to speak about an "invited colonialism" in eastern Europe, South America, and other parts of the world.

What all these examples indicate is that in discussing these matters we tend to stumble upon a recurrent error. The process of modernization is all too often attributed to some kind of clever contraption by the "white" northern societies and races to control the people of the Southern or Eastern hemispheres. In actuality, the same anxieties and animosities arose on all continents as soon as groups and individuals were obliged to face the reality of massive change. Where does the erroneous explanation stem from? I think that we lay too many intentions and rational motivations at the door of what seems to be, on the basis of solid and repeated evidence, mere evolution. No conspiratorial plan with clear aims has ever been unveiled behind what we conventionally call invention and construction of history. Mechanical applications of cause-and-effect relations lead us nowhere.[5]

On the other hand these developments were modulated and qualified on an intellectual level. True, many stark oppositions and approvals can be found there also, but these were accompanied by extremely detailed discussions in philosophical and literary, or openly political form, on the meaning of modernization and of our responses to it. We may wonder whether the abundant tradition of pastoral, and later idyllic works from the Renaissance on, and all the way to the late eighteenth century, was not also fueled by the resentment of agricultural societies that saw their mode of existence endangered. Be that as it may, there can be little doubt that much of the romantic and modernist literature expressed the bewilderment and the doubts of the authors, and certainly also of their audience, when faced with the implications of the modernizing process upon the human person.

Clearly a good part of the romantic debate already indicated a conservative bent and deep sorrow and anguish over the way rationalization was progressing. On the other hand many other models, such as those devised by Goethe, Scott, or Mme de Staël were clearly intended (to repeat) to be experiments in moderation and taming for Europe itself and, by implication, for imagining complex bonds with the rest of the planet. We may wonder whether ultimately the whole modern theory of multiculturalism could be conceived without the impulses originating in the romantic era.

Herder should be named here as a great turning point. Herder enunciated the principles that enable us to discard rigidly unifying standard classical measurements and replace them with *Stimmen der Völker*—principles of individual and group identity, ethnic, and cultural empowerments. While this was seen by some as a step toward relativity and a justification for fierce nationalism, Herder, in fact, cleared the road toward a new, more flexible kind of accord between local and universal principles, one based on multiple bonds. We can be convinced that the Herderian revolution was helped along by audience acquaintance with Kant's epistemological principle of the *Ding-an-sich;* the postulate that an absolute reality could well survive even without a full cognitive grasp or a restless reduction to our theoretical categories. Thus the two great thinkers collaborated unwittingly, in spite of their apparent or explicit adversity.

In the light of this great double initiative, it becomes increasingly difficult to attribute imperialistic, ulterior motives to Novalis's, Schlegel's, and even Hölderlin's veneration of Indian antiquity, to Schopenhauer's privileging of Buddhist religion as the one closest to the most convincing brand of philosophy, or to Goethe's choice of Persian poetry as paradigmatic of the most delicate balance between the spiritual and the earthy. Coleridge's selection of a Mongolian symbol for human creativity, Shelley's resort to Islam, Byron's proposal of Middle Eastern cultures as the realm of strongly profiled human energies, are equally telling.

I do not want to confine these mediating forces to literary humanism. In fact it is interesting to note that in the emerging field of political science statal modalities were often discussed in terms of the dialectics of cultural relativity and cultural typology. Thus in the seventeenth and eighteenth centuries early practitioners such as Montesquieu (1748) and Volney (1791) engaged, albeit gingerly, in extra-European comparisons.[6]

Post-Herderian scholars of quite different orientations developed such comparatist positions in various ways. Oswald Spengler (whose work has been justly criticized for many ideological as well as professional reasons) has the merit of having produced an imaginative system that discredits Eurocentrism. Spengler's system found ingenious ways to accord autonomous dignity to a great many non-European cultural systems, from Egyptian and Babylonian to Meso-American, and denied the Hegelian-Marxist monopoly of Europeanism in world history; it also provided significant parallels between various cultures and praised their achievements (Spengler 1980).

Looking at the other end of the ideological spectrum we find somebody like André Malraux whose general idea of the "imaginary museum," was that aesthetic principles and enlightened taste can survive and overcome the frontiers of time and sociocultural space. According to Malraux a level can be established on which artistic works from vastly different backgrounds can coexist and even illuminate each other. Although this approach never enjoyed, to my knowledge, a systematic theoretical underpinning, it proved remarkably tenacious, from Goethe's *Weltliteratur* seen as a kind of Olympian gathering of all that is best in each society and tribe to the contemporary practices, unreflective perhaps, of the Nobel Prize committees.[7]

We can conclude that, far from exercising a divisive and restrictive influence, the forces of literary aesthetics, as well as those of intellectual discussion, generally served more often than not as areas of experimentation and provided occasions for fruitful dialogue, for overcoming misreadings, and for paving the way toward sociopolitical solutions in history. They helped to soothe the asperities of historical emancipation, and it is not their fault that they were not used more often or more efficiently.

The unfolding of modernization was, and remains, agonizing in the Northern, not less than in the Southern Hemisphere, in communities of the most different cultural and racial origins. Let me now turn to some specific similarities encountered in literary and intellectual crystallizations of the dilemmas raised by modernizing pressures. A look at these examples shows that cultural relativism (the superficial version of multiculturalism, to speak more bluntly) falls far short of the absolute explanatory power it claims for itself: we find deep and unintended analogies at work in the dynamics of this process. Common patterns in the management of suffering and doubt are readily discovered, in spite of the vast differences of external codification.

The first comparative test I chose is that of a small east-central European culture, the Romanian one, which underwent a revival and metamorphosis in the early nineteenth century precisely because of its contact with the rapidly modernizing West and with the debates raging there. The relevance of these debates and changes was doubly and triply acute for a community placed at the margins of this zone, a community that felt internal and external pressures to keep in pace with the more central areas that it both desired and feared to join. The ambivalence of the West itself is another comprehensive subject that cannot be properly addressed here.

At the beginning of the nineteenth century, Romanian society, barely postcolonial, was only to some extent feudal and more largely traditional/ tribal/patriarchal. The preference for a modernizing evolution was confined to thin layers of informed and educated elites, who were persuaded that it was in the best interest of the community as a whole to adjust itself to changes that were deemed inevitable and unstoppable. In the nineteenth century, conservatives and liberals differed merely as to the degree and the methods to be used in order to attain the desirable goal of Westernization. Thus whereas the revolutionaries of 1848, the historian Nicolae Bălcescu, the radicals Ion Brătianu and C. A. Rosetti, the essayist Mihail Kogălniceanu, and others, sought an accelerated and vigorously steered revamping of society, the moderate *Junimea* group, particularly its mentors Titu Maiorescu and Petre Carp from the 1860s on, argued that measures of change should be calibrated to local possibilities and resources. The former advocated wholesale importation of the West's legal patterns, intellectual values, and economic structures. The latter, equally cosmopolitan, wanted adaptation rather than replication.

By the end of the nineteenth century the situation had changed. As the country was actually caught up in the network of modernizing changes (urbanization and alienation being the expression of a contractual-type society), an increasingly large section of the intellectual and political elite rebelled against this process and clamored for the maintenance of, or return to, indigenous values and modes of life. Here, too, the conflict between "Slavophiles" and "Westernizers," as launched in the Russia of the 1860s, was reproduced; it was the type of conflict that in just a few decades would shake Islamic, Hindu, and other societies around the world. The indigenous nationalists, inspired by the political essays of the romantic poet Mihai Eminescu (1850–1889) and energized by the historian and critic Nicolae Iorga (1871–1940), the poet Octavian Goga (1881–1938), and their *Semănătorist* literary movement, argued that Romania's natural vocation was that of an agrarian society, imbued and directed by the rhythms of nature, inward-looking, religious, traditional, and satisfied with a subsistence economy. Calm wisdom rather than curious inquiry, ethnic purity rather than cosmopolitan mixture, ought to be encouraged. Gradually their lines of conflict became sharper and the conflict grew acrimonious. A native variant of fascism emerged after World War I, based on a kind of revolutionary mysticism. Meanwhile, thinkers such as Eugen Lovinescu (1881–1943), C. D. Zeletin (1882–1934), and others extolled the merits of a society aligned to Western progress.[8]

What is truly interesting, however, is that between these two camps we find a surprisingly large body of thinkers who tried to devise a third way and reflected on the inevitable negotiation involved in the transfer of values: what is lost and what is gained in the process of displacement from one order of human existence to the other (Hitchins 1994). They proposed solutions and compromises that they thought were acceptable, even when these could be appropriated for self-interested, and therefore distortive, reasons by one of the extreme sides.

Thus Lucian Blaga (1895–1961), primarily a poet and playwright, also developed a complex philosophical system in which notes of relativity are clearly audible. Part of his system was a theory of culture in which he struggled to define some specific features of Romanian cultural identity starting from values embedded in folk poetry, for example the ballad "Miorița." According to Blaga, a characteristic cultural matrix for Romanian folk production is provided by a space feeling that is undulating in successions of ups and downs, corresponding to the natural landscape of hills and valleys from which it actually emerged. However, Blaga's essay "Mioritic Space" was inscribed in a much more elaborate general theory of the stylistics of culture and religion, in which the specific identity of Romanians becomes merely a modest case among a whole generic multitude (Blaga 1944, 16).

Older than Blaga, C. Rădulescu-Motru (1868–1957) learned much from the nineteenth-century moderate conservatives the *Junimists*. He composed a sociopsychology of the peasant world that would not necessarily clash with the prescriptions of an urban or even cosmopolitan society.[9] In an even more specific way, theories of this kind were articulated and transferred into practical blueprints by Virgil Madgearu (1887–1940), who was not only a professor of economics and sociology, but also, throughout the 1930s, the secretary-general of one of Romania's two most influential democratic parties, the National-Peasant Party. Madgearu proposed that capitalism be introduced sparingly in Romania, and combined with an encouragement of peasant cooperatives that would help preserve traditional households, modes of property, and values.

The greatest Romanian sociologist, Dimitrie Gusti (1880–1955), sought to devise his own formula for the combination of Western and local values. He set up the creation of sociological teams, consisting of students, that would descend upon villages in different parts of the country and spend longer periods of time there, trying to gather exhaustive data on the anthropology, linguistic dialects, economic situations and standards of living, local politics, folklore, and dress codes. Gusti also coordinated and supervised a very comprehensive encyclopedia of Romanian geography, history, and culture. At the same time, Gusti was careful to keep his work in line with international methodologies and to position himself inside the international sociological community on a theoretical level.[10]

On a more purely literary level, examples of such give-and-take were more frequent and more obvious. The poetry of the abovementioned Lucian Blaga is a good example: it is placed squarely in the formal and lyrical tradition of expressionism, even though many of its motifs and topics are taken from the world of the Romanian village. Numerous contemporaries of his followed the same pattern—for instance, the poet Adrian Maniu (1891–1968). Tudor Vianu (1897–1964), one of the leading critics of his generation, wrote often and ably about Romanian literature. In fact he was also the coauthor of a history of Romanian literature, but he wrote deeply imbued with German and French philosophy and literary theory.[11]

All the examples listed above have something in common. They represent the work of individuals who, no matter how different they were in their media of expression or in their ideological premises, were intensely aware of the recalcitrance to change of the sociohistorical environment in which they were functioning. Nor were they ready to dismiss such recalcitrance as simple reactionary inertia. They agreed that processes of emancipation and modernization could be very painful, brutal, and unattractive. They realized that, almost exactly as in ecological interventions, the dangers of losing something are as powerful and substantial as the chances of gaining something. The authors mentioned (and others in the area between the Oder and the Dnjester rivers) were trying to establish a space of negotiation and profit analysis between the values of a rich and still viable past and the pressures and needs of advance. The Romanian case abounds in valuable intellectual suggestions of all kinds, even though it is not encouraging in practical results; management of ideas could very well go hand-in-hand with the mishandling of actual socioeconomic affairs. This is of relatively small interest to us in this context. Our demonstration is much more theoretical: it proves that in this case, as in many others, multiculturalism is a process, not a simple monolithic fact, and that it is multiple rather than simple and direct.

Let us now additionally engage in a brief survey of the debates inside the African American intellectual community during the last hundred years or so. Earlier debates had used as primary medium a religious idiom. It would be fascinating to dwell upon the retrieval and the decoding of these debates, since the results would certainly be most rewarding, as some pioneering works have already indicated. However this would take us too far afield from the more specific goals of this examination. My argument will be rather that, beginning with the mid- or later nineteenth century, the intellectual voices of this ethnic and social community did not constitute a unified and simple block nor did they simply follow lines traced out by the liberal Left, as is sometimes believed.

For evidence it is enough to look contrastively at two of the founding figures of modern African American self-searching, namely Booker T. Washington and W. E. B. DuBois, both of whom enjoyed prominence and respect in the late nineteenth and early twentieth centuries beyond the boundaries of their community.[12]

On the surface the polemic between these two great figures centers on practical matters: the type of education most suitable for the full emancipation and assertion of the African Americans in a predominantly European American society. Booker T. Washington militantly promoted a practical-utilitarian education for his community, while W. E. B. DuBois eloquently proclaimed the need for a general college education that would provide leadership, and for organization at all levels (Harris 1991).[13]

The palimpsest inscribed in their texts offers an additional (and fundamental) difference: Washington argued for a thorough integration of African Americans in Western society, while Dubois was more emphatic on the identity and self-reliance of their community.[14] This distinction is as crucial as it is simplifying. DuBois's increasing inclination toward socialism and communism as he was aging can well be read as the gesture of one reaching out toward bonds that transcend racial lines; the distinction between himself and his influential contemporary, the radical nationalist Marcus Garvey, is obvious. By the same token there are enough passages in Washington's work that indicate that he did not wish to ignore distinctions between racial modes of existence. Nevertheless it is not absurd to detect here analogies to the Slavophile versus Westernizing distinction in eastern Europe.

The game was played out more fully a generation later (DuBois was still living) during what remains the high point of African American cultural achievement: the Harlem Renaissance. The abundance and diversity of figures in music, the arts, and literature expresses, I am sure, a struggle for inventing an acceptable and original mode of positioning in which identity could be preserved without loss of dignity, but also without losing the benefits of adherence to the modernization process.

The writings of the most prominent representatives of the Harlem Renaissance are a testimony to this. Wallace Thurman consistently used an ironic mode when recording the atmosphere and figures of the time and place, particularly in his 1932 novel, *Infants of the Spring*. Langston Hughes and Claude McKay zigzagged ideologically from right to left and back; both were basically expressionists who could write in ways close to a "national" African American mode as well as step outside ethnic status. Even more characteristically, Jean Toomer (perhaps the most talented of the group) cultivated a deep-seated ambiguity as to his own definition, somewhere between white and black; he, along with Nella Larsen, extended this all the way to their own physical definition on the basis of either skin complexion or ancestry.[15]

The echoes of the fascinating and passionate experiments of the Harlem Renaissance are still heard and are still enhanced and diversified. A major contemporary novelist like Charles Johnson describes himself as an American writer who happens to be of African ancestry. Most contemporary intellectuals (whether Afrocentric or not) could be seen as descendants of DuBois (Henry Gates, Houston Baker, Cornel West, and others), but the other side (Thomas Sowell, Glenn Loury, Walter Williams, Shelby Steele, and others) is also rich in talented representatives. One might debate whether some of the great musicians of big band jazz, or even rock and roll and rap, did not engage in a kind of reverse colonization by placing an indelible stamp of the sounds and forms of an African tradition upon Euro-American musical styles and popular imagination.

Perhaps many of the possible similarities above can be seen as mere broad analogies. Additionally, more specific cross-references can be sometimes pointed out. One of these must be the work of Houston Baker, whose most original theoretical contribution has to do with the specific ways in which African American literature manifested itself. According to Baker in *Blues, Ideology, and Afro-American Literature* (1984), early on in African American history a matrix was formed that thereafter constrained, guided, and informed any representative writing by African Americans. He regards this matrix as semantic (symbolically anthropological) rather than material, even though an ultimate socioeconomic determination is acknowledged.

> The blues are a synthesis . . . combining work songs, group seculars, field hollers, sacred harmonies, proverbial wisdom, folk philosophy, political commentary, ribald humor, elegiac lament . . . they constitute an amalgam . . . always . . . shaping, transforming, displacing the peculiar experiences of Africans in the New World. (1–14)

This matrix (defined as a vibrant network, fossil, or trace) is later recognizable, as Baker demonstrates, in writings by Frederick Douglass, Paul Dunbar, Zora Neale Hurston, Richard Wright, Amiri Baraka, and Toni Morrison. This fascinating attempt to define the creative cultural identity of a group resembles many similar eastern European attempts, and most specifically the abovementioned one by Blaga. Despite differences in sources (Foucault versus Spengler) and concepts, both authors postulate a kind of structured sociocultural subconscious that channels in specific ways the values of cultural producers functioning much later than the time in which the guiding paradigm is born. Both insist that there is something irreducible and recognizable in the cultural output of African American, or, respectively, Romanian writers. For the perceptive reader, the bottom line is that no cultural relativism can be recognized here, but rather that deep-seated dialectics can be observed in their functioning, contrary to the dogmas prevailing in current academic teaching.

After this quick survey of remote analogies we will now return to the early nineteenth century: I will refer to the masterpiece of James Fenimore Cooper, the five-volume sequence of the Leatherstocking narratives. Let me say right away that, far from dismissing Cooper as a mere author of childish adventure, I place him among the most serious thinkers of the period, in the same category with Chateaubriand, Walter Scott, Germaine de Staël, even Goethe, for the extent to which he, like these, detected early on and confronted with gravity and responsibility the oncoming changes. Cooper, even more than the enumerated contemporaries, reflected on the issue of what is nowadays called multiculturalism and the place of relativity in human culture, at the level of the individual no less than at that of the group. He had serious doubts about a centralized course of human history culminating in an unquestioning or absolutely general adoption of Western models. Like other leading minds of his age, Cooper succeeded in escaping the passive and frightened contemplation of alienation. Instead he tried to dramatize and to test out in his novels acceptable models of dialectic interpenetration of cultures.[16]

Although in the twentieth century, racial-cultural polarizations in North America are usually seen in the binary system of European versus African modes, it should not be forgotten that for two or even three centuries earlier the polarization was entirely different: newcomer versus original inhabitants, or European versus Amerindian. The enormous mass of anthropological and religious explanations and disagreements aired and published around this issue, particularly in Spanish and in English, cannot be touched upon here; suffice it to say that it proves, once again, that positions were not monolithic but rather covered a broad spectrum from justification to utter blame. After gaining independence the newly constituted United States were faced with the hard and delicate decision of whether they represented the past (and continuity) or whether they opted for a radically different future.

As we know the American choice went in favor of the future, but this was not always the case. The philosophical musings incorporated in the work of Thomas Cole, perhaps the greatest romantic artist in early America, show us a pessimistic spirit deeply preoccupied with the origin, the further course, the inevitable decline of any civilization.[17] Cooper falls within the same category: one that is in solidarity with a state of mind in which American optimism, confidence, and sense of mission were not yet indisputable dogmas.

At the same time there is another curious aspect that ties Cooper to the analogies just discussed. I refer to the extraordinary and enduring success of James Fenimore Cooper's novels (specifically the Leatherstocking pentalogy) in central and eastern Europe. True, Cooper enjoyed much success in America itself and throughout Europe (Balzac was one of his numerous west European high admirers, as a statement of 1840 indicates; see Wallace 1986, 168), and a great part of it can be easily explained: it was due to the subject matter itself, the suspense and the adventure (commodities much sought after in the later eighteenth and early nineteenth centuries on the European market); it also had much to do with the "exotic" material, the descriptions of faces of nature unknown to the audience, to races and customs alien to them. It is also the case, as has been observed (for example, Eggebrecht

1985, 81, 236; see also Muszynska-Wallace 1959–1960, 191–200; the latter contains detailed references to travelogs by Lewis and Clark, Charlevoix, and Mackenzie) that far from being just escapism, Cooper's novels were regarded by many European readers as a source of information on areas that were known by them in an unsatisfactory manner. *The Last of the Mohicans* was, until 1947 at least, one of the twenty-one best-selling American books—it has never been out of print since its first publication, and in 1994 there were no fewer than seventeen editions in print, with translations ranging all the way to Chinese, Arabic, and Japanese, and obviously every single European language (McWilliams 1994, 11).

This is hardly exotic and alien. Whoever has read the prose of Sergey Aksakov in his trilogy of memoirs, and above all its first volume, cannot but have noticed the similarities of experience and of conflictual framework between the Bashkir and Chuvash natives and the Russian settlers, as parallel to experiences in the forests and on the prairies of America as evoked by Fenimore Cooper. Similar encounters have been suggested between Russian expansion and the Caucasian ethnic groups by Lermontov and Pushkin.[18] A certain narrative tradition with its typologies (sometimes clichés) had been formed in the wake of Walter Scott and Chateaubriand, and it proved serviceable to a vast range of ethnic/social dichotomies. Therefore, in an important sense Cooper was addressing not the exotic and the alien but the familiar and the predictable. However, we can look for even deeper ties of kinship.

The dilemma facing the incoming population when confronted with the mostly nomadic aboriginals of North America was, in the ideological subconscious of the east Europeans, bound to their own by a rich web of oppositions and of homologies. Cooper's Amerindians, no less than his Euro-Americans, hover uncertainly between extreme youth and old age. The "redskins" are clearly old by virtue of their longstanding possession of the land, no less than by their preservation of uninterrupted tradition and by their organic connection with nature. They have remained young through their lack of sophistication, or, better said, through their avoidance of civilizational complication, and through their refusal of intellectual self-consciousness. In turn the incoming "whites" are old insofar as they carry in their baggage the commands and habits of many hundreds of years of cultural history, and insofar as a deep divide separates their intellect from natural apprehension.[19] They are nevertheless young in their willingness to renew themselves, to start all over again, to strip themselves bare and begin to build new homesteads for their families.

A second dilemma faces the characters in Cooper's Leatherstocking novels. How do the encountering races respond to each other on a practical and, no less important, on an emotional level? Should the main tone of their affect, the *basso continuo*, be one of adversity, resentment, and hatred? Should it be one of admiration and mutual learning? Should (or could) it be one of neutral, or, if possible, respectful coexistence, one possible in a vast land? These are questions that, as we will see in the novels, continuously preoccupy the members of both ethnic groups.

In my opinion many east-central Europeans believed that these novels were mirror images of their own situation. Like the Amerindians, they could argue that they were the original owners of ancestral lands that had become the prey of invading and uninvited newcomers, and, albeit with more self-consciousness, they claimed special bonds with the land on which they lived and with nature in general. Again, like Cooper's Amerindians, they could point to age-old customs, songs, habits, and to a tribal, even "savage," structure and mode of life. On the other hand, like the incoming colonizers, many of these ethnic groups (Czech, Hungarian, Polish, Romanian, South Slavic, and others) were convinced that theirs was now a second chance, a moment of rebirth or of awakening after a long winter sleep imposed by evil enchanters. Like the settlers, these populations looked towards a shedding of cultural baggage and a new beginning in pristine freshness. To add another layer of complicating irony to these readerly contradictions, it seemed for many in the striving political-intellectual elites that the national renaissance to which they aspired would be nothing more nor less than a kind of catching up with the Western models and evolutions. However, these very Western patterns served as a contrastive referential level to the self-definition of the local identities that were supposed to be preserved and revivified. In this way, too, an interface was discovered that resembled the Amerindian/settler dilemmas. Attraction to and emancipation from each other is how Cooper constructs the relationship between the two races and cultures—and that is exactly the relationship forged by the local elites of east-central Europe and their authoritative Western models.[20]

In Cooper's *The Pioneers; or, The Sources of the Susquehanna* (1980)[21]—the fourth volume of the Leatherstocking saga (the action is placed in 1793) but the first penned by Cooper in 1823—Cooper shows himself already fully obsessed with the theme of the mutual critique of cultural entities and of their coexistence in the same framework of time and space. The whole novel is a quest and battle for true and moral property, for legitimacy, and for cultural identity. Oliver Edwards, the grandson of Major Effingham, acts until the very few last pages of the novel as a Native Amerindian, with the proud resentment and chivalrous sensitivity of one hostile to an imported modern civilization that supersedes a natural and organic way of life that had grown for many centuries on the soil of America.

The young man has taken on the appearance of Native Americans both physically and in his lifestyle, an issue touched upon, among others, by Mr. Grant, the pastor (Cooper 1980, 135–36). His ambiguous words, expressing, as the reader finds out in the end, muted anger against the dispossession of his still living grandfather, seem to suggest a rebellion against the order of things installed by the European and Christian "pioneers." (Major Effingham had been adopted as an honorary member of the Delaware tribe [421].) Moreover Oliver Edwards is reinforced in the social role of spokesman for the oldest and most basic cultural stratum of the continent, by his association with the two old men who represent the second oldest historical phase being the one subtly recommended and morally preferred by the author, at least at the level of nostalgia, a phase of merger and interpenetration of races and cultures. These two old men are Natty Bumppo and John Mohegan, who can both stand as examples of the possibility of such a peaceful coupling of cultural systems.

John Mohegan is actually Chingachgook, an enormously powerful and celebrated leader of his tribe several decades before, who now lives in a marginal and poverty-stricken position in a European society that barely tolerates him. He has converted to Christianity and has relinquished the traditional dress of his ancestors. He seems basically resigned, but Cooper emphasizes a continuing pride and dignity that endows him with the aura, and perhaps the values, of a European aristocracy so conspicuously absent among the settlers.

> His forehead, when it could be seen, appeared lofty, broad, and noble. His nose was high, and of the kind called Roman, with nostrils that expanded, in his seventieth year, with the freedom that had distinguished them in youth. His mouth ... discovered a set of short, strong, and regular teeth.... The eyes were not large, but their black orbs glittered ... like two balls of fire.... As he walked slowly down the long hall, the dignified and deliberate tread of the Indian surprised the spectators. (Cooper 1980, 81–82)

Elsewhere we are told of "ordinary composure," "fierce and determined looks" and (again) "dignity" (132).

Natty Bumppo, in turn, though a white European, is seen as one who has grown up and lived his whole life among the legitimate owners of the continent. Without completely denying his own descent, Natty has adopted the way of life and thinking (even to the way of dressing and of gaining his livelihood) of the Amerindians. The "deerskin moccasins," "leathern pouch," and "foxskin cap" (20–21) were to become commonplaces of a globally adopted iconography, but more significantly we are told that "his face was skinny and thin almost to emaciation.... The cold and exposure had, together given it a color of uniform red" (20–21). He does not hesitate to speak up for rights alternative to the leveling laws increasingly being imposed by the new order, or even to stand up and suffer for his faith in such an alternative that he considers closer to natural and divine law. (For judicious characterizations of Natty Bumppo see Long 1990, 35–45, 52–71, 183, 193–94.) More generally, it has been justly observed that manners are very prominent in the Leatherstocking cycle (Darnell 1993, 44–67, 120–24).

Cooper repeatedly resorts to a kind of symbolic ecology (for discussion of moral/symbolic landscapes see also Bradfield 1993, 33–67) in order to reinforce the alternative validity of this "remnant":

> Although poplars had been brought from Europe to ornament the grounds, and willows and other trees were gradually springing up nigh the dwelling, yet many a pile of snow betrayed the presence of the stump of a pine; and even in one or two

instances, unsightly remnants of trees that had been partly destroyed by fire were seen rearing their black, glistening columns twenty or thirty feet. . . . The ruin of a pine or a hemlock that had been stripped of its bark . . . waved in melancholy grandeur its naked limbs to the blast, a skeleton of its former glory. (42)

The society of the settlers is by no means demonized in this novel. It is in its turn depicted as organic and cosy (as seen in the description of the colonial Christmas banquet in chapter 9, 102–4), engaged in peaceful and productive work. Its leaders, in particular Judge Marmaduke Temple, are fair and benevolent. Its foibles are laughed at benignly: the clumsy attempts at institution building are described in humorous detail, as well as the comic lack of professionalism of early medicine (ch. 6 on "Dr." Elnathan Todd), of academic life (94–97), of a judiciary system (ch. 33, 341–55), and especially of architecture (95–96, 39–41).

In fact the incongruous artificiality and the ridiculous pretensions of the latter are particularly highlighted. This ties in neatly with the character of Richard Jones, the squire-judge's cousin, the most aggressive modernizer, a man filled with racial hatred (106), one whose attitudes toward the environment highly irritate even his cousin (100–101), and one who is most cruel and relentless in his pursuit of Leatherstocking whose arrest and trial he instigated.

The malicious character of the architect is exceptional for Cooper. The overwhelming majority of the other settlers are depicted as laid-back, bumbling, and good-natured. They also suggest the beginnings of the melting pot, insofar as they include French, German, Welsh, and other individuals, depicted with kindly emphasis on their peculiarities and imperfections. Their conflict with the surviving interracial and multicultural society of the intermediate age is, according to Cooper, one objectively, though tragically, driven by the forces of property and the clash of alternative civilizational models (See also Eggebrecht 1985, 89, and elsewhere). Thus the aggressiveness and excesses of law and lawyers are a continuous source of discontent and threat for Cooper's societies (cf. the detailed discussion in Adams 1990, 1–24, 55–80).

In two separate novels, *The Last of the Mohicans* (1826; the action is set ca. 1758), and *The Pathfinder* (1840; the action is set ca. 1760), Cooper builds up the character of Leatherstocking by explaining his assumptions and by examining his actual interaction with Native Americans in a place and at a time when the latter and their way of life had not yet been routed or liquidated. The angles are multiple and they include gender and sexual issues, although just delicately and allusively. Thus, in the *Pathfinder* (1980) two determined and resourceful women of different races develop a close alliance and help each other in ways that clearly transcend the usual racial oppositions. The characters are Mabel and June, the wife of Arrowhead, chief of the Tuscaroras (chs. 22, 23, and elsewhere). (McWilliams 1994, 52–75, is one of the relatively few who understands the importance of race and gender for Cooper, but he remains mired in currently dominant cliches.)

Even more strikingly, the central theme of *The Last of the Mohicans* is that of Uncas and Cora's sexual love cutting across racial-cultural lines (in more ways than one, since there is a slight suggestion that Cora may be of partial African descent). Significantly in both novels these relations end in failure. Thus, Uncas perishes in battle, the friendship of Mabel/Agnes and June will be interrupted. Moreover the actual attraction of Mabel to Nathaniel, then at the height of his professional, sexual, and, one might say, ideological powers, leads to nothing: she will marry Jasper and return to New York to lead a life of contented affluence. Already the very young Deerslayer can be heard saying: "As for me, I have no offspring, and I want no wife" (458) when the young widow Sumach proposes marriage to save him from torture and death at the hand of his Huron captors. Deerslayer similarly declines Judith's advances in the same novel. In the *Last of the Mohicans* Bumppo's mulish sterility is further affirmed and deepened. (For the matters presented in the last two paragraphs see also the discussions in Peck 1992, 6–17, 47–65, 75–85, 87–112; cf. also Fiedler 1960, 207–12, on sterility, though he does not seem to fully grasp the issue.)

This is one of the key signals Cooper sends to the reader. The pairing of races and cultures as attempted by Chingachgook and Leatherstocking is hybrid and must remain without issue. No fertility is attached to it. To Cooper this is clearly neither a matter for rejoicing nor of cold pragmatic observation. On the contrary the whole tragic aura attached to the figure of Natty Bumppo is, there can be no doubt, derived from his loneliness and infertility, from the failure of his intercultural and interracial project.

Is Cooper able to suggest any solution? Actually there is much openness in the cycle, since it can be said to be endowed with two different conclusions. One is expressed in the chronologically final piece, *The Prairie* (1980) (1827; the action is set ca. 1805), when the venerably old Bumppo (cf. Motley 1987; also McWilliams 1994, 76, about "the barren patriarchs") becomes one with the landscape, identifies with the land itself, in a sense melts in or with it. Character, no less than author, thereby turns a defeat into victory: actual (that is, physically concrete) children would have had less power of generalization and less symbolic universality than a Wordsworthian metamorphosis: "Rolled round in earth's diurnal course, / With rocks, and stones, and trees."

Still, as if sensing that this process might be interpreted as something of an escape into abstraction, Cooper also provided us with an alternative ending at the very end of his life. Indeed that is when *The Deerslayer; or, the First Warpath* appeared (1841; the action is set ca. 1746), but the novel's topic is the very formation of Leatherstocking and his earliest options. Cooper examines minutely, insistently the concept of "gifts." The term recurs incessantly, almost morbidly, throughout the novel, designating the features and habits inherent to the different races and cultures trying to find not only respect for their differences but also common denominators. Deerslayer (young in age but old-fashioned in word and deed) explains to Judith the distinction between nature and gifts in the following fashion:

> A natur' is the creatur' itself; its wishes, wants, idees, and feelin's, as all are born in him. This natur' never can be changed in the main, though it may undergo some increase or lessening. Now, gifts come of circumstances. Thus, if you put a man in a town, he gets town gifts; in a settlement, settlement gifts, in a forest, gifts of the woods.... All these increase and strengthen until they get to fortify natur' as it might be, and excuse a thousand acts and idees. Still, the creatur' is the same at the bottom. ... Herein lies the apology for gifts; seein' that you expect different conduct from one in silks and satins than from one in homespun; though the Lord, who didn't make the dresses, but who made the creatur's themselves, looks only at his own work. (403–4)

The important thing is to realize that this theory is but an extended gloss on a short previous statement of his: "You find different colors on 'arth, as one may see, but you don't find different natur's. Different gifts, but only one natur'" (403). Translated in contemporary terminology, racial distinctions are sociohistorical constructs of coercive determinative force; they guide and limit human behavior. Nevertheless they are not, according to Fenimore Cooper and his main character, truly ultimates. Rather this ultimate is attributed to the relationship between creative Divine Providence and the individual human person, which in turn is part of a common fund of human substance.

The theory is, needless to say, not original with Cooper; we are less interested here in its sources or in what might be considered at the beginning of the twenty-first century its share of truth. What is important is Cooper's obvious compelling need to articulate some kind of dialectic between stable continuity and relativity, between the claims of the specifically local and those of universal common bonds. Deerslayer's long speech comes in the midst of highly dangerous circumstances in which he might be excused for a hardening of his feelings toward Amerindians. On the contrary, he takes a clear position against the views of characters such as "Hurry" March or Tom Hutter who are much closer to the coming phase of racist negation of Otherness. Nathaniel repeatedly emphasizes the varying gifts of the different Indian nations. In turn Cooper peppers the text with affirmations such as: "a woman is a woman, let her color be white or red; and your chiefs know little of a woman's heart" (359), as well as with gestures of moral rectitude and integrity distributed across cultural lines (as are gestures of aggression and ruthlessness).[22]

The double conclusion of the Leatherstocking saga expresses early on the polar dialectic that was soon to beset not only any theory of multiculturalism, but in fact also many sociopolitical actions aimed at solving multiracial issues. I refer to the polar opposition between the need for integration and the need for distinction (or specificity). These issues are undoubtedly part of the (as yet unhealed) agony of modernization. As may have been noticed, I have treated in the previous sections of this chapter ethnic/racial tensions as a kind of expression (phenomenal) or mediation of the movement toward streamlined and rationalized modernity. The topics of Cooper's novels provide, I am convinced, an appropriate parallel to the debates inside the eastern European and African American communities.

I have not insisted in this chapter on some of the most famous critics of Cooper. This was largely due to the fact that their observations were less than relevant to my line of argument. Thus the learned David Simpson (1986, 148–229) draws conclusions of remarkable subtlety on Cooper's intentions by a carefully positivist study of the language used by the novels' characters. He does not say however much that has not been submitted anyway to the reader in these pages. Leslie Fiedler (1960, 149–212) was in his day and age a critic of considerable visibility. Twenty-five years later many of his comments on Cooper have lost their interest, drowned as they are in Freudian and Marxist clichés (for example, 152, 155, 164, 190, 198). This is not to say that Fiedler's quick power of perception and articulation should be ignored. More than once he surprises us by well-justified observations on Cooper's mode of thinking and writing. Thus for instance he understands well the dilemma of history/fiction for historical novelists (151, and elsewhere) discussed by us in detail elsewhere in this volume, he understands the complexity and depth of gender treatment by both Scott and Cooper (169), and he is ready to accept Scott and Cooper as stagers of idea-wars, dedicated to attempts to portray the dialectics of conservative and progressive in their own day, or, for that matter in any age (177, 163, 187, 191, 193). Much attention has been gained of late by Dana Nelson (for example, 1992, 48–63) and his insistent preoccupation with race in American culture, and in particular its handling by prominent or widely read authors. While the topic itself is indeed one of the centers of organization of American values and worldviews, Nelson's treatment is often overheated or remains caught in the stridencies of habitual politics, and thus his learning is muted. Naturally I prefer the approach I put forward in these pages. Most important, none of these and other critics seem interested in a comparative approach (though it must be admitted that Fiedler's understanding of the connections between Scott and Cooper went a long way even when it did not exhaust this extremely rich subject). After these brief comments let us therefore return precisely to the comparative line of conversation that has been our central concern.

What else do the examples given in this chapter have in common and what do they prove in terms of relativity? In all of them we can see recognition of difficulty. Far from being a primarily joyful process of long-awaited liberation, progress (any progress) is a tough and tortured experience of advance, sometimes triggered from the outside, always controversial, accompanied by doubt, hesitation, and backsliding. The categories of power and control as promoted by Foucault and the post-Marxists explain little and obscure much of what was (and is) going on in reality. The most common effect encountered on all continents and in all cultures is, in the face of modernizing progress, neither enthusiastic approval nor gloomy reaction, but rather the feeling of reluctance, the instinct of reflective delay.

The best thinkers of different communities have engaged in a complicated dialectic of cost-benefit analysis once they tackled the issue of historical evolution. They tried to weigh suffering against need and hope. Circumstances perceived as inevitable (or overwhelmingly powerful) were turned into challenges to a given community for which adequate responses had to be sought. Discourses, concepts, and images for adaptation and assimilation were devised. The impulse to insert kinds of preservation (of tradition and identity) into an ongoing process proved to be irresistible. These efforts resulted in newly available and incessantly emerging resources, for example modes of "complexification," a deepening of the territory of moderation, more subtle engagements with reality. (Whether and how such resources are being used remains an entirely separate problem.)

In conclusion, multicultural theories and practices as expanded after the eighteenth century are a response to the objective process of modernization. They try to counteract it by erecting their own kind of dogmatism: that of absolute separation of cultures and communities often on racial/ethnic bases. Often this becomes a kind of oppressive rejection of universality and commonality. Can this oppressiveness be eliminated while at the same time answering the valid concerns for identity and locality which gave rise to it? My own answers resemble, let us say, the shape of a double helix.

I recognize an evolutionary process of streamlining and global unification, and acknowledge at the same time the impetuous growth of a theory of cultural relativism that opposes it but is not without a globalist and coercive potential of its own. I argue at the same time that the best way in which some kind of grotesque alliance between the two can be avoided is by deepening the foundations of both. By looking at the very process of response to the pressures of modernization and globalization, we discover a commonality of reactive dynamics. Since these are clearly not a historical imitation of one another we deduce that they correspond to dimensions of human nature.

We thus begin to outline the bare sketches of a new kind of humanism, based on the admission that while multiculturalism and its relativities have true validity they are themselves endowed with a relativity of their own. Precisely the idioms of literature and religion are among the best instruments that can be adopted when we sketch out the kind of universalist approximations that emerge (almost by default) as we concede the shortcomings of cultural relativism.[23]

Notes

1. To bring an ad hominem argument: in the 1980s Derrida led the unionized professorial struggle against cuts in the budget for philosophy departments that were considered redundant or irrelevant by administrative authorities. Governmental justification had been drawn not least from Derrida's own deconstruction of philosophy.

2. See James Frazer, *The Golden Bough*, 12 vols. (London: Macmillan, 1911–1915), as well as the whole group of "Cambridge ritualists" contemporary with him in the first half of the

century. It is worth noting that this attitude was widespread in a discipline where major figures such as Joseph Campbell, Karl Kerény, or Mircea Eliade did not adhere to Christianity with any firmness. It is also intriguing to note that even the most zealous of Christian militants (in the Middle Ages and later) were less incensed against religions that had preceded the Gospels than against deviancies posterior to Jesus's ministry (or to the way it was interpreted by His institutionalized successors).

3. The Jesuit Matteo Ricci (1552–1610) developed a theory of Confucianism as a system related to Christianity, and in practical terms exerted much influence among Chinese elites by his skillful invention of rites adapted to local traditions. Simultaneously attempts were made (less in the theoretical field than in that of ritual change) for approaches to Hindu and Shinto religions. Finally the Jesuit experiment in Paraguay deserves renewed full consideration. These are just a few examples.

4. Polanyi (1985) and Gellner (1988) both derived chiefly, whether directly or indirectly, from Max Weber's *Die protestantische Ethik und der Geist des Kapitalismus* (1905–1906).

5. Cf. the essay on unanticipated consequences in Merton 1976.

6. It should be emphasized that both Montesquieu (*L'esprit des lois*) and Volney (*Les ruines, ou méditations sur les révolutions des empires*) definitely have a comparatist orientation and were very influential for many decades.

7. See Malraux 1952–1954. Goethe used the term *Weltliteratur* first, to our knowledge, in his conversations with Eckermann (January 1827 and, again, in more detail, July 15, 1827). As to the choices of the Nobel Prize committee in the last twenty to thirty years, they included Japanese and Nigerian, Bosnian and Czech, Egyptian and African American authors, along with the more habitual English, Spanish, Italian, or Russian names.

8. It is not easy in these circumstances to apply the usual categories of Right and Left. The nationalist "Iron Guard" or "Legion" often used leftist egalitarian rhetoric; the establishment and pro-Western Liberal Party (between the two World Wars) was supportive of vested interests and property rights. In Central and Latin America "charismatic" features were attached to leftist groups such as the Sandinistas or the Castro/Guevara faction—yet their programs and modes of operation were surprisingly close to those of the extreme Right in Romania or Hungary. Both groups wanted to block by sheer force and utopian idealism the advance of what they dubbed "capitalism" and what was in fact simply the progress of history. See also Weber 1965; Hitchins 1994.

9. As written above, it is interesting to note how in these circumstances certain themes and social choices run athwart the conventional Left/Right divisions. Even though Rădulescu-Motru was a moderate conservative himself, his theory of peasant society and psychology overlaps to a good extent with that of some of his contemporaries who were of decidedly center-left orientation (e.g. Garabet Ibrăileanu and Constantin Stere, in fact the whole *Viața Românească* group, which started before World War I and continued in different ways until the late 1930s).

10. Gusti and his followers organized "Muzeul Satului," a very complex reconstitution (at the outskirts of the capital city of Romania) of a "village" formed out of dozens of specific traditional houses from all parts of the country with their wealth of differences: household objects, artistic styles, etc.

11. Vianu 1968, 1978a,b.

12. It would be even more interesting to thicken the complexity of the analysis by drawing in authors of the Euro-American South of the same period (1850–1950). Genovese 1994

shows how the negativity of the modern advance (often called capitalism) produced in that part of North America a respectable body of conservative thought that aimed for a defense of the "southern way of life" as a kind of viable alternative organicism against capitalist and industrial modernity. Earnestly thoughtful and subtly nuanced responses were offered by the southern intellectuals known as the Fugitives, or the New Critics, as well as by an impressive number of major novelists, including William Faulkner, Eudora Welty, and Walker Percy. Despite absolutely major differences, their kind of problematization outlines a common ground between them and the debaters of the African American intellectual world.

13. For usually less than sympathetic but thorough treatments of the subject see Mathews 1949 or Thornbrough 1969.

14. This general description is very widely accepted (barring slight qualifications from one commentator to the other). Supporting materials in Paschal 1971; Aptheker 1982, 1986; see also Andrews 1985; Rudwick 1969; and particularly Rampersad 1990. As to the marginal but real contribution of W. E. B. DuBois to Afrocentrism, see the masterful assessment of Early 1995. For an overview, see Zamir 1995.

15. I do not agree with the position of Robert Coles and Diane Isaacs that the Harlem Renaissance was a kind of "therapeutic effort": cf. Singh et al. 1989. See rather Wintz 1988, DeJongh 1990, or, as a kind of introduction, Andrews 1994.

16. Perhaps it is not futile to remind the reader that James Fenimore Cooper actually wrote a rather large number of meritorious small political essays, moderately conservative in tone, though critical of (Jacksonian) democracy. For typical comments on his evenhanded political thinking see Hanley 1996. More specifically on the basically liberal orientation of *The Pioneers,* see Otten 1972.

17. I refer specifically to the four-painting cycle "The Course of Empire" (1836), but the actual painting entitled *The Last of the Mohicans* is also significant, as are the 1844 landscapes in the Catskills, which had been visited and admired by Cooper's characters. Both topics (similarity with Cooper and scepticism toward human growth as mere vanity) have been often visited. See for instance Ringe 1958; Wallach 1968; Wallace 1986, 168. A short general assessment is found in Baigell 1981. A nice brief comment on Cole is found in Johnson 1991, 163–64.

18. See Aksakov 1983, 21–25, 40–44, 76–77, 92–93, 97–98, 107, 119, 143–44. The action is placed in the 1790s in the district of Orenburg, and is unapologetic in its embrace of the Russian settlers' point of view. See, in the same sense, Scotto 1992. The issue of the specific Russo-Asian colonial interaction was signalled in literary writing early in the nineteenth century, for instance by the bestselling Sophie Cottin (*Elisabeth, ou les exilés de Sibérie,* 1806) or Xavier de Maistre (*La jeune Sibérienne,* 1815, or *Les prisonniers du Caucase,* 1815).

19. All sides may be said to be beholden to the first of Wordsworth's two modes of vision, the prelapsarian one: "Whither is fled the visionary gleam? / Where is it now, the glory and the dream?" (lines 56–57 of the ode "Intimations of Immortality"). Philbrick (1964) offers a parallel with Thomson's *Seasons.*

20. Incidentally it may be worth mentioning that this inherent original contradiction was to have later results of a dangerous and destructive nature in the twentieth century continued to this day by the theorizing of interethnic conflict, recurrent revivals of right-wing extremism, and of de-Westernizing attempts.For quotation purposes I will use the handy paperback editions, as follows: *Deerslayer* (New York: Bantam, 1981); *The Last of the Mohicans* (New York: Bantam, 1989); *The Pathfinder* (New York: Signet, 1980); *The Pioneers* (New York: Signet, 1980); *The Prairie* (New York: Signet, 1980).

22. Dudensing (1991, 7–10, 21–24, 95–97, 102–14, 162–71) founding herself on the classical works of Dekker (1967, 1987), Berkhofer (1978), Kohl (1981), and others makes excellent arguments on parallels between the Amerindian and Scottish populations and civilizations, as well as on the character of Natty Bumppo, but unfortunately her arguments are marred by her adoption of the theory of "stadialism." See also Barker and Sabin 1996. There is in fact a tendency to read too much philosophy in Cooper's pentalogy: the attempt to recapture Arcadia, the break between the fragment and the whole, and similar issue (for example, Eggebrecht 1985, 9–32, 88–90, and elsewhere, often based on Georg Simmel's comments on the category of the novel of adventure). Even less acceptable and useful because of their formulaic structure and irrelevant orientation are some essays in Clark (1985, 15–37, 55–95, 96–142, 178). Rans (1999, 37–51, 198–201, 240–43) exaggerates the "mutual exclusion of nature and civilization" and thus mistakenly criticizes Cooper.

23. Cf. also Nemoianu 1996.

Bibliography

Adams, Charles Hansford. 1990. *The Guardian of the Law: Authority and Identity in James Fenimore Cooper.* University Park: Penn State University Press.

Aksakov, Sergei. 1983. *Years of Childhood.* Trans. J. D. Duff. Oxford: Oxford University Press. (Orig. pub. 1856; English edition 1924.)

Andrews, William L., ed. 1985. *Critical Essays on W. E. B. Dubois.* Boston: G. K. Hall.

———. 1994. *Classic Fiction of the Harlem Renaissance.* New York and Oxford: Oxford University Press.

Aptheker, Herbert, ed. 1982. *Writings by W. E. B. DuBois in Periodicals Edited by Others.* Millwood, N.Y.: Kraus-Thomson.

———. 1986. *Pamphlets and Leaflets by W. E. B. DuBois.* White Plains, N.Y.: Kraus-Thomson.

Baigell, Matthew. 1981. *Thomas Cole.* New York: Watson-Guptill.

Baker, Houston A., Jr. 1984. *Blues, Ideology, and Afro-American Literature: A Vernacular Theory.* Chicago: University of Chicago Press.

Barker, Martin, and Roger Sabin. 1996. *The Lasting of the Mohicans: History of an American Myth.* Oxford: University of Mississippi Press.

Berkhofer, Robert, Jr. 1978. *The White Man's Indian: Images of the American Indian from Columbus to the Present.* New York: Vintage.

Blaga, Lucian. 1944. *Trilogia culturii.* Bucharest: Fundatia Regala. (Orig. pub. 1935–1937.)

Bradfield, Scott. 1993. *Dreaming Revolution: Transgression in the Development of American Romance.* Iowa City: Iowa University Press.

Chateaubriand, François-René, vicomte de. 1979. *Essai sur les révolutions.* Paris: Gallimard. (Orig. pub. 1797.)

———. 1979. *Génie du christianisme.* Paris: Pléiade. (Orig. pub. 1802.)

Clark, Robert, ed. 1985. *James Fenimore Cooper: New Critical Essays.* London: Vision Press and Totowa, N.J.: Barnes and Noble.

Cooper, James Fenimore. 1838. *The American Democrat.* Cooperstown, N.Y.: H. & E. Phinney.

Darnell, Donald. 1993. *James Fenimore Cooper: Novelist of Manners.* London and Cranbury, N.J.: Associated University Presses.

DeJongh, James. 1990. *Vicious Modernism: Black Harlem and the Literary Imagination.* Cambridge: Cambridge University Press.

Dekker, George. 1967. *Cooper, the American Scott.* New York: Barnes and Noble.
———. 1987. *American Historical Romance.* New York: Cambridge University Press.
Dudensing, Beatrix. 1991. *Die Symbolik von Mündlichkeit und Schriftlichkeit in James Fenimore Coopers "Leatherstocking Tales."* Frankfurt am Main, Bern, New York: Lang.
Early, Gerald. 1995. "Understanding Afrocentrism." *Civilization* 2, no. 4: 36.
Eggebrecht, Harald. 1985. *Sinnlichkeit und Abenteuer: Die Entstehung des Abenteurromans im 19. Jahrhundert.* Berlin: Guttandin und Hoppe.
Fiedler, Leslie. 1960. *Love and Death in the American Novel.* New York: Criterion.
Gellner, Ernst. 1988. *Plough, Sword and Book: The Structure of Human History.* Chicago: University of Chicago Press.
Genovese, Eugene. 1994. *The Southern Tradition: The Achievements and Limitations of an American Conservatism.* Cambridge, Mass.: Harvard University Press.
Gerschenkron, Alexander. 1966. *Economic Backwardness in Historical Perspective.* Cambridge, Mass.: Harvard University Press. (Orig. pub. 1952.)
Gottfried, Paul. 1979. *Conservative Millenarians: The Romantic Experience in Bavaria.* New York: Fordham University Press.
Hanley, Wayne. 1996. "James Fenimore Cooper in France: One Man's View of the July Revolution of 1830." *Connecticut Review* 18, no. 1 (Spring): 131–43.
Harris, Thomas E. 1991. *Analysis of the Clash over the Issues between Booker T. Washington and W. E. B. DuBois.* New York and London: Garland.
Hitchins, Keith. 1994. *Rumania 1866–1947.* Oxford: Oxford University Press.
Johnson, Paul. 1991. *The Birth of the Modern: World Society 1815–1830.* New York: HarperCollins.
Kohl, Karl Heinz. 1981. *Entzauberter Blick: Das Bild vom guten Wilden und die Erfahrung der Zivilisation.* Berlin: Medusa.
Lewis, Clive S. 1947. *The Abolition of Man.* New York: Macmillan.
Long, Robert Emmet. 1990. *James Fenimore Cooper.* New York: Continuum.
Malraux, André. 1952–1954. *Le musée imaginaire de la sculpture mondiale.* 3 vols. Paris: Gallimard.
Mathews, Basil. 1948. *Booker T. Washington: Educator and Interracial Interpreter.* Cambridge, Mass.: Harvard University Press.
McWilliams, John. 1994. *The Last of the Mohicans: Civil Savagery and Savage Civility.* New York: Twayne.
Merton, Robert. 1976. *Sociological Ambivalence and Other Essays.* New York: Free Press.
Montesquieu. 1949. *L'esprit des lois.* In *Oeuvres complètes.* Ed. Roger Caillois. Paris: Gallimard, Pléiade. (Orig. pub. 1748.)
Motley, Warren. 1987. *The American Abraham.* New York: Cambridge University Press.
Muszynska-Wallace, E. Soteris. 1949. "The Sources of the *Prairie.*" *American Literature* 20 (May): 191–200.
Nelson, Dana D. 1992. *The Word in Black and White: Reading "Race" in American Literature, 1638–1867.* Oxford: Oxford University Press.
———. 1998. *National Manhood: Capitalist Citizenship and the Imagined Fraternity of White Men.* Durham, N.C.: Duke University Press.
Nemoianu, Virgil. 1996. "Globalism, Multiculturalism and Comparative Literature." *Council of National Literatures World Report:* 43–73.

———. 1996. "The Dialectics of Diversity: From J. F. Cooper to Eastern Europe." *Arcadia* 31, nos. 1–2: 127–45.
Otten, Kurt. 1972. "Cooper's *The Pioneers.*" In *Der amerikanische Roman, von den Anfängen bis zur Gegenwart.* Ed. Hans Joachim Lang, 21–49. Düsseldorf: A. Bagel.
Paschal, Andrew G., ed. 1971. *A W. E. B. Dubois Reader.* New York: Collier Macmillan.
Peck, Daniel, ed. 1992. *New Essays on "The Last of the Mohicans.*" New York: Cambridge University Press.
Philbrick, Thomas. 1964. "Cooper's *The Pioneers:* Origins and Structure." *Proceedings of the Modern Language Association* 79: 581–83.
Polanyi, Karl. 1985. *The Great Transformation.* Boston: Beacon. (Orig. pub. 1944.)
Pratt, Mary Louise. 1992. *Imperial Eyes: Travel Writing and Transculturation.* New York and London: Routledge.
Rampersad, Arnold. 1990. *The Art and Imagination of W. E. B. DuBois.* New York: Schocken.
Rans, Geoffrey. 1999. *Cooper's Leather-Stocking Novels: A Secular Reading.* Chapel Hill: University of North Carolina Press.
Ringe, Donald A. 1958. "James Fenimore Cooper and Thomas Cole: An Analogous Technique." *American Literature* 30: 26–36.
Rudwick, Elliott M. 1969. *W. E. B. Du Bois: Propagandist of the Negro Protest.* New York: Atheneum.
Said, Edward. 1978. *Orientalism.* New York: Pantheon.
Scotto, Peter. 1992. "Prisoners of the Caucuses: Ideologies of Imperialism in Lermontov's 'Bela.'" *Proceedings of the Modern Language Association* 107: 246–60.
Simpson, David. 1986. *The Politics of American English 1776–1850.* Oxford: Oxford University Press.
Singh, Amritjit, William S. Shiver, and Stanley Brodwin, eds. 1989. *The Harlem Renaissance: Revaluations.* New York: Garland.
Spengler, Oswald. 1980. *Der Untergang des Abendlandes.* Munich: Beck. (Orig. pub. 1923.)
Thornbrough, Emma Lou, ed. 1969. *Booker T. Washington.* Englewood Cliffs N.J.: Prentice-Hall.
Torgovnick, Marianna. 1990. *Gone Primitive: Savage Intellects, Modern Lives.* Chicago: University of Chicago Press.
Vianu, Tudor. 1968. *Estetica.* Bucharest: Editura pentou literatura. (Orig. pub. 1934–36.)
———. 1976. *Arta prozatorilor români.* Bucharest: Albatros. (Orig. pub. 1941.)
———. 1979. *Idealul clasic al omului.* Bucharest: Editura științifică. (Orig. pub. 1934.)
Wallace, James D. 1986. *Early Cooper and His Audience.* New York: Columbia University Press.
Wallach, Alan. 1968. "Cole, Byron, and 'The Course of Empire.'" *Art Bulletin* 50: 375–79.
Weber, Eugen. 1965. "Romania." In *The European Right: A Historical Profile.* Ed. Eugen Weber and Hans Rogger. Berkeley and Los Angeles: University of California Press.
Weber, Max. 2000. *Die protestantische Ethik und der "Geist" des Kapitalismus.* Weinheim: Beltz Athenäum. (Orig. pub. 1905–6.)
Wintz, Cary D. 1988. *Black Culture and the Harlem Renaissance.* Houston: Rice University Press.
Zamir, Shamoon. 1995. *W. E. B. Du Bois and American Thought 1888–1903.* Chicago: University of Chicago Press.

CHAPTER 6

Sacrality and Aesthetics in the Early Nineteenth Century
A Network Approach

IN THE YEARS PRECEDING and immediately following the French Revolution, organized religion in continental Europe was threatened in its very being in ways that had never before been equaled, nor were they to be paralleled in quite the same way during the two hundred years that followed. Thus the Jesuit order (a key support for Catholicism during the Counter-Reformation) was banned in virtually all European countries between 1773 and 1814, and indeed abolished by the Vatican itself, surviving precariously and in conditions of dubious legal validity in Russia and in America. Any practice of religion was virtually forbidden in France for approximately a decade, and the persecution of the clergy was nothing short of brutal. The head of the Roman Catholic Church was physically compelled to officiate the nuptial rites of the new French tyrant; Pope Pius VII was later (1809) dispossessed, arrested, dragged as a political prisoner across Italy and France, and kept in captivity until the collapse of the Napoleonic dictatorial regime. Between 1789 and 1815 the number of priests dropped by half in France, the number of annual ordinations by about 90 percent. In England, Catholics continued to be severely confined while Anglicanism, too, was in much disarray. In country after European country, for many decades, religious orders were dismantled in the name of social relevance, holidays scrapped, the state control of religious institutions (a control dating from the sixteenth and seventeenth centuries) ruthlessly reaffirmed (Bavaria, Portugal, the Habsburg possessions, and primarily Austria might be good examples). Only thirty of fifteen hundred Benedictine abbeys survived in all of Europe (among the victims: Cluny, Citeaux, and Clairvaux); likewise the number of Dominican houses dropped from five hundred to eighty (and the number of friars dropped from approximately twenty-five thousand to three thousand). Trappists were transported in chains to French Guiana, the Carthusians were particularly hard hit in that by 1803 they had lost all their sixty-eight houses and France and eighteen in Germany, while in Portugal all fifty Augustinian monasteries were forbidden. Joseph II of Austria, while not as brutal as the rulers of Bavaria and the French revolutionaries (who roundly declared that somebody choosing a monastic life was thereby forfeiting all civil and citizenship rights), was nevertheless one of the most relentless persecutors of monastic life. Moreover "Josephinism" imposed sermons that should limit themselves to matters of social morality and the functioning of orders that would serve practical purposes. Joseph II tried "to make the Austrian Church as thoroughly independent of the Holy See as a Church could be without ceasing to be Catholic," and "preaching was reduced to moral instruction in which little reference was made to the Christian mysteries" (McCool 1977, 22). In addition I would argue, without going into details, that the often-praised "Josephinist" policy towards the Jews in the monarchy was ambiguous and perhaps hypocritical.

It is therefore small wonder that in 1815, when normality and the rule of law were reestablished in Europe after decades of unbridled violence and upheaval, religiously minded people should have tried to reassess the function of religion in society. It might even be argued that the period 1815–1865 was one of the greatest ages of religious apologetics ever known, at least in the modern age. The sovereigns themselves changed their style—no more Joseph II, no more Friedrich II, no more Catherine the Great. Perhaps the most typical monarch of the post-1815 period was Friedrich Wilhelm IV of Prussia who reigned between 1840 and 1861 (rather than the much-maligned Charles X of France). He was deeply influenced in his youth by Pietism, thought ultimately of the state as a *Gesamtkunstwerk,* and had advisers that combined conservatism with religion and more than once with the Beautiful (Barclay 1995, 24–29, 32–34, 55, 66–68, 76, 78, 80, 85, 94). Ludwig I of Bavaria and other contemporaries might serve as confirmations and analogies (Gottfried 1979, 73–92, and elsewhere). Simultaneously Christian-Democrat and Christian-Social movements began to crystallize and to influence society, often in a moderate left direction. It is often forgotten that Christianity had played a key role in the emergence of industrial workers' trade unions (Sauvigny 1955, 252; Sevillia 2003, 225–46), or that decisive impulses for the abolition of the slave trade came from both Protestant and Catholic churches. Even before luminaries like Wilhelm von Ketteler and Adolf Kolping launched their proposals of Christian-Democrat social change, the Scottish preacher Thomas Chalmers (quite popular on both sides of the Atlantic) struggled quite openly with the way in which "the morality of the actions that are current among people engaged in merchandise" can be preserved with the possibility "for a man to give his hand to the duties of his secular occupation and, at the same time, to maintain . . . sacredness of heart" (1821, chs. 3, 4). Although Chalmers does not entirely relinquish the common views on the "dissipation of large cities" (124–40) he is clearly more interested in pointing to modes in which religious virtues can infuse "mercantile intercourse" (29–74).

In Anglo-American societies this process had begun even earlier. Suffice it to mention here the name of the great Hannah More (1745–1833) who, at the prodding of the Methodist hymn-writer John Newton, turned toward the publication of ethical and religious tracts and studies. She became the first person in world history to sell over a million copies of any single work; her novel *Coelebs in Search of a Wife* (1809) appeared in forty-one editions within months (eleven in Britain, thirty in the United States), her collected works appeared in four different editions during her lifetime, and it has been said that she set a pattern not only for popular religious discourses henceforth but even for the political propaganda of the nineteenth century. The popular success of Hannah More and of others like her indicates the tremendous thirst for restoring a more complete understanding of human nature (one that should take into account the transcendent horizons inherent in it) after the relentless pressures of the Enlightenment intellectual and political elites (See Demers 1996; Jones 1952; Johnson 1991, 381–83, for a short assessment). In fact it has been convincingly argued (Mellor 2000, 13–38) that More may have singlehandedly counteracted the revolutionary tendencies in England and may have strengthened thus the cause of moderate reform. This would make her, in our terminology, a typical Biedermeier figure.

What ensued in 1815 was therefore not primarily reaction, as the clichés of conventional history would have it, but rather an enormously expanded public debate as to the best practical ways in which the religious impulses and needs of mankind can be accommodated in a world that, by common agreement, was in the process of accelerated, unstoppable movement toward modernizing changes. This fascinating debate (in which women usually played a much more decisive part than in any other area of public manifestation) had as its theme not domination but inclusiveness.

Very few indeed were those who, as part of this continent-wide conversation— one that, more than cultural trends and at least as much as political discourses, went far beyond the social or intellectual upper strata and quite deeply into the masses of the population—clamored for a full restoration of church privileges, or for a framework in which religion should have powers of cognitive arbitration. Where such positions could gain a political foothold they did more harm than good to their stated aims and may well have contributed to the failure of the Restoration, at least in France and in Spain (Sauvigny 1955, 81–82, 87, 300–305, 414–17). Such was the case with those loosely inspired in France by the doctrines of Louis de Bonald. (A shrewd analysis is found in Dru 1967.) A good alternative example in the Austria of Metternich was that of the zealous and orthodox Catholic Klemens Maria Hofbauer (1751–1820), bishop of Vienna, later declared a saint and the second patron of the city. Hofbauer, though a man of modest education, had the knack of inspiring intellectuals and grouped around himself for a few years an astounding number of intellectuals interested in a Catholic revival, beginning with Friedrich and Dorothea Schlegel. Although he carefully avoided political involvements, he was under constant police supervision and suffered interrogations and house searches because of his comparatively moderate religious views and influence (Fleischmann 1988; Hofer 1923; Till 1951; and others). In France Prosper Guéranger refounded Benedictine monasticism starting from the abandoned priory of Solesmes (famous to the present day). In fact France witnessed after 1815 a spectacular revival of monasteries, seminaries, priestly vocations (Sauvigny 1955, 308, 312), and of reinfiltration of ecclesiastics in schools, universities, and public life (318).

An example somewhat similar to that of the intellectuals of the "Hofbauer circle" is that of Samuel Taylor Coleridge, who proposed in *The Constitution of Church and State* (1829) an organic concept of social organization with a certain entanglement of the religious and intellectual classes that together would act in a filtering and advisory capacity to society as a whole. Coleridge (and to greater extent than recognized, Southey) exerted influence not on a wider public but certainly on select intellectuals. This is particularly true of the "Tractarians" of the Oxford Movement, some of whom went all the way to becoming Roman Catholics (Newman and Manning in particular) while others (Keble, Froude, Pusey) reformed considerably the intellectual and cultural foundations of Anglicanism by reclaiming its century-old traditions and asking it to get again involved in the values of art and architecture, literature, and music (cf. also Johnson 1991, 357–90). They all drew sustenance from Coleridge's and Southey's doctrines (see, for example, Dawson 2001; even earlier the Church had described in detail how members of the movement had been connected with contemporary French religious authors). In fact it is not wrong to say that even a quintessential Victorian liberal like Gladstone drew on Coleridge and even Burke. In America figures like Isaac Hecker or Orestes Brownson illustrated an emergence of Catholic thinking among the much more widely spread Protestant and/or pansophist theorizing.

At the other end of the spectrum social utopians and mystics from Owen, Saint-Simon, and Fourier to Mme Krudener, Ballanche, and Saint-Martin, as well as the Poles Towianski and Skarga clamored for a kind of translation of religious hope into terrestrial paradises, or else for discovering direct (almost mechanical or magical) channels of connection and influence between spiritual transcendence and earthly affairs. Henri de Saint-Simon openly spoke about the creation of a "new Christianity," one so deeply imbued by socialism and sexual liberality that it appealed to Marx and influenced him. It is worth insisting that not only the socialist utopians but also (in their comprehensive schemes) figures like Auguste Comte and Victor Cousin (the first very clearly, the second only to some extent) as well as Jules Michelet and Edgar Quinet, were in effect endeavoring to secularize the aspirations of Christianity without entirely losing the values and substances of spiritual transcendence.[1] This was also the purpose (sometimes avowed, sometimes tacit) of German idealist philosophy (Nipperdey 1991, 404, 429). It is worth noting that the imminence of the millennium was a doctrine of long standing inside Christianity (and to a slightly lesser extent inside Judaism). It is therefore rather logical that while some of the utopians and millennarianists were distanced from religion or tried to find a substitute from it (Richard Godwin and Saint-Simon himself), others played around the margins of religious thinking (Joanna Southcott, Richard Brothers, William Blake, and numerous others; a good survey is found in Fulford 2002, 1–23; also the thoughtful Talmon [1961], as well as the largely ironic but well-informed study of Muray [1984], who works on the connection between occultism and socialism; in a more sociopolitical mode see Underwood 2002). Charlton (1963) offers a systematic treatment of the French situation (that can be easily applied to other European countries) and a division into eight categories: traditionalists, ideologues, eclectics, socialist reformers, liberals, positivists, neocriticists, and idealists. This division is useful quantitatively but not always reliable in terms of the classification; it also seems to include too many thinkers and doctrines; I regard the examination of the "socialist reformer" category (chs. 4 and 6 on the social and the occult and/or neo-pagan) as the most useful. Charlton has however the great merit of dealing in some detail with the important matter of the "cult of science" (intended by many as a valid replacement of religion) that was beginning in the early nineteenth century but would come to full fruition only in the second half of the century. Secularization, prophetism, and the desperate search for the wide, comprehensive system are common to all these orientations, which can be shown to take religion as a model and point of reference. Nevertheless the most characteristic case seems to me that of Edgar Quinet's career and doctrines. As a young man he started from Guizot, Thierry, Germaine de Staël, even Bossuet and Chateaubriand, no less than from German models like Creuzer and Herder. Nevertheless, by the 1830s and certainly by the 1840s he had moved far to the left (perhaps through the influence of Victor Cousin), arguing that while religion is the substance of humanity, which had been abandoned by the churches (the Catholic in particular), neo-Christianity was best expressed by revolutionary democracy, for instance by the extreme wings of the French Revolution, and also by an aggressive nationalism (Powers 1957, 28, 35, 38, 46, 48–51, 108, 126, 172; Seillère 1919, 14–19, 37–75). In short, mysticism and absolute democracy became synonymous for Quinet.

Of course between these two extremes we find, as is to be expected, a wide intermediate area in which the imaginary and the fictional combine in rich and unexpected ways with earnest examination and passionate search. The literary (and the aesthetic more generally) combines with and mutually engages in substitutions with religious discourses. One must mention the large number of romantic poets or prose-writers who found literary inspiration in religion, whether early in their career or later: Wordsworth and Coleridge (indeed Shelley also), Friedrich Schlegel, Tieck and Eichendorff, Lamartine and Mickiewicz, Gogol and Hugo, and dozens of others. Many tried to find a network of relations between all known religions and thus sketch out the deep-structure of human dealings with transcendence. A significant example of this kind is provided by Benjamin Constant. A true liberal (indeed, one recognized as a doctrinal originator of liberalism in Europe), Constant tried to indicate the overall ramifications of any religious idioms with the others.[2] In Germany slightly earlier Friedrich Creuzer, in *Symbolik und Mythologie der alten Völker* (1810–1812), laid the foundation of a science of myth and religion (dealing with the distinction between allegory and symbol that was so central for Goethe's theorizing) that was to flourish later under the auspices of Sir James Frazer, as well as of Kerényi, Eliade, Campbell, and other outstanding figures of a full-fledged discipline.

Even more complex are the cases of those who, like Creuzer and Constant, engaged in the same pursuits but also wanted to hang on to traditional Christianity as well as to respond to the political works of the day. A typical example among others is Joseph Görres (1776–1848) in his *Mythengeschichte der alten Welt* (1810); Görres at the same time moved from left to right and back again while still arguing for both a Catholic conservative framework and one conspicuously inclusive of Eastern religions; as a matter of fact he thought that all religions derived from one common trunk rooted in India, "the land of the world's youth" (Münk 1994, 575). These views are expressed quite well particularly in *Glauben und Wissen* (1805) and then, more methodically, in *Mythengeschichte der asiatischen Welt* (1810). He was influenced by Friedrich Schlegel and in turn tried to provide support for Brentano and the Grimm brothers in their rediscovery of fairy tales. In 1827 he was hired by the University of Munich as "professor of general and literary history" and wrote his *Christliche Mystik,* in which, among other things, he outlined some principles of Catholic social doctrine that were later developed by Bishop Von Ketteler. Görres may also have exerted some indirect influence also on Bachofen and Nietzsche.

An even more interesting zig-zagging can be observed in the case of Félicité de Lamennais (1782–1854), who moved from hardline Catholic apologetics (perhaps partly under the influence of Ballanche) to Christian liberal populism and finally to a kind of nondenominational democratic radicalism, working out evangelical values and teachings toward their sociopolitical implications (Bowman 1990, 78). His *Paroles d'un croyant* (1834) marked the turning point toward independent leftism for Lamennais. His style and ideological stance influenced many later French thinkers including Victor Hugo and Edgar Quinet.[3]

Even a cursory and incomplete enumeration such as the present cannot overlook the important figure of the Protestant Friedrich Schleiermacher (1768–1834), who developed a theory of religion founded on sentiment, intuition, and empathy, while at the time resorting to the judicious use of hermeneutics in order to bolster the above faculties (see, for example, very briefly Ziolkowski 1990, 330–34; Martin 1990, 54–58; Frame 1987, 77; Porter and Teich, 1988, 118–19). In some ways Schleiermacher is the closest to the authors that we will discuss in slightly more detail below, in as far as his theories of hermeneutics had a significant impact on the hermeneutics of literary criticism. Likewise Antonio Rosmini-Serbati (1797–1855), who was the friend and adviser of Manzoni, Cavour, and a good number of popes and cardinals, as well as the founder of a powerful Institute of Charity, although he was plagued by controversy throughout his life. He was an incredibly prolific author. The definitive critical edition of his works was started in 1934 by Castelli and is supposed to reach eventually one hundred volumes; an almost similarly ambitious undertaking is the edition of translations into English by British Benedictines at Durham. Rosmini is a highly interesting figure even though he is poorly known outside Italy; his intention was to create a system on Augustinian foundations that would answer the Kantian system and at the same time assimilate it, finding a modern, contemporary idiom for age-old Christian truths.

In eastern Europe at the same time two or three events stand out. One is the interest of a mixture between Christianity, pre-Christian mythologies, and folklore seen as a chief source of national memory. Prominent figures engaged in these endeavors are numerous: the towering folklorist researcher Vuk Karadzić (1787–1864) in Serbia; the philologist Bogdan P. Haşdeu (1838–1907) with his *Cuvente den betrani* (1878) in Romania; Ferenc Kazinczy (1759–1831) and a number of his followers including Istvan Horvath (1784–1846) or Ferenc Kölcsey (1790–1838) in Hungary; the so-called "Ukrainian School" of poetry, Antoni Malczewski (1793–1826), Seweryn Goszczynski (1801–1876), Jozef Bohdan Zaleski (1802–1886), and even more than these the thinkers August Ciezkowski (1814–1894), Bronislaw Trentowski (1808–1869) and J. M. Hoene-Wrónski (1778–1853) in Poland; but the process is general throughout the early nineteenth century all over eastern Europe. The revival of neo-Platonism can be noted in Sweden, the Netherlands and elsewhere (Porter and Teich 1988, 181, 206–7).

It must also be strongly stressed that most of the developments in Western Christianity on which we have dwelt (specifically the new forms of spiritual revival) find their counterparts in Eastern Christianity. Some of these were purely religious, as is the case with the prominent figure of Paissy Velitchikovsky (1722–1794). Of Ukrainian and Jewish ethnicity he soon left home and traveled widely in eastern Europe, being stationed for a while at Mount Athos. Most of his life was spent however in western and northern Moldavia, where he reformed the monastic system and wrote in Romanian; his emphasis was Christocentric, prayerful, and spiritual. Simultaneously, in 1782 the *Philokalia* was published in Greek in Venice, followed promptly (in 1792) by a Russian variant under the title *Dobrolubya* in Moscow. This was a collection of traditionally transmitted (sometimes apocryphal) texts of patristic origin (as well as medieval and later texts) that contained advice on spirituality and on the Beauty of the Good; it contributed in decisive ways to altering Eastern Orthodox modes of relating to religion. Meanwhile in Montenegro the ruler and archbishop Petar Njegos (like his contemporary the Croat Catholic nobleman Ivan Mažuranić) contributed in important ways to the revival of both religiosity and literature among South Slavs.

Others were openly and strongly combined with literature, as can be seen in the Hungarian "Aurora" circle, and other romantics, for instance Mihály Vörösmarty (1800–1855); Janos Arany (1817–1882); the late works of Adam Mickiewicz (1798–1855) (I have in mind specifically *The Books of the Polish Nation and Its Pilgrimage* [1832], written in biblical prose, but also the early *Forefathers' Eve* [1823]); the Romanian works of Fr. Eufrosin Poteca (1786–1859), the critic and poet Heliade Rădulescu (1802–1872), as well as Alecu Russo (1819–1859), in the works of Lithuanian Bishops Motiejus Valancius and Antanas Barnauskas, or of the Esthonian poets

Kristjan Peterson and Reinhold Kreutzwald. Again the process is widespread over the whole of eastern Europe and sometimes precedes or is richer than similar activities in western Europe.

Judaism, coexisting albeit often uncomfortably in that part of the world, can also be recognized as a powerful player in the ferment of the whole of Europe. From an almost secularized version of Enlightenment Judaism as illustrated by Moses Mendelssohn and others (and these had been bolstering the Reform Judaism that emerged soon after Martin Luther's Reformation) the two chief directions in the first half of the nineteenth century went toward the setting up of Conservative Judaism (the "Historical School" as it was called for a while) and, perhaps even more important, Hassidism, which emerged already by the middle of the eighteenth century and (in emphasizing joy and community) had great cultural impact and connections. A convincing example is provided by the brilliant Rabbi Nahmann of Bratslav (1772–1811), a leading Hassidic figure but also literary figure who is the romantic counterpart of the Enlightenment, rationalist, and "classical" stalwart Moses Mendelssohn. What is common to many of these of these movements (Christian and Judaic) is that they turned toward nature, culture, faith, and interiority rather than strict ethical principles and dogmatic epistemology.

One short note may be in order here. I would not like to leave the impression that I consider romanticism the exclusive vehicle or environment for all these changes. Preparatory signs, sometimes important intellectually and culturally, can be recognized early on in the eighteenth and even in the seventeenth century. Among these I would mention the tradition of Jansenism and Quietism (in France it has been recently argued that Jansenism is the unacknowledged source of the French Revolution [Van Kley]), the explosive emergence of Methodism in England, the Pietist movement (mostly in German-speaking lands) the revival of occult preoccupations in the eighteenth century (Swedenborg, Rosicrucianism, and scores of other names or movements come to mind), and the activities in Eastern Orthodox Christianity and, as mentioned, in Judaism. These all represent the appropriate context for the evolution of the nineteenth century, even when the immediate trigger was provided by the events of 1789–1815 as a response to the systematic eighteenth-century persecution.

For the intellectuals of the time, as well as for a rather broad slice of the general audience, perhaps the most stimulating and exciting were works that endeavored to vindicate God through His works, above all through the experience of the beauty of creation. I will mention a few of the most innovative, ambitious, and prestigious among these, not forgetting the turning point represented by Chateaubriand's *Génie du christianisme* discussed in more detail in the first chapter of this book. These include the almost forgotten *Die heilige Kunst* by Alois Gügler, a Swiss high-school teacher from Lucerne, as well as the contrastive examples of Jaime Balmes, the fiery and erudite Catalan preacher.

Chateaubriand's historical novel *Les martyrs,* although aesthetically rather modest, is historically important in as far as it was the forerunner of a whole subgenre of sentimental, melodramatic, and apologetic works in the nineteenth and the twentieth centuries. As explained in the first chapter, *Génie du christianisme* played an overwhelming political and ideological role in its own time, and for at least one hundred years later, in changing the mode of arguing for Christianity. This influence was due to the work's intellectual substance but also to sheer weight of circulation. It bears repeating that Chateaubriand was deliberately trying to remove the debate about Christianity from under the sovereignty of analytical rationalism. Of the essentials signaling divinity in its fullness, it is Beauty, at least as much as, and perhaps more than, Truth or Goodness that is the most accessible and reliable. The proverbial forces of sense-impression and emotion provide more convincing testimony to the nature of the creation and of God than rational debate and analysis.

It ought to be mentioned here that Chateaubriand's position differs nevertheless from the one that we encounter in the later nineteenth century when aesthetics, the arts, and literature become virtually replacements for religious experience, as in the writings of Schopenhauer, Mattthew Arnold, the pre-Raphaelites, and many others on the Continent. Chateaubriand in contrast to these understands Beauty as diverse abundance and harmony (what would now be called the ecological or the homeostatic). Chateaubriand's leitmotif is that of fertility and abundance of the concrete. He also emphasizes the continuity and fraternity between nature and culture. In *Génie du christianisme* we find numerous examples in which nature's creatures and events support human activity, while arguments in favor of the validity and worth of religion are drawn from cultural occurrences in an almost seamless way.

Like his direct predecessors Fénelon (see the detailed explanations of Richardt 1993), Malebranche, and many other divines in other centuries and countries, Chateaubriand thinks that we should speak about two successive acts of creation: the first of physical nature, as depicted in *Genesis* as well as observed by our own senses and examinations; the second of the spirit, as presented in the Gospels: the psychological, ethical, and spiritual teachings of Jesus Christ. This explains the correspondence between the cultural and the natural realms. The gestalt of a struggling humanity in the face of God could qualify and soften the impact of pure linearity and progress. The historical spectacle as vanity of vanities is but the theatrical scenery required by the beauty of absence.

Now a few words about Alois Gügler. His unfinished work *Die heilige Kunst, oder Die Kunst der Hebräer* appeared in five small volumes between 1814 and 1836 and has remained virtually unresearched, marginalized, and ignored even by Catholic theology or thinking.[4] Gügler seems to have influenced a few later, better-known theologians, such as Möhler. His emphasis on biblical poetry coincides with Chateaubriand's positions in *Génie du christianisme*.

Its first volume, the only one to which I will refer here, deals with the author's general assumptions, while two each of the subsequent volumes deal in some detail with the books of the Old Testament and those of the New Testament. It is not clear to me to what extent Gügler consciously draws on romantic philosophers and poets, or simply works along parallel lines with them. In any case the similarities are stark. Like Herder, Gügler believes in a "national creative spirit" and in a *Genesis*-oriented philosophy of history that we could describe as protological. The somewhat pantheistic or theosophical touches in the later (exegetical) volumes remind us of Fichte's style and thought, and even more of Schelling and Baader. The exalted and flowery style seems learned from Jean Paul. Like Hölderlin, Gügler sees ancient Greece as being somehow part of Asia, or of a broadly understood mystical-paradisal East, a universe of pure, unadulterated humanity still united with the Divine and the natural. Like Novalis, Gügler privileges "the holiness of the night," attributing to it the creative features inherited from divine parenthood. It is not impossible to conceive that Gügler acted as a gleaner and synthesizer of all these ideas and sources. Still, Gügler embodies better than many others what, as M. H. Abrams and others have argued, was the very core of romanticism: the paradigm of Edenic innocence–Fall–Redemption inscribed in the secularized (and yet spiritual) form of cultural (and particularly poetic) achievement.

According to Gügler's theory, the world should be regarded as God's piece of beautiful craftsmanship. As a consequence it is only natural that it is precisely in the aesthetic creativity of all races and climes that the divine and the religious will gain maximum transparency. Nevertheless, in the different local and national mythologies the experience of the Divine is either splintered, diffuse, or blocked. The chief exception is provided by the history and art of ancient Hebrew culture. There we have, according to Gügler, an exemplary relationship between the Divine steering of history and its narrative expression. The art-like unfolding of the Old Testament provides the durable model, as well as the measuring rod, for any human history whatsoever. By contrast, the New Testament narratives and the ecclesiastic time are less historical and less individually focused since, again according to Gügler, their salvational theme provides for less tension (or rupture) between the two fundamental levels of human existence.

However the mediation between the transcendent and the secular needs what Gügler calls *Stimmung* and *Gestimmtheit* (that is, tuning and harmonizing), but at the same time atmosphere and frame of mind. *Stimmung*, which is produced by music and other arts, is the environment or mode by which deepest reality is brought into agreement with human behavior. Therefore aesthetic activity is that which ultimately brings the universe to peaceful completion.

Gügler, though little known even inside his own country and religion, represented brilliantly a widespread trend. How attractive the aesthetic argument was for all those desirous to rehabilitate Christianity and to find a new, secure place for it in the radically modified world after 1815, can be seen by looking at the contrastive example of Jaime Balmes, who lived between 1810 and 1848. He became a priest in 1834 and received a doctorate in theology in 1835. He did not hold positions on University faculties but was elected a member of numerous academies, including those in Barcelona, Madrid, and Rome, on the strength of his publication record. Prominent among these publications is a parallel of Catholic and Protestant civilization (directed against the theories of François Guizot), a massive volume immediately translated into French and English (in 1844); he also published treatises on metaphysics, ethics, and the history of philosophy, started several journals, wrote volumes of Christian apologetics, and engaged in political writings and activities.

One interesting thing about Balmes from the point of view of the current volume is that he ostensibly did not pay much attention to aesthetic issues. He seems to have been unaware of the work of Baumgarten, who is never mentioned in his short *Historía de la filosofía* (pt. 4 of a comprehensive philosophical handbook published in 1840). He liked Chateaubriand and wrote on him, though not without some critical notes. Balmes understood by "aesthetics" only the theory of perception, and he placed his opinions on this merely as a kind of introductory section to the metaphysics chapter of his 1840 work, where he dealt with the senses and reserved just one dull page for the imagination. That is precisely the reason why it is so significant to discover that in the books of one seemingly so distanced from the aesthetic argument it manages nevertheless to break through at key points of his demonstrations.

Thus in *Cartas a un escéptico* (1840–1843) Balmes generally confines himself to the usual areas of reason and morality as he defends faith against religious indifference. Nevertheless, late in his text (letters 22, 24, and 25, out of a total of twenty-five) he turns energetically toward aesthetic points, some of which seem borrowed from the Kantian philosophy that Balmes usually criticizes. For him the beauty of Catholic religious services, the postulation of saints as intermediaries, and various rituals are justified because they provide sensorial props to the frailty of human nature in its effort to reach the infinite and the sublime; concrete sense perception expresses the ideal and the spiritual (letter 22). The point is picked up again even more explicitly in letter 24, when Balmes tackles the practical usefulness of the imagination: it places objects on the terrain of virtue to attract and captivate intense passions (such as those of St. Teresa of Avila, Bernard de Clairvaux, or St. Jerome) that otherwise would have been inevitably engulfed by the intensity of sin.

Finally, in letter 25 Balmes roundly admits that religion rhymes with poetry and fantasy more than with prosaic philosophy. In any case, he explains, language itself must be seen as a divine gift, the origin and existence of the universe is exceptional and unusual, and ultimately there is at the very heart of being mystery and the miraculous. Given these circumstances it is perfectly normal that the accounts provided by religion should be poetical.

In the abovementioned parallel study of Catholicism and Protestantism somewhat similar rhetorical strategies are used. Most of the work deals in polemics with

Guizot's theory of the growth of civilization in Europe, also with issues of historical ethics: what did Catholicism contribute to the abolition of slavery, the emancipation of women, softening of manners, compassionate giving, or, by contrast, coercion and inquisition? Many of Balmes's ideas, developed in greater detail in his sociopolitical essays, can be recognized in this work of philosophy of history: his inclination toward a liberal, benevolent Catholicism, in the tradition of Fénelon, toward constitutional monarchy, even, we might say, an early form of Christian-Democrat doctrine (Balmes once said, "Tengo la monarquía en la cabeza y la democracía en el corazón"). But here also, Balmes feels the need to turn toward aesthetic arguments by the time he reaches the end of his work. Thus in chapter 72, dealing with intellectual progress from the eleventh century to the present, he extols humanistic erudition and the function of Rome as a center for all the arts throughout many centuries and he quotes at great length from Chateaubriand on the cultural role of monastic culture. And this from one whom Menéndez y Pelayo thought prosaic and more inclined to understand Truth than Beauty.

Other actions and directions contributed to the new place of religious discourses inside the larger field of intellectual discourses of the West. We know that the biological sciences of the early nineteenth century (zoology, paleontology, botany, and the like), as well as many of the social sciences (anthropology, early sociology) or indeed even history and linguistics, had chosen a comparatist slant as their favorite methodology. Likewise many of the earliest scholars in religious studies used comparative lines of analysis to broaden their insights, avidly including non-European (or ancient) religions and myth-systems in their studies. The rise of this "science of religion" (the pioneering efforts toward which had of course started much earlier, centuries earlier, in fact) is nevertheless anchored by contemporary research (for example, Despland 1994, 1999) in France (and, I would add, also in Germany, and to a lesser extent, in England and the rest of Europe) and more specifically in the second Restoration (the Orléans regime of 1830–1848). It was largely due to Catholic initiatives (the names of Montalambert, Ozanam, Lacordaire, Lamennais, or the abbe Migne figure prominently and come immediately to mind), although Protestant and Jewish contributions were also important.

The process seems to have been developed as follows: scholars first set up systems of religious comparatism. The names and works of luminaries like Benjamin Constant, Görres, and Creuzer were mentioned above and they would all deserve a more detailed discussion for which this is not exactly the best time and place. These were based on the Renaissance and post-Renaissance doctrine of the "double revelation," which granted some dignity to other, non-Christian religions as either precursors or by simplified forms of Christianity. In turn such comparisons could lead to general theories of symbols. The interesting thing is that such theories of symbols (still closely connected with comparative religion and, by the way, much visited by literary writers) in turn gave birth to frameworks of the "civil religion" that loomed so large in the Third Republic, as well as to theories of natural religion, the latter in Michelet and Quinet in particular (Despland 1999, 284–99). These frameworks descended from comparative religion were as often as not revolutionary, pantheist, or atheist as others. We may venture the argument that despite enormous ideological differences there are structural similarities between Saint-Simon and Joseph de Maistre growing out of their common (and symmetrically opposed) utopian aspirations (see also Despland 1999, 46–49). Such intellective processes may be said to have laid the foundations of much later modern conceptions of history (and the philosophy of history) as secularized versions of religious thinking, as discussed by Löwith and Voegelin among others.

Be that as it may, the attentive reader cannot but observe with some fascination the stubborn persistence of Catholic imagery and thought traditions inside the most various (and often adversarial) discourses, from the political to the aesthetic. To a certain extent this was due to the desire of Restoration scholars to find a kind of middle ground between the aggressive secularization of the Jacobins and the inertia of the devout ultramontanist factions; these scholars in religious studies tried to bridge the obvious gaps between a much more assertive scientific worldview and the religious traditions of society. Another aspect is the connection between French literary aesthetics and romantic religion, described also as an "erased code" or a "reprise littéraire" of the latter by the former (Despland 1999, 489–502; see also Despland 1994).

The persistence of Christian imagery in French writing in the early nineteenth century is formidable. It is not limited to literary passages such as those in Nerval's *Aurélia* or in Lamartine's poems, or even in Victor Hugo's prose and poetry (Bowman 1990, 167–81). It moves on to insistent parallels between Jesus and Socrates, or even Napoleon (3–13, 34–60), to be found in both literary and paraliterary writings. It has been correctly pointed out that during the French eighteenth century, starkly and staunchly religious titles were no less numerous than those of deists or atheists, even though less prominent (Sevillia 2003, 195; Viguerie). Likewise after 1815 there is a profusion of the imagery of "religious blood" to be found in ecclesiastical writings (Jean-Baptiste Lasausse, Thomas Cardinal Gousset, and scores of others), in poetry (Victor Hugo, Musset, French and English romantics), even in scientific writings (Alfred Maury, Imbert-Gourbeyre) (see the excellent detailed analysis of Bowman 1990, 81–105). Walter Scott (see Bos 1932) represented a remarkable variety of religious creeds and views (in an objective manner) through his characters, but to me the best British example remains that of Shelley's *Prometheus Unbound*, where the avowedly atheist poet turns the figure of the God- and cosmos-shattering revolutionary (almost unwillingly) into a Christlike figure. On the other hand it is true that revolutionaries of the age (in 1848 during the antislavery campaign and on other occasions) resorted to Christlike imagery and modeling.

It is only fair to insist here in a few words on the mode in which writers themselves adapted the new discourses on religion and theology and used them. As said at the beginning, literature throughout the West felt itself responsible for and involved with a revamping of religion and the injection of more emotional dimensions over and above the somewhat rationalistic or even dry ways in which religion was taught, preached, or practiced throughout.

As known, a number of significant scholars (among them Meyer Abrams and Harold Bloom) highlighted already decades ago how the romantic enterprise as a whole was from the very beginning combined with religious intentions in different ways. Bloom spoke several times about the connection between Gnosticism and some chief romantic visions. Abrams posited that romanticism as a whole had a large subtext (a "plot") that was but a secularization of the biblical plot of Genesis-Fall-Redemption. Of course, for the early ("core") romantics this was usually an implicit combination, not one loudly or visibly articulated.

The nineteenth century provides fascinating examples of complex combinations of philosophy, literature, and religion. I discussed above briefly the example of Alois Gügler. It should be said that the latter is caught in a wide circle of figures active in southern Germany, Switzerland, and Austria. He himself was the direct "descendant" of Johann Michael Sailer (1751–1832), who along with the medical specialist Johann Nepomuk Ringeis (1785–1880) and others represented the ideological core of the University of Landshut and later Munich (see Gottfried 1979, 56–69; Münk 1994). This is just one example among the many modes of networking that characterized this area in terms of the religion/literature interface. It is precisely during the highpoint of this activity that Clemens Brentano, a Catholic but not conspicuously so in his earlier literary work, dedicated several years (1819–1824) to the recording of the visions of the stigmatized nun (later beatified) Katharina Emerick—the multi-volume lives of Jesus and of the Holy Virgin are the result of its recording; the written form probably owed much to Brentano himself.

This is not the place to review the amazing abundance of valuable theological works that emerged during this period. Nevertheless it is appropriate to say that some of these apologists either actively sought an alliance with literary art or simply found themselves inserted in the literary world and exerting some influence on it. Cardinal Newman would be an excellent example: he had learned much from Coleridge, his style of writing was exquisitely literary, and he was easily accepted as serious and distinguished essayist at the time as well as later (cf. also Alexander 1935, 21–24, among innumerable other judgments). In France, Chateaubriand could be mentioned again, even though he was not more than an occasional apologist and certainly no theologian. On the other hand, Félicité de Lamennais was clearly endowed with a good theological mind, albeit with an explosive and fickle temperament. He was soon adopted by the literary world as one of its legitimate members and interacted with his colleagues in interesting ways. Rosmini was not only perhaps the greatest Catholic philosopher of the age but he deeply influenced Manzoni.

Georg Hermes, Anton Günther, and Johann Sebastian von Drey were absorbed by intellectuals or writers either directly or indirectly. (McCool 1977, 31, 61, 67–69, 88–109, 119–24; see also Münk 1994). Of particular significance in German-speaking lands and elsewhere were the "circles" of religious intellectuals that acted as a link between literary intellectuals and theologians. The names of Cardinal Hofbauer in Vienna and Sailer in Landshut/Munich have already been mentioned. It is indispensable to add here particularly the scintillating Countess Amalie von Gallitzin (1748–1806), seconded by Franz von Fürstenberg (1729–1810), who in Münster acted as a kind of clearinghouse, connecting different wings of (especially) Roman Catholics. One of the Münster circle's most imposing achievements was obtaining the conversion of Count Friedrich Leopold zu Stolberg (1750–1819), who ultimately managed to write a fifteen-volume *Geschichte der Religion Jesu Christi* (1806–1818), a kind of world history from a Christian perspective, meant to counteract the Enlightenment. Although the work remained unfinished, it is fair to say that it had in German educated circles an influence almost comparable to that of Chateaubriand's *Génie* (Münk 1994, 569–70).

It is quite true that the "reawakening" of German literature had been from the beginning involved with religious thematics; it is enough to think of Klopstock's *Messias* for instance, but the names of Jung-Stilling, Hamann, or Matthias Claudius (even Lessing and Goethe to some extent) also come to mind. On the other hand what German romanticism in its different shapes brought was a much deeper processing and an almost systematic harvesting of the field.

The démarche of the philosophers and theologians of the time (particularly the Catholic ones) is best summarized by McCool (1977): refuting the rationalists either by demonstrating that "human reason was intrinsically incapable of reaching any true or certain conclusions about religious or moral issues" (a more traditionalist standpoint) or else adapting "one of the prevailing contemporary philosophies to Catholic apologetics and systematic theology." The advantages of the latter approach were clear. Christian faith was provided with a framework through which its revealed mysteries could be presented to the educated classes in a rigorous intellectual system, while at the same time undermining the habitual rationalist objections against religion (McCool 1977, 18). In fact this line of argument could attract major thinkers or bring them back into the fold. Probably the most spectacular example is that of Schelling who, throughout the second half of his life, concentrated on searching for the best rationalist framework inside which the religious and the aesthetic could be merged. Again the names of Görres and Creuzer could be adduced.

Among the writers who allowed their personal or biographical choices to overflow in and sometimes actually imbue their literary production one may mention in Germany Novalis, Gotthelf, Annette Freiin von Droste-Hülshoff, Mörike, Grillparzer (despite his accesses of political bitterness), later Stifter, as well as numerous others. In France perhaps Lamartine and Balzac are among the most outstanding cases. In England Felicia Hemans, the later Wordsworth, and a number of women novelists (including, arguably, Jane Austen) might be enumerated. The situation is somewhat more complicated in eastern Europe where the enthusiastic adoption of Western views blocked sometimes the open expression of religious views in literature. However it is precisely in this area of Europe where a deep-structure of religious views is the most fertile area of exploratory research and where an aesthetic religiosity became most powerfully entrenched until well after 1900.

I must reemphasize that in most of these literary cases sooner rather than later the aesthetic comes to substitute for the religious, almost against the wishes of the authors. One interesting episode of the post-1815 evolution, in Germany at least, was the outright struggle of a number of otherwise nonpolemical writers against the "Vormärz" and "Jung-Deutschland" groups: not necessarily or primarily from a political and ideological point of view as from the latter's opposition to religion. Examples might be the long review by Wolfgang Menzel, perhaps the leading critic of the time, of Karl Gutzkow's novel *Wally, die Zweiflerin* (1835), the arguments of which had wide echo and were in fact adopted by others. The Swiss Protestant parson and distinguished writer Jeremias Gotthelf, otherwise fairly left-wing in his views, lambasted "Jung-Deutschland" for having corrupted traditional liberalism and dragged it toward radical and socialist positions, not least through its utilitarian and antireligious standpoint. (This can be well seen in his two short stories *Doktor Dorbach der Wühler* and *Ein deutscher Flüchtling*, as well as in his prominent novel *Jakobs des Handwerksgesellen Wanderungen* of 1846, in which Georg Herwegh is the main target.) A rather timid and retiring figure such as Annette Freiin von Droste-Hülshoff wrote poems such as *Mein Beruf* or *Warnung* and *Die Weltverbesserer* in which she expressed worry and anguish against a potential de-Christianization of the world. (I follow here mostly the informative judgments of Bauer 1980–1990.)

I am not sure whether the captivating story of the destiny of "village bells" (Corbin 1998) in nineteenth-century France may serve as a kind of explanatory analogy to the switches and combinations between literary art and religion during the same period. Let us see. Despite various grumblings and setbacks from the Middle Ages on, the church bells had served as an absolutely decisive marker for the sensory culture not only in France but throughout Europe. They had sacralized time and its organization and had defined the sound landscape for centuries. The French Revolution, aiming to regenerate the human race, saw from the very beginning that it ought to annihilate this particular mode of sense perception. The respect and veneration toward the deceased (a foundation of all traditional societies all over the globe), the ritual solemnization of human rites of passage, the auditory certification of human emotions and time divisions became objects of destruction. Step by step over the course of a decade the revolutionary movement with all its power first successfully limited the usage of bells and later literally dismantled and melted them into coins or weapons, while also legislatively reducing or forbidding their use. This was done against sullen passive opposition (and only occasional outbreaks of exasperated violence) on the side of a population that in France until close to the middle of the nineteenth century was still 80 percent rural. The decision of the imperial administration after 1802 to allow again the sounding of bells was received with joy as a liberation. (Napoleon himself enjoyed considerably this particular harmony, as different sources tell us; see, for example, Corbin 1998, 384nn10–11).

The whole of the nineteenth century was marked by a long and highly interesting battle between the secular and the religious forces of society as to the ownership and uses of bells. Issues such as the length of pealing, the particular hours when they could be used, the secular purposes of the bells, access to bell towers, noise disturbances, and a score of others were debated on a local and even on a national level. Early French romantic literature tended to eulogize nostalgically the bell-sound-dominated sensorial culture, while later in the nineteenth century the emphasis was often on the mournful and the sinister connotations of bells. Ultimately the victory was won by the dogmatically laicized society. In the later twentieth century, while bells were not completely banished or abolished they were firmly restrained and marginalized. The sound landscape is dominated by sirens, motor and mechanical noises, radio and stereo blasters, and various cacophonies. Most important, bells were and are subordinated to practical uses such as announcing time. There is thus a kind of coexistence with the religious as a minor partner and its substitution by secular, de-Christianized practices (Corbin 1998, ix–xii, 3–44, 218–53, 287–308, and in fact the book as a whole).

Different as all this may be from literary activity, it nevertheless serves as a good reference. (On a sociopolitical level the number of former clerics, now laicized, is notable: Talleyrand, Baron Louis, and others yet). Like the bells, literature in the nineteenth century tended toward a conjunction of the aesthetic and the religious. Similarly, as I have stressed earlier, the aesthetic becomes the senior partner by the end of the century, but here our parallel ceases to be useful in as far as in literature the pairings, conjunctions, and dialectics continue in a much greater variety of shapes.

In summary, the eighteenth century and, after all, even the nineteenth century were engaged in the secularization of the religious horizon and weltanschauung. These are turned into a diversity of messianisms: philosophical, ideological, literary, political, ethical. The response of religion to this expropriating activity was an expropriation of its own, namely the conquest of the aesthetic, of vast realms of the feelings, and of the emotions, in a word, of the "expansions" of this modernizing, romantic-responsive world. There can be no doubt that the early nineteenth century witnessed throughout the West a marked reappraisal of religion. Governmental hostility toward organized religion subsided gradually. Largely because of pressures from below the opinion that societies are difficult or impossible to conceive in the absence of some kind of religious dimension was generally accepted.

At the same time, however, serious efforts can be noted on the religious side to revamp, renew, or modernize a whole range of its own forms, images, and positions.

Perhaps the emergence and success of Conservative Judaism is a most prominent example here: retrieval of the sacral beauties of traditional ritual but not radical return to strictly Orthodox disciplines. Anglican procedure was rather similar. The change in attitudes by Roman Catholics was, though slower, even more profound, in the sense that the Church's repositioning itself in a minority role was for the first time acknowledged along with the need to vindicate the utility of religion inside the body social.

The connection of the religious dimension to the realm of the beautiful was an extremely important part of this repositioning strategy. Religion began to claim for itself the role of a guardian of the emotional, imaginative, and symbolic resources of humanity. While not entirely relinquishing its ties to the Good and the True, there were numerous cases in which the beautiful was placed over and above them; at any rate, the beautiful was no longer relegated to a mere auxiliary role. While these initiatives came sometimes from institutional ecclesiastic sources and can therefore be interpreted as conscious and "constructed," they often arose among writers and artists in largely spontaneous gestures. The examples I have presented are quite early in the century, but it is fair to say that the mutual (and multiple) engagements of cultural work and religious faith were to become a prominent and highly characteristic feature of the nineteenth century as a whole. These events certainly had a stabilizing role and gave new life to religion(s) throughout the West.

The other side, however, was the growing and earnest conviction that the arts and literature could in fact somehow replace religion.[5] Thus in some fundamental ways nineteenth and twentieth-century aestheticism could be seen as an offspring of the entanglement between sacrality and the beautiful (see the perceptive article of Schmaus 2002). The entanglement of the two was not devoid of dangers for both. The humanistic realm began to be suspected of being just a mask, alibi, or coverup for reasons of religious proselytizing. Meanwhile religion could see itself occasionally subverted or vulgarized as being "merely" aesthetic or fictional. This set of issues was highlighted particularly by the end of the nineteenth and the beginning of twentieth century. It is still present and continues to deserve our full attention.[6]

Notes

1. See Bowman 1990, 155–66. This whole exceptional work is a true mine of information, intelligent reflection, and of discovery of the connection lines between the religious field and other areas of symbolization in early-nineteenth-century France. Additionally one may think of a multitude of details, often ignored. For instance the way in which the treatise of "Christian economics" by Alban de Villeneuve-Bargemont influenced Tocqueville's brother in his agricultural and natural economy principles (and, why not?, even Tocqueville himself, at least indirectly).

2. He begins by arguing that "S'il y a dans le coeur de l'homme un sentiment qui soit étranger à tout le reste des êtres vivants, qui se reproduise toujours, quelle que soit la position où l'homme se trouve, n'est-il pas vraisemblable que ce sentiment est une loi fondamentale

de sa nature? Tel est, à notre avis, le sentiment religieux" (bk. 1, ch. 1, p. 3). [If there is in the human heart a feeling alien to all other living creatures, one that always recurs, irrespective of the human being's position, is it not likely that such a feeling should be a fundamental of his nature? This is the case, in our view, of the religious feeling.] He continues by saying "les dogmes, les croyances, les pratiques, les cérémonies, sont des formes que prend le sentiment intérieur et qu'il brise ensuite" (bk. 1, ch. 1, p. 13) [dogmas, beliefs, rites, ceremonies, are all forms taken by the inner feeling and broken by it after a while.], and "Il y a ... quelque chose d'indéstructible dans la religion" (bk. 1, ch. 1, p. 250 [There is something indestructible in religion] and "tandis que le fond est toujours le même, immuable, éternel, la forme est variable et transitoire" (bk. 1, ch. 1, p. 26). [While the deep content is always the same, unmovable, eternal, the outside form is variable and ephemeral.] Quite promptly Constant links religion and freedom. "Prenez à la lettre les préceptes fondamentaux de toutes les religions, vous les trouverez toujours d'accord avec les principes de liberté les plus étendus, on pourrait dire avec des principes de liberté tellement étendus, que, jusqu'à ce jour, l'application en a paru impossible dans nos associations politiques" (bk. 1, ch. 4, p. 84). [If you take literally all the fundamental principles of all religions you will always find them compatible with the broadest principles of freedom, so broad that one might think that it is impossible to find them applied practically even nowadays in our political structures.]; or, even more strongly, "L'époque où le sentiment religieux disparaît de l'âme des hommes est toujours voisine de celle de leur asservissement. Des peuples religieux ont pu être ésclaves; aucun peuple irréligieux n'est demeuré libre" (bk. 1, ch. 4, p. 89). [Any age in which the religious feeling disappears in human souls is always related to their state of enslavement. There have been religious people in a state of slavery, but no irreligious people has maintained its freedom.] All these quotations are from vol. 1. (There is now a new one-volume critical edition Arles: Actes Sud, 1999, prepared by Tzvetan Todorov and Etienne Hofmann.)

3. Lamennais is sentimental to the point of hysteria, parabolic and grandiose, ecstatic and mawkish, intentionally rhapsodic and prophetic, he displays the nervousness of a lush passion. Nevertheless, in a curious way he is devoid of the intensity and ambition of a high-romantic rebuilder of the universe such as Blake, for instance. At bottom Lamennais tones down his aims; he constantly channels his energies into some kind of social utility, or else insists on the compatibility of religion with science. (cf., for example, 44–47, 68–82, 178–79). Admittedly these observations do not always apply to his orthodox ("ultra-montanist") works before 1834 (some of which were written together with his brother Jean-Marie). See also the balanced assessment of Woodward 1963, 248–55.

4. There is a short biographical work by J. L. Schiffmann, *Lebensgeschichte A. Güglers* (1833). The most serious study is included in Urs von Balthasar (1961, 1:89–97) and I drew on its conclusions. See also the articles (or "entries") by Härdelin 1967 and Klinger 1975.

5. Already somebody like Beethoven argued in favor of an art substituting for religion. See Johnson 1991, 120–21.

6. This chapter deals specifically with the varieties of intermeshing between the aesthetic and the religious. It is not intended as a comprehensive survey of the treatment and functioning of religion in Europe and North America during the early nineteenth century. I would like to emphasize here that in my opinion a perfectly good argument can be made in favor of a Europe that was being de-Christianized apace during these decades. We know very well that for instance the works of Voltaire and Rousseau were more widely read and circulated during

this period than the sum of their adversaries' writings. Major studies contributing to the dismantling of Christianity and/or the Bible appeared simultaneously with those mentioned above: not only scholarly works, but also productions of wider intellectual appeal such as those of David Strauss, Ludwig Feurbach, and soon Renan, Darwin, and Marx, to list just a few prominent names. My purpose was merely and precisely to explain why, in the face of this formidable social and intellectual activity, society maintained its stability and its allegiance to Christian traditions.

Bibliography

Abrams, Meyer H. 1971. *Natural Supernaturalism: Tradition and Revolution in Romantic Literature.* New York: Norton.

Alexander, Calvert, S.J. 1935. *The Catholic Literary Revival.* Milwaukee: Bruce.

Balmes, Jaime. 1844. *El protestantismo comparado con el catolicismo, en sus relaciones con la civilización europea.* 4 vols. Barcelona: Jose Taulo.

———. 1846. *Cartas a un escéptico en materia de la religión.* Barcelona: Brusi. (Orig. pub. 1840–43.)

Barclay, David E. 1995. *Friedrich Wilhelm IV and the Prussian Monarchy, 1840–1861.* Oxford: Clarendon Press.

Bauer, Winfred. 1980–1990. "Geistliche Restauration versus Junges Deutschland und Vormärz-Literaten." In *Deutsche Literatur: Eine Sozialgeschichte.* Ed. Horst Glaser. 10 vols. 6:97–111. Hamburg: Rowohlt.

Bos, Klaas. 1932. "Religious Creeds and Philosophies as Represented by Characters in Sir Walter Scott's Works and Bibliography." Ph.D. diss., Paris.

Bowman, Frank Paul. 1990. *French Romanticism: Intertextual and Interdisciplinary Readings.* Baltimore: Johns Hopkins University Press.

Chalmers, Thomas. 1821. *The Application of Christianity to the Commercial and Ordinary Affairs of Life.* New York: Campbell and Sons.

Charlton, Donald Geoffrey. 1963. *Secular Religions in France 1815–1870.* New York: Oxford University Press.

Chateaubriand, François-René, vicomte de. 1978. *Génie du christianisme.* In *Essai sur les révolutions. Génie du christianisme.* Paris: Nouvelle Revue Française / Gallimard, Pléiade.

Church, R. W. 1970. *The Oxford Movement 1832–1845.* Chicago: University of Chicago Press. (Orig. pub. 1891.)

Constant, Benjamin. 1824–1831. *De la religion considerée dans sa source, sa forme et ses développements.* 5 vols. Paris: Bossange Père et al.

Corbin, Alain. 1998. *Village Bells: Sound and Meaning in the Nineteenth-Century French Countryside.* New York: Columbia University Press. (Orig. French ed. pub. 1994.)

Dawson, Christopher. 2001. *The Spirit of the Oxford Movement.* London: St. Austin Press. (Orig. pub. 1933.)

Demers, Patricia. 1996. *The World of Hannah More.* Lexington: University of Kentucky Press.

Despland, Michel. 1994. *Reading an Erased Code: French Literary Aesthetics and Romantic Religion.* Toronto: University of Toronto Press.

———. 1999. *L'émergence des sciences de la religion: La monarchie de juillet: Un moment fondateur.* Paris: L'Harmattan.

Dru, Alexandre. 1967. *Erneuerung und Reaktion: Die Restauration in Frankreich 1800–1830.* Munich: Kösel.

Fleischmann, Kornelius. 1988. *Klemens Maria Hofbauer: Sein Leben und seine Zeit.* Graz: Styria.
Frame, John. 1987. *The Doctrine of the Knowledge of God.* Phillipsburg, N.J.: Presbyterian and Reformed Publishing.
Fulford, Tim, ed. 2002. *Romanticism and Millenarianism.* New York: Palgrave.
Gottfried, Paul. 1979. *Conservative Millenarians: The Romantic Experience in Bavaria.* New York: Fordham University Press.
Härdelin, Alf. 1967. "Kirche und Kult in der Luzerner Theologischen Romantik (Alois Gügler und Josef Widmer)." *Zeitschrift für katholische Theologie* 80: 139–75.
Hofer, Johannes. 1923. *Der heilige Klemens Maria Hofbauer.* Freiburg im Breisgau: Herder.
Jones, Mary Gwladys. 1952. *Hannah More.* Cambridge: Cambridge University Press.
Johnson, Paul. 1977. *A History of Christianity.* New York: Atheneum.
———. 1991. *The Birth of the Modern: World Society 1815–1830.* New York: HarperCollins.
Klinger, Elmar. 1975. "Alois Gügler (1782–1827)." In *Katholische Theologen Deutschlands im 19ten Jahrhundert.* 3 vols. Ed. Heinrich Fries and Georg Schwaiger. 1:274–302. Munich: Kösel.
Lamennais, Félicité de. 1913. *Paroles d'un croyant.* Paris: Payot. (Orig. pub. 1834.)
Martin, James Alfred. 1990. *Beauty and Holiness.* Princeton, N.J.: Princeton University Press.
McCool, Gerald A. 1977. *Catholic Theology in the Nineteenth Century: The Quest for a Unitary Method.* New York: Seabury.
Mellor, Ann K. 2000. *Mothers of the Nation.* Bloomington: Indiana University Press.
Münk, Hans. 1994. "Die deutsche Romantik in Religion und Theologie." In *Romantik-Handbuch.* Ed. Helmut Schanze. 556–89. Stuttgart: Kröner.
Philippe Muray. 1984. *Le 19e siècle à travers les âges.* Paris: Denoël.
Nipperdey, Thomas. 1991. *Deutsche Geschichte 1800–1866: Bürgerwelt und starker Staat.* Munich: Beck. (Orig. pub. 1983.)
Porter, Roy, and Teich Mikulás, eds. 1988. *Romanticism in National Context.* Cambridge: Cambridge University Press.
Powers, Richard Howard. 1957. *Edgar Quinet: A Study in French Patriotism.* Dallas: Southern Methodist University Press.
Richardt, Aimé. 1993. *Fénelon.* Ozoir-la-Ferrère: In Fine.
Sauvigny, Guillaume de Bertier de. 1955. *La Restauration.* Paris: Flammarion.
Schmaus, Marion. 2002. "Lebenskunst, Kunstreligion, Weltfrömmigkeit: Signaturen des Ich im Gespräch von Goethe und Novalis." *Goethe Yearbook* 11: 255–77.
Schrott, Ludwig. 1987. *Biedermeier in München.* Munich: Amira. (Orig. pub. 1963.)
Seillière, Ernest. 1919. *Edgar Quinet et le mysticisme démocratique.* Paris: Société d'économie sociale.
Sevillia, Jean. 2003. *Historiquement correct: Pour en finir avec le passé unique.* Paris: Perrin.
Talmon, Joel. 1961. *Political Messianism: The Romantic Phase.* New York: Praeger.
Till, Rudolf. 1951. *Hofbauer und sein Kreis.* Wien: Herold.
Underwood, Ted. 2002. "Historical Difference as Immortality in the Mid-Nineteenth-Century Novel." *Modern Language Quarterly* 63, no. 4 (December): 441–71.
Urs von Balthasar, Hans. 1961. *Herrlichkeit.* 7 vols. Einsiedeln: Johannes Verlag.
van Kley, Dale. 1996. *The Religious Origins of the French Revolution.* New Haven, Conn.: Yale University Press.

Viguerie, Jean de. 1995. *Histoire et dictionnaire du temps des lumières.* Paris: Laffont.

Woodward, Sir Ernest Llewelyn. 1963. *Three Studies in European Conservatism.* Hamden, Conn.: Archon. (Orig. pub. 1929.)

Ziolkowski, Theodore. 1990. *German Romanticism and Its Institutions.* Princeton, N.J.: Princeton University Press.

III

INFORMATION

The Moderating Force

CHAPTER 7

The Informative Narration
From Cultural Packaging to Psychological Geography

THE HUMAN RELATIONSHIP to space has long been recognized as a topic of major interest and even as a possible key to the contrastive definitions of various cultures (Spengler) or of human consciousness in general (Kant). Even those who find such a reliance on spatial coordinates and orientation excessive may admit at least a certain merit in a historical stylistics of cultural attitudes towards space (including movement) or in the self-conscious perceptions of space. The vast treks that are part of the originating myths of most traditional cultures; the subtle mixture of fabulous imagery and exact reports in ancient Greek, no less than in Chinese or Arabic travelogues; the exaltations of horizon expansion in the Renaissance; and the firmly ideological uses of alterity and exoticism in the eighteenth century are just some of the discourses of dynamic space-relationship and space-appropriation that come to mind. In the early nineteenth century the dilemmas of an emerging globalization—an event unique and unprecedented within the memory of the human consciousness—were translated, among other things, in deep and intensive reflections on spatial relationships. Did home, rootedness, and the local horizon lose their steadying role as the primary environment or as the placenta of the human creature? Do cultural and industrial (artificial or manmade) environments stand in hostile contrast to (God-made or nature-originated) physical/organic environments, or can we imagine a certain balance between them? Do they interact, and if so, how? Or at least how much credit should we accord each of them? Is the newly reached consciousness of globality, indeed sometimes the even more comprehensive cosmic awareness, a realistic option for the dwelling and functioning of human beings?

Many of the discourses of the early nineteenth century were predicated, I am convinced, on questions of this type, along with many of the anguishes and uncertainties in the European society of its time. It would not be difficult to show that these (like other features discussed in this volume) were by no means limited to a thin stratum of educated or affluent individuals. On the contrary, it seems likely that precisely the less verbal or less scriptic felt the impact more forcefully in terms of mobility (enforced or possible), the alteration of nature, emigration choices, transfers to urban environments, and the like. There is every reason to believe that the literary and philosophical questionings of the successive romantic generations articulated concerns perceived more dimly, but quite immediately, by most of society.

This is not to say that durable and continuing features of human existence (economic livelihood, social power, institutional tensions, erotic needs, transcendent/religious pursuits, creative impulses, or others) found themselves in a state of diminution, which would have been impossible in any case. It is only to say that they were now framed in new and additional ways when compared to the discourses current fifty or one hundred years ago. The earliest and most explosive romantic impulses, those of Blake, Wordsworth, and Hölderlin, can be seen as attempts to come to terms with globalization: the outlines of a cosmic awareness, the moments of absolute consciousness (even in the regret of their absence), the efforts of Hegel, Schelling, and Coleridge to theorize a state of spiritual comprehensiveness and totality, were simultaneous (even analogous) with the equally ambitious efforts of radical restructuring by revolutionaries in France and elsewhere.[1]

Travel literature in the early nineteenth century and its sudden enhanced importance and popularity (one reaching deep into a cross section of the readership, apparently) is based upon the convergence of several powerful factors. One was undoubtedly the need to find a manageable idiom for the overwhelming aspirations of romanticism and for dealing with the intimidating realities of a world that was immense, various, yet available to consciousness—not only available but also daunting like a task. The enthusiasm of sudden and absolute possession and assimilation and its assumption of oneness did not seem helpful or acceptable on a practical level. Byron's quick intelligence impelled him to move without delay from the cosmicities of *Childe Harold* and *Cain* to the pragmatic appropriation of space and difference exposed in *Don Juan*. The abundance of marginality displayed in nineteenth-century travel literature may be conveniently said to repeat Byron's démarche: to illustrate concretely (and to experiment from case to case) what can be done with vastness and with multiplicity.

Another conceptual source of this accumulating travel literature was just as undoubtedly the struggle of political philosophies: ideology as expression of existential options. Colonialism is a consequence of and a response to a new state of affairs present in the human mind: the planet as integrated reality. Exerting one's power, demonstrating one's superiority, was unquestionably an immediate temptation; physical possession was the crudest, most instinctive, and most immediate response of the "old Adam." Colonialism was strengthened by the desire to deny alterity and impose uniformity and similarity on all zones;[2] the utopia of brotherly equality was an equally instinctive and reductionist impulse overlaying the colonial desire, interfering with it but also nourishing it. Travel literature could be either an affirmation of these impulses or provide a substitutive sublimation.

Meanwhile other options were possible and in fact came into existence and competed vigorously. The knowledge of the close-at-hand, the exploration of small spaces, the revaluations of localism, the identification with originary environments, were equally attractive. It should not be overlooked that other responses (equally ideological) preferred a kind of leisurely savoring of difference: walking through space was replaced by a walking through capacious rooms of culture and custom. The vehicle of the travelog was at hand and the literary topos of the walk no less than the actual practice of walking as developed in the eighteenth century served well. The romantics continued the tradition of Dr. Johnson, Sterne, and Smollett, as well as of Rousseau, Volney, or Karamzin. Thus Wordsworth and Southey were mighty walkers. Johann Gottfried Seume (1763–1810) undertook a gigantic walking tour of Europe recorded in his *Spaziergang nach Syrakus* (1802). Hazlitt is rightly quoted as one who was able to articulate the experience of walking as a liberation of the self and the communion with nature (Robinson 1989, 17–18; in the wake of Hazlitt himself), better yet, the paradigm of the balance between the natural and the cultural. In this sense much eighteenth-century visual or scriptic textuality (from Fielding's novels to Gainsborough's *Morning Walk* of 1785) would seem to be based on some kind of idea of the walk as an archetypal human activity, the "pilgrimage of a soul" that accommodates both mutability and constancy and that provides the variety of experiences required for human ripeness (and/or salvation).

Travel writing has been discussed from diverse other points of view. Blanton (1997, 2–3, and elsewhere) underlines the narrative character of these writings and their production by the interaction of the self with the world (beginning with Wordsworth and others). This is true and useful but it simply would modify my focus. Wallace (1993, 62–66, 11–18) makes a number of fascinating points, such as the connection between the walking-narratives with the age-old tradition of the georgic, in its connection with the contemplation and inscription of the human in nature, or else the way in which the rise of the railways almost imposed the alternative of walking by foot. These and other angles are highly meritorious, but they would imply a departure from my own purposes; thus for instance it is easy to notice that in this chapter I do not deal just with walking but with travel by all kinds of means. That is the reason why I had to shape my intentions more strictly.

My own enumeration of converging and influential factors would be, however, incomplete without listing sheer curiosity: the epistemological availability or cognitive thirst that was opening up in Western societies and was growing exponentially. Readiness to ingurgitate large masses of reports and information in the nineteenth century is an enormously important social fact that has not yet been investigated, let alone explained, in satisfactory fashion. This applied to everybody. Thus, according to some calculations, 13 percent of Goethe's reading was formed out of travel literature (Furst 1992, 13). Likewise, 14 percent of the texts published in *Revue des Deux Mondes* in 1842 were devoted to travel (Wolfzettel 1986, 11–12). Travel narratives were excellently suited as a vehicle for dealing with at least one aspect of this enormous increase of cognitive material. Travel literature could incorporate, in balanced fashion, packets of information presumed reliable and imaginative satisfactions that served as lubrifiers, as well as modes of streamlining and processing this information. John Murray III's *Redbook* guides were launched in 1836 (his first guide to continental voyagers appeared in 1820), and in Germany Karl Baedeker started his own series in imitation in the early 1840s (the first of his books came out in 1827). In just slightly more literary and less utilitarian fashion, France produced from the 1820s on numerous *guides pittoresques*. Thomas Cook's travel agency, the model of all the others, was founded in 1841, and it is in the 1840s that popular journalism began to include travel accounts as a constant feature. These are documentary and utilitarian Biedermeier products, but they tie in easily with the travel literature of the time in which romantic empathy served as an additional cognitive instrument intended to provide a higher kind of knowledge, an enhancement of objectivity through subjectivity.

It is for all these reasons that a close look at travel literature is very fruitful. In the present chapter I will examine comparatively several sets or groups of authors in terms of their diverse foci. These will include: travel as the viewing of moral-philosophical landscapes (humanistic geography as it is sometimes called, or landscape as scriptural history); travel as space variation and displacement; and finally the study of cultural physiognomy as a(n) (un)satisfactory substitute for travel. It is here that the connection with two other generic modes of the time becomes obvious. The historical novel and the historiography of the time had as their purpose instruction in an indirect, sophisticated and delightfully elegant way. Likewise the chatting or even chattering discourse of Biedermeier travel literature brings it in line with the conversational essay and with the products of *costumbrismo* (in Spain or in eastern and central Europe), as exercises in fusing the aesthetic and the utilitarian.

Finally I will try to draw some short conclusions and offer some explanations. How does individual consciousness respond to and wrestle with cognitive accumulation as one significant expression of modernity? Is it the case that the weakly telic and nonstructured nature of the travelog is building up toward freedom for fragmentariness? Equality or quasiequality between the episodes makes travel literature particularly responsive to the needs of the early nineteenth century. In a word how does travel literature shade into or blend with other contemporary forms of secondariness and dispersion?

Chateaubriand's first and only visit to Constantinople took place between September 13 and 18, 1806, and his impression of the capital of the Ottoman Empire was summarized in a few memorable pages published five years later in his *Itinéraire de Paris à Jérusalem:*

> We landed in Galata: immediately I noted the stir on the wharves, and the mob of porters, merchants and sailors; all these revealed by the diverse facial hues, by the

differences in their language, demeanor, clothing, hats, bonnets and turbans that they called from all parts of Europe and of Asia in order to dwell on this frontier of two worlds. The almost complete absence of women, the lack of wheeled carriages, and the packs of masterless dogs—these three features were the first to strike me as I stepped into this extraordinary city. People walk around only in felt slippers, the noise of carts and carriages cannot be heard, there are no church bells, and virtually no hammer-wielding craftsmen, and so a perpetual silence reigns. You look around and see a voiceless crowd, that walks by as if it wished to avoid notice, in stealth, always with the air of hiding from its master's vigilant eye. You pass all the time from a *bazaar* to a cemetery as if Turks were around only to buy, to sell and to die. These wall-less cemeteries, placed in the middle of streets are splendid cypress groves: doves build their nests in these cypress trees and share the peace of the dead.... No sign of joy, no appearance of happiness meets the eye: All that can be seen is not a nation, but a herd shepherded by the imam and slaughtered by the janissar. Here the only pleasure is debauchery, the only punishment death. The mournful sounds of a mandoline sometimes emerge from the back of a coffee-house and one can observe ignoble children engaged in obscene dances in the front of apelike figures seated around low tables. Surrounded by jails and prison-houses a seraglio rises, the Capitol of servitude: there, a sacred guardian anxiously preserves the germs of the past and the original law-tables of tyranny. Pale-faced adorers ceaselessly prowl around this temple, bowing their heads to the idol.... The despot's eyes attracts the slave, much as the serpent's glance hypnotically fixes the birds that will become his prey. (Chateaubriand 1968, 204–5; my translation)

We will immediately have a chance to make some comments upon this passage, but first let me provide another quotation from another traveler, the Romanian aristocrat and politician Dimitrie Ralet. True, Ralet was writing half a century later; even given this time lag the difference remains striking. He notes:

> We reached the hotel, where we first noticed some policemen; until then, their absence had been striking. Nobody had inquired after our passport, nor had we received a residence card, two shapes in which many a civilized country expresses its sempiternal anxiety, and perpetually admits its weakness and mistrust. (Ralet 1979, 65; my translation)[3]

Constantinople is for Ralet what London had been for Dr. Johnson, "a portrait of human life itself." He says, rhapsodically:

> One moment you forget all your unhappiness, another you weary at the mere idea of its numberless climbs and descents, and then again you feel at peace and forget all your worries in the face of the enchanting beauties that touch all your senses surrounded by a nature that unfolds its harmonious grandeur by and through its own confusion, a nature that surpasses any paradise you may have dreamt of, by a

sea that mirrors the hues and tints of heaven. Much as in the course of your life you encounter love with its flattering delights and with its deceitful hopes, as you encounter power preceded by so many vain illusions and accompanied by so many real disappointments—so you will encounter on your travels the Bosporus with its multifarious beauties, with limpid waves, but true reality is not far away; you will come to shore and find the most hurting contrast between soothing waves and dirty lanes, between [. . .] luminous and elating azure and a reeking, dismal ugliness, between an infuriating luxury which is, as you know, inseparable from oppression, and a misery that irritates you since it is accompanied by sloth. (Ralet 1979, 82)

The cypress trees in Constantinople's graveyards are for Ralet both melancholy and majestic (102), contributing to the unreal mirage-like beauty of a city that he regards as a great urban and cosmopolitan center, and, in many ways, a model of modernity.[4] What can account for these radically different evaluative as well as descriptive propositions on the same environment even admitting, as I suggested before, that there had been some significant changes in the fifty years that had elapsed from Chateaubriand's to Ralet's visit? To answer this we have to remind ourselves once more of Chateaubriand's crucial position in European self-consciousness, as Western societies were beginning to explore the dynamics of evermore completely alienated modernity, with all their attractions and pitfalls. Chateaubriand's capacious mind and soul provided space for the playing out of the dialectics of conservatism and liberalism, of religion, nature, and art, and of various other essential conflicts emerging at the time. Chateaubriand provided an imaginative vocabulary that for one hundred years and more served in France and elsewhere for expressing the dilemmas of an advancing modernity. One of the ways in which he did this was by using the travelog as a vehicle for symbolic messages. This became possible at the time because "the walk," both as eighteenth-century practice and as a discourse topos in the eighteenth century, was gradually being replaced first by the grand tour (still inside the confines of the European world), and soon by even more adventurous explorations of areas all over the globe. Geographical mobility of larger social masses was a nineteenth-century phenomenon, as opposed to migration (basically a one-way trip), an age-old manifestation of human groups. It is also in the early nineteenth century that tourism ceased to be the appanage of a handful of eccentric aristocrats or poets and became a middle-class custom.

Chateaubriand was among the few who seized upon these sociocultural trends and shaped them in meaningful, value-carrying models. The first of his two great expeditions took him into a realm of the exotic, the primal and the pristinely unhistorical: extra-western North America, described not only in *Atala* and *René* but also in *Mémoires d'outre-tombe* and in other works.[5] His second great journey was to take him to the sources of an historically constituted culture, that is to Athens and Jerusalem. The first of the journeys was reinterpreted (by Chateaubriand himself, no less than by most of his readers) as a powerful response to Rousseau and Diderot;

its ideological implications were fully expounded in *Génie du christianisme*. The world of primitivity was indeed one in which Beauty and religion were unsevered; it confirmed Chateaubriand's search for a "conservatism with human face" or a harmonious traditionalism—the kind of convergence of or cooperation between opposing values that Walter Scott in England and Goethe in central Germany were also trying to formulate.

By contrast, the journey to Athens and Jerusalem turned out to be a much darker and more pessimistic undertaking. With increasing lucidity Chateaubriand came to realize—even while continuously fighting back—that the future was pregnant not with his humanist conservatism but with a society of alienated egalitarianism and neutral democracy. The text of the *Itinéraire* is full of anxious hopes and doubts, it is breathlessly grasping for the certainty of Western Christendom's roots. Bitterness, gloom, and dark irony abound. The results of the journey are disappointing: the Hellenic as well as the biblical roots of culture seem dispersed and lost to the sense experience and to a real empirical access. They have become elusive and ambiguous textual realities at best.

The description of Constantinople is therefore an almost inevitable given inside Chateaubriand's plot. Midway between the Hellenic and the Hebrew realm (and almost exactly at the center of the narrative account) Constantinople is the empire of death. It wields a stifling or destructive supremacy over both Athens and Jerusalem, and it has the dread majesty of "time-the-destroyer" (another age-old topos). That is why Constantinople itself becomes the center of pale silence and the metropolis of graveyards. Going even beyond this fairly clear structural function one may speculate whether for Chateaubriand Constantinople was not an emblem of the dawning age of leveling and indifferentiation. In any case this seems more plausible than suspecting Chateaubriand of orientalist prejudice. His cast of mind and narrative practice were different—much like Volney he was interested in the cyclicity of the rise and ruin of empires and cultures. Therefore using an Islamic macroimage for a Western-engendered reality would not have bothered him: still I will not claim more than an uncertain suggestion of lethal modernity.

By contrast, for Ralet Constantinople (granted, a generation later) could become an ideal, almost utopian text. Ralet was a progressive Moldavian localist. He wanted his native country to become Westernized, to join in the benefits of modernized societies such as openness, variety, freedom, and social and economic advance. Nevertheless, like many of his generation, intellectual outlook, and social class, he had doubts as to whether such a joining to the West was feasible at all, and, if feasible, he wondered what the consequences and side effects might be. Visiting Constantinople filled him with elation. Here was a city that must certainly be described as a metropolis and that had still remained deeply oriental. Building on this key perception Ralet generates a text in which the local and the traditional are harmoniously interwoven with the cosmopolitan and the progressive, and likewise the rural with the urban, the natural with the manmade. For Ralet, Constantinople, far from being an image of death and silence, is an aesthetic construct of hope: the potentiality of Western-like environment built out of local substances and materials, not the mere imitation or imposition of an alien civilization, is powerfully affirmed by the Romanian author.

Dimitrie Ralet's travelog is, like Chateaubriand's *Itinéraire* and so many other travelogs, an exercise in value choices and meaning selections. Beyond that, however, both share some other features. First, they carefully cultivate ambiguity and multivalence. They evade action but also act through the form of evasion, flight, and the search of new horizons. They refuse canonical stability by choosing a marginal generic vehicle, but there is equal denial in the replacement of a prescribed or predictable environment with a noncanonical, remoter one. These negative ambiguities are balanced by something else: travel literature in the early nineteenth century proclaims the unity of knowledge and desire, and seeks to present this unity as incorporated in the text. Noncanonical marginality can provide, according to this scheme—in travel literature, the historical novel, the conversational essay, and in similar vehicles of Biedermeier romanticism—much of what high romanticism had tried but not achieved. Indirect achievement is thus deemed to be more probable and more powerful, or at least more efficient, than the direct approach to theoretical and practical dilemmas.

If this first kind of ambiguity or double-writing may seem a little abstract, there is a second feature that comes out much more obviously from reading Chateaubriand, Ralet, Leigh Hunt, Hazlitt, and others. It is the way in which the remote, the unexpected and the secondary are assimilated to the permanent, the known, and the possessed. Low romanticism after 1815 is a golden age for armchair traveling in time and space. The absolutism of a consciousness identifying itself with the universe, absorbing in itself all of nature, and/or allowing itself to be absorbed into nature is now scaled down to the somewhat more realistic aim of roaming over the globe and bringing the unknown back to familiarity. This travel literature is by and large a literature of (re)familiarization, as I will immediately show by adducing some examples from Leigh Hunt.

Before I do so, however, let me mention briefly a third feature that we can find in many fields of the age and that is discussed in many chapters of this book, but that I feel I have to repeat because it provides another broad framework for the functioning and self-definition of travel literature in the early nineteenth century: the substitutive animus of the age. In Biedermeier romanticism we find characteristic switches of the aesthetic and the pragmatic, mingling of the feudal and the bourgeois, and hence in a trading of the past for the future and the alienated for the traditional—and vice versa—in what are irregular patterns (Sengle 1971–1980, vol. 2).

Keeping in mind this third proposition, we can briefly look at some passages in Leigh Hunt. Hunt published his *Autobiography* in 1850; he had started jotting down and partially publishing reminiscences since 1810. In September 1821 Hunt went to Italy and stayed there until the summer of 1825. This experience is related in chapters 17 to 22 of the *Autobiography*.[6] To what extent dwelling abroad and thinking of home are combined and turned into mutually substitutive values can be also seen in the way in which, together with Shelley, Byron, and some other expatriates, Hunt created there a small and rather closed English society. It can also be seen in the fact that his main creative endeavor in those years was precisely the publication of a journal in England (*The Liberal*). It can best be seen in the reflections themselves as they pertain to Italy and to Hunt's life there. Indeed the experience of Leigh Hunt in Italy is meant to be and does emerge from these pages as an experience of unfettered alienation, or an escape from the roots and other organicities and from the multiple crossing ties of a traditional society. In this sense Leigh Hunt and other expatriates in Italy were plunging headlong into a futuristic situation, sampling a kind of life that was to become more general one hundred or one hundred and fifty years later, precisely in their homeland and similar sociogeographic areas. "All the insect tribes, good and bad, acquire vigor as they get southward," Hunt says introducing an exposition on scorpions, cicadas, fireflies, and other creatures about which "it is impossible not to think of something spiritual in seeing" their progress. This is an apt emblem of the flitting state repeatedly alluded to, for example:

> I lived with the true human being . . . and my own not unworthy melancholy; and went about the flowering lanes and hills, solitary indeed, and sick to the heart, but not unsustained. In looking back to such periods of one's existence, one is surprised to find how much they surpass many seasons of mirth, and what a rich tone of color their very darkness assumes, as in some fine old painting. (Hunt 1850, 2:209–11)

Elsewhere the imagery suggests even more strongly detachment from environment and from predictable matrices:

> The first novelty that strikes you, after your dreams and matter-of-fact have recovered from the surprise of their introduction to one another, is the singular fairness and new look of houses that have been standing hundreds of years. This is owing to the dryness of the Italian atmosphere. Antiquity refuses to look ancient in Italy. It insists upon retaining its youthfulness of aspect. The consequence at first is a mixed feeling of admiration and disappointment; for we miss the venerable. (2:137)

Leigh Hunt is not inclined towards idealizations. Ugliness and lack of feeling figure prominently in his Italian descriptions. The young beggars in the port of Genoa are memorable:

> They had no foreheads, and moved their hands as if they were paws. Never did we see a more striking look of something removed from humanity; and the worst of it was, they had no sort of comfort in their faces; their laugh was as melancholy, yet unfeeling, as their abject and canting whine. They looked like impudent, squalid old men of the world, in the shape of boys; and were as pale and almost as withered. (2:165)

The reader finds elsewhere in these chapters symptomatic details, such as "nine out of ten persons in the room have dirty socks on" (2:219), or "the chicanery, sensuality, falsehood, worldliness ... [of] the Court of Rome" (2:216) as well as abundant social-critical barbs (the much criticized syndrome of orientalism is visible in these accounts of southern Europe no less than in other nineteenth-century presentations of the Middle East).

However, what predominates is a long line of images of estrangement and separation. Here is a pointed and significant example: "To me Italy had a certain hard taste in the mouth. Its mountains were too bare, its outlines too sharp, its lanes too strong, its long summer too dusty. I longed to bathe myself in the grassy balm of my native fields" (2:198). This passage of landscape criticism, as we might call it, is truly emblematic for Hunt's predicament. He seeks and finds release from the constraints of his native historical matrix in the alienation of a remote land, but he turns the new environment back into the originating home base, arguably at a broader range and certainly at a higher level of abstraction. The tensions between freewheeling individualism and structured or repressed existence are rediscovered, highlighted, and then translated into the arid stridency of the environment.

Nor is it the case that alienation is depicted as evil and devoid of compensations. Leigh Hunt the character projects himself into an Italy that is not only an area of freedom but also of aesthetic enjoyment: "The cherries were Brobdingnagian, and bursting with juice," and "Returning through the city, I saw a man in one of the by-streets alternately singing and playing on a pipe, exactly as we conceive of the ancient shepherds" (2:175). The space of alienated liberty is thus filled with artworks and reminiscences of the Renaissance and classical antiquity. This aesthetic enjoyment provides a key to Leigh Hunt's technique of dialectical transformation of the real into the imaginary, back into the real, and again into the imaginary. A scene observed of an August evening in the cathedral of Pisa is iconic in more ways than one. Hunt notices the multitude of wax candles surrounding a gigantic picture of the Virgin and muses:

> It is impossible to see this profusion of lights, especially when one knows their symbolical meaning, without being struck with the source from which Dante took his idea of the beatified spirits. His heaven, filled with lights, and lights too arranged in figures, which glow with lustre in proportion to the beatitude of the souls within them, is the sublimation of a Catholic church. (2:143)

Long, almost infinite vistas open up here. The material-empirical models of Dante's imaginary construct are in their turn based upon a preexisting ideal vision of paradisal reality, while at the other end it is the concrete reality of Dante's verse that becomes the trigger for Hunt's own pseudomimetic outlines and considerations.

I would argue that the same kind of relativization and dissolution of (or disillusion with) causality pervades and colors the whole of Leigh Hunt's discourse. The estrangement of foreign travel and residence is a recapturing of home and hearth, in other words a variant of familiarity.

> When I put on *my* cap, and pitched myself in imagination into the thick of Covent Garden, the pleasure I received was so vivid, I turned the corner of a street so much in the ordinary course of things, and was so tangibly present to the pavement, the shop-windows, the people, and a thousand agreeable recollections which looked me naturally in the face, that sometimes when I walk there now, the impression seems hardly more real. I used to feel as if I actually pitched my soul there, and that spiritual eyes might have seen it shot over from Tuscany into York-Street, like a rocket. (2:197)

This passage can be read with and through the Dante passage: Hunt is in Italy in order to restore and modify (simultaneously or in subtle overlappings) the environment of his own *Heimat*. Armchair traveling as a mode of reading becomes a mode of writing and of grasping the world even when this is not how things literally happened. Essentially what we have here is a taming of alienation, the inclusion of alienation among the accepted and familiar modes of dwelling in the world.

These are perhaps examples that are chosen with excessive care for their moral and even ideological purpose. Many other texts of the age can be submitted to similar focused analyses, but in as many or more the purpose is much more diffuse and the roving eye is more amiable, detached, mildly amused, and (deliberately?) superficial. Quantity seems to prevail over quality. The writings of the Prince of Pückler-Muskau's abundant work is an even better case in point.

Pückler-Muskau was an eccentric dandy, a wastrel, and a low-key, easygoing adventurer whose sub-Byronian wanderings were jotted down in overwhelming abundance and were duly noticed by his contemporaries. Grillparzer and Herwegh dedicated poems to him, and Goethe wrote one of his last (1830) reviews about the Prince's account of his residence in the English Isles; one of his formulas was impeccably exact: "He reports on the most monotonous things with the highest attention to individual diversity."[7] This is not to deny that Pückler-Muskau had his share of political biases. As a young man he was a liberal, close to Heine[8] and Laube, who thought of him as one of their own. Even later, when his views became more erratic, confused, or fantastic, he was able to produce pages of devastating irony on the parallels between slavery and modern Western forms of labor exploitation.[9] Nevertheless, Pückler-Muskau's greatest early work, *Briefe eines Verstorbenen*, is fundamentally a relaxed, horizontally roving depiction of English and Irish society, with an emphasis on the castles and parks of England (he speaks of himself as a "Parkoman"),[10] the curiosities of social life, and different prominent figures of the national scene. The narrative is quickened only by the piquant purposes of the tour: to support his extravagant expenses the Prince had divorced his eight-year-older wife and, with her knowledge and blessing (she is the addressee of his letters), was looking for a suitable and affluent new wife. The search turned out to be fruitless, but the press of the time had a field day with the story. Pückler-Muskau was inevitably dubbed "Prince Pickle" in England and became the object of a hilarious caricature in Dickens's *Pickwick Papers* (ch. 15 as Count Smorltork). None of these things deterred Pückler-Muskau, who continued energetically his traveling and published several volumes in the 1830s and 1840s, one signed "Semilasso" ("the half-tired one"). Some of the best or most meaningful episodes in these volumes are reenactments of cultural gestures or itineraries that had already acquired authoritative status. Thus in his Mediterranean pilgrimages Semilasso dutifully hunts out Byronian traces,[11] as well as occasional relics of Greek antiquity. Pückler-Muskau's voluble amiability obfuscated much, his readers must have thought, but it clearly also revealed much. The subordination to cultural models, the epigonic relish in hermeneutic description of an already existing order of monuments, the broad unfolding of natural and cultural intertwining, all struck a chord with the Biedermeier public and faithfully expressed mentalities widely encountered on both sides of the Atlantic. (This explains the considerable circulation of these works in several European languages, including American editions.)[12]

A somewhat similar figure, though from a totally different environment, was I. G. Codru-Drăgușanu (1818–1884), who published in 1865 an account of the travels undertaken from 1835 to 1844 in western Europe under the title *Peregrinul Transilvan* (the full title of which, in translation, would be The Transylvanian peregrine, or letters written from foreign countries to a friend in the homeland, from 1835 through 1848).[13] His picaresque expeditions were to take him from a remote Transylvanian village to the Romanian principalities, Austria, Switzerland, Germany, France, Italy, Russia, and England. Naturally enough his viewing angle is not that of a refined dandy like Pückler-Muskau, rather that of a quick self-tutored mind of enormous curiosity, naive and calculating at the same time. Much like Pückler-Muskau (or Leigh Hunt for that matter), he engaged in comparisons of the newly discovered realities with those in his homeland. Codru-Drăgușanu is neither overawed nor cowed in the face of the West. As a matter of fact his book often has the air of an orientalism turned inside out, with sarcastic and belittling notes towards the West. Still, most of Codru-Drăgușanu's text is at bottom a relaxed, benevolent meandering through the natural and cultural landscapes of Europe with some indifference towards further theorizing or a deepening of meanings. Such an attitude was of course not unusual in European writing of the time. Weakly structured blends of entertainment and information are quite frequent among the publications of the age and they need not detain us here.

It is of more import to ascertain that—deliberately or not—some of the best travelogs organize themselves not only as moral-allegorical imagery but also as meditations upon the relationship between mind and space. Scientific instruments (microscopes and telescopes) and technological advances (speed of transportation) had already shaken the traditional confidence in the stability and limitation of existential horizons. As mentioned above, opportunities for vertical social mobility and displacements of large masses of people (horizontally by emigration or war) had enhanced the need for rethinking the relativity of space in terms of a much more powerful, even arbitrary, subjective mind. Thus the ensuing travel literature found itself intimately involved in a renewed wrestling between space and mind, as well as in the dialectic effort to redefine a satisfactory balance between the two.

Investigating a good part of Thomas De Quincey's literary prose (*The Spanish Military Nun, The Revolt of the Tartars,* and *The English Mailcoach* for instance) shows that De Quincey's conception of travel was based on evasion and flight. To be sure, every travel story that we know is constituted out of alternations of nodes (or stops) and journeys or travels. However, in *The Spanish Military Nun* the latter make up only a small section (perhaps 25 percent or so) of the narrative, while the stops are long and prepare well the explosions that project the main character from one end of the world to the other. In *The Revolt of the Tartars* this kind of explosive flight covers the whole of the story, while in a key passage of *The English Mail Coach* a perfect fusion is achieved between cause and movement, idea and material (Nemoianu 1972). Clearly (and like Pückler-Muskau in a different way) De Quincey was trying to reproduce the travel experiences of the high romantics: the cosmic journeys of Byron's and Shelley's characters, the symbolic and consciousness expeditions of Wordsworth, Coleridge, and Southey (even leaving aside the universal or aesthetic expeditionary myths of Blake and Keats). At the same time De Quincey, partly through lack of creative energy, partly through intentional reluctance, tended to pull down these cosmic-symbolic expeditions to the level of historical concreteness, in other words towards the episodic and subjective. Up to a point the ambiguities of De Quincey's travel prose just express his personal discourse, but they also illustrate the more general (and more philosophical) tendency to use space and travel as a tool by which to examine the collapse of the large and the small, as well as the intimate intertwining of subjective consciousness with the objectivity of external space. A brief glance at two otherwise quite different writers of the 1820s and 1830s (William Cobbett and Karl Immermann) will confirm and expand this affirmation, and an equally quick look at a somewhat earlier writer, Xavier de Maistre, will encourage some tentative general conclusions on the connection between the conversational essay of the European Biedermeier and the uses of travel literature.

Among William Cobbett's numerous works,[14] *The Rural Rides* is perhaps the most famous and the one that was most often reread in later generations. I believe that the cause of its influence in Cobbett's own time, as well as later, was the masterful way in which the great radical populist combined several generic strands—political pamphlet, didactic treatise, conversational essay, patriotic proclamation, diary—into a coherent unit under the heading of the travel narrative. He began writing his reporterial essays, as one might call them, in September 1822, after he had given up farming for good and had turned definitively to publishing and politics as a career, and continued until October 1826, with interruptions. *The Rural Rides*[15] appeared in book form in 1830, but much of this material had already been known to the readers of Cobbett's *Political Register*. Cobbett was preoccupied at that time with two main issues. One was political: the need for an electoral reform to abolish the "rotten boroughs" and to give the middle and lower-middle classes an increased participation in running the affairs of the country. The other was economic—to stop the comprehensive spread of capitalist and transactional modes of production, consumption, and socioeconomic relations from liquidating the traditional agricultural patterns of existence in England. We have to add to this Cobbett's ardent patriotism, his romantic love and understanding of nature, his firm individualism, and his aesthetic preference for the harmonies of nature, history, and moral-religious sociability. *The Rural Rides* shows Cobbett's skill in structuring a material that is and remains empirical—indeed often drily factual and statistical—into a dramatic enactment of his purposes and leading values. Cobbett summons all the energies of the concrete, of palpable reality, in an attempt to block the "flight of substance" (as later philosophical generations were to call it) and the advances of a world of reduction and abstraction. His cavalcades in the countryside can be seen as a mobilizing effort, as a calling forth of the spirits—or better, of the spirit, of a sturdy and self-contained reality and of the worth of singular things—against levelling, alienating, transactional, and dissolving modes of relating to the outside world. He marshals all his forces: compassion for individual cases of hardship and suffering vividly described; indignation and insult at a high pitch, often akin to ranting; obsessive repetitions and returns to specific themes and enemies, the didactic mode drawing on his considerable store of farming, botanical, geological, marketing knowledge, and shrewd evocation of natural beauties. I will confine myself to a few examples of each.

Cobbett was a good hater and every few pages he explodes into imprecations against "the most cowardly, the very basest, the most scandalously base reptiles that ever were warmed into life by the rays of the sun!" (Cobbett 1983, 320).[16] The list of Cobbett's enemies is long and diverse. It begins with the conservative British governments of the 1820s seen as repressive wretches (205, 276), and Cobbett is not beyond gloating over the suicide of Castlereagh whom he had already declared mad.[17] It continues with the aristocracy and country gentlemen, fellows whose "foul ... stinking ... carrion baseness" is an object of wonder and indignation (320). It continues with the population of those he thinks of as parasitical "budgeteaters": "a tribe of pensioned naval and military officers, commisaries, quartermasters, pursers" (161), as well as the local parsons. It includes what Cobbett repeatedly characterizes as an "infamous press" (221), and it culminates with the financial middle classes—the stockbrokers and loan-jobbers and paper-money people—about whom he says, "The hellish system of funding must be blown up" (221).[18] And last but not least Cobbett's hatred often crystallizes in vituperation against religious or ethnic groups such as the Scots, the Jews, or the Quakers ("a sect a great deal worse than the Jews"; 225),[19] all groups that are engaged in mediation, circulation, displacement, and the unravelling of stable relations, productive activities, and natural creativity. This is in fact Cobbett's point, beyond his litanies, beyond his ranting, boasting, and cursing, beyond his paranoia and his continuous state of excitement, like that of a Blake having to deal with the minutiae of everyday life. His point is that the "paper system," the substitute reality of artificial concoctions—credit, fictional values, abstract transactions, debt, and taxations—in a word, modern capitalism—is oppressive, destructive, and exploitative, that it undermines the dignity of work and cuts off human ties with nature.

Cobbett's *The Rural Rides* thus becomes an inspection of the author's rightful inheritance and a surveying of his property—the age-old English countryside. He reports on the yet undecided battle between what he sees as common sense, truth, and justice, and an expanding spider's web of parasitism, artificiality, and alienation, which he still hopes will be just a passing historical aberration. Cobbett sometimes engages in veritable odes to production as opposed to exchange, as in the beautiful inset piece of October 22, 1826, from Hambleton: "Does not every one see, in a minute, how this exchanging of fairs and markets for shops creates idlers and traffickers; creates those locusts, called middle-men, who create nothing, who add to the value of nothing, who improve nothing, but who live in idleness, and who live well, too, out of the labour of the producer and the consumer" (479).[20] More often however he uses his surveying rides as an occasion to emphasize and place under the reader's eyes all the reasons why his own wounded countryside is a better and more desirable environment than the other one, slowly taking shape under his very eyes.

Cobbett's world is one of natural delight: "the high land upon my right, and the low land on my left. The fog was so thick and white along some of the low land, that I should have taken it for water, if little hills and trees had not risen up through it here and there" (189). It includes human oddities: "An immense house stuck all over with a parcel of chimneys, or things like chimneys; little brick columns, with a sort of caps on them, looking like carnation sticks, with caps at the top to catch the earwigs" (213), or more pastoral scenes: "Large sweeping downs, and deep dells here and there, with villages amongst lofty trees, are my great delight,"[21] and "This is my taste, and here, in the north of Hampshire, it has its full gratification. I like to look at the winding side of a great down, with two or three numerous flocks of sheep on it, belonging to different farms; and to see, lower down, the folds, in the fields, ready to receive them for the night" (257).[22]

To this defense of the natural Cobbett musters the voices of earlier authors. Here is Defoe: "The spot where the tree stands is about a hundred and twenty feet from the edge of a little river, and the ground on which it stands may be about ten feet higher than the bed of that river" (40).[23] Here is Smollett: "When I enter a place like this (the watering-place Cheltenham) I always feel disposed to squeeze up my nose with my fingers" because these "gluttons, drunkards and debauchees of all descriptions, female as well as male, resort at the suggestion of silently laughing quacks, in the hope of getting rid of the bodily consequences of their manifold sins and iniquities" (401). He comes across wandering beggars much like Wordsworth's solitary figures (112). Sterne's ironic drawings can also be encountered (142), and Cobbett reaches Swiftian intensities in his bitterly sarcastic defense of the productive poor.[24] However it is Goldsmith's voice above all that Cobbett borrows when he puzzles about the perils of American emigration, when he rants against the taxation system, even in a reference to a village called Auburn (115, 226, 266, 412) or more openly in the antithetical inserts: "Every thing about this farm-house was formerly the scene of *plain manners* and *plentiful living*. Oak clothes-chests, oak bedsteads, oak chests of drawers, and oak tables to eat on, long, strong and well supplied with joint stools. . . . But all appeared to be in a state of decay and nearly of disuse" (this passage is continued and developed in detail; cf. 226–27), or "The semicircular paling is gone; the basins, to catch the never-ceasing little stream, are gone; the iron cups, fastened by chains, for people to drink out of, are gone; the pavement all broken to pieces; the seats, for people to sit on, on both sides of the cave, torn up and gone; the stream that ran down a clean paved channel, now making a dirty gutter; and the ground opposite, which was a grove, chiefly of laurels, intersected by closely mowed grass-walks, now become a poor, ragged-looking Alder-Coppice" (250).[25]

The nostalgic-contrastive mode is one that Cobbett resorts to abundantly and over vast periods of time. Thus, although a Protestant himself, he extols the merits of Catholic medieval England—according to him an age of harmony, prosperity, and respect for the individual needs and dignity of simple rural laborers (230–31, 125–27, 249, 254–55, 351, 383, 387, 474). He does not fail to bring up the matter of the curtailed holidays, of the abolition of leisure, a typical anticapitalist battle-cry all over Europe (316).[26] As if intuiting early on the Weberian theories about the connection between Protestant ethos and the rise of capitalism, Cobbett compares unfavorably the English situation to that of France and Italy (120–21),[27] and he reserves a particular loathing for "Scottish feeolosofers" like Adam Smith, (315, 362, 395, 161), and to the liberal antislavery rhetoric that focuses on remote sufferings in order to hide the very real injustice and exploitation at home.[28]

Cobbett is particularly effective in limning little self-explanatory scenes of poverty and injustice, accompanied by almost biblical-prophetical appeals to pity and indignation: "What injustice, what a hellish system it must be, to make those who raise it *skin and bone and nakedness*, while the food and drink and wool are almost all carried away to be heaped on the fund-holders, pensioners, soldiers, dead-weight, and other swarms of taxeaters," or, in red-hot indignation after describing how men enlisted in the military forces, out of their mercy and pity, subscribe to help the poor: "Is not this one fact; this disgraceful, this damning fact; is not this enough to convince us, that *there must be a change;* that there must be a complete and radical change; or that England must become a country of the basest slavery that ever disgraced the earth?"[29]

In no case can it be said that Cobbett confines himself to mere evocations of pastoral beauty. His self-taught expertise as a geologist, botanist, or zoologist allows him to mix the esthetic, the didactic, and the scientific in pleasing and original ways that remind us of seventeenth- and eighteenth-century discursive modes, but that also—more closely and more revealingly—remind us of the dainty connoiseurship of his Biedermeier contemporaries De Quincey or Hazlitt. Cobbett is a Beau Brummell of farming sights and implements. He speaks of soils with the elegant preciousness that others might reserve for descriptions of wine vintages: "Upon the hill, begins, and continues on for some miles, that stiff red loam, approaching to a clay, which I have several times described as forming the soil at the top of this chalk-ridge. . . . At Riegate you find precisely the same soil upon the top of the hill, a very red, clayey sort of loam, with big yellow flint stones in it" (197). The qualities of the hops and beans are compared and earnestly judged (211), geographical itineraries are mapped out (214–15, 298), and as to the turkeys, the narrator avers

> that we had, this year, raised two broods at Kensington, one black and one white, one of nine and one of eight; but that about three weeks back, they appeared to become dull and pale about the head; and, that, therefore, I sent them to a farm-house, where they recovered instantly, and the broods being such a contrast to each other in point of colour, they were now, when prowling over a grass field amongst the most agreeable sights that I had ever seen. (230)

Arthur Young is declared to be wrong in calling "the vale between Farnham and Alton *the finest ten miles* in England" since Cobbett can prove that the "ten miles between Maidstone and Tunbridge is a great deal finer," and he explains why: the fruit orchards are more abundant, the river and the vale are three times as large, and the rising grounds six times as broad. These considerations in turn are the neighbors of comparisons to a completely different natural and geological formation— "that sort of beauties which we see about Guildford and Godalming, and around the skirts of Hindhead and Blackdown, where the ground lies in the form that the surface-water in a boiling copper would be in, if you could, by word of command, *make it be still,* the variously-shaped bubbles all sticking up" (256).[30]

Cobbett can be compared to the German essayist Justus Möser, with whom he was partly contemporary, in his keen sensibility to the values of local production and craftsmanship, to distinctions that go all the way down to the individual producer.[31] He thus in effect proclaims a state of things in which craftsmanship is still individual authorship, a nonalienated and highly personal production. Thus the wheat of Earl's Court is unfavorably compared to that grown "in the wealds of Sussex or of Surrey," and it dwindles to insignificance when we compare it with "the wheat on the South Downs, under Portsdown Hill, on the sea-flats at Havant and at Tichfield, and along on the banks of the Itchen!" (166). He bemoans the end of local clothmaking, and in reporting about the south English countryside he literally zooms in on individual figures—"The owner of the farm, who knew me . . . it was Mr. Hinton Bailey, of whom and whose farm I had heard so much" (258)[32]— country-gentlemen, farmers, or great landowners of the upper-aristocratic reaches. Despite all the similarities with Möser there are important differences also, dramatically illustrated by their different attitude towards hunting rights and poaching. Möser was ready to support feudal privileges as a bulwark against the fastcoming alienation and uniformity, even when he recognized their drawbacks. By contrast Cobbett worked very hard to prove that tradition is the best ally of the workingman, that the severe sentences against poaching[33] were inhuman, abusive, and a breach of the kind of natural humanity in which any type of legal and social tradition must have been rooted, positions akin in some ways to that of the American Founding Fathers or of some of J. F. Cooper's characters. Cobbett never accepted that the rights of man are inferior to the rights of or to property, as conservatives from Möser to P. E. More sometimes did.

Reading Cobbett's *The Rural Rides* we draw two main conclusions, both connected with perceptions and usages of space. The first is that the walks and rides in nature become, for the author no less than for the readers (contemporary, or of later generations), walks and rides through lines of discourse, ideas, and arguments directed in turn towards a defense of nature and of the natural way of life. Cobbett both identifies and substitutes the lines of ideological discourses with his meandering rides in the countryside, and he does so in order to defend and fortify the latter through the former. The second is a general relativization of space. On one level *The Rural Rides* is a response by Cobbett to farflung accounts of continental or, indeed, transcontinental expeditions. His bulky collection of reports is meant to prove that there is enough material even in a very limited area of a few counties and shires. The rural rides are meant to show infinity in smallness. "Endless is the variety in the shape of the high lands which form this valley" (298), Cobbett exclaims at one point, thus summarizing the spirit of his book: a recognition of the relativity of space. The increased structuring, the multiplicity of the contents, no less than the enhancing and organizing activity of the eye expand space, enrich it, and turn smallness into a satisfying universe.

Writing almost simultaneously with Cobbett was Karl Immermann, who published four different travelogs (one in 1833, two in 1835, and one in 1843) presenting his journeys through German-language areas between 1831 and 1837, during vacations taken from his duties as a judiciary official (*Landesgerichtsrat*) in Düsseldorf. In essential ways Immermann's narratives (I will refer only to the first and longest of them, *Reisejournal in drei Büchern*, 1833)[34] differ from Cobbett's texts. Immermann shuns political topics and shows no acquaintance with farming or the natural sciences. His social comments, when present at all, are mild and oblique. He is instead passionately interested in the cultural life of the cities he visited and gives rather detailed reports on theatrical performances, engraving cabinets, museums, and sundry architectural curiosities. There are also very great stylistic differences: Immermann has long and sinuous sentences while Cobbett uses a direct and aggressive discourse studded with appeals to facts and intense sentiments.

Despite all these differences—and others yet—Immermann shares with Cobbett the dilemma of concrete versus abstract space. On the one hand he relates with heavy irony the lightning tour of a group of students and their French schoolmaster who in the Saxon Alps are frankly indifferent to anything but "l'idée du Kuhstoll," (*Werke*, 4:125–26), and he thus comes out clearly in favor of narrative diversity while pleading against ideal portraits and ideological allegories; this is particularly obvious because in the text of book 2 the episode referred to is preceded by an excellent nature description of the same mountain scenery, representing thus Immermann's own approach. On the other hand large parts of Immermann's travelog are little else but leisurely walks through literary genres. Thus book 3, with small connective passages, merely steers the reader through the parabolic ballad, medieval legend, realistic story, short story, and so on. As a matter of fact the whole of book 3 is much closer in style to the novels of Peacock, with their underlying spoken, dialogated, and even dramatic structure, and are also close to Immermann's own novels, as has been shown by several critics.[35] Immermann seeks to reconcile these opposing pressures by turning towards cultural landscapes and human curiosities. He says quite early in his narrative: "Die Natur macht noch wenig Eindruck auf mich, ich habe das schwärmerische Versenken in das tote Zeug satt. Die Rheinlandschaft steht weit über Gebühr im Preise. Die Menschenwelt ist *meine* Welt. . . . Die Gruppe bleibt mir Hauptsache, Strom, Fels und Wald sehe ich als Nebenwerk an" (4:15). [Nature now impresses me rather little; I am fed up with the pathetic plunge into all this dead stuff. The Rhine landscape is much overrated. *My* world is the human world. . . . For me the main thing is the social group, stream, rock, forest I regard as secondary.] Thus Immermann, with all his repeated declarations in favor of concreteness, of the dignity of details and exterior diversities (4:142–43, 189), concentrates more on subjective, emotional, intellectual, and personal reactions. However, each time these larger effects are triggered by small occasions, a technique somewhat similar to that of De Quincey, as described above. For Immermann thereby traveling becomes an occasion for digression, for the stringing together of disparate thoughts. A romantic unity or even desire for the unitary coherence of cosmos, nature, the divine, the human, and the social is for Immermann irretrievably lost—what survives is a realm of dissimilitude. The thoughts and the actions that left by themselves would be patchy, motley, and even absurd borrow a kind of order from the time-space logic of traveling. This is good Biedermeier strategy, a taming of the universe for practical individual or social purpose, much as Cobbett's replaceable use of farming didactics and extolled natural beauties had also been Biedermeier strategies.[36]

At one point during a trip Immermann meets and frequents Ludwig Tieck, hears from him some opinions about Elizabethan stage arrangements, exclaims: "Welch ein Glück liegt im Empfangen einer neuen Idee!" (133) [What happiness one finds in the reception of a fresh idea!], and immediately launches into a disquisition on the possible combination between Greek, Elizabethan, and modern stagings. The beautiful and the useful merge under the impulse of a travel incident. It is also travel as a dynamic of displacement that empowers the narrator to defeat his own anxiety and to master huge realities such as the past, or the grasp of space. Charles Lamb had, less than fifteen years earlier, presented London in effect as a small cozy country town, a place of familiarity and security (*Geborgenheit*), and Immermann reports similar experiences. Thus for Immermann the Kingdom of Hannover is nothing but "ein grosser Pachthof" (one large leasehold estate; 214),[37] and the whole of the past is treated usually ironically, not with the hushed awe of the purer romantics (Novalis or Arnim), or of the great rhapsodes of ruins (a Volney, a Chateaubriand). Perhaps the most typical example is the description of Goslar as a city fallen from the heights of might and of the romantical sublime into the realm of the shabby-idyllic. (The remnants of the lofty past are grasped in the tones of professional and objective curiosity, not with exaltation, melancholy, or even nostalgia.)[38]

There is no need to argue that this approach towards space and travel (as a form of relating to space) requires certain discourse strategies and certain basic choices in the positioning towards space and its borders. Subjectivization of travelogs was not unheard of in the eighteenth century: it is enough to think of Sterne or Diderot. The dramatic opening up of spatial horizons on a global scale is however more in the nature of a sudden irruption, accompanying/causing romantic consciousness. For the travel narratives of the 1820s and 1830s such an expansion is taken for granted, and at the same time oddly unsatisfactory rather than surprising and spectacular. The prototypical response to this kind of dilemma was provided early on by Xavier de Maistre. This is not to say that he exerted much influence: Cobbett was certainly unaware of his writings, and it is quite unlikely that Immermann had heard of or read Xavier de Maistre. The point here is another one: for informed later readers he appears to express in a simple and exemplary way some basic options in the negotiations between consciousness and spatial movement.

Le lépreux de la cité d'Aoste (1811)—which was enthusiastically received by Lamartine and his friends and may have influenced *Jocelyn*—is an exploration of enclosed space and radical solitude. Its unabashed sentimentalism is only the reverse side of genuinely humane empathies and of a rather successful attempt to respond to existential solipsism by extending the boundaries of an internal universe. (Xavier de Maistre is in a sense a disciple of Leibniz, whose monads are occluded and hermetically sealed and yet, being structured like the universe, possess thereby a visionary communication with it.) The exploration of wide and exotic spaces is undertaken in *La jeune Sibérienne* (1815) and *Les prisonniers du Caucase* (1815), both narratives of flight, evasion, and wide-open spaces. The first of them in fact has strong similarities with De Quincey's narratives and Prascovie, the young Siberian girl struggling for the release of her parents from exile, resembles in certain ways the Spanish military nun.[39] The Caucasian prisoners also are caught between restraint into enclosed spaces and the dangers of huge, unstructured spatial unfoldings (steppes and high mountains). However Xavier de Maistre's most masterful treatment must remain his double work: *Voyage autour de ma chambre* (1795) and *Expédition nocturne autour de ma chambre* (1825), the second a deliberate resumption or repetition of the first; a comparison of the two in terms of the romantic (Wordsworthian or Hölderlinian) practice of repeated observations would be worth its while but has no place here. All the features of Biedermeier travel stories are combined here: flimsy pretexts leading to long subjective speculations and flights of imagination; the dwelling on details and small spaces; the prevalence of digression over a central concern; the relativization of space; and, not less important than these, a commingling of allegorical ideologies and value choices with descriptive concreteness. Xavier de Maistre gives his readers topographical information by sending his mind on expeditions. The "Voyage de quarante-deux jours autour de ma chambre," is full of "observations intéressantes" (interesting observations) and of a "plaisir continuel que j'ai éprouvé le long du chemin" (Maistre 1984, 31) [the continuous pleasure I experienced along the road], but also of mock-factual information: "Ma chambre est située sous le quarante-huitième degré de latitude . . . sa direction est du levant au couchant, elle forme un carré long qui a trente-six pas de tour, en rasant la muraille de bien près" (33–34) [My room is placed at forty-eight degrees latitude . . . its direction is from east to west, it forms a rectangle with a length of thirty-six steps along its walls], or "Après mon fauteuil, en marchant vers le nord, on découvre mon lit, qui est placé au fond de ma chambre, et qui forme la plus agréable perspective" (34). [After my armchair, walking north one discovers my bed, placed at the back of the room, which offers the most agreeable perspective.] Chapters on charity or imagination, comic disputes with Joannetti, the valet, or the faithful lapdog, Rosine, alternate with such descriptions. The tone is that of a more frivolous and lightly graceful Lamb rather than of a Sterne—a comparison often made. The enclosed space is defeated through a revelation of the thickness of existence and the delights of limitation. At the same time proximity is invested with the glamorous attributes of distance: thus each of them is appropriated by the other.

We are faced here, therefore, with a travel literature in the guise of the conversational essay: a dialectic of reality is bound up with the more formal yet more playful dialectic of narration and conversation, of ideology and moral didacticism. Xavier de Maistre in a prototypical way, but De Quincey, Immermann, Cobbett in broad variations, show how the close can become the distant and how the intimate can become the picturesque and the unusual. This kind of boundary displacement is a symptom of the small/large relativization and a (sometimes nervous) meditation thereon. It also exemplifies the meshing of social or moral concerns and a descriptive contemplation of the concrete.

The perception of space and movement, distance and boundary, by some of the less overtly aesthetic authors of the 1820s and 1830s—those placed between the broad range of passive readers and the most active shapers of philosophy and poetry—can also allow us to link them to larger themes of their age. The generations of later romantics, poetic realists, Biedermeier writers, and the Age of Restoration were the first to come to terms with the full impact of modernization: disjoining, atomizing, transactional modes of being, first in the West, but then increasingly on a global scale. The wrestling with this phenomenon still continues, even in the West, but even more so in the wide worlds of Asia, South America, and Africa, and an attentive scrutiny of responses in the first few generations is therefore a highly topical issue. After all, this analysis is one of our constant concerns in this book. Generally the responses to historical onslaughts (for example, of the breathtaking events of romantic challenge, revolutionary upheaval, rationalized terror, and world war—all experienced in a span of less than a quarter century) were remarkably creative and imaginative. The writers we just discussed are a case in point. The opening of spatial horizons and obliteration of boundaries through the violence and aggression of revolutions and wars, no less than the romantic fantastic raid to transcontinental targets, into the cosmos and beyond, found as a response the Biedermeier leisurely walk and the survey of confined domains. A delicate space organization repudiates the savagery of pure nature no less than the utilitarian exploitation of it, through an option in favor of a park-like, lightly controlled landscape, lovingly surveyed with a lingering on details and a continuous reference back to their multiple levels of significance.

Even more specific outcomes could ensue (even when they did not necessarily). Cobbett proved to be a seminal figure: one of the earliest and most characteristic spokesmen for modern populism. The bewildering combination of features that were later to be assigned to either the Right or the Left was specifically taken over by the distributism of Chesterton and Belloc in the early twentieth century, but was replicated on a broad scale, on left and right (as well as center), as images of good living and moderate and virtuous existence. The beauty and desirability of smallness was repeated from a poet and artist like William Morris to a social economist like E. S. Schumpeter. William Cobbett's *Advice to Young Men* (1829–1830)[40] is an outline of the Biedermeier ethos as convincing as any that was ever issued in Germany or central Europe at the time. The monogamous nuclear family is strongly affirmed; husbandly dominance in the house is explicitly requested (secs. 185–86, 190–93), but paired with the imperatives of conjugal fidelity (secs. 198–99, 203, 136–40) and of fairness in the sharing of housework (secs. 160–61, 173, 251–52) and maternal medical authority and competence (secs. 230–34). Over and above these are placed frugality (secs. 14–17, 24–25, 73, 91), a dislike of capitalism (sec. 21) and of the Protestant Reformation (secs. 50–51, 29), cleanliness (sec. 114) and a genuine learning ethos (section 44) not unlike the central-European one (see chapter 8 in this study). Section 99 presents a perfect short image of Biedermeier contentedness. It would be exaggerated to pretend that Cobbett's populist ethos was "learned" as part of his traveling in southern England (or even Canada and the newly independent United States, as he himself sometimes hints). Nevertheless there is a strong connection between the two. The density of the world, the importance of detail, the packed multiplicity of small things are all fundamental features of a worldview inside the horizons of which a Cobbettian kind of populism becomes possible.

Moral landscapes, travel as the philosophy of space and time, literary voyage as "fabula mundi," natural and cultural reports as intersections of informational structure and narrative urges—all these possibilities come together when travelogs gradually tend to coincide with the already existing subgenre of the "cultural physiognomy." Oliver Goldsmith's poem "The Traveller" (1764) was an example of this mode of synthesizing and generalizing description.[41] Volney's *Les ruines* (1791), a work quite different in purpose (philosophy of history), scope, and expressive medium acted in the same philosophical-cultural direction. While these and other eighteenth-century attempts always tended to remain somewhat abstract (and seemed to obey neoclassical traditional rejoinders towards general typology and allegory), after the French Revolution and the Napoleonic wars pressures towards immediacy and concreteness tend to gain the upper hand. In the early nineteenth century this well-established genre of cultural physiognomy became usually much more detailed, a peregrination through the mind and customs of a nation, and that is why it merged with the travelog. We have just seen how in the most typical of the time's travel literature intellectual processes and patterns hidden behind and in the surface details of reality are thrown into relief. The cultural physiognomy is even less bashful about its aims. The presentations of physical details are kept to a minimum, incidents and anecdotes that do not feed the argumentative discourse become scarce, moral and ideological elements are highlighted. Nevertheless these texts can still be regarded as contiguous and solidary with travel literature: their purposes are the same. Hazlitt and others provided transitional examples (missing links), but Germaine de Staël's *De l'Allemagne* remains perhaps the foremost example of this writing mode and the (unclassifiable) Karl Julius Weber (1767–1832) will provide confirmation.

William Hazlitt's *Notes of a Journey through Italy and France* (1826)[42] is not only a lively and substantial work betraying multiple interests, but one in which the chief typologies of romantic/Biedermeier travelog are incorporated. Thus comments on place and space abound: Hazlitt is masterful in individualizing locality:

> I grant the Simplon has the advantage of Mont Cénis in variety and beauty and in sudden and terrific contrasts, but it has not the same simple expansive grandeur,

blending into one vast accumulated impression; nor is the descent of the same whirling and giddy character, as if you were hurried, stage after stage, and from one yawning depth to another, into the regions of "Chaos and Old Night." The Simplon presents more picturesque points of view; Mont Cénis makes a stronger impression on the imagination. (280)

In only a few sentences or paragraphs Venice, Bologna, Florence, or Turin gain precise identities. About Venice: "you view it with a mixture of awe and incredulity . . . Genoa stands *on* the, sea, this in it. . . . You feel at first a little giddy; you are not quite sure of your footing as on the deck of a vessel" (267).

At the same time Hazlitt surpasses most of his contemporary travel writers in his uses of intertextuality and in deliberate references to previous literature (of actual travel or of pure imagination). His references, reiterations, and resumptions span an area from Sinbad the Sailor (121) to Chateaubriand (133, 235–36), the papal and Vatican descriptions, or the descriptions of Venice in chapters 22 and 23 and to the abundantly mentioned or quoted Walter Scott (141, 151, 158, 173, 202, 206, 254, 279).[43] Actual replications, rewritings, counterwritings, or referential frameworks for the traveler are furnished by Milton (218), Rousseau (155, 182, 297), Sterne (178), Dante (251), and Stendhal (250), among many others.[44] The process reaches a kind of culmination with the defiantly playful interjection of the fund of imagery common to the romantic sublime: Wordsworth and Coleridge, Byron and Shelley on Alpine impressions are placed together in a kind of brilliant collage. A good part of chapter 14 (188–93) is a weaving of quotations or allusions from Shelley, Scott, Byron, and Wordsworth into a general image of the lofty, desolate, and horrid, "wild grandeur and shadowy fears," or Albrecht von Haller's idyllic freedom ("rustic simplicity and . . . pastoral grace," 193). The Grand Chartreuse is thrown in for good measure ("Life must there seem a noiseless dream; death a near translation to the skies," 189), while a Coleridgean "headlong turbid stream" in a "dark wood of innumerable pine-trees" with "On our left, a precipice of dark brown rocks" appears against "summits . . . bright with snow and with the midday sun," all in the manner of Kubla Khan's creation. Similarly the presence of Mont Blanc is evoked a little later in patently Shelleyan language ("You stand, as it were, in the presence of the Spirit of the Universe, before the majesty of Nature," 292). These rewritings are bolstered by passages of textual interaction with Byron (287), Wordsworth ("Might I once more see the coming on of Spring as erst in the spring-time of my life . . ." [217]) and Leigh Hunt (1850, 2:193).[45] As a matter of fact in what might well be considered a key to the whole enterprise Hazlitt offers some metadescriptive considerations: "In traveling we visit names as well as places" (281), an opinion well understandable in one who had just declared: "Words may be said, after all, to be the finest things in the world. Things themselves are but a lower species of words, exhibiting the grossness and details of matter" (207), and "traveling confounds our ideas, not of place only, but of time" (282). He concludes by saying that "a thousand miles from home ... every object one meets is a dream" (282), an idea developed in the last two paragraphs of the narrative-alienation (that is, the oneiric quality of the experience abroad) is necessary in order to "dispel false prejudices," as well as "enlarge one's speculative knowledge" (303), or, in contemporary discourse, discover and experience Otherness.

Hazlitt's could equally well be classed with travel accounts of ideological and moral geography; if anything the political element is in the pages of *Notes of a Journey* more emphatic than elsewhere. His anti-Catholic prejudices are robust and eloquently expressed (214–16; also 235–36). His nationalism is equally unabashed (129–35, 139–41), and the Bonapartist sympathies come through occasionally (175), while the full-blooded liberal attitude is present everywhere, for example, on the issue of Jewish rights (233) or in a piece of fine sarcasm on the Biedermeier fear of the written word and the sealing up by Piedmontese border authorities of a box containing books by Bacon, Destutt de Tracy, and the *Edinburgh Review* as if it had been "filled with cartridge paper or gun-powder" (186). Similarly remarkable is the passionate diatribe against the Stuarts (244–45). Hazlitt is preeminently the representative of a historical moment (in Germany and eastern Europe as well as in Italy or in England) in which nationalism was thought to be the best expression of liberal intentions: "I would not wish to lower any one's idea of England; but let him enlarge his notions of existence and enjoyment beyond it. He will not think the worse of his own country, for thinking better of human nature" (301, in the guise of a conclusion).

Despite all these rich interests and multivalent intertextualities, Hazlitt's *Notes of a Journey* will have to be judged on the whole as an exercise in cultural physiognomy. Hazlitt validates his writing as a kind of survey of cultural mentalities, a political gesture to some extent (as the quotation in the previous paragraph indicates) but also as the ideally superior form of travel—armchair traveling at its most exquisite and distilled. One of Hazlitt's chief passions and curiosities to which he returns time and again is national comparison and characterization. "In France, one lives in the imagination of the past; in England every thing is new and on an improved plan" (92), and the long passage, full of malicious jabs, on French behavioral patterns (95–99)—"licentious in his pleasures, nay gross in his manners," "inconsequentiality in the French character," "passes over the most offensive smells," "inordinate desire to shine," among others—set the tone from the beginning. This is followed up with free and frequent incursions into the area of national physiognomy. "A Frenchman has no object in life but to talk and move with éclat and when he ceases to do either, he has no heart to do anything" (172) he muses, while on the Milanese he says, "Their animation was a little exuberant; their look almost amounts to a stare, their walk is a swing, their curiosity is not free from an air of defiance" (278). The rapid strokes used in depicting Holland seem inspired by Goldsmith's *The Traveller:* "The rich uninterrupted cultivation, the marks of successful industry and smiling plenty, are equally commendable and exhilarating;" and "The towns and villas in Holland are unrivalled for neatness, and an appearance of wealth and comfort," but also "There is something lumpish and heavy in the aspect of the country;" and, more trenchantly "Holland is, perhaps, the only country you gain nothing by seeing. It is exactly the same as the Dutch landscapes of it" (300–301). Meanwhile Hazlitt is not beyond questioning his own writing and thinking habits, the cast of mind that sets some kind of implicit human standard (arbitrary yet nationalistically subjective), the deviations from each (that is, the Otherness of national characteristics, such as Spanish gravity or French lack of it) are ironically stigmatized (143). Yet it is a procedure that he and his contemporaries use; a main difference is precisely Hazlitt's resolute conclusion: "These things are extensions of one's idea of humanity" (301).

Furthermore Hazlitt is intelligently perceptive of the historical dimensions inherent in geographical difference. He notices distances in degree of modernization and urbanization between England and the Continent (118–19, or 200). His grasp of the "spirit of the age" (261; "Not a Madonna scrawled on the walls near Rome, not a baby-house figure of the Virgin, that is out of character and costume," or 117; "I am inclined to suspect the genius of their religion may have something with the genius of their poetry. . . . Their churches are theatres; their theatres are like churches") confirms here as elsewhere that Hazlitt is a true forerunner of such cultural morphologists as Taine, Spengler, and Friedell.

The largest and best evidence of Hazlitt's transitional status—halfway between real traveling and cultural diagnostic—is provided by the aesthetic civilizational passages in the *Notes of a Journey*. These show Hazlitt stepping beyond the game of national physiognomy that Karl Julius Weber was contemporaneously raising to perfection (and that would still continue far into the future, all the way to the turn-of-the-century writings of Count Keyserling) and outlining a type of discourse that, as we know, was to reach maturity with Burckhardt and Pater. It is not just that Hazlitt describes with vigor and discrimination great museums and artistic styles, for example the Louvre (107–10) or "the Gallery at Florence" and the Pitti Palace (220–27) or the treasures of Roman collections (237–41). The point is that, at their best, Hazlitt's works literally turn geography into cultural history: a tapestry of human achievement with all its material and spiritual achievements. Nor is this procedure confined to cultural artifacts, because it can be seen at work equally well elsewhere, for instance in the description of Appenine village mountains: the landscape is transformed into a romantic cultural artifact ("suspended on the edge of a precipice," "bleak tract of . . . dark morass," "lonesome still loftier peak saluted the sky," "a brook brawled down," and so forth [208]). Hazlitt's *Notes of a Journey* is therefore situated on the exact dividing line between straight description (albeit on an ideologically or philosophically tailored material) and the wandering through the worlds and words of sociocultural landscapes and physiognomies.

That particular dividing line had already been crossed by Germaine de Staël in a book that was received with much more acclaim than Hazlitt's and was to become many times more influential than Hazlitt's. De Staël's *De l'Allemagne* had been finished in 1810 after six years of work. Napoleonic police officers stopped the book's publication, destroyed all five thousand printed copies, and exiled the author. She and her son managed to save the manuscript and one or two sets of proofs when crossing the frontier by hiding them on their person. *De l'Allemagne* first appeared in 1813 in London, but the French original had already been preceded by German and English translations. The book has never since been out of print. Its influence was enormous, particularly on the literary generation that occupied the French literary scene in the 1820s and the 1830s (Hugo, Vigny, Musset, and their generation). It is divided into four parts, moving roughly from the more material and circumstantial to the ineffable and spiritual. Thus the first part deals with geography, climate, manners, and sociopsychological environment. The second part deals with German language and literature. The third part deals with German philosophy and ethics (as philosophical theory and social practice). The fourth part deals with religion and *enthousiasme* (that is, spiritual fervor and subjective intensity).

Several short remarks on de Staël's literary strategies are worth noting if we are to understand the originality of *De l'Allemagne* and its place as a typological turning point inside travel literature. The first is that she tends to avoid causal statements. The different levels of German culture are not overtly placed in causal relationships, even though they are seen as concentric circles and even though cross-connections and analogies are often pointed out, hinted at, withdrawn again, or surprisingly sprung on the reader. The second observation is that in *De l'Allemagne* de Staël confirmed once again her position as the true originator of modern comparatism. Goethe and Herder alone among her contemporaries are close to her in that respect, but I believe she surpasses the former in the actual praxis of cultural comparatism and the latter in theoretical acumen and critical lucidity. (Even academic comparatism grew out of the Coppet circle[46] that had assembled around her: both Sismondi and August Wilhelm Schlegel had been her friends and, one may say, satellites.) In each part of *De l'Allemagne*[47] shrewdly detailed comments on French (or English, or Italian) literature and philosophy provided the referential and contrastive background to the German description (for example, pt. 3, chs. 2, 3; or pt. 2, ch. 1; or pt. 1, ch. 9, among many others). *De l'Allemagne* stabilizes, articulates, and furnishes examples for the theoretical space de Staël had staked out for herself ten years earlier in *De la littérature.*

Another key rhetorical strategy used by de Staël is the dispersal of the text. The continuous digressions in *De l'Allemagne,* the flight in several directions at once, the play at the margins, the unpredictability of textual directions, ultimately find expression in the veritable fireworks of witty bon mots and in the pulverization of textual coherence in separate, pointed, discontinuous, needle-sharp sentences. (Such explosions of wit can be found everywhere, but to give an example, pt. 2, ch. 9, as well as most of pt. 1 are successions of brilliant aphorisms and memorable ironic diagnostics.) These dispersals can be seen under two different angles, one connected with gender, the other with genre. In the first case the reader is struck by the proximity of Germaine de Staël's discourse to the description of French feminist critics such as Luce Irigaray or Julia Kristeva of "le parler femme": dispersal and marginality, multiplicity and refusal of strict logic (Moi 1985, 102–73). In the second case one is bound to recognize the chapters in *De l'Allemagne* as excellent examples of conversational essays, well in the mode of Lamb (or even Addison or Montaigne). Chapters such as pt. 4, ch. 6 ("De la douleur"), pt. 4, ch. 10 ("De l'enthousiasme"), pt. 2, ch. 14 ("Du goût"), as well as any chapter in part 1 do not hide their autonomy as disquisition, digression, and displaceable unit. The pointillist character of Mme de Staël's writing is further enhanced generically by its connection to the powerful line of French moralist writing (from La Rochefoucauld to her contemporary Chamfort, who had been adapted as a model by Friedrich Schlegel also).

An array of these and other rhetorical strategies is put firmly in the service of de Staël's psychological geography. It is not as if she had invented the research of national cultural traits. As I said before, this mode of travel writing was a commonplace. In the eighteenth century it was often derided, and already in the seventeenth century guides to the formulaic presentation of travel accounts (detailed point-by-point outlines and the like) were prepared (for example, William Davison in 1633 and Count Leopold Berchtold in 1789; in fact the abovementioned *Demokritos* by Weber is an elaborate variation upon the topos of national characteristics).[48] However, Germaine de Staël was innovative in several important ways (as well as displaying superior strategic intelligence). Mme de Staël was quite conscious and deliberate about what she was doing and clearly set herself in the mode of Xavier de Maistre and of all those who transferred the aura of the mysteriously exotic to the space of near immediacy. In the introduction to *Corinne ou l'Italie* she wrote warmly about the "moment où les objets nouveaux deviennent un peu anciens, et créent autour de vous quelques doux liens de sentiment et d'habitude."[49] She showed how to apply this approach not to a room or a house but to a whole culture by analyzing in depth one national culture and mapping out its internal structures and contradictions. She connected deftly sociogeographic and linguistic features with literary and cultural ones, in ways that established her as a pioneering zeitgeist theorist on the same level with Hazlitt and other contemporaries (cf. pt. 3, chs. 8–11, or pt. 1, ch. 5).[50] She seeks her equal in the perfect way in which she blends cultural geography with ideological intention, that is, the proclamation of romantic ideals and principles. This of course had been done for centuries in the treatment of Rome and Greece, but the use of Germany as physical embodiment of an alternative canon must have been perceived as a witty and defiant paradox precisely by contemporary readers with a very powerful referential background on classical antiquity: Germany was set up as the counter-Greece.

While de Staël can easily trip on details (one example is "Walstein" for Schiller's "Wallenstein," presumably following Benjamin Constant's version, in pt. 2, ch. 18, and everywhere else; another is "Cornelie" for "Cordelia," in pt. 2, ch. 27), she emerges as a superb critical analyst: her portrait of Elizabeth in Schiller's *Maria Stuart* (pt. 2, p. 18), as well as those of Joan of Arc (pt. 2, ch. 19) or of Mephisto and Faust (pt. 2, ch. 23), are masterpieces that Coleridge would have envied. Her hierarchy of the age's six great figures (Goethe and Schiller, Klopstock and Wieland, Lessing and Winkelmann [pt. 2, chs. 3–8]) was endorsed canonically for over a century thereafter (with the sole replacement of Winkelmann by Herder, who is otherwise well presented in pt. 2, ch. 30). More importantly these separate portraits and cameos combine into a configuration of the golden age (pt. 1, ch. 19: "Ne croit-on pas rencontrer un trait de l'âge d'or") with touches of the idyllic society in the description of the rural feast at Interlaken (pt. 1, ch. 20).

In turn, the spirit of Germanness, as described by de Staël coincides with romanticism (pt. 2, ch. 1; or pt. 4, ch. 15, as well as pt. 2, ch. 24, on Zacharias Werner, a personal friend and protégé). In an even more general sense this intermeshed romantic/German/idyllic discourse is identified with the spirit of chivalry (pt. 1, ch. 4)—a subversive element in the protototalitarian Europe being erected at the time by Fouché and the Duc de Rovigo for Napoleon. However this "esprit de chevalerie" [the modern equivalent for the heroic age] can be now perceived only dimly; it is "une empreinte effacée" [a pale trace] and "(il) règne . . . pour ainsi dire passivement" [it reigns . . . so to say, passively], and the cause is clear for Mme de Staël to state: "Rien de grand ne s'y fera désormais que par l'impulsion libérale qui a succédé dans l'Europe à la chevalerie" (vol. 1, p. 73) [From now on nothing great will be accomplished in Europe except by the liberal impulse, the successor of chivalry.] Following consistently this insight, the author preserves as the most general outline for her abstract "travelog" a movement through the German psyche as a search for signals against absolute dictatorship and its leftist roots. The ruthless reaction of French censorship is evidence of its correct and intelligent assessment of the long-range subversive dangers posed by *De l'Allemagne*.

Germaine de Staël is, no less than Benjamin Constant, the author of deliberate and efficient efforts to provide a coherent centrist, liberal, and moderate alternative to dictatorship, revolution, and stagnation—an alternative that (as European Biedermeier) was in fact to shape in depth the first half of the nineteenth century. In the Coppet group this moderating discourse had been discussed and formulated as a comprehensive ideological framework: republican, aristocratic, Protestant, Enlightenment, constitutional, and other elements were blended in it. De Staël's own version acknowledged this loosely common system (pt. 2, ch. 31) and highlighted a number of personal features. A certain distaste of Voltaire (pt. 3, ch. 3) and Rousseau (pt. 1, ch. 19) is noticeable, as well as a preference for the Schillerian dialectic of "naive" and "sentimental" (pt. 2, ch. 11). Philosophically de Staël may well be more astute than other members of the group in applauding Leibniz as the true source of romantic ideas (pt. 3, ch. 5) and, perhaps by implication, of her own rationalist/romantic discourse; further proof of originality is the bold inroad into a (yet unknown) chaos theory and new-age type scientific spirituality (pt. 4, ch. 9, in de Staël, 2:297–98).

Similarly personal additions to the same common fund of ideas are de Staël's thoughts about women's situation in society. She does not share Condorcet's energetic appeal for full civil rights and legal equality of women (Gwynne 1969, 176–80). Nevertheless, in keeping with her centrist efforts she outlines a kind of "feminism within the family" that is not without interest (see pt. 3, ch. 19, and pt. 4, ch. 12), and she certainly proclaims loud and clear the right of the outstanding and creative individual (man or woman) to be heard and to influence society.

De Staël's own version of liberalism descends from the views of Montesquieu and runs parallel with those of Destutt de Tracy, but perhaps also of Mallet du Pan (whom she apparently did not know): a virtuous republic or a constitutional monarchy in the English mode are both desirable possibilities (Gwynne 1969, 102–13).[51] But unlike these—and more strongly than even Benjamin Constant—she emphasizes the ethical and religious sources and dimensions of classical liberalism (pt. 3, ch. 13). (It is a well-known fact that in the last years of her life and career Mme de Staël was moving back closer to mainstream Christianity [Balayé 1979, 174–75, 185–90].) The morality of sentimental attitudes (pt. 3, chs. 17–19) is, in her view, what must envelop and inform existentially any true liberalism, one exempt of materialism and rationalism (pt. 3, ch. 2).

This rather coherent ideological project is, I submit, a chief blueprint behind *De l'Allemagne*, a book meant as a psycho-cultural diagnostic, a voyage of and through the mind, but also as a discourse of moderation and depth, an allegory of centrist idealism.

In a sense any survey of travel literature in the early nineteenth century must come full circle, from centrality to marginality and back to centrality, because that is the route of travel literature itself. The discourse of entertainment, escape, and serene description is continuously being devoured by the discourse of cultural concern, utilitarian alert, and earnest cognition. The flight from pure and major literature towards extracanonical fields is soon reversed. Formally travel literature develops its own conventions,[52] content-wise it joins in the urgent spiritual and mental preoccupations of the age. After all, typologically *De l'Allemagne* is not the final stop. Tocqueville's *Democracy in America* goes farther yet: it is a political treatise in the guise of a travel book.

Travel literature in the first half of the nineteenth century is marked by a defeat; it suffers in its vain wrestling for a preservation of the immediacy and concreteness of space. On the contrary, through (willing or unintended) participation in the colonial impulse travel literature contributes to globalization and the endangerment of Otherness that, programmatically, it had tried to counteract. This is the point made with passionate fury by Mary Louise Pratt on travel writing about South America. It is at best a very partial argument. In the most penetrating and suggestive passages of her book, Pratt refers correctly to the key role of extra-European perception in the emergence and the sustained growth of romanticism (137–38).[53] This, to put it in my own words, is the globalizing, comprehensive vision (or attempted vision) on which any or all high romanticism is predicated. The more modest Biedermeier approach deals of course in specifics. Even assuming that all of Pratt's indictments will stand up in court (and they will not, and do not), any fair observer will admit that there is another side here: the emancipation of the reader of travel writing, the liberation of consciousness from the shackles and prejudices of unvarying environments and preimposed and prescribed modes of seeing and thinking. This expansion and liberation may have been vicarious and muted, but it was real and important nevertheless, a kind of transition and awakening. There is in each travel account a genuine and honest "effort to overcome cultural distance," to turn the travel report into a vehicle for mediating "our knowledge of things foreign" and the arduous climb towards neutralizing the shock inherent in the "perception of similarity within radical difference." The positions taken by Pratt and by other contemporary Western critics, while rife with generous indignation and ruthless self-criticism, express, ironically, the provincial limitation, the Western-centeredness, and indeed the domination desire that they castigate so loudly in their predecessors (Porter 1991, 1, 12). For instance they ignore almost entirely the accounts of the writers at the "dominated periphery" about their travels in Europe. The travel notes of the Hungarian József Irínyi in France, England, and the German lands (1846), the excursions of the Romanian Nicolae Filimon in Austria and southern Germany (1858), Józef Ignacy Kraszewski's Italian and German notes transmit chiefly their authors' admiration for the West and a desire to emulate its mode of life and capitalist and rationalist structures. A very interesting case is that of Russian literature, which was very rich in Asianist (orientalist) no less than in Europeanist expeditions. Perhaps the most influential over the years proved to be the voyage reports of Radishchev and N. M. Karamzin, forefathers of Russian romanticism. Karamzin visited the West and expressed his admiration for the modernizing progress and the liberal intellectual movements there, offering them as examples for his native land. Radishchev described his trip from St. Petersburg to Moscow and, while negative towards his homeland, implicitly applied Western rationalist categories in judging the observed realities. Eastern European reports of this kind are matched by those of visitors to the "center" from Asia, the Middle East, and South America. It is only by the end of the nineteenth century that an awakening right-wing nationalism began to generate anti-Western comments and travel materials supportive of indigenous modes of life. A convenient turning point for travelogs of this kind is provided by Dostoyevsky's disappointed relation of contacts with the West (1863), in which many Slavophile tones are sounded. Later texts coming out of eastern Europe often adopt anticapitalist, antidemocratic, and anti-Semitic stances.

Finally, an important point has been made by Friedrich Wolfzettel in his commentaries of the "picturesque" and the "exotic": that French travel writers of the nineteenth century, far from wishing to impose imperialist conformity on peripheral areas, were desperately seeking spots on the globe where rationalist and industrial streamlining had not yet become prevalent. The quest for the picturesque is a defensive gesture; travel authors are allies of the about-to-be-colonized, they seek areas of organic history / nature interaction, areas where the unique rather than the stereotype and repetitive should prevail. Mary Louise Pratt sets against the Linnean aggression of the West the creativity of Peruvian women—communal, ecological, non-Western, female—that is, she finds there all the marks of a late-twentieth-century Western utopianism (Pratt 1992, 201–29). Much of nineteenth-century travel literature is similar: it seeks, in a utopian fashion, in exotic alterity salvation from the pressures of the home situation. Both manipulate and distort (to some extent) the other to achieve their own purposes, but it would be unfair to accuse any of the sides of invidious aims or adherence to domineering impulses when in fact they are grasping nervously for enclaves of avoidance. It is more often the stern-faced critics who distort the dialectic of alterity and identity by reifying both (Europe and the Orient) and by denying the multistrandedness of their reality, as Henry James had recognized already in 1875 ("If cleanliness is next to godliness, it is a very distant neighbor to chiaroscuro," 129).

In short, an adequate examination of the role of travel literature in serving the interests of one constituency or the other and in shaping an authoritative world image can be obtained only after examining the abundant dialectic of mutuality and alterity that this type of literature uncovers. A good first methodological step is provided by an older article from Henry H. H. Remak,[54] which painstakingly placed face to face the reciprocal images of Otherness together with their semantic connotations (and reductions). What Remak did on a European level can be interestingly transferred to a global scale, thus providing the foundation for a truly dialectical and interactive understanding of travel literature. This would be a good way of turning the defeat of Biedermeier travel literature into a kind of strength.

At the same time this very kind of writing registered two clear resounding victories. The first was to adduce, through its very existence, conclusive evidence that pleasure in general and aesthetic patterning in particular could act as powerful and efficient vehicles of cognition, that the sublime and the individual could serve very comprehensive social goals such as the assimilation of the world, packaging of information, and expansion of existential possibilities. Romantic universality could be translated or parceled out (much in Biedermeier fashion) into space sections and organized into practical units. The travel of the age was placed between a yearning search for the picturesque (or, better said, escape from the pressures of modernizing rationality and social conformity) and an effort towards ethnography (that is, almost the opposite: the attempt to integrate through an adequate discourse the values of a pristine and organic vitality into modern civilization). For most of travel literature the task of harmonizing these models was taken up with alacrity and joy, and, I think, solved in a satisfactory way if we look at the larger picture. The picturesque must be seen as a defensive category, a mode of saving the traveler's own zones of subjectivity, irrationality, and subversion by an alliance with extra-European, or at least "uncivilized" landscapes. The purpose of the images is to evoke the memory of a lost unity of humanity and its natural environment.[55]

The second great victory of travel literature was its continued ability to function as "a central vehicle and symbol of intellectual growth in ... life ... morality, and ... society" (Curley 1976, 1). Whether the early-nineteenth-century writers still clung to the view of their traveling grandfathers—that of a certain common ground in rational, psychological and moral homogeneity in all climes—is not at all clear and probably varies from case to case. Nevertheless, along with the epistemological value of travel writing, its continued ethical energy is preserved.[56] As I suggested from the very beginning, the most general referential level of travel literature remains the idea of the pilgrim soul, of the *homo viator*. The temporary nature of human existence and our yearning to return elsewhere, to our true homeland, are Christian topoi most explicitly (and with greatest popular appeal) expressed by Bunyan in *Pilgrim's Progress*. Echoes of these spiritual meanings and value-laden concepts can still be heard in the secularized versions of Biedermeier travel writing, and the resulting indeterminacy has its own piquancy; the imaginary poetic travel of Coleridge, Southey, or Byron contributes to the satisfying complexity of these discourses.

While generalization of this kind must always remain somewhat dubious, we can nevertheless say that the body of travel literature acted, at least in the early nineteenth century, as a surprisingly effective moderating discourse. Like historical fiction, like the learning ethos, like the numerous variants of conservative liberalism or the forms of religiousness founded on aesthetic harmony, travel literature sought to provide an area of centrality and compromise. Travel literature tried to respond to the assaults and dilemmas of an accelerating historical process and to the unraveling of organic textures and bonds of tradition by enacting solutions and proposing alternative forms of conjunction and cohesion. Its archi-text was definitely one of compromise and negotiation.

Notes

1. For a more complete development of the historical-literary assumptions in this chapter, see Nemoianu 1984. For the philosophical underpinning, see Nemoianu 1989. For a full presentation of German travel literature of the time see Sengle 1971–1980, 2:238–77. Cf. also Popa 1971 and the theoretically interesting book by Papu (1967). For an overview cf. also George Gingras, "Travel," in Seigneuret 1988, 2:1292–1331. It is interesting that the romantics themselves had an intuition of the impact of globalization on themselves (see Hummelt 2003).

2. Though marred by exaggeration and injudicious partiality, Pratt manages to add something to our understanding of the encounter between the consciousness of modernity and traditional organic structures of existence.

3. The first edition, later amended, was published in Paris by De Soye et Bouchet, 1859. Ralet lived ca. 1817–1858.

4. Another interesting contrast is provided by the conservative Austrian author Jakob Fallmerayer (1790–1861), who was considered a great stylist throughout the nineteenth century but was later forgotten. He was a great admirer of both Byzantium and Istanbul. He

called Istanbul "the metropolis of the globe" and concluded a glowing and baroque descriptive passage by saying: "This is a world in itself, an Atlantis of bliss, a store-house of human delight, the seat of contradictions, lonely and full of movement, earth and water, the huge global preserve filled with the aroma of flowers, lights, shadows and long caravans, filled with the musically rushing play of waves, crowded with gondolas and cruising dolphins. This is the enormous fortress of the old continent, separated from the East and West by large deserts, from the South and North by raging water straits. To rule powerfully here is to be obeyed by the whole world," from "Fragmente aus dem Orient" (Stuttgart und Tübingen: Cotta, 1845, originally serialized in 1840 in *Allgemeine Zeitung*), 339, and Sengle 1971–1980, 2:256.

5. The *Mémoires* were written from 1811–1841 and first published in serialized form between October 21, 1848, and July 3, 1850, in *La Presse*. *Atala* appeared in April 1801, *René* in 1802, as part of *Génie du christianisme*. *Les Natchez* (conceived much earlier) appeared in 1826 and the *Voyage en Amérique* in February 1827.

6. Hunt 1850. References in the text are to this edition.

7. Goethe's review appeared in *Jahrbücher für Wissenschaftliche Kritik* 56 (September 1830): 468–72. Cf. Weimarer Ausgabe, Abt. 1, vol. 42, 55ff. Goethe later had some correspondence with Pückler-Muskau and is reported to have expressed privately high appreciation of him. Grillparzer wrote his verses in 1840, Herwegh in 1841. Immermann, who had himself written travel literature, also praised the Prince. Pückler-Muskau's book was published as *Briefe eines Verstorbenen. Ein fragmentarisches Tagebuch aus Deutschland, Holland, England, Wales, Irland und Frankreich, geschrieben in den Jahren 1826 bis 1829*, vol. 1 (Munich: Franckh, 1830), vol. 2 (Stuttgart: Hallberg, 1832), but the authoritative editions are considered those of 1836 and 1837.

8. Heine wrote in complimentary ironic tones about him, calling him "a romantic Anacharsis, the most fashionable of all eccentrics, a Diogenes on horseback" (1854). Cf. "Lutezia: Berichte aber Politik, Kunst und Volksleben" in Heine 1893, 4:131–38.

9. Pückler-Muskau 1841, 2:416–425 (passage on Zante), ending in the words: "Oh slavery is sweet! Do believe me, dear liberals!"

10. Pückler-Muskau 1991, 1:545, in the seventeenth letter of 1827. Indeed the numerous and subtly discriminating park descriptions are among the most striking features of the book. The voices of Smollett, Scott, Hazlitt, Hunt, Wordsworth, the Gothic novelists, and even Dickens can be recognized in its pages, along with the admiration of civilized order and misgivings about it. Pückler-Muskau 1841, 3:2, in the passage on Cephalonia.

11. Pückler-Muskau 1841, 3:2 (passage on Cephalonia).

12. A sizable though less than complete edition of the "Tour in England, Ireland and France" translated by Mrs. Sarah Austin appeared in 1832 in London and was promptly published in Philadelphia also (1833). "Tutti frutti" (translated by Edmund Spencer) was released by Harper and Brothers in New York in 1834 and seems to have been taken over in 1836 in London; in 1845 a three-volume narrative of Pückler-Muskau's Egyptian travels appeared in London. The earliest French translation appears to have been a six-volume *Mémoires de voyages* in Brussels, 1833–1834. This account of just a few years can give some idea of the prompt international response to Pückler-Muskau's output. Among the numerous monographs on Pückler-Muskau I will mention only the one by Ohff.

13. The trip took place between 1835 and 1848, the account first appeared in 1865 in Sibiu, and the first modern edition came out in 1910 Cf. Sanda Golopenția-Eretescu, "The European Connection: Ion Codru Drăgușanu's Transylvanian Peregrine," paper presented at

the 1989 Modern Language Association Convention, and Negoițescu, 1:95–98. An opposite case is that of Dinicu Golescu whose travel notes from central Europe in the 1820s have been seen as a "cultural utopia" by Mircea Anghelescu. See his introductory study to Dinicu Golescu, *Scrieri* (Bucharest: Minerva, 1990), v–lxi. The least one can say is that Golescu's pedagogical purposes are transparent.

14. Cobbett is said by some to have been the most abundant writer in English literature. See Spater 1982, 1:2. A rough estimate puts the production at 120 printed volumes or 120 million words.

15. The full title of the original edition is William Cobbett, *Rural Rides in the Counties of Surrey, Kent, Sussex, Hampshire, Wiltshire, Gloucestershire, Herefordshire, Worcestershire, Somersetshire, Oxfordshire, Berkshire, Essex, Suffolk, Norfolk, and Hertfordshire: with economical and political observations relative to matters applicable to, and illustrated by, the State of those counties respectively* (London: W. Cobbett, 1830). My references are to the only handy modern edition.

16. Cf. also Cobbett 1983, 396, 310, 383, and many other places.

17. Cobbett was verbally inventive in his abuse. For him Canning was an "impudent mountebank," a "jack-pudding," a "loathsome dish;" Castlereagh was a "shallow pated ass," Liverpool a "pick-nose wiseacre," and so forth. Cf. Spater 1982, 2:452.

18. Cf. also Cobbett 1983, 271, and many other places.

19. Cf. also 344. For the Scottish-Jewish connection see Cobbett 1983, 407, 386. Cobbett thought that in the early seventeenth century displaced Scots acted as nonproductive traders and bureaucrats and weakened the organic bonds of the community. References to the Jews, barbs or outright attacks in Cobbett 1983, 120, 150, 223, 271, 280, 395, 402, 409, 428, 446, 480. Anti-Irish exclamations in 126, and elsewhere.

20. See also Cobbett 1983, 314, 276.

21. Cobbett 1983, 251—a scene almost picked out of the romantic painting of the Hudson River School at 189.

22. Unfortunately too long to quote here is the beautiful piece about Stanford Park, Wednesday 27th September (Morning) (1826), Cobbett 1983, 392–93, where the tension between idyllic peace and social struggle is masterfully evoked.

23. Cf. also Cobbett 1983, 85, 88.

24. See Cobbett 1983, 250, for a direct reference to the house of Swift's early patron Sir William Temple. Others yet are there: Shakespearean cadences (92) or the voice of Benjamin Franklin (149).

25. For a masterful ode to change see Cobbett 1983, 268–71, where by turns Cobbett is filled with fury, awe, anger, disagreement, and pleasure surveying, along a few rivulets, the transitoriness of property and power.

26. For a specific attack against the Protestant work ethic, see Cobbett 1983, 370. Attacks against intermediation, growing abstractness, "Parasites," that sometimes gel fully into an anti-capitalist mentality can be found in Cobbett 1983, 97, 109, 120, 145, 161, 221, 265–66, 276–77, 421, 444, 450.

27. Cobbett also repeats obsessively that the population of England is in decline compared to the Middle Ages and he brings as evidence the size of the country churches, that are much too capacious for present-day rural populations. See Cobbett 1983, 311–12, 336, 463–66.

28. A passage of radical and conservative mixture, a Cobbett specialty. See also Cobbett 1983, 118, 75, 92.

29. Cobbett 1983, 309 and 342, respectively. Examples are legion. The full power of Biedermeier sermonizing is unleashed by Cobbett (as it had been by P. L. Courier in France) by playing on the borderline between the religious and the social. See Cobbett 1983, 216–17, 228–29, 309, 203–7.

30. Scenes or episodes combining discourses of the beautiful and the useful in Biedermeier fashion can be found in Cobbett 1983, 44, 72, 82, 211, 214, 230, 240, 257.

31. Cf. my study of Möser in Nemoianu 1989, 97–112. Möser specifically refers to merchants able to distinguish by the quality and texture of linen the producing family. Cf. Cobbett 1983, 332, also 166, 258. To give just one example, the decline of concreteness is deplored in these terms: "In some counties, while the parsons have been pocketing the amount of the tithes and of the glebe, they have suffered the parsonage-houses to fall down and to be lost, brick by brick, and stone by stone" (Cobbett 1983, 460).

32. In a superbly eloquent passage on the Duchess of Bewley (and almost addressed to her [Cobbett 1983, 458–59]), Cobbett orchestrates all his talents for irony, nostalgia, description and sarcasm in order to put face to face the populist order of the Middle Ages with the aristocratic individualism of modernity.

33. A long and exemplary discussion in Cobbett 1983, 430–33.

34. Immermann 1971–1974, vol. 4.

35. Cf. Windfuhr, also Benno von Wiese in the introductions and comments to Immermann 1971–1974, and particularly Sengle 1971–1980, 3:857–60—short but admirable comments.

36. Cobbett 1983 contains long passages of hilariously arbitrary statistics that the modern reader can read only as literature.

37. On Lamb see Michael Gassenmeier, "Vibrating City versus Dead Nature: Some Remarks on the Singular Urban Vision of Charles Lamb" in Ahrends and Diller, eds. 1990, 133–47. Also, earlier, Nemoianu 1984, 49–50.

38. See for example the description of the city of Hannover in Immermann 1971–1974, 4:213, and the ironic but friendly discussion of the aesthetically restored monastery in Immermann 1971–1974, 4:210–11, 216. Sengle (1971–1980) highlights Immermann's excellent creation of a "Biedermeier forest," in a fully anthropomorphic manner.

39. In 1806 Sophie Cottin published her novel *Elisabeth, ou les exilés de Sibérie*, which became a bestseller. De Quincey's story was similarly inspired, though not by a novel, at least by a sensational French report. For general information on Xavier de Maistre I am endebted to Lombard (1977) and Berthier (1921).

40. I used Cobbett 1980. References in the text are to this edition.

41. Geographical-descriptive poems were extremely popular in the seventeenth and eighteenth century and are sometimes considered forerunners of the literature of travel.

42. Hazlitt 1930–1934, 10:89–339. References in the text and notes are after this edition, which in turn follows the 1902 edition of A. R. Waller and Arnold Glover.

43. Chateaubriand was ambassador in Rome in the late 1820s and secretary in 1803 (but the first version of the very first three books, not including Italian experiences only, appeared in 1826, the earliest Italian chapters having been written around 1838). Therefore we can have not the shadow of a doubt regarding direct influence. The parallels (and their detailed examination would be well worth a full-length study) are even more interesting. Equally striking (and chronologically as impossible) are the stylistic and descriptive overlaps with Cobbett (241, beginning of ch. 20), and De Quincey's mail coach (177, ch. 13).

44. Just a few examples from Hazlitt and Howe, 1930–1934 include: Keats (109, 145, 174), Lamartine (182–83), Cervantes (186), Boccacio (211), Bunyan (229), Shakespeare (92, 102, 106, 107, 113, 115, 133, 151, 157, 159, 161, 162, 165, 170, 173, 177, 183, 184, 186, 188, 190, 191, 202, 204, 220, 226, 245, 248, 249, 253, 255, 262, 272, 282, 287, 292, 294, 299, 302), and Milton (100, 106, 107, 159, 161, 177, 194, 200, 214, 226, 245, 265, 272, 279, 287, 294, 296) are the most abundantly quoted. Biblical references, quotes from authors of classical antiquity, and from other authors such as Alexander Pope, are also in good supply. Sometimes Hazlitt literally goes on a binge: Milton is quoted four times on page 109; on page 145 we find four tags from Shakespeare; on page 107, six quotations from various authors, almost as in Eliot's *Waste Land*. These lists here have no claim of completeness (all in vol. 10).

45. Other romantic, "preromantic," or contemporary references: Cobbett 1980 (91, 107, and elsewhere), Goldsmith (93), Wordsworth (54, 132, 152, 159, 266), Byron (164, 165, 177, 225, 258, 275), Sterne (113, 133, 178), along with Cowper and Coleridge.

46. For a good discussion of the pedigree and contour of the ideas of the Coppet circle see Clarissa Campbell Orr, "Romanticism in Switzerland" in Porter and Teich 1988, 146–48.

47. References in the text are to the 1988 edition.

48. Batten 1978, 86–88. For a few further examples see Curley 1976, 9–10. Fielding in *Tom Jones* made fun of these "national" conventions. Mention could be made also of guides to polite behavior and sightseeing techniques, for example, Franz Posselt, *Apodemik oder die Kunst zu reisen: Ein systematischer Versuch zum Gebrauch junger Reisenden aus den gebildeten Ständen,* 2 vols. (Leipzig, 1795). A short but excellent generic definition of the "national" conventions is provided by Louis van Delft, "Espace, frontières et anthropologie: Les caractères des nations à l'âge classique" in Bauer and Fokkema 1990, 2:130–36.

49. A good discussion of the whole topic in Wolfzettel 1986, 17–19.

50. See also her interpretation of synaesthesia as a kind of basic model for correspondence in sociocultural morphology (pt. 3, ch. 10, or de Staël, 2:168).

51. Gwynne 1969, 102–13. It should also be said that after 1815 de Staël was close to the emerging "juste milieu" or "doctrinaire" group through her relative the Duc de Broglie and her friend Prosper de Barante; though she did not entertain direct relations with Guizot and Royer-Collard she shared their intellectual backgrounds and assumptions and offered similar diagnostics of current political issues.

52. I have not referred here to the very fruitful semantic and narratological analysis of Lotman 1977, 233, and elsewhere: a spatialized view of the world, a "shifting of a persona across the borders of a semantic field." This has helped "poly-systemic" investigations, for example, Lieven d'Hulst, "Le récit de voyage et la littérature française à l'époque romantique" in Bauer and Fokkema 1990, 2:299–304.

53. Many of Pratt's (1992) impulses turn into positions that can only be described as reactionary, for example, the indictment of Linnaeus and rationalism (for example, 27–31), which harks back (as does Foucault's theory) to typically archconservative, nineteenth-century populist critiques.

54. Henry H. H. Remak, "West European Romanticism" in Stallknecht and Frenz, 123–59.

55. An argument beautifully developed by Buzard 1993, 30–44. Almost exactly the same points are made in Wolfzettel 1986, 6–17. I think both err in separating too sharply between the two elements, the former methodologically, the latter historically (eighteenth century versus romantic nineteenth century). Wolfzettel, however, is excellent on intergeneric ties with the diary, the conversational essay, and history (cf. 147, and elsewhere).

56. In analyzing the conversational essay (to which, as I showed in this chapter, travel literature is closely related), Bromwich states that for the author it is a way of exploring how "self-knowledge is a condition of his knowledge of the world."

It would be an error to consider this chapter an attempt at an exhaustive presentation of travel literature and/or at studies about travel literature. To emphasize this point, I will mention here a few books that were *not* used, even though they are recent, meritorious, and indeed akin to the arguments I have made: Dolan 2000; Gilroy 2000; Morgan 2001; Clark 1999; Leask 2002; Hadfield 2001; let alone the quickly expanding field of "romanticism and ecology." It might be appropriate to note here that there were also "anti-travel" writers, for example, Heine, Laube, Börne, or Willibald Alexis, who spoke about writing in disappointed, sarcastic, or even hostile modes (Wulfing in Glaser 1980–1987, 6:180–204; also Schivelbusch 1977).

Bibliography

Ahrends, Günter, and Hans-Jürgen Diller, eds. 1990. *English Romantic Prose: Papers Delivered at the Bochum Symposium 1988.* Essen: Blaue Eule.

Balayé, Simone. 1979. *Madame de Staël: Lumières et liberté.* Paris: Klincksieck.

Batten, Charles. 1978. *Pleasurable Instruction: Form and Convention in Eighteenth-Century Travel Literature.* Berkeley: University of California Press.

Bauer, Roger, and Douwe Fokkema. 1990. *Proceedings of the 12th ICLA Congress.* 4 vols. Munich: Iudicium.

Berthier, Alfred. 1921. *Xavier de Maistre.* Lyon: Vitte.

Blanton, Casey. 1997. *Travel Writing. The Self and the World.* New York: Twayne.

Bromwich, David. 1983. "The Originality of Hazlitt's Essays." *Yale Review* 72: 366–84.

Buzard, James. 1993. "A Continent of Pictures: Reflections on the Europe of the Nineteenth-Century Tourists." *Proceedings of the Modern Language Association.*

Chateaubriand, François-René, vicomte de. 1968. *Itinéraire de Paris à Jérusalem.* Paris: Garnier-Flammarion. (Orig. pub. 1811.)

Clark, Stephen, ed. 1999. *Travel-Writing and Empire: Post-Colonial Theory in Transit.* London: Palgrave.

Cobbett, William. 1980. *Advice to Young Men and (Incidentally) to Young Women.* Ed. George Spater. Oxford: Oxford University Press. (Orig. pub. 1829–1830.)

———. 1983. *Rural Rides.* Ed. George Woodcock. Harmondsworth: Penguin. (Orig. pub. 1830.)

Curley, Thomas. 1976. *Samuel Johnson and the Age of Travel.* Athens: University of Georgia Press.

Dolan, Brian. 2000. *Exploring European Frontiers: British Travellers in the Age of the Enlightenment.* London: Palgrave.

Furst, Lilian. 1992. *Through the Lens of the Reader: Explorations of European Narrative.* Albany, N.Y.: SUNY Press.

Gilroy, Amanda. 2000. *Romantic Geographies: Discourses of Travel 1775–1844.* London: Palgrave.

Glaser, Horst Albert, ed. 1980–1987. *Deutsche Literatur: Eine Sozialgeschichte.* 10 vols. Hamburg: Rohwolt.

Gwynne, G. E. 1969. *Madame de Staël et la révolution française: Politiques, philosophies, littérature.* Paris: A. G. Nizet.

Hadfield, Andrew, ed. 2001. *Amazons, Savages, and Machiavels: Travel and Colonial Writing in English 1550–1630.* Oxford: Oxford University Press.

Hazlitt, William, P. P. Howe, eds. 1930–1934. *The Complete Works.* 21 vols. London: Dent and Sons.

Heine, Heinrich. 1893. *Sämtliche Werke.* 21 vols. Ed. Ernst Elster. Leipzig and Vienna: Bibliographisches Institut.

Hummelt, Norbert. "Eichendorff und Magellan oder die Anfänge der Globalisierung." *Neue Züricher Zeitung,* August 30, 2003.

Hunt, Leigh. 1850. *The Autobiography of Leigh Hunt with Reminiscences of Friends and Contemporaries.* 2 vols. New York: Harper and Brothers.

Immermann, Karl. 1971–1974. *Werke.* 5 vols. Frankfurt: Athenäum.

James, Henry. 1893. *Translatlantic Sketches.* Boston: Houghton. (Orig. pub. 1875.)

Jones, Stanley. 1989. *Hazlitt: A Life, from Winterslow to Frith Street.* Oxford: Oxford University Press.

Leask, Nigel. 2002. *Curiosity and the Aesthetics of Travel-Writing 1770–1840.* Oxford: Oxford University Press.

Lombard, Charles. 1977. *Xavier de Maistre.* Boston: Twayne.

Lotman, Yuri. 1977. *The Structure of the Artistic Text.* Ann Arbor: University of Michigan Press.

Maistre, Xavier de. 1984. *Nouvelles.* Ed. Pierre Dumas, Piero Cazzola, and Jacques Lovie. Geneva: Slatkine.

Moi, Toril. 1985. *Sexual/Textual Politics: Feminist Literary Theory.* London and New York: Methuen.

Morgan, Marjorie. 2001. *National Identities and Travel in Victorian Britain.* London: Palgrave.

Negoițescu, Ion. 1992. *Istoria literaturii române.* 2 vols. Bucharest: Minerva.

Nemoianu, Virgil. 1972. "The Spanish Military Nun and the Importance of Journey for De Quincy." *Anale University Bucharest* 21: 77–83.

———. 1984. *The Taming of Romanticism: European Literature and the Age of Biedermeier.* Cambridge, Mass.: Harvard University Press.

———. 1989. *The Theory of the Secondary: Literature, Progress, and Reaction.* Baltimore: Johns Hopkins University Press.

Ohff, Heinz. 1993. *Der grüne Fürst: Das abenteurliche Leben des Hermann Pückler-Muskau.* Munich and Zurich: Piper.

Papu, Edgar. 1967. *Călătoriile Renașterii si noi structuri literare.* Bucharest: Editura pentra Literatură.

Popa, Marian. 1971. *Călătoriile epocii romantice.* Bucharest: Univers.

Porter, Dennis. 1991. *Haunted Journeys: Desire and Transgression in European Travel Writing.* Princeton, N.J.: Princeton University Press.

Porter, Roy, and Mikula Teich, eds. 1988. *Romanticism in National Context.* Cambridge: Cambridge University Press.

Pratt, Mary Louise. 1992. *Imperial Eyes: Travel Writing and Transculturation.* London and New York: Routledge.

Pückler-Muskau, Fürst Hermann von. 1841. *Südöstlicher Bildersaal.* Stuttgart: Hallberg.

———. 1991. *Briefe eines Verstorbenen*. 2 vols. Ed. Gunter J. Vaupel. Frankfurt and Leipzig: Insel.

Ralet, Dimitrie. 1979. *Suvenire și impresii de călătorie*. Ed. Mircea Anghelescu. Bucharest: Minerva.

Robinson, Jeffrey C. 1989. *The Walk: Notes on a Romantic Image*. Norman and London: University of Oklahoma Press.

Schivelbusch, Wolfgang. 1977. *Geschichte der Eisenbahnreise: Zur Industrialisierung von Raum und Zeit im 19ten Jahrhundert*. Munich: Hanser.

Seigneuret, Jean-Charles, ed. 1988. *Dictionary of Literary Themes and Motifs*. 2 vols. New York: Greenwood Press.

Sengle, Friedrich. 1971–1980. *Biedermeierzeit*. 3 vols. Stuttgart: Metzler.

Spater, George. 1982. *William Cobbett*. 2 vols. Cambridge: Cambridge University Press.

Staël, Germaine de. 1988. *De l'Allemagne*. 2 vols. Paris: Garnier-Flammarion. (Orig. pub. 1810–1813.)

Stallknecht, Newton and Horst Frenz, eds. 1961. *Comparative Literature: Method and Perspective*. Carbondale: Southern Illinois University Press.

Wallace, Anne. 1993. *Walking, Literature, and English Culture: The Origins and Uses of Peripatetic in the Nineteenth Century*. Oxford: Clarendon Press.

Windfuhr, Manfred. 1957. *Immermanns erzählerisches Werk*. Giessen: W. Schmitz.

Wolfzettel, Friedrich. 1986. *Ce désir de vagabondage cosmopolite: Wege und Entwicklung des französischen Reiseberichts im 19ten Jahrhundert*. Tübingen: Niemeyer.

CHAPTER 8

Learning over Class
The Case of the Central-European Ethos

OVER A LARGE AREA of central Europe—roughly covering what is now Austria, Czechoslovakia, Hungary, Romania, and the former Yugoslavia—society was pervaded by a common ethos, one that differed in many key points from the Protestant work ethic. The latter had been indispensable in the formation of modern capitalism and liberal democracy in Anglo-Saxon lands and in northwestern Europe in general. The central-European ethos was focused not on gainful labor and individual achievement, but rather on the acquisition of information and on the communitarian recognition of the primacy of learning as a standard of merit and social advancement. It reached its highpoint precisely during the period on which this book concentrates, 1815–1848, and is intimately connected with other manifestations here described, pointing without any doubt toward the moderation and taming of the modernization movement.

I will first try to explain the ideological origins and the manner of dissemination of such an ethos. Second, I will try to show the social and class dimensions of this ethical and historical phenomenon. Specifically I will adduce examples indicating that the central-European ethos was widely spread in all social classes, from the poorest classes through the middle classes to the aristocracy, and in all ethnic groups; this can prove that the whole area shared a belief in epistemology as the provider of valid, orderly, and moderate rules for social mobility and social organization. Third, I will examine the cultural geography of the phenomenon, that is, the historical-geographical range of the learning ethos, the extent to which it defines a common cultural identity for central Europe, and similarities and differences with other parts of Europe (Germany and Russia, France). Other issues will be touched on in passing including, for example, the decline and/or end of the central-European ethos in its area of birth, its unexpected survival/revival in North America, as well as the relevance of this central-European ethos for the world at the turn of the twenty-first century. The solidarity with other forms of moderation such as the interaction of the aesthetic and the religious, information processing and organization, the connections between the historical and the fictional, the establishment of conservatism as an alternative to and yet a branch of liberalism will, I trust, be easy to deduce even when I do not present them in detail.

My first and broadest framework is the concept of modernization, in the Weberian sense, as modified by Rostow (1960), Berger (1986), and others, and as repeated several times in this volume (a repetition the usefulness of which comes from my insistence on its importance). A reminder therefore: I will use "modernization" (here as elsewhere) as a simple and handy term to describe the break between the old biological and/or organic social structures of the medieval and early modern world and the world of the last two centuries. The latter is shaped by increasing rationalization, by the growth of individual, unattached, alienated elements, by industrialization and the forging of a man-made environment, by enormously accelerated rates of information gathering, and (to use Weber's own term) *Entzauberung,* the progressive discarding of instinctive and emotional modes of relating to society and the world. This kind of existential framework was, I believe, generated by the whole development of Western culture (biblical categories and the experience of Greek-Latin antiquity, medieval Christianity, and Renaissance capitalism), but it began to acquire a clear shape and to develop its own dynamic only towards the middle of the eighteenth century in what is sometimes described as the "core area," that is, the north and west of Europe (England first and foremost, but also northwestern Germany, northern France, the Netherlands, Denmark, Sweden, northern Italy, and, later, the northeast United States). From the core area, this framework of human existence was adopted in a seemingly irresistible movement of expansion all over the planet. Indeed the history of the last two hundred years may be said to have been a history of coming to terms with the process of modernization.

Whenever the exigencies of modernization impacted a traditional society, the result was considerable tumult: enthusiastic approval, violent opposition, attempts at compromise, economic and social turmoil, intellectual ferment, anxiety, elation, and unhappiness. Vastly different as they may be, Leninism and fascism, Mao's Cultural Revolution, Russian Slavophilism, Islamic fundamentalism, and the intellectual version of négritude, all have this in common: they are responses to and consequences of the clash between the slow and sure course of earlier history and the desegregating velocities of a new kind of human behavior and vision. I postulate that in the deepest sense the constitution and adoption of what I call the central-European learning ethos was an attempt to come to terms with the same situation and to provide strategies of moderation and of balancing at least for one region of Europe, if not for the whole of it.

How did this process begin? What were the mechanisms and the materials that engendered the central-European learning ethos in a particular area and at a given period in time? As is the case, I believe, with all historical events, the root causes are multiple. I will briefly describe a few, without claiming that my list is exhaustive.

First, there was a sociohistorical situation—a difference in fact. In the core area of northwestern Europe modernization intervened usually against the background of a rather well-defined structure of class differentiation: urban classes of all kinds (commercial, professional, intellectual, court-attendant, and so on), multiple landowning and land-working classes (free, half-free, land-bound, and so on). This was not so in central Europe. The class system there was rather simple and immature. There were large parts of the area (Transylvania, Slovakia, the Balkan areas, and the Austrian Alps, for example) where powerful survivals of a patriarchal-tribal organization could still be encountered around 1800, when individualism was still a highly unusual phenomenon. Cities were small and commerce and industry in a nascent stage. Landownership and land-working were defined in more sharply polarized ways.

What all this amounts to is that concepts of community and "sacrality" (in Durkheim's [1912] and Girard's [1972] sense) were still active. Therefore society could not be averse to a unifying, communitarian framework, one that could be or seem to be responsive to each and everyone. (At least in more massive way than in other parts of Europe and of the world in general.) Moreover, in the Habsburg lands, which comprised most though not all of the area being examined here, modernization was initiated (as it was to be initiated in other parts of the world) from above. Rationalism came about through rationalist decisions, so to speak, not through experience and habit, as was the case in key parts of the core northwest. The best example in this respect is governmental Josephinism, but both earlier and later examples could be adduced.

The second cause or set of causes has to do with the Weimarian neohumanist and neoclassical paradigm and its ramifications. Unquestionably the impact of modernization in German-speaking areas several decades before and after 1800 had considerable intellectual consequences. True, in Germany itself the practical sociopolitical responses were often rather incoherent and devoid of pragmatic drive. By contrast the mental responses were nothing short of prodigious, and they constitute to this day a rich store of ideas, many of which are still usable. As has been suggested, Germany was one of the first areas to experience dilemmas that we now observe in the so-called third world (Dahrendorf 1967), and therefore its cultural-intellectual responses became exemplary for the rest of the world. They included Sturm und Drang, idealist philosophy, romanticism, and Weimar neoclassicism, and ranged all the way from enthusiastic acceptance through puzzlement, doubt, irony, and attempts at synthesis. Central Europe, as has been repeatedly shown, drew immediately and heavily upon the store of images provided by these German reactions. Relevant to the growth and spread of the central-European ethos were first the theories of Herder, later the human models of the Humboldt brothers, Goethe, and Schiller, and finally the model of *Kulturbürgertum,* which was developed in Germany in the wake of Weimarian neoclassicism and was later influential in many parts of Europe.

The third large set of causes has to do with the institutionalization of Biedermeier concepts and attitudes and their persistence well into the twentieth century over large areas of central Europe. As I have explained elsewhere (Nemoianu 1985, 120–60—and this remains a fundamental premise of our whole enterprise in this volume), the nature of romanticism differed in western and eastern Europe. The essence of the former was visionary and revolutionary, aiming at a regeneration of the human race and a breakdown of the separations between the faculties (reason and imagination in particular) as well as those between consciousness and nature or reality. These superhuman and utopian goals could not be pursued over long stretches of time, nor could such visionary and revolutionary tension be sustained in writing. High romanticism in England, Germany, and France was soon replaced by a more tempered and moderate set of intentions and writing modes, a lower romanticism that, in its central-European form at least, came to be often called Biedermeier; this lower romanticism flourished mainly between 1815 and 1848.

Central and eastern European literatures hardly experienced at all the intensities of high romanticism. Instead they forged their own amalgam of Enlightenment, romantic, and preromantic elements, and combined this with the social realism and intimate microharmonies of the age of Biedermeier. In a word, these literatures and cultures (thirsty for moderating techniques) skipped high romanticism, somehow pretending that they had already experienced the upheaval and effort towards human regeneration by revolution and the romantic cosmic embrace by totalizing consciousness. Scott and Byron (rather than Wordsworth and Hölderlin) were immediately understood and accepted all over eastern Europe. Biedermeier literary attitudes are apparent everywhere. Mickiewicz and Słowacki among the Poles explored the relationship between dream, relativity, rebellion, hopelessness, and *Geborgenheit.* The Czechs Josef Kajetán Tyl and F. J. Rubés, or the Hungarians Mihály Vörösmarty, János Garay, and Miklós Jósika, could be immediately recognized as coevals and coequals of Western lower romantics, while the Serbian Jovan Sterija Popović and the Croats August Senoa and Ante Kovacić, with their pastoral-idyllic bases, can be easily perceived as Biedermeier writers.

Not only is it the case that this kind of Biedermeier literary writing was continued for well over a century and remained a favorite of large popular and middlebrow audiences, but the social resonance was even more powerful. Biedermeier literature reflected a certain state of mind and a certain social situation, which in turn it influenced or even shaped. At this point we can, as mentioned earlier, speak of a certain institutionalization of Biedermeier attitudes, at least in central Europe (perhaps elsewhere also) and their integration in the perception of national identity. After all, these first responses to the impact of modernity coincided with a revival of national consciousness on the part of, among others, Czechs, Hungarians, Jews, Romanians, and Serbs. The types of sensibility discovered and expressed in the

Biedermeier age, the intellectual debates initiated at that time, the great names produced then, shaped the community consciousness of such groups and channeled their modes of thinking until at least the middle of the twentieth century; further progress in social activity, literature, and science used this Biedermeier framework as a background or even as a foundation. The development of the central-European learning ethos thus took place in close dialectical interpenetration with the values of Biedermeier and at roughly the same time (that is, the decades before and after 1800).

Of course both the Biedermeier idyllic tradition and its Weimarian roots came out of an effort at synthesizing Enlightenment rationalism and romantic communitarianism and organicity that went on in other spheres as well and produced important results. (It would not be wrong to say that Marxism sprang from the same sources.) Besides these three main traditions other factors can be seen as contributory or accommodating. One of them is the Catholic tradition that prevailed over large areas of central Europe for many centuries. The Catholic framework had been characteristically one in which orderly upward mobility was possible: an avenue to success by test and competition. The rationalism that imbued the ideological and even the theological discourses of Catholicism in the seventeenth and eighteenth centuries fit with the demands of modernization and fed the new ethos. Additionally, the rationalism that Catholicism shared with most of European public life in those two centuries was intermeshed with an organic conception about nature and society (Johnston 1972). This post-Leibnizian, Theresian, and then romantic view carried with it solidarist and communitarian implications that diminished or weakened the tendencies towards individualism and competitiveness.

Another contributory element may well have been—although I would like to be more tentative on this point—a trust in science that could go all the way to its reification or fetishization. This was true in one way or another all over Europe in the nineteenth century. It would be worth investigating whether indeed, as I believe to be the case, one can detect in central Europe more often than elsewhere a specific, almost aesthetic delight in the face of scientific laws and discoveries, as well as a kind of almost childish or innocent trust in the power and goodness of science.

One highly important additional factor in the development of the ethos was the way in which it was unabashedly reinforced by officialdom and by governmental power for over a century. Under Maria Theresia and Joseph II the whole considerable weight of the state was brought to bear in the direction of a transformation of Catholic harmonization into learning impulses and motivations. This was a highly deliberate kind of decision that was followed by some of the smaller neighboring countries (east and west), but that otherwise sharply differentiates the Danubian basin from western Europe.

It will be useful to summarize briefly what is generally meant by the Puritan/Protestant work ethic and then contrast it in very simple terms with the concept of a central-European learning ethos. In the course of what follows I hope to flesh out more fully and qualify the definition of the latter by actual examples taken from different fields of social and cultural action.

Max Weber expressed his central ideas in a seminal article published in two parts in the journal *Archiv für Sozialwissenschaft und Sozialpolitik* (1904–1905). This was later expanded into *Die protestantische Ethik und der Geist des Kapitalismus* (1920), the first of three volumes comprising Weber's own edition of his essays on the sociology of religions, in which Weber responded to critics besides developing his ideas more fully. I am fully aware of the numerous critiques (from many sides) as to the explanatory usefulness of Weber's theory, and there is no point in recapitulating the whole debate or in taking sides. The simple fact remains that, at least in a loose sense, the Protestant work ethic has come to be widely recognized as hard reality not only in the context of seventeenth-century England and America, but down to our own times. The disputes about it have to do more with the weight of the Protestant work ethic inside a given time period, with the nature of its connection with capitalism (cause or effect), with its historical sources, and less with its reality as a sociohistorical phenomenon.

Weber started from the fact that in the seventeenth century capital accumulation can be widely seen as an aim in itself, not as a means to an end, and he attributed this to the Calvinist/Puritan ascetic worldview. True, similar views and attitudes can also be found inside scholastic Catholic discussion and elsewhere. But only in the Anglo-Saxon countries and in northwestern Europe does the capitalist/Protestant link acquire a systematic character—bookkeeping systems, a bureaucratized nation-state, a formalized and codified legal system, and other features are connected with it. A certain congeniality or "elective affinity" between capitalism and Calvinism made the two reinforce each other; the Puritan-Calvinist-capitalist nexus blossomed into a full-fledged system of moral-religious virtues. Individualism was bolstered through the doctrine of personal saintliness and private direct relationship with God. Justification takes place through work, success, human self-discipline, and perfectibility, both moral and material. Acquisition is placed on a pedestal. Temperance, resolution, industry, frugality, cleanliness, and chastity are declared foremost virtues. Failure and poverty could be regarded as signs of God's disfavor, while wealth, as acquired through industriousness, could be taken as an indication of divine approval.

There is no question but that these features played a key role in many societies in the seventeenth and eighteenth centuries (Furnham 1990), and in America (through the somewhat secularized version of Benjamin Franklin or simply through family tradition) they continued and continue to play an exceptionally important part in shaping public discourse and both private and public behavior.

I would argue that among the numerous competing ethical strains in Western societies (Furnham 1990, 214–32) the central-European learning ethos should be considered as particularly prominent. As I said earlier, it grew out of a combination of Enlightenment and romantic features (to be even more specific: the tempering of romantic impulses through the respect and preservation of Enlightenment traditions). It posited that the liberation and advance of the human individual or group was tantamount to increasing access to science, information, and humanistic values. The immersion in the values of high culture and professional competence were supposed to be rewarded (indeed, as often as not, in the Danubian area, they *were* rewarded) by access to a higher level of humanity, integrative acceptance, broader horizons, and ultimately by liberation and growth. The central-European learning ethos was truly comprehensive and inclusive. It applied to the peasantry: ceaseless toiling, a deliberate limitation of living standards, stinting, and hoarding were justified by the hope that a younger generation would be able to pass the barrier separating it from full liberated humanity. It applied massively to the middle classes and perhaps most emphatically to the Jewish middle classes in their effort at social integration and cultural acceptance. It applied to the working class and to the large bureaucratic apparatus of the Double Monarchy and its successor states, shaping and pervading the civilizational framework and the sustaining values of duty, fair order, honesty and legality, punctuality, and responsible behavior (the symbolic embodiment of which became for a while Emperor Franz Joseph I). It informed the aristocratic strata in their search for an existential rationale and for some positional legitimation in a gradually modernizing world. The central-European learning ethos postulated the world as a vast arena in which affirmation and promotion were possible through orderly and fair tests, struggles, and strategies. It was a vast framework but a coherent and unified one. The fairness was implicit in the fact that what was at stake was the acquisition not of wealth but of information, a nonmaterial but quantitatively measurable element. Information or knowledge, as I will try to show later, was in this context the basis even for pursuits that are difficult to reduce to merely rational moulds, such as literary-artistic creation and warcraft. Learning could justify wealth and high position, and it was an avenue open to all classes. It was also the locus of Truth, Beauty, and Goodness that became man's part through learning.[1] Increased learning carried of course its own rewards, but also became the focus for industriousness, discipline, polished manners, socialization skills, and many other virtues that it helped channel into society at large. It was, therefore, considered fitting that it should also be recognized and rewarded by God and society, the more so as the learning ethos seemed to provide a happy reconciliation between the individual will and striving on the one hand, and society-wide needs and integrations, on the other.

It is not at all part of my argument that these attitudes were limited to the north-south strip of land between Germany and Russia. Obviously, meritocratic and Enlightenment concepts of the same kind existed elsewhere, West as well as East (I have already referred to the *Kulturbürgertum* of Germany and its roots in the Weimar-Jena of the early nineteenth century). "Revolutions" in literacy and readership in the seventeenth and eighteenth centuries were common throughout northern and western Europe; phenomena as diverse as the action of Booker T. Washington in the nineteenth-century African American community, the reorientation of the Brahmin tradition in India towards progress by learning (as evoked by V. S. Naipaul 1990), the idealization of intellectual pursuits in Russian novels, and the efforts by the *Narodniki* to enlighten the people and uproot illiteracy can also be cited, though these phenomena do not seem to have been organized in society-wide structures. In a different but parallel case, Jewish communities in both western and eastern Europe combined traditional (religious) learning motivations with newer incentives for upward social mobility. Similarly I will not quarrel at all with the contention that both horizontally (geographically) and vertically (socially) there are irregularities in this zone, that is, areas in central Europe in which the functioning of the learning ethos can be recognized better, or is stronger, than in others. These irregularities do not bother me because I regard them as features of any historical phenomena. Two facts remain decisive in my opinion. First, the learning ethos is recognizably deeper, more widely spread, and officially sanctioned in the Danubian basin, among Austrians, Czechs, Hungarians, Slovaks, Jews, Poles, and Romanians, than elsewhere. Second, separate features of this ethos are connected in a systemic pattern among these groups rather than elsewhere, and that for a long while there was a kind of general government support and encouragement for it. Only towards the middle of the twentieth century, with the advent of Marxist-Leninist tyrannies in central Europe, can we speak of the demise of this ethos, although traces of it still linger. It is also interesting to note that in North America, where it was brought by central-European immigrants and particularly by Jewish middle-class communities, this Biedermeier artifact continues to persist in some ways up to the turn of the twenty-first century.

Perhaps the best way to begin adducing some evidence is by recalling the name of Joseph von Sonnenfels (1732–1817), who has become a figure of much historical interest in the last few decades. Sonnenfels is an emblematic figure for many reasons: because of his rise and career but also because of his ideas and his actual influence in central-European society. His grandfather, Rabbi Michael the Pious (Kann 1960, 147) was chief rabbi of Brandenburg; his father, Lipman Perlin, emigrated to the Habsburg lands, converted to Christianity under the name of Alois Wiener, was appointed in 1745 professor of Oriental languages at the University of Vienna, published grammars and theological treatises, and in 1746 was ennobled with the title of Von Sonnenfels. One of Perlin-Wiener's sons, Franz, became a governmental bureaucrat. His eldest son, Joseph, studied at the Piarist college in Nikolasburg and twice at the University of Vienna (philology and law), learned to speak nine languages, became a journalist, writer, and Freemason activist, worked as instructor at the Theresianum college, and ultimately, after 1765, engaged in governmental service. He was an Aulic councillor, a censor, and a university president. His old age, after 1790, was marked by numerous awards and honors—elevation to the rank of baron, honorary citizenship of Vienna, praise by great Europeans (Mirabeau, for example) and, not least, the dedication of a sonata by Beethoven. Sonnenfels was close to Empress Maria Theresia (Kann 1960, 236) and to some extent to Joseph II, insofar as he was a spokesman for the values of the Enlightenment.

In his political philosophy, Sonnenfels strongly advocated a coherent and stratified society within a strong "state" framework. A Rousseauesque *Gesellschaftsgeist* was meant to be enhanced by general education, to strive for social welfare, and to operate within the framework of constitutional government (Kann 1960, 168). Such an enlightened monarchic or aristocratic regime, with self-imposed restrictions upon its privileges, was meant to preserve "the amenities of social stratification for the higher classes and at the same time protect[s] the lower ones from license. Extraordinary merits and abilities may even open to the burgher the way to those exalted offices which by right of tradition belong to the noble" (170–71).

There were two main directions in which Sonnenfels acted either in a theoretical or in a practical way (or in both) in order to mold the state/society relations. One was education. He argued eloquently in favor of the social utility of young aristocrats, who ought to match birth with merit, virtue, and cultivation, and be turned into a bureaucratic class. At the same time he contended for upward mobility, openness, and advancement by competition on the basis of knowledge, ability, and professional competence.

The other field in which Sonnenfels's contribution may well have been decisive was that of legislative and administrative texts. He wrote a manual on style in affairs of government and was a key player in the commission for the creation of the new Austrian law codes (Kann 1960, 152–53). In the long term, the legal language thus generated had a considerable effect on the shaping of the learning ethos. As much as any other single person, Sonnenfels must be considered an architect and prime mover of the central-European learning ethos.

It is clear that Sonnenfels was only one participant in a much broader movement, including cameralists (like Justi), mercantilists, and, gradually, even the romantics he despised. It is significant that Sonnenfels was extremely active in a society for the promotion of the vernacular, *Deutsche Gesellschaft*, in the 1760s. Societies of this type were soon to become crucial features of the political-cultural landscape throughout eastern Europe. *Matice česka* (founded in 1831), *Matice srpska* (1826), *Matice hrvatska* (1842), and the Transylvanian Romanian *Astra* (1867) are just some of the more prominent. They were all predicated on the idea that political actions and—even more broadly—national identity, are dependent upon and located in the area of the cultivation of knowledge and beauty and the protection of the language. These societies acted as pools of talent and think tanks for politicians and ultimately served as a referential level for what was good and what was practicable. They were also designed as models of ideal societies in which social interaction would transcend class interests by establishing common standards of learning and of striving for intellectual and spiritual betterment. Specifically these societies worked towards creating national museums and libraries, collecting funds for student fellowships, editing manuscripts, and publishing cultural journals, but at the same time bringing out primers and textbooks, disseminating science, and encouraging arts and crafts as well as an awareness of history. At the same time they provided a forum for debates regarding the future orientation of the community. Naturally there were differences between the various societies. The Romanian *Astra* may be said to have emphasized schooling in its different forms. *Matice česka* seems primarily to have encouraged literature in the vernacular, translations, and scientific pursuits; significantly, it was formed in connection with, and almost as a subsidiary of, the National Czech Museum (est. 1818). The promotion of national consciousness, the regularization of linguistic rules, and editorial work prevailed in *Matice srpska;* through its leader, Jovan Hadzić, it also engaged in substantial polemics on the tradition versus progress issue. The idea for *Matice hrvatska,* interesting to note, came up in 1829 during discussions with Czech circles (specifically the poet Jan Kollár), and its founder, Count Janko Drasković, strongly emphasized from the beginning the link between sciences, literature, and patriotic (general) education. Similar societies were organized by the Hungarians (1825), Slovenes (1864), and Slovaks (1863). The Hungarian association was turned into a national academy in 1830; Romania established its own national academy in Bucharest in 1867; Austria did so in 1897; in the course of the century national academies were also founded in Prague, Zagreb, and Cracow.

National affirmation was a declared purpose of all these cultural organizations. Despite this it would be erroneous to regard the movement as nationalist, separatist, and antimodern. National affirmation was seen as a contribution to universal culture and science, as a way of inserting the community in the general progress of learning and civilization. Another way of looking at these cultural-political societies is to note that they were part of a whole associative wave in the Danubian basin in the nineteenth century. At that time, democratic processes (as opposed to their much sounder constitutional and legal bureaucratic framework) were unevenly and incompletely developed in this area when compared to the state of affairs in France, England, or the United States. This flourishing associative life was a very effective substitute for some of the missing features of democratic activity. They provided outlets for a variety of groups and a mode of exercising rights and faculties, thus contributing to intellectual as well as to political growth.[2]

It has even been suggested that associations came into being as a kind of substitute for vanishing "organic" forms (for example, guilds, corporations, and so on) (Bruckmüller 1985, 337; Cohen 1981, 38). In any case their original models emerged first in Austria in the 1740s, either as learned academies or as patriotic-economic associations devoted to agricultural or artisan pursuits. It is interesting to note that very different things such as chambers of commerce, labor unions, insurance companies, mutual credit associations, and cooperatives of various kinds, grew out of these beginnings a century or so later (Bruckmüller 1985, 338–39, 400–405). The total number of all such organizations grew, in the Austrian half of the monarchy, from 4,331 in 1867 to over 15,800 in 1880, and they functioned in urban as well as in rural areas (399).

In the Hungarian or Transleithanian half of the Habsburg monarchy, less than 7 percent of the population was endowed with voting rights as late as 1910. In 1881, however, in this country of sixteen million inhabitants, no fewer than 3,995 different associations were registered. This number had grown from 579 associations in 1862, a mere twenty years earlier, and was to continue growing up to an estimated 11,000 just before World War I (Molnár and Reszler 1989, 55). By contrast, only fifty-five such organizations existed in the eighteenth century in the same territory. Also by contrast, late-nineteenth-century France had only a fraction of this number (590). It is appreciated that about 50 percent of these associations pursued cultural and intellectual aims: reading circles, singing groups, *Schulvereine* (that is, groups for the setting up of private schools), groups for the dissemination of scientific knowledge and religious cultivation, clubs for political debate. (The most prestigious association of this kind in Hungary was the National Casino Club of Budapest, which was very exclusive but which built a considerable library and spent considerable funds on supporting cultural activities.) What all this shows is that, whether sponsored by ethnic Hungarians or by minorities, societies of this type fell into a category that by definition placed the values of a common humane civilization uppermost and sought specific ways of inhabiting it.

In Bohemia, and notably in Prague, we can witness the coexistence of Czech associations, headed by the vibrant and flourishing *Matice česka* (supported primarily by the Czech nobility and middle classes; its founders had been Counts Klebelsberg and Kolowrat, along with scholars, journalists, and clergy), with a network of associations of the declining but still vigorous German Bohemian minority. These provided interactive opportunities for a cross section of the intellectual and productive middle classes (Cohen 1981, 172, 57). The Romanian *Astra*, while founded and sustained by the community's middle and upper classes, also received warm support from rural communities (Matei 1986, 37).

Through its discourse structures as well as through its avowed value goals, the central-European learning ethos mediated interethnic tensions and, at the very least, provided the common ground of a debating arena. The same is true on a social level. In different ways all social classes admitted the primacy of this ethos or paid lip service to it—no mean feat in itself—and accepted its implicit rules of subordination and advancement. This is definitely not, let me state it once and for all, to claim that class conflict, economic inequalities, or social consciousness had been abolished in any way, which would be obviously absurd. It is merely to point out that there were strong and specific countervailing forces in this geographical and historical area. In a sense the strength of the central-European learning ethos derived precisely from the variety and intensity of the conflicts (national and social) that it counteracted. With these thoughts in mind, I will engage in a cursory review of some class attitudes in relation to this ethical framework.

In the Austro-Hungarian Empire, in the independent Balkan states, and in the different Polish provinces, the aristocracy had preserved strong economic and social positions, sometimes even legal privileges. Nevertheless these countries or areas were modernizing fast, their very structure was changing, the authority of the West was looming large. In different ways local aristocracies (and not only their socially and ethically alert members but also those who, in an intelligently selfish vein, wanted to preserve some sociopolitical relevance for their class and kin) pragmatically adopted an ethos of learning and service as a convenient road towards modern relevance. It may be useful to note here that between 1800 and 1850 in all the areas under discussion, sizable sections of the aristocracy (higher or lower) saluted the coming of radical historical change and contributed a lot to it. This was also the case in England, France, and Russia, but it remains nonetheless striking what a large part of the nobility in Hungary, Romania, and particularly Austria worked towards sociohistorical change in the late eighteenth and early nineteenth centuries. In Austria, families such as Fürstenberg, Auersperg, Stadion, Colloredo-Mannsfeld, Schwarzenberg, Schönburg-Hartenstein, and Thurn und Taxis, belonged to the highest and most select stratum of the Austrian aristocracy; but they were often described as the "Austrian aristocratic Whigs" as early as 1848, but particularly in the second half of the nineteenth century (Gollwitzer 1956, 188–92).

Service and knowledge came together most logically, of course, in the military careers that were a traditional and favorite field of activity for the central-European aristocracy. In the Habsburg army in 1896, 22 percent of commissioned officers and 72 percent of generals bore titles of nobility (Hajdu in Molnár and Reszler 1989, 66–68). These were not swaggering mercenaries or swordsmen but, as was often said, "bureaucrats on horseback," whose behavior, duties, and level of knowledge were prescribed in great detail. Moreover the army, like the church (or churches), was traditionally an instrument of social mobility and provided interaction on meritocratic bases for all kinds of individuals (Rothenberg 1976, 118–28). Already in 1843, the officer corps, while in majority of German descent, included "officers of Spanish, French, Walloon, Danish, Irish and English derivation" (11). In the nineteenth century the supreme command of the *K. u. K.* Army was a highly politicized affair, largely in the hands of a centrist-liberal coterie (76–81) that emphasized meritocratic and political motivations rather than origin (social class or ethnic background); professionalism had to prevail over voluntary and sentimental modes of relating to the army (83). Conrad von Hötzendorf, the last major figure in the leadership of the Austro-Hungarian army, is a good example of such a mixture of professionalism, technical knowledge, aristocracy, and meritocratic and dynastic attitudes transcending class barriers.

Here is the place to emphasize that the high percentage of aristocrats in the military has also to be seen in the light of the fact that large numbers of commoners who reached the upper levels of the military ladder were absorbed into the nobility by titles granted on merit. A first- or second-generation nobility of merit was thus created that served as a bridge between the nobility and the commoners, but also as a model for the latter. This was true not only in the military but in many other fields: business, statecraft, engineering, the sciences, and so forth. Perhaps the best example is provided by the Jewish minority in the Austrian, as well as in the Hungarian half of the empire. William McCagg's classic study of Jewish progress (for example, the number of Jewish nobles in Hungary grew from four in 1824 to 346 in 1918; see McCagg 1972, 25) presents case after case of association between economic advance, ennoblement, and vigorous intellectual pursuit, each successive action justifying and legitimizing the previous one and reinforcing an image of the aristocracy as a class with intellectual and educational relevance, one connected equally with social achievement and cultural accomplishment. Throughout the Habsburg monarchy the purpose of attracting into the aristocratic class the achievers in the most varied fields (and of varied ethnicities) was pursued energetically (the parents of György von Lukács, Von Neumann, and Robert von Musil were so honored): this can be explained only by admitting that there was a guiding social model of the aristocracy as a class of knowledge and cultural merit. The process had begun already in the eighteenth century. Thus in the first four decades of the century only 4.5 percent of nobiliary creation was justified by economic achievement, whereas by the end of the century, the figure had risen to 18.2 percent (Bruckmüller 1985, 253). Ethnic groups devoid of a traditional aristocracy (for example, the Transylvanian Romanians or the Serbians of Hungary) were endowed with a peerage based on military, clerical, economic, or scholarly achievements. In the period 1804–1918 a total of 8,931 nobiliary titles were granted, over 4,000 of which went for military achievement, 2,157 for bureaucratic or political merits, over 1,000 for financial or manufacturing prominence, and almost 300 for science and art (Siegert 1971).

In any case, the percentages of educated or highly educated members of the aristocracy were quite high, superior to those of the same class in the past and to other social classes. Such percentages can be found in the politically active class in Hungary, Romania, Austria, and Croatia. There is impressive evidence of the feverish efforts of the Hungarian nobility around 1800 and in the first half of the century to provide their offspring with suitable collegiate academies and, where this was not possible, to generate themselves syllabi and educational tools for their own family (Csáky 1981, 213–17). It is also in the first decades of the century that the pursuit of higher education in the West (mostly in France and Germany, much less often in England or Italy) became a standard procedure for Hungarians, Romanians, and Poles. Young aristocrats pioneered this kind of experience, and played a decisive role in disseminating reforming and progressive ideas in their countries of origin.

I tend to see this as a parallel and analogy to revolutionary ("romantic") actions but also as a tempering substitute for them.

There were other narrower but highly efficient ways in which allegiance to the learning ethos could be expressed. One was the protection and encouragement of the arts; collecting art, Maecenas-like patronage, and the funding of intellectual pursuits provided the conditions for a lively interaction between meritocracy and aristocracy. Rilke at Duino, in the castle of Princess Marie von Thurn und Taxis, is a famous example, as is the patronage of the Esterházys for Haydn and, on a smaller scale, the protection of the Fürstenberg family in Bohemia for the poet Karl Egon Ebert and the historian Frank Xaver Kraus, and their support for the publication of the first authoritative Bach edition (Gollwitzer 1956, 313). The Romanian composer George Enescu was protected by the Cantacuzino princes and later married a princess of the family, while Count Ferenc Széchenyi founded Hungary's National Museum and Library (Janos 1982, 50).

More than a few members of the nobility became active and creative themselves in the intellectual life of the time. Baron József Eötvös (his son was an illustrious physicist) and Count Széchenyi are difficult to match in importance in the intellectual and cultural life of the Hungarians in the early and mid–nineteenth century. (later a member of the Bánffy family became a distinguished novelist). The role of the Croatian count Drasković in the cultural life of his country has already been mentioned. Romanian aristocrats played key roles in setting the foundations of mathematical, scientific, and historical education and research in the nineteenth and early twentieth century. Romanian linguistics would have been impossible without Alexandru Rosetti; G. M. Cantacuzino and N. I. Ghica-Budeşti were leading historians and theoreticians of Romanian architecture; Aristide Caradja and Emil Racoviţă were internationally known figures in entomology and speleology respectively; Ioan Cantacuzino founded immunology and experimental pathology in Romania; Alex I. Ghica was a leading mathematician while Henri Catargi, Hélène Vacaresco, Lucia Sturza, Martha Bibesco, and Matyla Ghyka were outstanding figures in their country's arts and letters. Similar lists could be drawn up for other central-European countries.

In politics the numbers of aristocratic figures is overwhelming—at least until World War I—in Hungary, Austria, and Romania: Metternich and Schwarzenberg, Apponyi and Andrássy, Ştirbey and Cantacuzino, among many others. Nor was this presence confined to the top national leadership. Of the bureaucracy in four key offices in Hungary (interior, commerce, finance, and the prime minister's chancery), gentry represented an average of 56.7 percent in 1899 and 45.9 percent in 1910 (Janos 1982, 110–11). Also in Hungary the number of aristocratic members in the house of representatives varied between 10.8 and 16.4 percent during the three decades 1875–1905 (100). This activity and presence should not be seen merely as an expression of socioeconomic interests or as power exercises, but also as a defense and legitimation of status by achievement. Moreover, in most of these cases education, knowledge, and taste accompanied or even superseded descent, ancestry, and wealth. Statesmanship, no less than the military profession, can be seen as an area of vocational specialization and applied cognitive activity for many members of the nobility (Gollwitzer 1956, 304–6). They were also modes of channeling creative and explosive energies (at all social levels) into more sedate and orderly constructive directions.

Passing to the middle classes the case becomes much clearer. Indeed it can be stated as a general proposition that in central Europe the middle class was largely a product of the complex intermeshing of Enlightenment, romanticism, and Biedermeier, rather than the producer of these as may (or may not) have been the case in the West. Sociodemographic movements were captured, directed, and regulated by these mental (and sometimes organizational) frameworks. Thus the learning ethos was "naturally" adopted or absorbed by the growing bourgeoisie in the nineteenth century.

Probably the most striking example is provided by the Jewish middle class and upper-middle class of the region. The studies of Victor Karády make frequent use of the term "sur-scolarisation" (over-schooling) in connection with the Jewish middle class, to indicate primarily their massive orientation towards the liberal professions as an avenue to socially upward mobility. Around 1900, close to half the physicians, lawyers, managers, and entrepreneurs, and over 30 percent of the engineers, journalists, and veterinary surgeons in the Hungarian half of the empire and in selected parts of the Austrian half (for example, Bukowina or Galicia) were of Jewish descent (Karády in Molnár and Reszler 1989, 89). At the University of Vienna, 30 percent of the students in medicine were Jewish in 1869–1870 and 48 percent in 1889–1890; at the school of law the percentages for the same years were 19.8 and 22 percent, respectively (Pollak 1984, 54). Just prior to World War I, 18 percent of the reserve officers in the Habsburg army were Jewish, even though only approximately 5 percent of the monarchy's total population was Jewish (Rothenberg 1976, 128). This is an excellent gauge since the reserve-officer effectives were traditionally stocked with and drawn from middle-class and professional categories. Between 1870 and 1910, pupils of Jewish and partly Jewish descent represented approximately 40 percent of the alumni of eleven *select gymnasia* (elite high schools) in Vienna (Beller in Oxaal, Pollak, and Botz 1987, 39–58). If one takes into account all *gymnasia* in Vienna the statistical proportion is 30 percent Jewish, corresponding to a population slightly higher than 10 percent in the Vienna metropolitan area (Rozenblit 1983, 99). For this Jewish section of Vienna this was the highway to integration in Western culture. As one researcher writes, "The educators who constructed the curriculum firmly believed that the study of Latin and Greek grammar was instrumental in developing logical thought patterns; that the study of classical literature was essential for the development of a taste for beauty and simplicity; and that concentration on ancient history and philosophy would inculcate noble and heroic sentiments in young scholars" (101). Even if George Steiner's quasi-identification of *Kulturbürgertum* with Jewishness in central Europe (Steiner 1967, 170–72) seems exaggerated, it remains clear that by the turn of the century the role of the Jewish middle and upper classes was decisive in fields such as psychology (Freud), music (Schönberg, Mahler), philosophy (the logical positivists), economics, and political and legal theory. It may be worth repeating that a double motivational line may have strengthened the adherence of central-European Jews to the learning ethos—a Talmudic tradition as well as an eagerness to grasp social opportunity.

However, an intense internalization of an adherence to the central-European learning ethos was not confined to the Jews alone. As Steven Beller says, "in Austrian German society as well there was a tradition of learning, especially among the bureaucracy, in order to keep [and earn] one's status as a family in the governing elite" (Beller in Don and Karády 1990, 169). In Hungary "by 1846 there were 33,000 people who qualified as college graduates and it was calculated that there were twice as many licensed attorneys per capita than in the Western or Cisleithanian (on the whole, more developed) part of the Empire" (Janos 1982, 42). The number of bureaucrats increased by leaps and bounds. The central administration grew from 60,776 in 1890 to 119,937 in 1910, and the total number of administrative employees to 387,922 in 1914, that is, 3.5 percent of the active labor force. (By contrast, in Germany the figure was 0.9 percent in 1913, and in Great Britain 0.8 percent in 1920 [Janos 1982, 94].)

It seems clear that in a broader sense "sur-scolarisation" was an area-wide feature. Bohemia had 1,500 elementary schools in 1822; by 1918, the number had grown to over 6,100. By 1930, illiteracy in the whole of Czechoslovakia was down to 4.1 percent, the best percentage in the area (Korbel 1977, 64), but also a much lower rate than in the Iberian peninsula at the time, or perhaps in the United States today. In the independent half of Romania the number of students in primary and elementary schools rocketed from 186,403 to 727,588 in just one decade (1895–1905), and literacy rose from 22 percent in the nineteenth century to 43 percent in 1915 (59 percent for the population of military age) (Janos in Jowitt 1978, 98).

In Austria and its provinces the number of administrators grew from 130,000 in 1841 to 336,000 in 1900. To process this increasing number of highly educated bureaucrats and to establish fair rules of advancement, a series of increasingly detailed provisions was enacted between 1873 (*Rang und Gehaltschemata*) and 1914 (*Dienstpragmatik*). These indicated what educational assumptions, degrees of knowledge, tests, and promotion principles should be checked or applied (Bruckmüller 1985, 397). Similar but somewhat laxer appointment and selection procedures were set up in the Hungarian half of the empire (Janos 1982, 96).

Obviously, rules of this kind could not be applied to the entrepreneurial middle and upper-middle class. There is every indication, however, that the capitalist and merchant class felt not liberated but frustrated and unfulfilled because it had not been legitimated by a more complete submission to a methodology of advancement derived from the learning ethos. A good part of the sociocultural behavior of this upwardly mobile population can be explained by a desire to compensate, even to overcompensate, for this perceived lack. Thus the breeding of educated, creative, and brilliant offspring (McCagg 1972) can be seen as such a compensatory legitimation. More generally it is difficult to exaggerate the almost unanimous allegiance of the middle class in central Europe (in Germany also) to the slogan *Besitz und Bildung* (property and culture), or to the linkage of the civilian component of the word *Bürger* to its connotations: *Bildung, Aufklärung, Vernunft* (cultivation, enlightenment, reason; Bruckmüller 1985, 319–20, 342). Clearly the strategy of neutralizing or slowing radical impulses was working here with brilliant success.

Bourgeois patronage of the arts and aesthetic habits closely imitated those of the cultivated nobility. In Bohemia and Austria during the eighteenth century, aristocratic patronage in music and art had encouraged the development of artistic creativity, particularly in music and architecture, somewhat less in painting, and least effectively in literature. In Prague such patronage was expressed by several dozen *Hauskapellen* of the high aristocracy (Auersperg, Claus-Gallas, Lichtenstein, Lobkowitz, Questenberg, Wrtby, and many others; Bosl 1979, 570). This sociocultural form was imitated in the nineteenth century in two different ways. First, by the emergence, at least in the large urban centers, of upper-middle-class patrons of the arts who tried to emulate the high nobility (Reissberger, in Zeman 1982, 762, on art collecting). The Wittgenstein and Todesco salons and patronage were famous in Vienna just before 1900; Em. Gozdu and the Hurmuzaki brothers acted in similar ways for the Romanians, and so on. The second, more modest, but much more widely spread form of imitation was the emergence all over central Europe of cultural associations devoted to reading, cultural betterment, and musical practice; perhaps most widely spread were music and reading (even theatricals) exercised in small family groups or among friends (Bosl 1979; also Schamschula in Zeman, ed., 1982, 120).

Architecture was an equally expressive medium for the values of the middle classes and for their conviction that class differences could be overcome by cultural-epistemological means. Thus, while the whole Biedermeier cast of mind is undoubtedly implicated in the central-European learning ethos, it may be argued that Biedermeier architecture and interior decoration in particular expressed an attempt by the middle classes to appropriate historical tradition for itself in a specific way and with a certain reduction in scale (Bosl 1979, 569). Different as the imposing Ringstrasse in Vienna might be from Biedermeier quaintness in its appearance, it seems to be the consequence of similar aspirations: to recapitulate historical traditions in a modern environment and to fortify them. In both cases liberal architectural statements were both syncretistic and pluralistic: the tradition of creativity and high value was being conquered from the inside (Schorske 1981, 24–115). We can even venture further and wonder whether the phenomena described by Arno Mayer as "the persistence of the old regime" (Mayer 1981)—for example, the way in which capitalist and middle-class contents found expression in the garb of century-old structures (feudal, monarchic, traditional)—could not perhaps be seen under a different and more favorable light. The rising middle classes were adopting and assimilating traditional structures because these were generally perceived as crystallizations of Truth and Beauty. Dealing with them on a modern level, negotiating a relationship between such durable values and newly emerging social modes, was considered as essential to the common good.

Be that as it may I find it significant that in an official classification of 1815 the nobility came in first, followed by a variety of middle-class categories, the first of which was that of academics and professors, the last (or seventh) that of economic producers (Bruckmüller 1985). The mediatory role of cultural and intellectual pursuits on the ladder of upward mobility appears clearly and openly stated on such occasions. Even the much debated role of a phenomenon like Freemasonry appears to make more historical sense and to find a fuller cultural justification when placed in this family of circumstances. This role was not primarily politic (that is, the engineering of sociohistorical change through political means), but rather one of initiation through knowledge, the education of middle-class elites in processes of decision making, the transfer from the mystical to the cognitive. In some ways, Freemasonry is another example of Mayer's "persistence of the old regime" in its contriving to integrate emerging phenomena into a common (and pacifying) value framework.

Undoubtedly, similar demonstrations are more difficult in the case of the broader population, that is, of working people in urban and rural environments. Nevertheless, we do have plenty of evidence—sociological as well as literary—indicating that the learning ethos had largely permeated these strata of society also, even though more diffusely. The first point to be made has to do of course with the dramatic increase in literacy and in participation in primary, secondary, and vocational education. Both private and governmental powers collaborated in this effort. Manufacturers had started vocational schools for orphans in Vienna and Klagenfurt in the early 1750s (Bruckmüller 1985, 266). The institution of *Hofbefreiung* (privileged taxation status) for Jews and, more generally, all kinds of artisans and professionals, was based of course on economic interest, but also on the recognition of competence (250–51). Furthermore a systematic and painful recycling of the religious class took place under Joseph II in particular, but also earlier. An estimated minimum of seven hundred to eight hundred monasteries were abolished between 1783 and 1787 in Austria, Hungary, and elsewhere in the empire. The clerics in question were reoriented towards practical issues: pastoral and social care, teaching, and "enlightenment"; 3,200 new parishes were created (325–26) and the funds of lay religious brotherhoods were transferred to educational purposes. The sudden leap in general schooling was due in some part to this process of secularization or pragmatic reorientation of the church. In Bohemia the number of rural schools doubled from 1,200 to 2,400 in the 1780s alone; already in 1781 the number of school-going children had reached 42 percent. In eastern Austria the figures stood at the same time between 33 and 70 percent, though they were much lower in mountainous western Austria. The secularization of the Jesuit school model also meant a system whereby hierarchy by merit and arduous competition became institutionalized (275, 322–23). By the end of the nineteenth century, illiteracy was receding and on the way out in most parts of central Europe. In eastern Austria by 1857, less than 20 percent of youngsters of draft age were still illiterate. By 1900, illiteracy had dwindled in Vienna to 3 percent, a figure close to that of England and considerably better than in, say, Italy or Portugal (Engelsing 1973, 96–99). By 1838, the percentage of school-going children had reached close to 99 percent in Vienna, and was thus higher than the one in Berlin around the same time (Bauer, in Zeman 1982, 382).

Against this background it is significant to note the change in attitude of the peasantry itself, from frequent opposition to governmental instrusiveness and Enlightenment "do-goodism" and a clinging to patriarchal modes of life, to a passionate embrace of the new possibilities for equalization or betterment (Csáky 1981, 206–9, as well as his conclusion on the homogenizing role of *educatio nationalis*, 224–25, 230–31; see also Engelsing 1973, 102, and Bruckmüller 1985, 274, 323). Numerous literary works in Romanian, Hungarian, Serbo-Croatian, and other languages describe the case of poor parents, usually peasants, who make every conceivable sacrifice in order to ensure the educational progress of their offspring.

One example among many is *Budulea Taichii* (Daddy's Budulea, 1880) by I. Slavici (an author of Romanian Transylvanian descent), a short story that presents realistically the dialectic of education against a peasant background: encouragement, fear, and uncertainty. It relates the story of a gifted and hardworking peasant boy, Mihai (or Huțu) Budulea, who by dint of scholastic achievements steps up the social ladder and becomes first an elementary school teacher, then a seminarian, episcopal bureaucrat, and archivist, and finally is being groomed to become a bishop: joining the elite of Romanian, indeed, of central-European society as a whole, might not be a prize beyond his grasp. Slavici notes the gradual alienation of this up and coming young man who suddenly, however, changes and returns to his village to become eventually a *protopop* (an Orthodox priest of a higher rank, equivalent to a monsignor in the Catholic hierarchy), and to build a family. Slavici's human ideal was the Transylvanian intellectual (teacher, pastor, lawyer) who, after serious studies in the world outside, returns to his native village and works there for the moral and economic enlightenment of his fellow man. During Budulea's trek into the world of higher learning his family and other villagers do express periodically the fear that they will lose him (linguistically, ethnically, socially), but hardly ever act in hostile or chauvinistic ways. They all agree that the main avenue to progress is learning, the acquisition of intellectual skills and of higher degrees of knowledge. The fairness of this mechanism for advancement and the implicit equality of chances for betterment is accepted unquestioned in *Budulea Taichii*. What is being questioned is not the need for progress, but the degree, the pace, and the aims of progress.

A kind of belated and nostalgically idealized image of this kind of learning ethos, synthetic and simplified, and yet for that very reason convincing and clear, is presented by Heimito von Doderer in his novel *Die Dämonen* (1956). A polyphonic and complex novel, set in the 1920s, mostly in Vienna, *Die Dämonen* describes with both accuracy and sardonic humor the tensions, anxieties, and the pettiness of central-European society after World War I and the ways in which these inevitably feed into anarchic violence, revolution, and fascism. One of the few figures to stand out from the teeming variety of characters is the young industrial worker Leonhard Kakabsa, an individualist driven by the sheer desire for knowledge and love of reading. One of the socially humblest figures in the novel, Kakabsa becomes a librarian to Prince Alfons Croix. The young prince, who is one of the most exalted (though secondary) characters in the book—seen as the embodiment of high moral and intellectual values, noble descent, and wealth—immediately recognizes in the self-taught industrial worker a kindred spirit and an equal. To emphasize this point further, Leonhard is shown to fall in love with Mary K., a cultivated, middle-aged, middle-class woman, who is herself staging, by sheer indomitable will, a comeback from a crippling traffic accident. The novel by Doderer (started in the 1930s) can be said to pinpoint very accurately the way in which an ethos becomes retrospective myth: equalization and growth through cognitive development. Learning overcomes social class here in most demonstrative way.

One last example of the extension of the central-European learning ethos into the broad masses of the population is provided by altered reading habits and the enormous extension of publications of all kinds. The evidence is abundant, and I will only cite a few instances. The circulation figures reached by the large Viennese dailies in 1853 were slightly lower than those of their counterparts in London and Berlin (Engelsing 1973, 95; see also Pollak 1984, 61, 73); nevertheless this indicated a spectacular achievement, particularly when correlated with the composition of the readership. *Neue Freie Presse* in 1873 had a significant number of subscribers from among artisans, domestic servants, and soldiers, along with the more predictable middle-class and professional readership (Engelsing 1973, 123). Around 1900, "in Budapest alone twenty-one daily papers were published averaging four hundred printed pages and weekday circulation of one million" (Janos 1982, 102). In the whole of Habsburg Hungary, one hundred fifty newspapers in German were published, forty-four in Romanian, eleven in Slovak, along with the majority of Hungarian-language publications (102).

Regular scholarly publications began to appear in Bohemia in the 1770s in German and Latin (Bosl 1979, 554–55) and soon thereafter in Czech. The circulation of schoolbooks in the Austrian half of the Habsburg monarchy reached up to 1.31 million in 1863 alone (639,000 of which were in German). These and other figures for the circulation of newspapers and books are comparable to those in western Europe, a phenomenon that is remarkable given the lower technological and socioeconomic state of development of the east-central European area.

There are two additional, somewhat more specific, phenomena inside the world of reading and literacy that seem to me clearly connected with the mass appeal of the central-European learning ethos. One of them is the institution of the "reading cabinet" along with the reading club—true, institutions otherwise not unknown in the West, or without their equivalents there.[3] Reading cabinets were set up in the Romanian Danubian principalities in the early nineteenth century. They were well stocked with a variety of foreign books and had a broad readership. Over and beyond the usual middle-class reading clubs and associations there were *Lesevereine* in Vienna as early as 1848, one for printers' apprentices with three hundred members as well as two other similar organizations with 2,800 members (Engelsing 1973, 109). In Bohemia such societies for workers were equally frequent.

The second phenomenon is the reading of calendars and almanacs, which is a specifically nineteenth-century phenomenon, even though the genre is not entirely uncommon in either the eighteenth or the twentieth centuries. Almanacs and calendars provided a mixture of the scientific and the literary, of the secular and the religious, of the practical and the entertaining that filled exactly the needs of a popular readership. Austria was superior to Prussia in terms of resort to this kind of reading material. Thus, in Prussia in 1853 the ratio was one published calendar copy per sixteen inhabitants; in Austria it was one per eight inhabitants, close to the rate of France (Engelsing 1973, 118). I will try to address briefly in my last section the general cultural implications of these phenomena.

In the last decade or so many attempts have been made to define the common features of central-European culture and to provide a description of its common physiognomy. Authors as different as Timothy Garton Ash, George Konrad, Milan Kundera, François Fejtö, and George Steiner (all of them with rather broad appeal) are just some of those who have engaged in such exercises, following the earlier and more scholarly works of William M. Johnston (1972) and (with much more limited and more precise purposes) Roger Bauer (1974). Pluralism, tolerance, organicism, and the special place between East and West are just a few among the numerous definitional features proposed. These are useful analytical categories and they do not in the least contradict the considerations put forward here; to a certain extent they combine and overlap with a pervasive ethos that can be encountered area-wide at all levels of society. It goes without saying that no single ethos can ever claim the full and total allegiance of all members of a society, particularly of one so polymorphous and with such a low definitional profile as the central-European one. Obviously I do not mean to suggest that in this area mechanisms and features of sociohistorical functioning generally encountered in Western societies were somehow suspended or negated. Class conflicts did exist, no less than the dilemmas of modernization, marginality, and dependency, and so did the efforts to define an ethnic-national identity. (Nevertheless we should also point to phenomena and trends such as "Austroslawismus" and "Bohemianism," in which the cultural-intellectual elements overwhelmed direct ethnic affirmation or interest [see, for example, Bosl 1979, 560–62, 637].) The presence of a strong and conscious option in favor of the socialization of cognitive search (that is, the search for knowledge, the accumulation of knowledge, and the acceptance of a hierarchy based on knowledge) qualified other historical realities, interacted with them, and contributed to their alteration in specific ways. It would take us too far afield to investigate in detail each of these kinds of interactions. Instead I will focus on a number of discursive phenomena that can indicate the specific coloring and structuring of the cultural-intellectual universe in central Europe.

The first group of phenomena involves the many different images that shaped social imagination in depth. They included the idyllic topos (Nemoianu 1978), the image of moderation, serenity, balance, harmony, and interaction, organicity reduced to scale. The credibility of an actual societal foundation for this discursive construct was enhanced in the environment of the kind of evolutionary order posited by the learning ethos. Other variants of harmony—religious, secular, even purely frivolous—were provided by the dramatic productions of the nineteenth century, from Friedrich Raimund and Johann Nestroy (Bauer 1974) to Johann Strauss and Franz Lehar. More powerful still were the images of paternal and benevolent monarchs, their benignity actually enhanced by their ineffectiveness; constitutional restraints and the disappearance of absolutism liberated the monarch for milder pursuits. In the area, Franz Joseph I (1848–1916) was the model of the exemplary monarch who became a legend in his lifetime. He had enjoyed an exceptionally thorough education that included military science, astronomy, law, philosophy, political science, along with fencing, dance, and music, and was topped off by extensive linguistic studies (French, Czech, Hungarian, Polish, and Italian) (Bled 1987, 17–21, 118–19). More important, a lifetime of very orderly and conscientious labor, a self-positioning as an embodiment of duty, fairness, and punctuality, the quality of *Anständigkeit* (decency, reliability, proper and correct behavior), all combined to constitute a powerful role model of the ruler as referee at different levels of social life (Reszler, in Molnár and Reszler 1989, 144–56). These combined together into the specifically central-European strategy for reining in revolutionary, radical, or explosive tendencies (nationalism and socialism among them), as well as moderating for a span of time the unleashing of creative energies in society as imagined and triggered around 1800 by romanticism all over Europe.

To move on to another discursive phenomenon: the images of pluralism and organicism found themselves ingeniously merged in the project of the federalist framework—which was (and remains) central to the area, whether as political reality, as mere aspiration, or simply as the focus for a utopian value search. The history of plans to restructure the whole area by rationalist federalization according to ethnic boundaries—the plans put forward by F. Palacký, K. Renner, A. C. Popovici, and F. Naumann, among others—is very well known and has often been discussed (Wierer 1960; Nemoianu, in Molnár and Reszler 1989, 31–41). Some of these plans were aimed only at the Habsburg Empire in its existing form; others were area-wide, that is, they specifically sought to attract and to combine outlying areas beyond the existing political borders. In any case it must not be forgotten that a kind of vaguer federalism was already inherent in the blueprint of the Habsburg lands, seen as a congeries of overlapping sovereignties and autonomies (Csáky, in Molnár and Reszler 1989, 19–29). In an even broader and deeper sense, federalism is tied in with the central-European learning ethos, the area of coincidence being the relationship between individual and community or between local and general concerns. Any federalism is an arrangement intended to preserve particular identities within the overarching harmony of general interests. Much in the same way, the central-European learning ethos was trying to ensure affirmation of the individual person within a communitarian framework and in orderly, prescribed structures. This logical-structural parallel led to the mutual reinforcement of federalism and the learning ethos.

A third discursive phenomenon was the prominence of didactic literature. Didacticism (a social posture of Biedermeier descent) permeated central Europe. Everybody was teaching everybody, while enlightenment and awakening were considered the equivalent of additional quantitative packets of information. (The issue itself was of course Europe-wide, as our chapter on Southey, to take just one example, indicates.) This is proved among other things by the enormous growth of popular learning-literature alluded to above (calendars, almanacs). Another specific genre of half-literary, half-didactic writing was the travelog (Nast, in Zeman 1982, 719–32; or Schmidt, in Zeman 1982, 668–69, to give just a few references to an enormous body of research on the topic), which provided geographical initiation, expansion of horizons, apprehension of a globalized horizon, liberation from biological attachments (see chapter 7 in this book for its broader implications). As a matter of fact it may be said that historical novels acted in similar fashion, extending the reader's frames of reference and providing informational contexts for the present. The work of Walter Scott was, to be sure, of interest to the literatures of western Europe, but its reception in eastern and central Europe (including Germany and Russia) was more intense and more influential in inducing the emergence of the local historical novel as a key vehicle for expressing ethnic identity. The historical genre, fictional or factual, could become a vehicle for national affirmation, for enacting the present, for outlining the future, as well as being a didactic tool that combined the pragmatic and the pleasant. (Two further chapters in this book can provide a more detailed analysis.) As a matter of fact this tenacious search for a blend of utility and entertainment was extremely widespread and rather typical. One case that is rarely studied or cited is that of the *tableaux vivants,* which, from the salons of Vienna all the way to the provincial high schools of southeastern Romania, witnessed great popularity. These were attempts to bring historical scenes to life, usually in imitation of famous large-scale paintings, contemporary or from the past. The *tableaux vivants* were less than historical plays, since there was no action or development, but they were considerably more than a mere masked ball: not amateurish and capricious, but held in check by a given model and by the intention of meticulous reproduction. Instruction prevailed over diversion. A mixture of nobility, rich commoners, and (in some parts) even governmental agencies set up such *tableaux vivants* (Reissberger, in Zeman 1982, 748–49, 759).

While this type of activity may be said to be a mere oddity—albeit a symptomatic one—it is squarely framed by a context in which the cultivation of the aesthetic (and, I venture to say, even aestheticism itself) was seen as a kind of shortcut towards a better and deeper knowledge. Already some early romantics (for example, Novalis or Jean Paul) had outlined this idea, and the suggestion that art was epistemologically momentous remained alive and well in central Europe at least until the end of the nineteenth century. (The enormous success of the paintings of Hans Makart, with their mixture of the historical, the allegorical, and the phantastic, signals the same aesthetic/epistemological configuration; see, for example, Pollak 1984) This aesthetic knowledge was, in a sense, an archaic-magic belief in the human capability to absorb patterns through behavior that would incline cognition to resonate with the rhythms of the universe. A propensity for reflecting the universe and internalizing it, the argument went, can always be educated into individuals, can become part of the human experience. Southey, Coleridge, and Newman would have said the same. However nobody was better at this game than Adalbert Stifter in his *Nachsommer* (1857).

Stifter chose a genre that was by then well-established in European literature, the bildungsroman, that is, a long narrative tracing the growth and evolution of a young man into full maturity. His characters are not described with particular depth or subtlety. This because Stifter's emphasis is on the progress of cognition itself, on advancement and growth. Many critics writing about *Nachsommer* have pointed out the utopian and retrospective nature of the "life as museum" portrayed in Freiherr von Risach's "Rosenhaus" (Schorske 1981, 288–300). Others have emphasized that Risach's real-life model (Baumgartner) rose from peasant's son to imperial high office. However, in the context of the present investigation, the most important feature of the novel is the smooth and logical cognitive transition from natural science—step by step, widening circle by widening circle—to a higher state of harmony and healing, and of culture of the soul ("seelische Kultur," in Zeman 1982, 301–2). Thus Heinrich Drendorf's interests and knowledge shift gradually from botany and geology to carpentry and orchard cultivation to the psychology of love and society. A framework, equally conservative and liberal, of spiritual ecology is outlined. Stifter's ethos is one of progress by work. In the end, knowledge is transformed into Beauty, Enlightenment ideals into a harmony of completeness.

A review of the facts leaves little doubt that an ethos of learning prevailed in eastern and central Europe. Each of its features, whether part of social reality or mere intellectual principle, can be found in other parts of the West and even, simultaneously or slightly later, in other parts of the world. A dramatic pressure towards the acquisition of knowledge has been building up consistently in the last two hundred years all over the world and has played an enormously important part in motivating social and individual actions. This historical factor is, curiously enough, highly underestimated in most available historical explanations of the modern age. Foregrounding the epistemological factor in one area of the world is intended as a signal of its functioning everywhere; it does not mean that it is absent everywhere else. On the contrary, I consider it one of the major strategies used in the Western world (and partially and gradually elsewhere also) in order to absorb the avalanche of accelerated changes occupying society. The same is true about almost every other feature enumerated in this article: the role of the aesthetic, upward mobility, the recycling of aristocratic strata, the legitimation of the middle classes, the eradication of illiteracy, and so on. Both in the east and the west of Europe (for example, France), in India, and in many other places, some or several of these features can be pointed out; it is just that some of them appear thicker in central Europe. What counts, at bottom, is their combination, the figure thus constituted. In central Europe this figure appeared early on—thus polytechnical colleges were established in Prague (1806) and Vienna (1815) earlier than in Germany (1825), and only slightly later than in France (1794), while in the "personal emancipation of the peasant and the removal of custom barriers," the empire preceded both France and Germany (Gross, in Komlos 1983, 4)—and it was adhered to despite relative socioeconomic and technological backwardness. This undoubtedly endowed the central-European area with a number of peculiarities, and among them, I believe, was a certain toning down of class conflicts.

Are we in a position to evaluate these peculiarities? Can we retrospectively judge them as relatively favorable or unfavorable in some developmental scheme? Such enterprises always produce ambiguous results. Many of the most endearing qualities of central Europe, coziness and decency, legality and respect for intelligence, among others, can be shown to be linked to the learning ethos. However many of the area's most discouraging and backward features were also generated by it (in part or entirely): slothful modernization, excessive nostalgia, deficiencies in the relationship to reality, and the chronic addiction to all kinds of retrograde populism are just some of those that acted as historical handicaps. The political behavior of these learning classes was far from irreproachable, and any idealization would be unwarranted. The legacy, therefore, of this mode of acting was far from unambiguous. By the time of World War I the central-European ethos was seriously eroded. It is doubtful whether in the 1920s and 1930s the *Kulturbürgertum* any longer performed a progressive or even useful role in most of central Europe (or in Germany). Nationalism, fascism, and above all the long decades of Marxism-Leninist oppression destroyed or at least minimized the efficacy of the ethos as a real social factor. Nevertheless its historical role was something that could not be eroded. Not the ethos itself but the way in which it decisively shaped the historical memory and the actual makeup of the area's populations still remain clear and, indeed, powerful realities.

At the same time it is remarkable to point to the continued relevance of the central-European learning ethos in today's world. It had, for instance, a direct influence on attitudes inside American society through central-European (and in the first place Jewish) immigration. Many of these immigrants saw learning as the chief avenue to upward mobility; they also promoted an attitude of reverence for culture and science in society at large. More generally, recognizing the crystallization of a general epistemological human drive into a local ethos is, I think, of great interest. At the turn of the twenty-first century definitions of the human (individuals, societies) as somehow informationally oriented are becoming more frequent. Whether these are valid in any conclusive sense is hard to decide. Suffice it to say that they touch upon some central features of human existence in our day and that hence, a historical experiment of the recent past, such as the central-European learning ethos, must remain of primary interest. [4]

Notes

1. In much of the Danube basin not only class barriers but even gender handicaps could sometimes be overcome by means of access to learning. Thus women could be recognized as writers or scientists even when they had no electoral rights.

2. The multiple and polymorphous function of these voluntary associations is remarkable; it went from the provision of funeral insurance, to bowling and feasting, to cultural issues (a subject to which I will return later), to openly political issues.

3. The first circulating library proper in the British Isles may be said to be the one established by Allen Ramsey in Edinburgh in 1725 (Altick 1957, 59); book societies, or book clubs, were set up at least as late as the early nineteenth century as "more or less informal organizations(s) of middle-class families in a given neighborhood for the buying and exchange of books" (218). Broad-based attempts were made to establish village and "mechanics' institutes," lending libraries, and reading rooms. Nevertheless both Thomas Carlyle in 1840 and an official and distinguished special committee of the House of Commons in 1849 declared the situation unsatisfactory in terms of the access of the working people to the world of reading (214–25).

4. I would like to thank Professors Milan Dimić (Alberta) and Andrew Janos (California) for valuable bibliographical indications in writing this chapter.

Bibliography

Altick, Richard. 1957. *The English Common Reader: A Social History of the Mass Reading Public 1800–1900*. Chicago: University of Chicago Press.

Bauer, Roger. 1974. *Die Welt als Reich Gottes: Grundlagen und Wandlungen einer österreichischen Lebensform*. Munich: Europa.

Berger, Peter L. 1986. *The Capitalist Revolution*. New York: Basic Books.

Bled, Jean-Paul. 1987. *François-Joseph*. Paris: Fayard.

Bocşan, Nicolae. 1986. *Contribuţii la istoria iluminismului românesc*. Timişoara: Facla.

Bosl, Karl, ed. 1979. *Handbuch der Geschichte der böhmischen Länder*. 4 vols. Stuttgart: Hiersemann.

Bruckmüller, Ernst. 1985. *Sozialgeschichte Österreichs*. Munich: Herold.
Cohen, Gary. 1981. *The Politics of Ethnic Survival: Germans in Prague 1861–1914*. Princeton, N.J.: Princeton University Press.
Csáky, Moritz. 1981. *Von der Aufklärung zum Liberalismus: Studien zum Frühliberalismus*. Vienna: Verlag der Osterreichischen Akademie.
Dahrendorf, Ralf. 1967. *Society and Democracy in Germany*. New York: Doubleday. (Orig. pub. in German, 1965.)
Doderer, Heimito von. 1956. *Die Dämonen*. Munich: Biederstein.
Don, Jehuda, and Victor Karády, eds. 1990. *A Social and Economic History of Central European Jewry*. New Brunswick, N.J.: Transaction.
Durkheim, Emile. 1912. *Les formes élémentaires de la vie religieuse*. Paris: Alcan.
Engelsing, Rolf. 1973. *Analphabetentum und Lektüre: Zur Sozialgeschichte des Lesens in Deutschland zwischen feudaler und industrieller Gesellschaft*. Stuttgart: Metzler.
Furnham, Adrian. 1990. *The Protestant Work Ethic: The Psychology of Work-Related Beliefs and Behaviours*. London: Routledge.
Girard, René. 1972. *La violence et le sacré*. Paris: Grasset.
Gollwitzer, Heinz. 1956. *Die Standesherren: Die politische und gesellschaftliche Stellung der Mediatisierten 1815–1918*. Göttingen: Vandenhoeck.
Janos, Andrew C. 1982. *The Politics of Backwardness in Hungary 1825–1945*. Princeton, N.J.: Princeton University Press.
Johnston, William M. 1972. *The Austrian Mind: An Intellectual and Social History, 1848–1938*. Berkeley: University of California Press.
Jowitt, Kenneth, ed. 1978. *Social Change in Romania 1860–1940: A Debate on Development in a European Nation*. Berkeley, Calif.: Institute of International Studies.
Kann, Robert. 1960. *A Study in Austrian Intellectual History: From Late Baroque to Romanticism*. New York: Praeger.
Komlos, John, ed. 1983. *Economic Development in the Habsburg Monarchy in the Nineteenth Century*. Boulder, Colo.: East European Monographs.
Korbel, Joseph. 1977. *Twentieth-Century Czechoslovakia: The Meanings of Its History*. New York: Columbia University Press.
Matei, Pamfil. 1986. *Astra: Asociaţiunea Transilvană Pentru Literatura Română si Cultura Poporului Român 1861–1950*. Cluj: Dacia.
Mayer, Arno. 1981. *The Persistence of the Old Regime*. New York: Pantheon.
McCagg, William O., Jr. 1972. *Jewish Nobles and Geniuses in Modern Hungary*. Boulder, Colo.: East European Monographs.
Milisavats, Zhivan. 1988. *Matice srpska y Vukova reforma*. Belgrade: Matice Srpska.
Molnár, Miklós, and André Reszler, eds. 1989. *Le génie de l' Autriche-Hongrie: État, société, culture*. Paris: Presses Universitaires de France.
Naipaul, V. S. 1990. *India: A Million Mutinies Now*. London: Heinemann.
Nemoianu, Virgil. 1978. *Micro-Harmony: The Growth and Uses of the Idyllic Model in Literature*. Bern: Peter Lang.
———. 1985. *The Taming of Romanticism: European Literature and the Age of Biedermeier*. Cambridge, Mass.: Harvard University Press.
Oxaal, Ivar, Michael Pollak, and Gerhard Botz, eds. 1987. *Jews, Anti-Semitism and Culture*. London: Routledge.
Pollak, Michael. 1984. *Vienne 1900: Une identité bléssée*. Paris: Gallimard.

Rostow, Walt W. 1960. *The Stages of Economic Growth.* Cambridge: Cambridge University Press.

Rothenberg, Gunther E. 1976. *The Army of Franz Joseph.* West Lafayette, Ind.: Purdue University Press.

Rozenblit, Marsha. 1983. *The Jews of Vienna 1867–1914.* Albany: State University of New York Press.

Schorske, Carl. 1981. *Fin-de-siècle Vienna: Politics and Culture.* New York: Vintage.

Siegert, Heinrich. 1971. *Der Adel in Österreich.* Vienna: Kremayr.

Slavici, Ioan. 1892. *Novele.* 2 vols. Bucharest: Socec.

Steiner, George. 1967. *Language and Silence.* London: Faber.

Stifter, Adalbert. 1977. *Nachsommer.* Munich: Deutscher Taschenbuch Verlag. (Orig. pub. 1857.)

Wierer, Rudolf. 1960. *Der Föderalismus im Donauraum.* Graz: Böhlau.

Zeman, Herbert, ed. 1982. *Die österreichische Literatur: Ihr Profil im 19. Jahrhundert (1830–1880).* Graz: Akademische Druck und Verlagsanstalt.

CHAPTER 9

National Poets in the Romantic Age
Emergence and Importance

I BELIEVE IT IS APPROPRIATE at this point to concentrate, as briefly as possible, on the institution of the national poet as it appears in its fullness toward the end of the eighteenth and the beginning of the nineteenth century. This I regard as a subdivision, so to say, of the interests in education and of the modalities of handling the knowledge revolution and therefore I will limit my presentation. On the other hand, inevitably the accent must be here also on east-central Europe, although the background of western Europe ought not to be ignored. Besides, I will deal less with the how of these events, important though it is, and try to focus for the moment on the matter of why this set of events occurred and gained importance. Why did German-speaking lands need Goethe and Schiller; why did (an absent) Poland need Mickiewicz; why do Petöfi and Eminescu still seem indispensable; why do even Shakespeare, Dante, and Cervantes grow so considerably in importance? (Obviously, the list could be lengthened.)

Admittedly we are dealing here with an ongoing process, not limited exclusively to the romantic age; attempts at poetic sacralization began quite a bit earlier. Thus, albeit in a sketchy manner, Dante and Shakespeare had been informally proposed for this kind of status already during the Renaissance, and the same can perhaps be said also about Corneille and Racine, Cervantes and Lope de Vega. In Greek and Roman antiquity Homer and Hesiod certainly, Pindar, Aeschylus, and Sophocles possibly, and Virgil quite deliberately had enjoyed a very special position. Nevertheless as long as the referential level for any poetic and rhetoric was the classical one we can speak of a certain unity and predictability: a poetic achievement is measured by the extent to which it approaches the standards and values prescribed by a venerable and firmly reliable tradition.

What is more special about the eighteenth and the early nineteenth centuries is the emergence and/or consolidation of the nation-state that feels that it has to legitimize itself by a number of features that some call institutional, others simply ideal.

Even in cases when such nation-states do not yet exist (in fact particularly under these circumstances) validation of an ethnolinguistic ("national") group by a personal and autonomous literature is seen as indispensable. This is, of course, abundantly exemplified in eastern Europe, as explained in earlier chapters, but also in southern, and sometimes even in northwestern Europe (Scotland, Ireland, and some Scandinavian countries).

However, this explanation would limp if we did not take into account and repeat for emphasis another fact. The sociocultural framework of Europe in the given period was one in which reaching and demonstrating to others a certain level of intellectual and aesthetic achievement had become of high importance. This had to do with several factors. On the one hand the ever-increasing valuation of scientific accomplishment and of cognition in general, implied obliquely a heightened demand for broadly conceived educational values, including the humanities and aesthetic production. On the other hand, the reassessment of religious understanding and vindication was now done (particularly since Chateaubriand's pioneering *Génie du christianisme*) through the Beautiful, and no longer exclusively (or even primarily) through the True and the Good. Both these factors were pushing toward justification by means of high literary (and other artistic) accomplishments.

This was the state of affairs which motivated the tenacious search after a substantial national literature and its organization in a historically coherent manner. It is important here to remember that the emergence of national poets was not an isolated phenomenon. Rather it went hand in hand with the writing of histories of national literatures, with the attempt to discover early foundational myths (preferably in epic form), and, at bottom, with the investigation of group histories (in which the groups were ethnic, linguistic, racial, social, or all of the above).

As I have indicated, such phenomena had roots in the remote past. One of these, perhaps the most fundamental, was the emergence of vernaculars (languages and literatures) out of the common Latin trunk. "Battles between ancients and moderns," or justifications of "vulgar tongues" as vehicles for sophisticated ideas and poetic expressions had become almost critical topoi. Dante had felt the need for this justification (in the incomplete *De vulgari eloquentia*, 1304–1305); in the French Renaissance we can find several examples (one of the first is Du Bellay's *Défense et illustration de la langue française*, 1549, followed by Corneille's intervention in 1660, the "Querelle des anciens et des modernes" in 1687–1716, and others yet; for a more complete survey see Hubert Gillot, *La querelle des anciens et des modernes en France*, Geneva: Slatkin, 1968); Swift had mulled over the issue in his characteristically sarcastic way (in his *Battle of the Books* written in 1697 in Sir William Temple's library, published in 1704).

Closer to the age discussed here, the romantic movement, rising simultaneously in several countries, had met decisive resistance on the part of those who found it parvenu, devoid of solid back-up in the past, and simply the outcome of whimsical, arbitrary, invention. To counter this serious set of objections, romantic theorists decided to construct a solid pedigree of their own, one that would respond to the genealogical superiorities claimed by their adversaries. That is how the line of Dante-Cervantes-Shakespeare (briefly speaking) was set up as a viable romantic alternative to the classical and the neoclassical tradition. At the same time the search for the equivalents of the great epics of the past was sometimes replaced by the literal invention of such foundational works. James McPherson's *Poems of Ossian* (1773) is a fictional work, and not a very remarkable one at that, based upon vague scraps of surviving Gaelic texts, but its popular success throughout Europe was extraordinary. *Beowulf* is a genuine poem written around 700–750 A.D., preserved in a manuscript of around 1000 A.D., but largely unknown and actually first published in 1815: for a long while it remained without much echo. The *Nibelungenlied* of ca. 1200 circulated in manuscript, but in a limited area of southern Germany and was rediscovered only by the romantics, widely imitated, and rewritten in the nineteenth century by such luminaries as Friedrich Hebbel and Richard Wagner, among many other enthusiastic fans. Likewise *La chanson de Roland* and *El Cantar de mío Cid* (ca. 1100 and twelfth century respectively) were never truly forgotten or uninfluential, but they reached the status of founding myths only around or after 1800. Vörösmarty in Hungary and Eminescu (as well as B. P. Hașdeu) in Romania tried to invent or structure national mythologies. Serbian and other Balkan epic materials have more authenticity. The Finnish *Kalevala* (1835–1849) is openly acknowledged as the work of Elias Lönnrot, even though the author did use some genuine surviving oral lyrical and epic traditional verse. There are many doubts as to whether *The Tale of Igor's Host* (twelfth century) is genuine or a later Russian construction and the scholarly debate has so far remained inconclusive. No such doubts are possible in the case of the "Old Czech" manuscripts of Králóve Dvúr and Zelená Hora, which are now generally accepted as the fictional work of Vacláv Hanka, Josef Linda, and perhaps others. It is fair to say that in all these cases Homer and the Bible were the great authoritative models, although gradually and later similar overwhelming works in Sanskrit, Chinese, and other languages (including eventually African) came to join this family of writings. Perhaps a very few words about some of the more prominent cases of individual national poets would be useful before we try to reach some conclusions.

In Romania, to begin with a later case, Mihai Eminescu (1850–1889) was discovered by an assertive and influential group of young critics, essayists, theoreticians, and politicians, the *Junimea* group in Jassy and was quickly elevated to the rank of national poet, "morning star of Romania," and the like (already in the 1870s). To be sure, the merits of Eminescu are incontestable. He had an enormously powerful control of the language, a resourceful and deep imagination, a personal metaphysics and philosophy of history, was well educated, having studied at German and Austrian universities, and being cognizant of several foreign languages as well as informed in a number of areas of knowledge. Additionally his personal life was tragic: he lived mostly in poverty, was pessimistic and unhappy, his personal and erotic life were unfortunate and disorderly, and during the last years of his life he suffered from severe nervous illnesses, so that he ended his life in a mental asylum. The combination of substantial intellectual and poetic achievement with personal tragedy proved irresistible for a wider audience. The *Junimea* group, which had tried out different others for the role of national poet (Vasile Alecsandri, Samson Bodnărescu), had found not only somebody able to replace the traditionalist and somewhat stale poetry of the previous generation, but a durable, major figure who even nowadays continues to have a stable hold on the minds of very broad audiences. It helped, in the process, that Eminescu revealed himself as a staunch nationalist, as a man preoccupied with the greatness and the happiness of his conationals, on whose history he partly projected his own psychology: undeserved misfortune, inner greatness, and a persecution complex.

Ironically there is some debate on the ethnic roots of Eminescu, who according to some scholars may have been partly or entirely of Slavic descent (although this is uncertain). The same is true about the national poet of neighboring Hungary Sándor Petőfi (1823–1849), who was of Serbian descent. However a number of other features also coincide. Like Eminescu, Petőfi was an ardent nationalist, he died quite young, bravely, on the battlefield, and he contributed substantially to articulating a national mythology. His poetry was rich and diverse and it did contribute to the adaptability and the flexibility of the Hungarian language. He was almost immediately embraced and admired. One interesting difference ought to be mentioned, however. Petőfi belonged to a more abundant literature, one with a longer tradition, and the cool aesthetic observer may actually wonder whether some of his contemporaries (Arany, Vörösmarty) were not in true fact his peers or his superiors as poets. This ultimately makes Petőfi more rather than less interesting as a case study: he may be seen more clearly as a figure singled out in a very special way, according to historical and biographical indicators rather than just artistic ones.

The canonization of Adam Mickiewicz (1798–1855) is at least as fascinating. Here was a writer of surpassing merit, of European stature indeed, who spent most of his life abroad, outside of the confines of a homeland that he had already lost. Let us recall that by the end of the eighteenth century, after three divisions by neighboring empires (Romanov, Habsburg, and Hohenzollern), Poland had ceased to exist and its proud multisecular history during which it had been sometimes a major player on the European scene had (apparently) come to an end, despite the vague Napoleonic gesture of establishing briefly a grand-duchy around Warsaw. By 1815, as the future of Europe was in broad outline decided for a whole next century, Poland found itself in the unusual situation of having its whole generation of (as it happened) brilliant poets (not only Mickiewicz, but the likes of Słowacki, Krasiński, and many others) living and writing abroad. If, as may be argued, some of the latter figures of this poetic elite seem more attractive to some readers in our own day, owing to their unusual imagination and philosophical depth, Mickiewicz early on in his career plunged into the historical past of the Polish people and summoned unforgettable scenes, partly realistic and jocular, partly tragic and symbolic (I am thinking in particular of *Pan Tadeusz* and *Dziady* of 1834 and 1823–1833, respectively) that could act as referential signals to the plight of the nation. Furthermore Mickiewicz later in his life became engaged in political action meant to maintain and promote inside European public opinion the topicality of the Polish future. He taught Slavic history and culture at the University of Lausanne and at the Collège de France (1838–1844); he tried to raise a "Polish legion" (1848) to fight for the liberation of Italy and Poland; and, most relevantly in a way, he developed a kind of philosophy of history in which mystical religiousness and national aspiration would be merged (see the 1832 *Books of the Polish Nation and Its Pilgrimage* and the companionship in ideas with the mystic Andrzej Towianski in the 1840s). The latter tendency, while less known at the time, gradually seeped into the consciousness and the common discourses of Poland and may be said to be active even to this day. His rise is thus due partly to his own judicious combination of the poetic and the social, and partly to his adoption by leading French intellectual circles and the impact this had on the imposed powerlessness of a Poland devoid of independence.

There can be no doubt that these eastern European examples (others might be easily added) were up to a certain point influenced by Western models. The examples abound here also and they are often paradoxical or unexpected when related retrospectively to the situation on the terrain at the given time (late eighteenth and early nineteenth centuries). In England, let alone in Europe, William Blake was literally unknown, the number of his readers being a couple of dozen at best during his lifetime. Wordsworth and Coleridge were known but not widely read, understood, or even respected; they were certainly unknown quantities to readers outside the English-speaking world. Shelley was hardly known beyond a circle of professional connoisseurs, and Keats was admired by few except some very personal passionate friends. As opposed to these, Byron and Scott had gained almost immediately enormous public success both in Europe and on the Continent. In the case of Scott there is no question in my mind that the selection was a highly democratic one: it was due to his innovative generic experimentation—after all he literally invented the new (sub?)genre of the historical novel, set its patterns and typologies, and responded promptly and shrewdly to public demand. It may be illuminating at this point to compare the route traced by his *Waverley* (and all the ensuing novels, by himself or by others) with the one of Mary Shelley's *Frankenstein*. After all, here we have two novelistic species invented almost simultaneously, by people who belonged, roughly speaking, to the same circles. Nevertheless, Scott's invention was the one that enjoyed explosive and immediate success. This is due in my opinion to the fact that the historical novel corresponded to the spirit of the age, to the sociocultural concerns of the time, and tapped into a set of burning concerns, having to do with issues such as historical development, continuity and change, national community, victory and defeat, revolution and tradition. Scott was seen as a model for national glorification, a place that was much contested given the slightly earlier enthronement of Robert

Burns. By contrast science fiction was well ahead of its time; only in the later nineteenth and particularly in the twentieth century was it in a position to surpass by far in popularity and broad-based popular interest the historical novel; only at that time was Mary Shelley rediscovered—when the zeitgeist imposed concerns that had to do with science and its ramifications into the existential and imaginative modes of the human species.

Byron in his turn set up the model of which Mickiewicz, Petőfi, Eminescu (among others) were variants. He was a spectacular figure, well versed in the art of self-advertising, able to critique the social present while still leaving room for encouraging alternatives. He balanced masterfully the image of self-victimizing with that of tough individualism, and equally well physical prowess with intellectual brilliance or wit. Pessimism and audacity went hand in hand with human assertion as against sacralized humility. The violent untimely demise (cleverly altered into battlefield sacrifice for liberty by the spin doctors of the age) became a topos for the national poet: we find it in variants in Petőfi, Eminescu, Pushkin, even Hölderlin and Poe, and as late as Charles Péguy (1873–1914) in France, who died as a volunteer on the front in the first weeks of World War I, or Yukio Mishima (1925–1970), who ended his life by committing hara-kiri in a traditional ceremony in protest against Japan's postwar direction.

For many generations of Continental readers, Byron was placed at the same level as Shakespeare, whose full canonization happened at about the same time, promoted, yes, by Coleridge and Hazlitt, but not less so the Schlegel brothers and by Tieck, by his Polish and Russian admirers, by Victor Hugo and the circles around him. In England specifically, the fact that a number of Shakespeare's plays dealt with the national past bolstered his central position.

The situation was perhaps slightly different in France, Italy (which did not exist yet as a nation-state), or Spain. Italy, despite the respect for Foscolo and Leopardi (and despite a few striking similarities of theirs with the exalted national poet-victims mentioned above) placed a prose writer rather than a poet in the status of national grandeur: namely Alessandro Manzoni. This may have been due in part to the continuing and renewed glorification of Dante, partly to the fragmentation of Italy that was to continue until around 1870. Similarly it would be difficult to speak about any surge in Spain over and beyond the rediscovery or reinforcement of Cervantes, Calderón, and Lope de Vega, to a good extent by external agents, in Germany, England, and France. Even the revaluation of some great mystical writers like St. Teresa of Avila or San Juan de la Cruz came a little after the romantic age. Likewise in France, although we cannot entirely ignore the halfhearted attempts to set up Victor Hugo or Chateaubriand as national poets, the neoclassical tradition of the seventeenth century and the reverberations of the Enlightenment Age were simply too strong to allow alternative competitions except at most in a complementary role.

The German-speaking area occupies an intermediary role here between northern and eastern Europe on the one hand and southern Europe on the other. The "telescoping" of the classical and the romantic contributed to the process. Decisive however was something else. Unlike in Italy political fragmentation acted in a challenging and energizing way. The spiritual, cultural-intellectual sphere became an alternative unifying homeland; the social imaginary gained weight and was endowed with additional reality. For a while the idea of "the great six" found favor in scholarly and educational circles. Lessing, Wieland, Klopstock, Herder, Goethe, and Schiller seemed to constitute a group in which the classical and the romantic were neatly balanced. However there were presumably too many tensions and potential conflicts between these, as well as some inequalities in stature. So Goethe and Schiller emerged as major figures. Schiller was in some ways closer to pattern because he had had a short life and his passions and idealism were more obvious. Also, despite mighty efforts it was difficult to square the work of Goethe with any kind of nationalist aspiration. However, precisely for that reason Goethe enjoyed genuine international appeal (in France, England, Russia, America, and elsewhere). It was also, I would contend, a matter of Goethe's centrism, of his moderate conservatism, of his adroit maneuvering between extremes: a Biedermeier attitude, one in keeping with the moderation of the "silver age." Goethe did not share—in fact he dismissed—the early radicalism of the romantics, but he did not join the later reactionary conversion of many of them either. A rather revealing parallel could be made with August von Kotzebue (1761–1819). The popularity of Kotzebue at the time was overwhelming (and not only in Germany—English translations of his plays came promptly, thick and fast). Moreover Kotzebue was a convinced reactionary, a political instrument of the Czarist regime, and he ended up assassinated by the nationalist and politically radical student Karl Sand. Any disciple of the doctrine of cultural materialism would have to predict that, on the face of it, Kotzebue ought to have been the prime candidate for canonization. However, precisely because of his political stance (and, no, I do not discard the matter of objective and intrinsic value) Goethe emerged as the dominant figure of the age and has remained to our own days the (improbable and untypical) figure of national poet.

What can our conclusions be after this cursory review? One important factor in the emergence of national poets was the multitude of new data reaching scholars and ordinary audiences alike: the growing energy of the nascent informational revolution. Once Herder and others (Michelet and Quinet, to name but a few) had asserted eloquently the verities and necessities of a multicultural understanding of the world, it seemed indispensable to expand the fixed canon of classical descent and of narrow but powerfully streamlined models. On the other hand this expansion could not, realistically speaking, comprise the multitude of actors and producers in each of the additional countries and/or languages. Establishing a national poet was a kind of shorthand, a summary of the achievements and of the profile of each of these sub-cultures. It may also be seen as a kind of compromise. Yes, the Western decisional centers (obviously a metaphorical expression here) were saying, "We will make room for you, but not too much; what we need is a token representation, an 'ambassador' to our courts, a recognizable sample of your endowments and achievements. You can decide yourselves who that will be or else *we* are the ones who will make the choice for you," the argument continued.

It is also the case that, in the spirit of compacting and telescoping, whole societies found it useful to resort to somebody or to something able to provide coherence and some kind of unity to their past and their present. It was soon recognized, consciously or intuitively, that Homeric and Virgilian texts had been at their time quite useful to the respective societies. They had provided at least a broad, general, and ideal level of solidarity to otherwise diverse societies. How much more urgent and indispensable would such unifying myths prove if they could function as nation-building elements. Let us not forget that we are talking here about countries with a fragmented and discontinuous past, one full of gaps and interruptions, whose history had been based on stop-and-go rhythms. Or else these were aspirants to nationhood devoid of independence and of coherence. Under these circumstances one either looked toward the past for some unity or else assigned this duty and obligation to more recent, national poets. In either case a certain degree of coherence could be achieved.

Political/ideological needs of self-assertion have already been mentioned here at the beginning and in other chapters; there is no need to repeat them. Their importance remains untouched. Likewise dramatic biographical appeal and, equally important, intrinsic aesthetic merit. (Theories of serendipity or of conspiratorial decisions by hegemonic sociopolitical groups have scant credibility for me.) Finally one other factor has to be taken into consideration. It is Goethe's proposal of what *Weltliteratur* ought to look like. Goethe's view, as expressed in his old-age conversations with Eckermann and as widely known, was inclusive and elitist at the same time. It was inclusive in as far as he genuinely (and there is no reason to question Goethe's honesty in the matter) wanted to see present on the high Olympian plateau of world imagination representatives of as many cultures, societies, and literatures, as possible. It was elitist in as far as only "the best and the brightest" could gain admission in this select society of super-achievers. We might think of Olympian here not only from the point of view of ancient divinities but also from that of the modern Olympic games.

In any case what is worth emphasizing is that, once established, the position of national poet remained fairly stable until the end of the twentieth century and probably beyond. Other countries followed the example. (Ireland is not the least typical case with its Joyce or Yeats, or even early epic writing.) Particularly for smaller countries it seems rather difficult and improbable that a rapid displacement of such figures can take place. Even in the case of highly modernized and sophisticated cultures, where the hegemony of cynical and dogmatic skepticism seems for the moment rather firm, the attempts to shake the positions of Goethe and Shakespeare have been so far singularly unsuccessful. It remains to be seen what the future will bring to this peculiar mode of viewing literature.

Perhaps a final note would be in order. Does the institution(alization) of the national poet contribute at all to the moderating efforts toward pacification, moderation, and reconciliation present in the age? I think that in a paradoxical and ironic way, it does. The establishment of the nation-state had many progressive advantages, at least from the point of view of its initiators, but it became soon rather obvious that it carried with it also some dangers, not least an exacerbated sensitivity, going all the way to martial readiness. Alternatives to violent competition had to be set in place; many could be thought of, much as (to take an ultra-modern example) soccer and other athletic competitions are hoped to take the place of military clashes. Proclaiming and encouraging achievement, talent, and genius in the arts and particularly in literature, seemed a sensible decision. Competitiveness could be channeled into more peaceful directions. Thus encouraging the glorification and symbolic altitude of a grand national poet could satisfy national egotisms, and at the same time it did not demand too much of a sacrifice from one or the other of the neighboring nation-states to admit the merits or accomplishments of one or several of such poets, artists, scientists, and other peaceful creative figures. In this sense fiddling with the canon was preferable to toying with cannons.

Obviously this was not a definitive or a decisive answer. Armed conflicts did not disappear in the nineteenth century inside Europe, and even less outside the continent. It might however be an interesting exercise to try to measure the extent to which literary pride mitigated the dangers of war (perhaps even of revolution) and contributed to a kind a general harmony and fraternity between ethnic and other groups.

CHAPTER 10

The Conservatism of Voracious Reading
The Case of Robert Southey's The Doctor

THE ENGLISH RADICALS and the progressive Left found themselves in a difficult and ambiguous situation during the first fifteen years of the nineteenth century, when their country was engaged in the Napoleonic wars. The best comparison that can be suggested is the situation of their Western counterparts during the decades of the cold war. Neither side could easily deny the tyrannical and aggressive nature of the adversary—Napoleon or Brezhnev, respectively—nor were they willing to break completely with their own communities and governments. Yet they also felt a deep allegiance to the revolutionary leftist values that these dictators continued to represent albeit in a less than pleasing form. Hazlitt and Hunt, Shelley and Byron did not hide their admiration for Napoleon, and they criticized the Tory governing forces with the loud stridency used by Russell and Chomsky one hundred and fifty years later, while the eminently reasonable *Edinburgh Review* was publishing article after article explaining in great detail how detente and peaceful coexistence were much preferable to a state of war with France, again in a tradition that was to be continued enthusiastically by the informational elites of the late twentieth century.

The situation was nevertheless frustrating and infuriating, and under the circumstances some outlet for pent-up anger was clearly needed. Conservatively inclined intellectuals seemed the most convenient target, yet even these proved elusive. Thus Scott didn't care much, and besides, his mixture of amiability and belligerence was difficult to assault. Everybody realized that it would have been counterproductive to attack Coleridge whose overwhelming medical and personal problems made him more an object of compassion than anything else. Wordsworth was a canny and eccentric curmudgeon who isolated himself in the countryside and knew well which governmental advances to accept and which to refuse. By contrast Southey seemed healthy and in 1813 had cheerfully picked up what Scott had turned down: the laureateship.

As a result Southey became the object of relentless adversity,[1] particularly since he naively or serenely refused to maintain a low-key stance and actually published poetry laudatory of the monarchy and works of political debate in which many tenets of the reform forces were engaged aggressively. Whatever one may think of the manner in which Southey fulfilled what after all were his duties as a poet laureate, he certainly also expressed in an open and articulate way a number of conclusions that he had reached together with (though separately from) Wordsworth and Coleridge. The main difference is that whereas Wordsworth's idiom was that of metaphorical indirection, and whereas Coleridge's style, fragmentary and tortuously metaphysical, cloaked his intentions, Southey's sinewy prose and his tendency to blurt out his truths, biases, and preferences turned him fast into a more visible foe.

What were in fact some of the main features of Southey's conservatism after (and a little before) 1813? These can be culled chiefly from looking at the articles written between approximately 1809 and 1828, and collected in two two-volume works, *Sir Thomas More* (1829–1832) and *Essays, Moral and Political* (1832).[2]

They certainly included a clear-cut nationalism, one that gradually went beyond the mere patriotism of the citizen of a country at war. *The Life of Nelson* (1813) is arguably the most eloquent piece of uplifting nationalistic prose ever penned in English; it was followed by the even more explicit though less accomplished *The Lives of the British Admirals*, 5 vols. (1833–1840). Southey had moved from the tradition of eighteenth-century English localism (which still rings in some of the verses of Wordsworth and Coleridge) to a kind of passionate interest in global comprehensiveness (expressed equally in his large epic poems and in such works as the three-volume history of Brazil). His nationalism therefore was like the return swing of a pendulum: he became convinced that it was in fact a kind of judicious middle-of-the-road—the providential way in which values of universal merit could be channeled to the world through a firm and faithful allegiance to Britishness. (His concern was with ethical values primarily, but he prominently displayed his concern for those connected with cognition also.) In the process colonial endeavors suddenly became acceptable as carriers of emancipating practices and discourses, let alone as solutions to internal social problems.[3] Britishness was for Southey the idiom of progress, and he came to believe that the price of colonialism seemed a light one to pay given the advantages of the unifying message carried by it. Southey's next prominent Tory conviction was an antiindustrial one. There is no question but that he harked back (like other romantics) and, in the age-hallowed English tradition of pastoralism and Horatian mediocrity, to a contented rural world.[4] His vision was that of a precapitalist or premodern England: a harmonious, modestly self-satisfied environment in which the contact with nature would be preserved at all times, with the admission of just, slow, and carefully selected movements toward progress. Southey combined the dislikes and suspicions belonging to Wordsworth and Blake with the more indignant tones of a Goldsmith and a Smollett.[5]

This position was rendered more complex by a genuine and passionate defense of the lower classes of society, by outrage against conditions of poverty, and by anger at any Darwinian competitive liberalism. We can say that in many respects the man was a close cousin of Cobbett's more than of Burke's.[6] Cobbett, like Southey but in a more radical, even violent manner, was an anticapitalist nostalgic for the rural past.[7] They both expressed genuine anger against a system that maintained a large part of the population in total poverty.[8] Southey was however more flexible and more inclined to accept inequality in different shapes. A good way of formulating things is that Southey inscribes himself with part of his thinking in the tradition of Cobbett-Dickens-Chesterton, with another in that of Burke, Scott, and Adam Smith.[9]

A third feature of Southey's conservatism was precisely his acceptance of inequality through a firm, authoritarian, paternalistic mode of governing. When parliamentary reform was at the door in 1831 Southey actually began thinking of emigration, and he sometimes said that the prereform system was too generous, lax, and comprehensive.[10]

Finally, the picture would not be nearly complete without mentioning the specific way in which Southey understood religiousness. Although he was a relentless adversary of Catholic emancipation, Southey could see aesthetically pleasing and traditionally acceptable features of Roman Catholicism or express liking for a moderate thinker like Fénelon.[11] Southey's firm insistence on Anglicanism grew out of a sense of tradition, stability, and dutiful patriotism (as understood by him), but also out of the genuine conviction that this religious form was rational and truly walked the middle of the road in matters religious, whenever it was wisely managed.

What are we to make of this combination, which seems to be coherent and incoherent at the same time? The first and most important observation will have to be, I believe, a historical one. Southey heralds the main features of the Victorian social-intellectual and historical framework. In fact it seems to me almost impossible (or at least a great self-inflicted handicap) for any cultural historian to speak about the Victorian Age without beginning with Southey: yet virtually all writers on the subject seem to ignore this most convenient entry gate. Victorian England was forecast by Southey better than by the other romantics. It seems clear to me that Southey's writing (more than that of Coleridge or Shelley) became a paradigm for many key aspects of nineteenth-century British aesthetic, intellectual, and even political behaviors.[12]

Thus some of his ideas indicate a kinship to Carlyle: like him, Southey was a defender of the working classes and also an advocate of the "leadership principle;"[13] not to mention that there are some obvious similarities between *Sartor Resartus* and *The Doctor*. In other ways Southey was rather a forerunner of Disraeli's renewed Toryism and the "young England" movement: for example, in the manner in which it put a premium on abolishing class war and advocating unifying national and communitarian ties (depicting a corporate nation). A direct connection would be his friendship to Lord Ashley. In other ways yet Southey prefigured (stylistically speaking) the Victorian yearning for the return to chivalry, and finally both Southey and Coleridge can be seen as godfathers to the Tractarians and the Oxford Movement and of the Anglican renaissance of the nineteenth century.

The second chief observation when we seek some kind of coherence inside Southey's conservatism (or some connection between it and his both amiable and pugnacious personality), as well as some motivation for it, is to understand that this conservatism is actually a branch of liberalism, that it derives from it even though it chooses to go its own way and to harden (up to deforming them) some of its features. This is what I meant when I said that part of Southey's thinking can be classed with that of Scott, Burke, and Adam Smith, who also derive from the Whig tradition, rather than from hard Toryism, let alone the armored "old regime" line of absolute monarchy of divine right.

The third and most important tendency on which I want to dwell in the present chapter is that toward fanciful meditation and serenity (and its connection with some of the—progressive—Enlightenment ideals). This inclination cannot be uncoupled from the essayistic discourse of leisurely ("both ... and") debate, of digression, of relativization, and of massively lowered ideological tensions and passions. Southey's gravitation toward the essay can be seen even in some of his poems such as *The Battle of Blenheim* (1798) or, in a more humorous vein, *Snuff* or *The Pig* (both 1799). Southey's writing covers the whole range of essayistic discourses. We recognize, of course, the pamphlets of (particularly) the 1820s and 1830s, but earlier also, in which he gave expression to the abovementioned conservative views. These are longer, well-structured, thesis-driven pieces of argumentative prose. At the other end of the spectrum of essayistic modes of writing one finds Southey engaged in the short, dry notation of odd facts, particularly in *Omniana* and the *Common-Place Book*.[14] As often as not Southey behaves like one overwhelmed and enthused by the explosion of knowledge in history and geography, in the natural sciences and in humane letters that occurred around the turn of the century. He plunges deep into the sea of knowledge and comes up with various objects and episodes that are held up to attention. These are supposed to have an eloquence of their own so that readers can easily draw their own conclusions. The rhetoric of small, weird facts becomes a kind of subjective alternative to the vast ordering and disciplinary systems that were emerging in Southey's time. He finds observations by more-or-less credible travelers in the Southern Hemisphere or by recondite chroniclers of the past and eagerly pounces upon them.

There are other ways in which Southey showed himself close to the spirit of essayism. The bibliographical annotations to his long poems (sometimes they double the total length of the text) are charming: naive and learned at the same time, full of a sense of wonder but also of the desire to demonstrate how wonder is inherent in historical and natural reality. Furthermore we have Southey's ceaseless fascination with marginality: he has clearly a passionate desire for Otherness in time and in space (other cultures and historical periods: Arabic, Brazilian, Indian, Gothic), does not avoid feminine discourse, and even tries to imitate it (above all in *The Doctor*, as will be noted shortly). He is a determined canonical revisionist: who else among his noisy leftist contemporaries would have gone to the trouble of examining the lives and writings of the uneducated poets?[15] (Among the figures examined by Southey are Stephen Duck, Taylor the Water-Poet, the "old servant" John Jones, Ann Yearsley, and others.) Certainly neither Byron nor Shelley, with their aristocratic fastidiousness in matters of taste, would have deigned to study such figures.

We cannot be wrong in claiming for Southey a key role as a transition and/or synthesis between several essayistic modes. One is the eighteenth-century approach to the familiar essay, as outlined by Addison and Steele and continued by Oliver Goldsmith. This was a rational writing mode aiming toward social psychology and classical ethics but in a relaxed manner. The other is the tradition of Burton and Thomas Browne, a postmedieval discourse full of pleasing learnedness and of arbitrary theoretical invention. Finally there is the energetic whimsicality and playful erudition of the romantic contemporaries. Lamb, De Quincey, Leigh Hunt, and others were masters of this newer kind of familiar and conversational essay. It is important to note that (at least) by this time we can no longer speak about a purely English phenomenon, since the Spanish *costumbristas* and a little later many east Europeans exercised themselves in a somewhat similar mode. A very major synthetic achievement of the kind was Karl Julius Weber's *Demokritos, der lachende Philosoph* (1832–1835), therefore exactly contemporaneous with Southey—a twelve-volume work in which laughter was examined chiefly by abundant examples, but also by short aphoristic statements, ultimately turning the comic into a universal principle: laughter and nationalities, laughter and psychological temperament, laughter and history, laughter and social occupations, and so forth.

Be that as it may, *The Doctor* can be rightly seen as the crowning magnum opus, Southey's "Prelude" or "Biographia." It is itself a synthesis of Southey's different attempts at essay writing, as well as of the different approaches to this genre as outlined in the preceding centuries in English letters. Moreover the book uses as a framework the destructured and debunking discourse strongly affirmed a half-century earlier by Laurence Sterne in *Tristram Shandy*. At the time it was a matter of some outraged wonder that an author would write a book so full of digressions that its titular character would be born only well after the middle of the book and that chapters would be reduced to a few sentences, while some pages would be left blank. (Such naughty writing strategies became widely acceptable in other European literatures only a century or more later.)

In explaining this choice of discourse, our most reliable background will prove to be the exponential growth of information and the increasing doubt as to the reliability of the frameworks that were supposed to contain, streamline, and order it. Categories such as taste or neoclassical doctrine (and of course, even earlier, scholasticism) can signal the confidence in the meganarratives and comprehensive explanations available for a few centuries to European intellectuals. However, by the end of the eighteenth century there was wide lack of trust, a feeling of collapse, and the need to find alternatives. Such alternatives appeared abundantly: the theories of Enlightenment philosophers, the visions of the romantic poets, the systems of the idealist philosophers are among them. One of the things all these have in common is precisely their self-understanding as progressive, even revolutionary, systems.

I would propose that in opposition to them the conservative attitude did not primarily try to maintain the older systems (of medieval or Renaissance descent) although there were enough individuals who attempted to work in this direction also. No, more frequently it tried to protect a certain kind of disorder that was appealing to it in the old thinking models and that seemed to be lacking conspicuously in the new, alternative, meganarratives.

Southey creates instead of a theoretical scaffolding (that is, instead of any system at all) a concrete situation: the idyllic environment of microharmony centered around the Horatian man of modest affluence and ample leisure. The topos habitually used was that of the country gentleman:[16] the independent man of sufficient affluence, but not necessarily rich, living without the pressures of labor and relatively isolated from society a life of contemplation, mentally agile, benevolent, and in close touch with nature. We encounter this type in Addison and Steele, Fielding and Smollett ("Humphry Clinker"), Goldsmith and Sterne. At the beginning of the nineteenth century this recurrent human model is significantly replaced by the equally calm professional, the practitioner of the liberal arts, a medical doctor in a provincial and largely rural environment. Southey's Dr. Daniel Dove lives in a minuscule historical town surrounded by library and family; he becomes the epitome of the contended man. The books in his library harken back particularly to the traditional roots of Anglicanism in the early seventeenth century (see chs. 7 and 226, for example). Books, family, and modest income are the boundaries of self-containedness in the ocean of individual realities.

This construction of normality is not reserved to the novel's early chapters but is significantly spread out throughout *The Doctor*, as if to indicate its continuing relevance in this sea of digressions. Chapters 97–99 (1:200–225, or ch. 79, 1:176–78) offer Parson Bacon, Dove's father-in-law, as a model of Christian stoicism and an embodiment of calm Horatian existence. The retired tobacconist Allison and his whole life are also paradigms of such normality (ch. 101, 1:229–31), and this is even compared in its quiet dignity to the mode of life of a duchess, that is, to high nobility (ch. 107, 1:250–56; further Horatian notes are found in ch. 109, 1:264–67). Chapters 232–33 (2:627–31) neatly move from Daniel Dove's "family feeling," to an ideology of smallness, to an examination of benevolent small power, and thence to the example (much in a Biedermeier spirit) of the beneficial nature of small principalities inside Germany, the example of Weimar being naturally adduced as the most prominent. More generally the chapters on Doncaster (particularly chs. 42–46), with their ramifications—the praise of topographical poetry such as Drayton's *Polyolbion* (ch. 36, 1:86), the praise of local attachments (ch. 34), local government (ch. 41), the considerations on the connection between local history and individual history (chs. 46–47, 1:108–11ff.)—constitute together an ode to normality. That Southey, in authentic romantic fashion, was able to keep in mind always the opposite is seen in the satirical chapter 74 (1:157–59) on Miss Trewbody whose normality was "no blessedness either to herself or others."

The action of *The Doctor* is reduced to a minimum and the characters proper are very few in number. The years of childhood and youth of Daniel Dove are sketchily presented (he studies at Leiden in Holland), we are told about his courtship of Deborah, the daughter of Parson Bacon, their marriage, and the few friends they have. The clerical father-in-law of Dove and his friend Allison belong to the same social category and human psychology as himself, they are engaged in the same mode of life. (The same is true of the mentors and benefactors who influenced the doctor's early years and helped shape him: his father as well as the teacher Peter Hopkins and the benefactor Richard Guy.) This whole action comprises (put together quantitatively) about 10 percent of the total text. The rest is reserved to various considerations and comments. The reader may sometimes get the impression that the writing strategy resembles that of Scheherazade in the *Arabian Nights:* a deliberate postponement of action through further and further digression. Unlike the author of the *Arabian Nights* or the Jan Potocki of the *Manuscript Found in Saragossa* (written only a couple of decades earlier), Southey uses digressions that are not other coherent narratives but rather short essays and considerations, references to the multitude of what exists.

The Doctor contains plenty of prefaces, postfaces, and particularly a whole ballet of mottoes and (mostly self-justifying) quotations. This was not entirely unusual at the time. Carlyle theorized the approach in the "onion theory" of Teuffelsdroeckh, but Walter Scott similarly resorted to protective clothing for the narration: several layers of prefaces and final (historical) notes and quotations. Southey uses the same discursive strategy in order to admit subjectivity, to relativize the text no less than to find a way in which it can grow organically. In this sense Southey seems closer to the ironic relativism of Jean Paul or certain German romantics such as the Schlegel brothers, Tieck, or Grabbe, who, like Southey, were convinced that there is some merit in juxtaposing incongruous elements and in quick displacements from the higher to the lower registers of style and of referential signifieds.

There is a message to the reader in this procedure. A quiet world such as the one inside which the general action of *The Doctor* is placed contains nevertheless a mass, perhaps an infinity of ideas and possibilities (illustrated neatly, one might say, precisely by the unfinished nature of his novel). The connection between each and all of these sectors of reality (as well as the multiple branchings of further possibilities from each and all of them) is that of chains and links of association, of analogies (numerological, alphabetical), of synonymy, not of hierarchical ordering and of dialectical *polemos* and *agon*. The apparently disjointed considerations of Daniel Dove (and/or Southey) suggest an early form of computer linking. They also foreshadow a kind of postmodernist chaos theory.

The deeper philosophical argument underlying Southey's *The Doctor* appears to run as follows. Human informational progress is such that any attempt at organizing it comprehensively must collapse or be illusory. If we reject metanarrative as a mere illusion of radicals and progressives then we seem to be faced with two choices. One is silence and complete passivity. The other is falling back to some older and more "naive" modes of thinking. These are connected with essayism which offers itself as a handy substitute. Quantity and variety go together for Southey, no less than for De Quincey for instance, who had reflected on these matters. Abstract philosophical reflection tends to level down the multitude and diversity of all that is or that can be thought. By contrast the anecdotal and informal nature of the essay comes to the rescue of both time and space.

Additionally there is a certain dialectic between the essayistic discourse and narrativity. Nowadays, at the beginning of the twenty-first century, it is not infrequent to hear it said (from Foucault to Hayden White) that any theoretical writings are at bottom narrative and fictional. We should remember that the eighteenth century and early nineteenth centuries were periods when this kind of connection was for the first time pursued consciously and deliberately.

What Burton, Sir Thomas Browne, and before them Walter Map and even earlier Macrobius and Aullus Gellius (to mention just a very few names in an otherwise illustrious genealogy), had done in a less intention-laden manner (namely to blur the distance between the argumentative and the anecdotal) was now turned into a much more highly motivated, targeted, and deliberately experimental pursuit. Lamb, Hunt, Hazlitt, and De Quincey certainly understood it as such. Southey not only inscribes himself in this project, but is one of its top figures. *The Doctor*, rarely read though it may be, excels as a generically undefinable text that blends and overcomes narrativity and essayism in the same way in which it relativizes ironically both conservatism and liberalism.

If I am right about the philosophical assumptions behind *The Doctor* then two conclusions impose themselves. The first is that Southey was trying to deal with the information explosion of the age while at the same time bridging the gap between an older epistemology and a newer one. He thought that radical intertextuality, disorder, and the hidden harmonies of analogy were more effective epistemological tools than streamlining and organization. Already this is an implicitly conservative attitude, in as far as it mirrors and reinforces the preference for the natural and random that was (then as well as now) associated with a conservative stance. However, over and beyond this inclination (which could be said to act as a kind of bridge), there was something else: Southey's conviction that a truly liberal attitude could be only one that was very broadly based upon a consensus with the past and with global breadth. His liberalism was conservative to the extent to which it refused to let itself be cut off from the foundations and even methodologies of the human past.

On the other hand it is truly impressive to discover in Southey's text certain less predictable positions and attitudes, such as his total separation from any anti-

Semitism, as well as tokens of a kind of protofeminism. Such views, expressed in a rather unselfconscious manner, were less than frequent in the early nineteenth century, and, again, they seem, like Southey's chaotic postmodernism, more closely comparable to an age that was to dawn almost a century and a half later. Already in Colloquy 13 of *Sir Thomas More* (2:208–42) a long debate between the two characters of the book had developed the idea that there is a need for an active role and presence of women in the social sphere. While the discussion there is tortuous and indicates that Southey had not shed all the habitual prejudices of his age and society, the characters nevertheless argue for institutional frameworks (secularized equivalents of religious orders) in which women could make a public social impact. *The Doctor* shows more flexibility and variety in this respect. Its very first chapter proper (one that introduces and explains the emergence of the book) is dominated by female presence, and it might be argued that the book as a whole is placed in a kind of feminine space. More detailed apologies or vindications are to be found in chs. 205–8 (2:549–58) where the issue of "equality of sexes" is discussed in partly serious manner, partly in the tone of jocular eccentricity, and in ch. 117, where Dove defends Job's wife against different unfavorable biblical interpretations; see also ch. 116, 1:283–85 and 2:492 (interchapter 20). To these one could add the highly complimentary presentations of the theories of Dona Oliva Sabuco on the connection between the human soul and the composition of the natural world, in chs. 216–18, 2:581–88.

Likewise Southey speaks always with perfect equanimity, in a respectfully grave and accepting tone about judgements and wisdom culled from Hebrew traditions (ch. 76, 1:161, or ch. 117, 1:286–87, or chs. 234–35, 2:633, 636). There is even a wholesale and deeper-reaching condemnation in indignant tones of the anti-Semitic prejudices frequent in his own time (or earlier) and the defamatory myths connected with them (ch. 120, 2:649; though with a tendency to attribute to Catholics most of the blame for these).

Obviously such progressive-radical aspects are more than balanced out by Southey's muted but unapologetic support for the values of religious and political traditionalism, which are as clearly promoted in *The Doctor*, as in the rest of Southey's writings, over and beyond the laudation of idyllic normality referred to above (see ch. 102, 1:232ff.). Daniel Dove's conservatism is cheerful and positive. He sees dancing (a subject, we remember, much debated with its pros and cons in England from Elizabethan times on, and continuing through the Commonwealth era right into the early nineteenth century when even Byron branded the waltz as a form of excess) as a normal and beneficent activity. Dr. Dove (chs. 190–91, 2:503–6) considers dancing as a way to channel superfluous energy; orderly pleasure is thus part of the ethical life and "moderate vice" finds itself vindicated. (Likewise, ch. 244, 2:644ff. proclaims the cheerfulness of religion and the goodness of rational mirth.) Moreover, like Michael Oakeshott later on, Dove argues in favor of gratuitous activity as an essence of conservatism (ch. 113, 2:511).

However the most sincere and most eloquent ideological message sent by Southey's text is to be found in the structure of the novel rather than in the text's statements. The disproportion between the plot / action / narrative skeleton of the book and the overwhelming quantity of digression, of encyclopedic and miscellaneous trivia is, it has been argued (at least about other works), a deliberately comic element.[18] Yet surrounding this comic dimension there is a deeply serious one. Southey depicts the world as one overrun by the multitude of real events and facts. The world is one of details, of secondary elements and occurrences. The world is an inextricable vegetal immensity of theories, opinions, and explanations that may be contradictory. The relentless classificatory and simplifying drive of many contemporaries must remain pointless. The appropriate attitude is rather one of benevolent indifference and of delighted, perhaps grateful contemplation. Similarly, while we may be dazed or bemused by the multitude of opinions and theories in the world, we have to accept them as part of reality and enjoy them as best we can even if we disagree with them. Changes in the world can arrive only by local action, by individual human compassion and kindness. Change can be only in the nature of alleviation and partial compensation, never of radical restructuring.

Any revolutionary measure, Southey believes, can only be destructive of the abundance of potentials embedded in what we call reality. Therefore given the way in which things advance in the world it is better to relativize in order to preserve, to treat humorously what he still thinks are "the essentials," or to let them be obfuscated in a fog of multitudinous details, hoping that truths will still shine through, now or later. The most formidable instance of this technique of multiplicity (much anthologized and even admired in a perplexed way) was that of Southey's poem on the cataracts of Lodore (1820), where through well over one hundred fifty lines synonymy runs wild, either by onomatopaeic and other sound effects, or through lines of sense connection. I detect in many parts of *The Doctor* the same effects: synonymy is used as a confirmatory force, it is supposed to reinforce the unity of the world: cosmic unity is affirmed allusively, through local and individual connections, no matter whether they are comic, tenuous, or substantial.

Here we have to remember once more Southey's quite unusual knack for hitting upon apposite if recondite references and examples. Thus there is virtually no one among his celebrated contemporaries who would have called William Blake a "great but insane genius" and would have given a long quotation from his commentary on the painting *The Ancient Britons,* as Southey does in a chapter on ugliness (ch. 181, 2:473–75). Likewise obscure elements of support to, say, the bolstering of the Horatian model are found in *The Village Curate* by one Hardis (ch. 189, 2:498). The point however is the cascading nature of digressions and of associations. Anagrams and numerology are among the favorite devices, partly in the Talmudic tradition but partly, as I said before, as a kind of (intuitive and primitive) early form of hypertext computer-linkage (chs. 175–81, 2:458–71 or 2:537–38—interchapter 22, on styles; the letter symbolism in ch. 111, 1:268–69). A good example of this method in action can be seen in chapter 189 (2:498–501), which starts with merely anecdotal and observational anthropological comments, moves toward the area of national stereotypes (a topic much favored in the eighteenth and nineteenth centuries), goes from there to a kind of literary cosmology, and finally seeks reassurance yet again in references to Burton and Browne, let alone a splendid quotation from a poem by Sir John Davis in which echoes from Milton blend with foreshadowings of Hamann. This might be called a kind of essayistic equivalent of the stream of consciousness in fictional prose, as admitted by himself in the metacritical chapter 169 (2:419ff.), an ironic synopsis in seventeen points of preceding chains of thought. The text waxes particularly animated when it comes to discussing names, not only that of its main character or of his horse but also, for example, in the praise of the name Thomas (interchapter 15, 1:290ff.). In fact in chapters 222–23 Southey explicitly proposes a theory of names (and language) based upon the correspondence between sound and meaning, much in the vein of Plato's *Kratylos* (as opposed to the arbitrary-contractual views of Hermogenes).

Similarly the combination of astrology and science in chapter 93 (of past and present cognition, as it were, at the turning point of the traditional toward the rationalist-empirical discourse, but still with sweet naivety) can serve as an apt emblem of the book as a whole. In a sense, however, it is not needed, as the text abounds in methodological explanations. Thus chapters 11–12 tackle the issue of digression, and interchapter 14 (1:259; also interchapter 12, 1:245–47) offers a theory of interchapters that might well apply to the book as a whole:

> Any subject is inexhaustible if it be fully treated of; that is, if it be treated doctrinally and practically, analytically and synthetically, historically and morally, critically, popularly and eloquently, philosophically, exegetically and aesthetically, logically, neologically, etymologically, archaiologically, Daniologically and Doveologically, which is to say, summing up all in one, Doctorologically. (ch. 93, 1:212)

The narrator of *The Doctor* repeatedly justifies himself by reference to previous authors and shows himself aware of the possibility of a canon of disorderly accumulation and voracious reading. This is of course to be seen in the avalanche of mottoes where along with Rabelais, Shakespeare, Homer, Castiglione, or Apuleius, we find much less celebrated names such as those of Davies of Hereford or Sir John Harrington. Chapters 112–14 (1:270–81) are devoted to books and the book trade. In other parts of the text the narrator self-referentially (and self-supportively) refers to various literary-intellectual ancestors. This can be seen in chapter 6 (1:17–19) with its cursory description of the Doctor's pantagruelic appetite of variegated range and catholicity of taste. It can be seen in chapter 118 (1:288ff.) with its explicit parallel to Sir Thomas Browne. Similar parallels are established to Montaigne in chapter 123 (1:304) and several times to Sterne (notably, for example, interchapter 17, 2:428).

The canonical pedigree once established, Southey unleashes freely his comic fantasy, by dealing with archaic/popular medicine (ch. 24, 1:58–59), by dwelling on the stylistics, genders and names of bells (ch. 30, 1:74ff.), by the (inevitable) chapter on tombs and graveyards (ch. 235, 2:634ff.), by a fragment on beards (2:671ff.), by the parody of philological and hermeneutic techniques as applied to a popular ballad (interchapter 17, 2:427–29), by the delight taken in the meticulous description of musical instruments (ch. 196, 2:521–22), by indulging in the presentation of sums of astrological information in rather illogical ways (ch. 197, 2:524–27), by mixing actual information with fantasy as in the chapters on Doncaster (chs. 33 and 35, 1:78–80 and 82ff.).[17]

An area visited and revisited with particular insistence is that of nature in general (Southey might be called an early ecologist) and that of animals in particular. Southey concerns himself in mock-serious fashion with the ethics and sociology of the animal world (ch. 209, 2:563ff., or 199, 2:530–36); he lectures with gravity on fleas in literature (ch. 89, 1:196–98); he turns his chapter on rats into a brilliant essay, comparable to those of Buffon (chs. 228–29, 2:617–20); he dwells on (his own) cats, much like T. S. Eliot (2:683–86; this is an ulterior fragment); and of course much of the first part of the book turns around the horse Nobs.

These considerations on animal and vegetal nature are complemented by medical/physiological speculations on human constitution. Thus, to give just one example among many possible, in chapters 215 (2:580–81) and 217 a theory is presented on neuro-induced maladies and remedies, as well as in a more quirky vein, of humans as former trees (or connected to them). Ultimately (in the latter example specifically but, I believe, in the book as a whole) all these considerations are loosely linked into a theory (of clear neo-Platonic descent, one well connected with the age-hallowed "great chain of Being") of the harmonious universe. Chapter 216 is expanded into such a framework of general analogies. Chapters 212ff. (2:571–79) speak (only half tongue-in-cheek) of the salvation of plants and animals from their own formal anarchy into a neo-Platonic divine embrace. The doctor draws freely from Brahmin wisdom, Druidical tradition, Moses and the Psalms, and the sayings of George Fox (the Quaker leader) in order to justify a somewhat conservative combination of universal interconnectedness.

This places Southey in the same family of thinkers with Chateaubriand, Goethe, and perhaps Schelling—all, I would argue, influenced by the tradition of neo-Platonism. The multiplicity of facts and events has its correspondence in the multiplicity of theories (ch. 127, 1:318ff., where even Buddhist views are jocularly accepted). Southey, like the few enumerated contemporaries (and, of course, many others) was both shocked and pleased by the exponential accumulation of human knowledge and was engaged in earnest reflection on the meanings of cognitive growth and on the ways to manage or to respond to it. One of his fears was that new knowledge should not displace the gains in knowledge and thinking that had preceded them. Another fear, as suggested before, was that either these masses of information would swamp and drown the amenities and civilities of society or else would be ordered in some kind of brutally disciplined and artificial way. That one can distinguish the faint outlines of a political subconscious here it would be difficult to deny. Southey's response is that what must be saved above all is disorder, the practice of spontaneous thought associations, digression, details in ever-changing patterns. This was to become an important feature of the tradition of Western conservatism in the nineteenth and twentieth centuries. It is also however a feature of much late-twentieth-century thinking on issues such as "spontaneous order," "complex adaptive systems" deriving out of "aggregation," "building blocks," "tagging," "strange attractors," and the like. Contemporary information theory may have had in Southey a naive but intuitive forerunner (Holland 1995).

Notes

1. This is well documented in Madden 1972, 218, 219, 233–34, 265, 267, 269, 272, 284, 285, 287–88, 290ff., 293, 312, 315, 323, 327. These pages contain a selection of negative (sometimes insulting) opinions by contemporaries.

2. Southey 1829, 1832, and new ed. 1971.

3. See, for example, Southey 1971, 1:154, 189. Cf. also 2:275, "On Emigration" (1828). This opinion is openly expressed in a number of private letters. "I am as ardent for making the world English as can be," he writes in a letter to Rickman (1811), quoted in Carnall 1960, 125. Cf. also Curry 1975, 83.

4. See the whole of Southey (1829, 1832) as well as the essay "On the State of the Poor, the Principle of Mr. Malthus's Essay on Population and the Manufacturing System" (1812) in Southey 1971, 1:111–16, 142, and the essay "On the State of the Poor, and the Means Pursued by Society for Bettering Their Condition" (1816), 1:178, 185, 208ff. See also Raimond 1968, 356–57, 371.

5. Sekora 1977. In *The Doctor* (interchapter 25, 2:598–99), Southey lashes out openly against this "luxury;" were he rich he says "I would live in it at the rate of five thousand a year, beyond which no real and reasonable enjoyment is to be obtained by money.... I would neither solicit nor accept a peerage.... I would not wear my coat quite so threadbare as I do at present; but I would keep to my old shoes, as long as they would keep to me." He thus on the one hand inscribes himself in an old-age tradition, on the other further indicates his kinship with Cobbett, of which more below. See also his Horatian irony against fame (chs. 124–25, 1:312–16). My references throughout (that is, both in text and notes) will follow the edition in two volumes (1849) prepared originally in one volume by John Wood Warter in 1848. Southey had brought out *The Doctor* in seven volumes (London: Longman, Rees, Orme, Brown, Green, and Longmans, 1834–1847). The first two volumes had appeared anonymously, the last two had been prepared by Warter. The one-volume edition is now the only one we have; I am aware of its imperfections. In citing I always place the chapter number first, followed by volume number, a colon, and then the page numbers.

6. See specifically *Rural Rides* (1830) and *Advice to Young Men and (Incidentally) Young Women* (1830).

7. I am not deterred by Southey's furious outbreaks against Cobbett's journalistic radicalism; see "On the Rise and Progress of Popular Disaffection" (1817) in Southey 1971, 2:98–105. Deep down there are more similarities than differences in the positions of the two. For the opposite view see Carnall 1960, 115–16.

8. He earned the meticulous examination and merciless chiding of Macaulay in an unsigned, enormously long, and very thoughtful review in *Edinburgh Review* (January 1830): 528–65; reproduced in Madden 1972, 341–79. Macaulay saw Southey as a statist adversary of free enterprise and as one inclined toward welfare programs. Macaulay's arguments resemble strikingly those of American Republicans of the 1990s. Cf. Curry 1975, 75–83, for a detailed presentation of Southey's life-long and consistent social sensitivity and indignation; virtually all attentive modern readers seem to see things in the same way (for example, Bernhardt-Kabisch 1977, 164, 169). Indeed he was sometimes compared to Friedrich Engels in the strength with which he exposed the condition of the working classes and earned a place in at least one history of socialism in Britain (See Carnall 1960, 193). Williams (1958, 20–29) compares Southey to Robert Owen in terms of analysis and remedial solutions proposed. Southey relates in fact that in 1819 during his journey to Scotland (of which he published an account) he was given a tour of the "socialist-utopian" community of New Lanark by Owen himself, and the relations between the two were courteous, even friendly, even though Southey expressed a number of reservations (fully justified ones, in my opinion); (see Curry 1975, 116).

9. The following is a good example of Burkean thinking:

> The British constitution is not the creature of theory. It is not as a garment which we can deliver over to tailors to cut and slash at pleasure, lengthen it or curtail, embroider it or strip off all the trimmings, and which we can at any moment cast aside for something in a newer fashion. It is the skin of the body politic in which is the form and the beauty and the life, . . . or rather it is the life itself. Our constitution has arisen out of our habits and necessities; it has grown with our growth, and been gradually modified by the changes through which society is always passing in its progress. Under it we are free as our own thoughts; second to no people in arms, arts and enterprise; during prosperous times exceeding all in prosperity, and in this season of contingent, partial, and temporary distress suffering less than any others, abounding in resources, abounding in charity, in knowledge, in piety, and in virtue. (Southey 1971, 1:378–79)

10. See his pamphlet "On Sir Francis Burdett's Motion for Parliamentary Reform" (1810) in Southey 1971, 1:9–12, 17–18. See also his repeated attacks against the pernicious effects of the print media in "On the State of Public Opinion and Political Reformers" (1816) 1:366–67, or 1:420, or in "A Letter to William Smith, Esq. M.P." (1817), 2:23–25.

11. See Southey 1971, 1:233–34, and 2:263–443, the three highly partisan and, in my view, intemperate essays of 1809, 1812, and 1828. It is interesting to note that despite Southey's anti-Catholic rantings—to some extent triggered by anti-Irish prejudices, one suspects—many later Catholics reacted favorably to him. Among his few genuine admirers in the later nineteenth century were Cardinal Newman and Gerard Manley Hopkins (cf. Carnall 1960, 192). Similarly Southey's life of Wesley was a work of ambiguous empathy: Southey did not share the views of the great Methodist reformer (or generally the emphasis on "enthusiasm"), yet he could not suppress a genuine admiration for Wesley's achievement and religious authenticity (Southey 1820). See also Southey 1971, 2:127–29. A further good example in *The Doctor* is in chapters 167–68 where Catholic ideas on natural unity and interconnectedness are made fun of, while chapter 170 quotes respectfully and approvingly a Jesuit.

12. It is remarkable that what might be dubbed Southey's overview of the Victorian Age can already be captured in an early work: *Letters from England by Don Manuel Alvarez Espriella* (1807). See also Raimond 1968, 346–53.

13. I am not aware of much research on the canons of British literature that German scholars close to National Socialism were beginning to outline in the 1930s. In any case Carlyle was one of their great favorites, seen as a truly "northern" and Germanic figure partly because of his Prussophilic sentiments—and his erudition in matters German more broadly—but partly also for ideological reasons: his antiplutocratic sentiments, his populist religiousness, and his emphasis on "the great men" in history.

14. Warter 1850, thereafter expanded in several editions. This is merely a collection of quotations arranged partly by subject, partly chronologically. It "belongs" to Southey in a Borgesian sense, one might say, in as far as it gives by oblique intertextuality an image of the collector's interests and preferences, indicating at the same time the tremendous range of his curiosity and cognitive variety. There is some slight commentary in *Omniana, or Horae Otiosiores* (London: Longman, Hurst, Rees, Orme, and Brown, 1812). Here are included forty-five contributions by Coleridge, along with the 210 by Southey; some of the latter were collected from previous journal publication.

15. "An Introductory Essay on the Lives and Works of Our Uneducated Poets" in Southey 1831. Along the same lines see also *The Doctor* (ch. 193, 2:510ff.).

16. Nemoianu 1977.

17. Bernhardt-Kabisch 1977, 171, 177, 180.

18. If we look more closely we observe that many of the topics and strategies employed by Southey were more widespread at the time than one would believe. Thus Chateaubriand also wrote on bells and graves in his *Génie du christianisme;* and a brilliant parody of biblical criticism as applied to the Napoleonic historical adventure was being written almost simultaneously. Cf. Whately 1985.

Bibliography

Bernhardt-Kabisch, Ernst. 1977. *Robert Southey.* Boston: Twayne.

Carnall, Geoffrey. 1960. *Robert Southey and His Age: The Development of a Conservative Mind.* Oxford: Clarendon Press.

Curry, Kenneth. 1975. *Robert Southey.* London: Routledge and Kegan Paul.

Holland, John. 1995. *Hidden Order: How Adaptation Builds Complexity.* New York: Addison-Wesley.

Madden, Lionel, ed. 1972. *Robert Southey: The Critical Heritage.* London: Routledge and Kegan Paul.

Nemoianu, Virgil. 1977. *Micro-Harmony: The Growth and Uses of the Idyllic Model in Literature.* Bern: Peter Lang.

Raimond, Jean. 1968. *Robert Southey, l'homme et son temps, l'oeuvre, le rôle.* Paris: Didier.

Sekora, Jean. 1977. *Luxury: The History of a Western Concept from Eden to Smollett.* Baltimore: Johns Hopkins University Press.

Southey Robert. 1808. *Letters from England by Don Manuel Álvarez Espriella.* London: Longman, Hurst, Rees, and Orme.

———. 1829, 1832. *Sir Thomas More; or, Colloquies on the Progress and Prospects of Society.* 2 vols. London: John Murray.

———. 1849. *The Doctor.* 2 vols. London: Longman, Brown, and Longmans.

———. 1885. *The Life of Wesley and the Rise and Progress of Methodism.* 2 vols. London: Bell and Sons. (Orig. pub. 1820.)

———, ed. 1925. *Attempts in Verse by John James.* Ed. J. S. Childers. London: Humphrey Milford. (Orig. pub. 1831.)

———. 1971. *Essays, Moral and Political.* Shannon: Irish University Press. (Orig. publ. 1832.)

Williams, Raymond. 1958. *Culture and Society.* London: Allen and Unwin.

Wood Warter, John, ed. 1850. *Southey's Common-Place Book.* 2 vols. London: Longman, Brown, Green, and Longmans.

Whately, Richard. 1985. *Historic Doubts Relative to Napoleon Bonaparte.* Ed. Ralph S. Pomeroy. Berkeley: University of California Press. (Orig. pub. 1819; 4th ed. 1862.)

VI

Conclusions?

CHAPTER 11

Romanticism
Beginnings, Explosion, Epidemic

ROMANTICISM, to try to draw some obvious conclusions, is regarded in this volume as the prevailing discourse and mode of writing (or even thinking) in Europe and North America during the half-century 1780–1830. Later impacts can be recognized, wave after wave, until the end of the twentieth century, not only in literature proper, but also in adjoining fields of writing, in the arts and in music, in philosophy and religion, and above all perhaps in the popular levels of entertainment, instruction, and media communication, which reached the widest strata of population available in the nineteenth and (at least indirectly) the twentieth century.

Both a broad and comprehensive concept of romanticism (as promoted by Lovejoy and numerous others)—one of repeated and pendular categories—and a holistic and coherent one (Wellek's for instance, without being the only) are credible and serious, but neither should be absolutized; even less the cultural-materialist approaches with their mixture of relativism and exclusivism (for instance as exercised by the disciples of Raymond Williams).

In the present book the romantic discourse and state of mind at the turn of the nineteenth century (as repeatedly suggested in different chapters) is seen as being based upon a dramatic expansion of human consciousness and cognitive horizon in the West, and this in turn is justified by the attempt, no, the *need,* to account for the beginning globalization of the human society and of human experiences taking place at the time and for the processing of an almost overwhelming avalanche of informational data becoming available and imposing themselves upon human consciousness. While it is true that random or deliberate engagements with cultural and ethnic Otherness can be detected throughout human history and in all societies, it is only around and after 1500 that such an engagement becomes a systematic, worldwide project, pursued by one culture, for gain (of wealth, power, knowledge, Salvation) no less than for the earnest pursuit of the good and of progress, but radiating from several centers and using a varied number of procedures. It should not be difficult to admit that by or just before 1800 this project reached fruition and that indeed the first shape of globalization (still uncertain in outline and in foundations) was facing human consciousness, first in the case of a few capacious or lucid minds but soon spreading to an ever larger number of diverse people.

It might be useful to remark that the terms "data" and "information" are used here, and have been used throughout this book, in the broadest possible sense. They do not refer simply to an expanded consciousness as just sketched out. They do not designate simply some advances in human knowledge in one scientific field or the other, although this was highly important, particularly in the spread of such ever newer and ever more numerous facts. They also designate the range of varieties of art and literature. They also designate the expansion of social chances and mobilities (vertical, lateral, and so forth). They emphatically include the unstoppable explosion of economy in general, of industry in particular (Sauvigny 1955, 199–235; Nipperdey 1991, 130–247; Johnson 1991, 541–626; Glaser 1980–1987, 6:23; among an enormous mass of other studies). It has to do (I will enumerate here things in a random fashion) with the growth in the number of translations (Glaser 1980–1987, 4:42) or to the publishing industry in general (Glaser 1980–1987, 6:31–39; Nipperdey 1991, 587–94). It is expressed most prominently in the explosive growth in the number of museums, universities, academies, and the like (Ziolkowski 1990; Nipperdey 1991, 451–84). It is most spectacularly expressed in architecture, where the typically representative buildings (church or cathedral and palace or mansion) are considerably diversified and expanded by other representative buildings: theaters, museums, concert halls, schools and universities, administrative buildings, and eventually industrial and railway buildings, no less than by the wide range of styles revived and utilized. It is not a mere coincidence that the cultivation and practice of music is also suddenly widened and goes deep into the middle classes or that the musical discourses extend beyond romanticism to a variety of forms and tonalities (Nipperdey 1991, 535–69; also Bernhard 1983; Lankheit 1988; Geismeier 1979; Böhmer 1968). All these are in different ways (but almost in equal measure) part of the "data avalanche" I mentioned.

Simultaneously we remark also an awareness of globalization as process: that is to say a recognition (or impression) of a modified dynamics of human history. Again, this awareness belonged perhaps to a relatively small number of individuals first, but these were followed quickly, almost immediately, by an amazingly large number of others who acquired the impression that they witnessed an unheard-of acceleration of human affairs going hand-in-hand with the expansion of these affairs: urbanization, industrialization, alienation, informational explosions, tendencies towards egalitarian democracy, individualist emancipation, rationalism and empiricism, a contractual and negotiated relationship between individuals, and the gradual ending of organic or tribal interactions and bonds.

Romanticism thus is, I would maintain, the attempt of human subjectivity to come to terms with these twin phenomena of expansion of human scope and of quickening of pace in historical dynamics. As might have been easily expected, the responses of the human mind in adjusting to events that radically modify human behavior and the very existential foundations of the species had to be in turn very broad and highly diverse. It should not have been hard to predict (and it is even easier to demonstrate) that some of these reactions would be violently hostile and/or fear-filled: the process and its pace were seen by many as categorically adverse to the human state of affairs until then. This adversarial attitude emerged quite naturally in zones of the planet that were often the passive object of modernization, but they can also be recognized in Europe and North America themselves, which were supposed to be the motors of the process. Philosophers and poets, political leaders, and fairly large and diverse strata of the population responded with sullen or brutal enmity to all that was happening and tried more than once to stop and reverse the trends of history. In all fairness it must be said that the events themselves had a harshness that encouraged such hostility. Counterrevolutionaries were not exclusively, and as a matter of fact not even primarily, part of the upper and privileged classes, but more often and in larger numbers the members of poor peasant societies who felt threatened in their traditions and identities by the newly emerging order of things (Johnson 1991, 221).

Simultaneously, of course, we notice (and sometimes celebrate) all those who acted as carriers and energetic forces pushing forward the movement: revolutionaries, visionaries, inventors, and creators of all kinds. As in the previous category, such individuals are not confined to a single continent: Simon Bolívar is a typical symbol for all those who modified deeply South America; the revolutionary Framers of the Constitution did something similar in North America; and beginnings of urbanization and technological advance can be observed early on in sundry parts of Asia. In Europe the movers of the English technological revolution or the leaders of the French political revolution, along with their admirers throughout the Continent, provide even more obvious cases. The fascinating thing, as I said in the preface and elsewhere in other chapters, is the fact that in the early decades of the nineteenth century methods were devised and discourses were constructed that acted as relatively satisfactory ties or forces of stabilization: imperfection was acknowledged at the time but can be even better recognized in retrospect. (The argument for the whole age as one of revolution was often made and in fact may be said to be adopted by the majority of the scholarly opinion, typically Hobsbawm.)

Thus in between the two strong extremes we find a bewildering multitude of combinations, of intermediate solutions and proposals and explanations, of attempts to mediate. Without them Western society would have easily disintegrated. The mediations were addressed to the extremes themselves: of enthusiasm and of recoil but equally so to the relationship between the older state of affairs of mankind and the newer one that seemed to arise. These mediations aspired to smooth over the asperity of emancipatory change and to inject kindness or graduality in the pace of progress while not actually denying the validity of this emancipatory progress itself.

As a matter of fact, for what statistics are worth in situations of this kind it is striking to notice that the numbers of variegated mediators is considerably larger than that of the defenders of more extreme attitudes, at least among intellectuals. It is therefore fully justified to describe this age as one of moderation, a period in which the invention of moderating and mediating strategies is astoundingly rich.

Indubitably the consequence of this multifaceted universe of responses, the consequence of this state of ferment (anxiety, joy, rational judgments, and so forth) was also an unusual productivity. It would be difficult to deny that the decades before and after 1800 brought us a wealth of images, concepts, projects, and ingenious plans such as we have rarely seen at any time in history. Even today, over one hundred and fifty years later, we still hark back to this world; we still use it as a reservoir to refresh our own ideas, to solve dilemmas, to draw analogies, to shape concepts, and so forth.

Naturally this reservoir, or to switch metaphors, this arsenal, can be found in imaginative writing above all: in poems, in novels, in dramatic plays, and in short stories. I say naturally because such literary vehicles are admirably suited to enacting scenarios of possibility: good or bad. And of course the abovementioned agitation had to do in decisive ways with future possibilities. The literary vehicles and genres could provide, as always, the widest freedom for options and for experimenting with what might be or what might have been. In fact a quick look suffices to classify the romantic age among the most experimental literary ages of the world. Our key question was, given these conditions, how did society manage to survive, to maintain its stability, its continuity? Is imperfection something beneficial or at least acceptable in itself, contrary to the general way of judgment? Does imperfection lead to moderation? Is it the common denominator of all the strategies that the present study presented?

It is the case, I think, that more pedestrian prose can be usefully explored as part of larger endeavors. As a matter of fact different kinds of nonimaginative or nonliterary writing must be seen as not less effective than the traditional genres in coming to terms with the rapidly transforming world outside and in moderating its impact upon ways of life and thinking. The writing of history and geography for instance may well have been a more objective exercise than the writing of a Gothic novel. This is true in the sense that historical and geographical description, when honestly pursued, endeavor to provide us with accurate images of zones in space and in time, to present correct and abundant raw information. Yet it cannot be denied that in the process of writing history and geography elements of narrative and rhetoric become necessary. The structuring and ordering of the information must be devised according to rules that have much in common with those of poetry and novelistic fiction. Thus it becomes in fact difficult to distinguish paraliterary genres from literature proper.

Precisely because they are more immediately involved with levels and angles of the signified, nonfictional prose genres can in their turn play with a vast array of possibilities. At the same time these margins of the literary must deal with the threatening (or surprising, or hopeful) possibilities themselves, they cannot claim to relegate them in the world of the merely potential (but not actual). In a word, a very good part of the writing activity of the period here chosen for examination is itself an attempt at examining the state of affairs of mankind at the given period, much as poetry or imaginative prose were. However, vision and outright invention can more easily be reduced to a minimum, they can more easily serve as reins to the explosive impulses of an age of revolution and counterrevolution.

Inevitably the current volume is not less fragmentary and episodic than the writing universe of the early nineteenth century with its center and its margins. If indeed the common denominator of romantic literature and romantic criticism is precisely that the right and the duty of the literary creator is to engage in visions that might help solve the conundrums and the uncertainties of the surrounding world, then their incompleteness can act as a moderating and a pacifying force.

This is true of romantic philosophy also. There we are often faced with a kind of writing that wanted to provide an explanation of the world in which the religious values of the past can be preserved in secular translation. This *écriture* could thereafter stand as an example of the best way of mediating between past and (postreligious) future. Yes, certainly, many philosophers, including Hegel and Schelling, also wanted to compose a historical explanation of why things unfold as they do. Still, I would maintain that the more general (though more hidden) purpose was the writing of idealist philosophy itself, through whose very existence a smooth continuity in the historical existence could be reestablished. The ominous rift between the contractual modes of alienated existence and the organic (or biological) ways of organizing human society (which had persisted in various shapes over several millennia, had been common to virtually all the planet's cultures, and perhaps could be traced to the earliest forms of tribal organization of hominids) might, philosophers believed, be bridged by an appropriate theory. That the search for a common denominator between God, nature, and humanity could easily lead toward indeterminacy and skepticism, and irony was noted early on, but it deterred few.

Thus criticism and philosophy were, during the decades that most everybody tends to call romantic, closely allied with literature. A few years ago, say at the time of Dr. Samuel Johnson (and inside his oeuvre), poetry and criticism were clearly separated. But in William Blake's rage-filled lines against Sir Joshua Reynolds this was no longer the case; Wordsworth's preface to the *Lyrical Ballads* is virtually part of that poetic volume; Coleridge's *Biographia Literaria* was supposed to be the counterpart of *The Prelude*; Shelley, even Hazlitt, let alone Keats, combined the poetic, the critic, and the philosophical. The "Tübingen triad" (Hegel, Schelling, Hölderlin) was to remain paradigmatic; Victor Hugo's prefaces to some of his dramas are part and parcel of the literary work. Goethe, Schiller, and Chateaubriand engaged freely in critical essayism; Byron's *English Bards and Scotch Reviewers* was a critical work and a poetic satire simultaneously; east Europeans such as the Hungarian Földi, or the Romanians Asachi and Heliade-Rădulescu were deeply involved in poetry and equally in criticism. Italian and Portuguese writing provide further examples. That romantic poetry and prose were philosophical is too obvious to require further demonstration. That romantic philosophy and theory from Schelling and Goethe through Carlyle, Emerson, and Nietzsche all the way to twentieth-century figures like Oswald Spengler or Lucian Blaga was more than once poetic is also well known.

Perhaps this was the remote cause for the vast, almost unfettered expansion of aesthetics, a branch of human speculation that was to maintain a high profile for well over one hundred and fifty years. Let us remember that the very term "aesthetics" (not to speak of the recognition of aesthetics as an autonomous discipline) dates only from the middle of the eighteenth century, even though activities that can be retrospectively annexed to the aesthetic are considerably older. However, the central role assigned to the Beautiful by people as different as Chateaubriand, Shelley, the Humboldt brothers, Kant, Coleridge, or Schiller, to name just a very few, must give us pause. What these and others have in common is, I think, once more, the pacifying power that they attribute to the Beautiful. According to this theory, in the realm of aesthetics, progress and tradition, creativity and stability, can coexist and collaborate. The very education of mankind hinges on the cultivation of the beautiful, and somehow the Good and the True can be seen as its consequences. This theory may now sound odd, but it was passionately believed in and defended during the period we are talking about. In fact it was seen by many as an excellent and judicious substitute for revolutionary, violent, action. There are numbers of authors in whose texts the aesthetic, the theoretical, and the theological are so closely connected as to be virtually inseparable: Schleiermacher, Coleridge, Schopenhauer, and perhaps Solger might be numbered among them. It is also the case that the major philosophers of the age felt that it is part of their orderly duty to write on aesthetics or even to elaborate a systematic aesthetics: Kant, Hegel, and Schelling come immediately to mind.

It is only fair to add here that the informational avalanche of which we just spoke impelled the growth and the development of a large number of sciences during the very same decades: linguistics, sociology, psychology, child pedagogy, ethnology, zoology and botanics, different branches of medicine, and others yet could be adduced as examples. From Buffon to Lamarck and Cuvier the distance is long. Carl Linné, Stephen Hales, and Joseph Priestley preceded by very few years the decades of romanticism. Close contemporaries like Sir William Jones, the Grimm brothers, Franz Bopp, and Rasmus Rask effected a true revolution in philology. Görres, Creuzer, and Benjamin Constant were just a few among those who thought of foundations for a comparatist examination of religions, myths, and symbols. Why did this happen? There are probably several explanations. Some of them have to do simply, as I said, with the momentum of accumulating information and the desire to structure it; they need not further concern us here. Others however are related, more or less closely, with the advances in philosophy and in literary criticism. To be more specific, such developing sciences tried to give account either of social phenomena or of individual (subjective) ones and to provide in a rational way explanations for historical events that anybody could notice. Indeed, we can go even a step farther and speak about a certain romantic "stylistic" or slant in well-established hard sciences. Thus the way in which magnetism and gravity were foregrounded as expressions of the law of universal love and attraction are highly significant (by Faraday, Ampère, Arago, and so many others). The transformation of geology into a system of symbols by literary figures like Novalis, Hoffmann, and others is equally interesting. Ornithology emerged in precisely the decades we are talking about (Farber 1997). The foundations of psychology by Oken, Carus, and even Mesmer, and the innovations in physics by Volta and Galvani have been often studied in great detail. Oersted, Berzelius, Liebig, Ohm, and Gay-Lussac are figures characteristic of the age as much as any poet or king. Alexander von Humboldt, as a historian of the earth (geology and geography combined,) was once described as the "Napoleon of science." The fact that Goethe considered it as appropriate, perhaps necessary, to engage in scientific (physical and biological theorizing) is symptomatic for the process of merging and substitution so prominent for the age. Together they indicate how a certain (Foucauldian? Spenglerian?) episteme pervaded the discourses of the world at the time in most sections of intellectual endeavor, or at least reverberated in a multiplicity of forms.

Among these multiplicities one that ought not to be forgotten because it was much visited by writers and because it was placed almost exactly at the borderline between the fictional and the nonfictional was the familiar or conversational essay, revived from what had once been its glorious age in the seventeenth and early eighteenth centuries. This vehicle was extremely convenient for authors of the romantic age because it was flexible, it did not oblige them to definitive and disciplined statements, and yet it opened up a field of speculation in which all kinds of values could be played out one against the other. In England there was a veritable explosion (Lamb, De Quincey, Hunt, Hazlitt, Landor, Cobbett), the Spanish *costumbristas* added their own stylistics, and the "physiognomies" of Russian, Hungarian, Romanian, and South Slavic authors are their close correspondents. Many of these authors, English and Continental, resorted to old-fashioned methodologies, but often in an ironic way. It remains, in my strongly held view, the most admirable example of articulating the kind of imperfection that, when all is said and done, was the solution of all these individuals and branches of mediating comportment.

The expansions of a consciousness that tended to merge with natural reality could be seen in numerous ways at the time (and later) and have been observed by many students of the age (M. H. Abrams, Herbert Grierson, Harold Bloom, the early E. D. Hirsch, G. Hartman, Marshall Brown, and others yet). Probably historicity can be singled out as the most typical aspect. This is not to say that history as such was ignored until then: who could ignore that interest in the values and events of the past had been strong and frequent from Herodotus and Plutarch in Greece, as well as others in virtually all cultures that we can think of? However, recognizing the validity of the past as an extension of and as a continuing impact on the present had been much less frequent. What the romantic age was able to bring was an awareness of the presentness of the past, of its equality of rights with the present, or even with the future. Imagination of course played a central role here. The historical novel as set up by Walter Scott and as continued by Manzoni, Cooper, Pushkin, Balzac, Willibald Alexis, Arnim and dozens of others, aspired to be closely related with historiography itself, indeed, perhaps one of its branches. In turn, historiography as written by Augustin Thierry, Jules Michelet, Thomas Carlyle, the Czech Palacký, the German Friedrich von Raumer, the Romanian Nicolae Bălcescu, the Lithuanian Daukantas, or the Russians Karamzin and Solovyov, openly resorted to artistic devices in its efforts to bring back the past. Rhetorical techniques, psychological inroads, pictorial modes, imaginative completions of information gaps, all became part of historical writing. More important even, a passionate love of different periods of the past conferred upon them a certain dignity well over the mere precursor role to which they had been usually confined.

This referred naturally to the Middle Ages, to classical antiquity, to the Elizabethan Age, or other such more or less familiar historical episodes. However the circle was gradually expanded to include less familiar ages and even categorical Otherness, in the form of cultures that could not be seen as directly related to or paving the way for the current world. Dealing with the "northern" antiquity (Celtic, Germanic, Scandinavian) was one step in this direction. Placing Hebrew first and Sanskrit thereafter among the sacred and inspiring originary languages, on the same level as Greek and Latin, was another. Valuing Polynesian (Diderot), Mesoamerican (Southey), Chinese, Indian (Hölderlin, Southey), Arabic (Shelley), Persian (Goethe), and other cultures or even religions had to follow logically. It is here that expansion in time and expansion in space had to combine. The otherwise strange fad of Ossianism can serve as the foremost example. However the Scandinavian *Kalevala* might also be enumerated here, along with quasihistorical works by Scott and Southey, or with the numerous Hungarian poets and prose writers speculating on the historical/geographical status of their nation.

At the same time the decades of romantic preoccupation witnessed a marked increase in the field of intersections (that is, of cultural activities in which two or more fields of endeavor went hand in hand). It is variety itself that engendered imperfection and thereby moderation.

Some of these intersections were not more than cross-generic activities. The sharp separation between genres (tragedy and comedy, prose and poetry, and so forth) on which the stricter neoclassicist critics used to insist became a pleasurable game of transgression. The novels of Scott and of the German romantics were, as we know, riddled with short lyrics. Tieck, Grabbe, Słowacki, and Büchner showed a marked preference for the tragicomic. New genres (the historical novel, science fiction) emerged. The idyllic and the didactic were interwoven already in the eighteenth century in literatures as different as Portuguese, Czech, and Hungarian, or even Lithuanian (Donelaitis).

In other cases whole fields (the arts, music, philosophy) were combined with literature. Delacroix, Géricault, Bryulov, and Haydon (see also Johnson 1991, 160–62) are among the many who took subjects from literature for painting, and Berlioz, Weber, Schumann, Schubert, and (slightly later) Liszt for music. In the same way descriptive literature tried to approach painting while music was (for the first time in the history of aesthetics) proclaimed as the model for and the target of all other creative arts. E. T. A. Hoffmann was not the only figure to exercise himself creatively in both music and literature. Such efforts had not been unknown until then (let us remember that in the Renaissance and indeed earlier also they had been quite frequent), but the practice of combination becomes much better established and, in a sense, represents itself as an expansionary activity on the part of the realm of letters; efforts were made to justify such combinations theoretically also. As to painting, the (sometimes newly formed) academies of art supported and strengthened it. The power of J. L. David in revolutionary France, Benjamin West's enormously admired "Death of General Wolfe" (1770), and the Napoleonic hagiography of Baron Gros, were among those that paved the way. In Germany Munich was a center, with Peter Cornelius sponsored by King Ludwig I, and Wilhelm von Kaulbach and Karl von Piloty following in his tracks. A truly spectacular school of historical painting was to develop soon under the auspices of Hans Makart, Leibl, Lenbach, Piloty, and Kaulbach. Karl Friedrich Schinkel (1781–1841) in turn straddles both "travel painting" and local intimist Biedermeier. Carl Spitzweg (1808–1885) and Ludwig Richter (1803–1884) might be seen as typical Biedermeier artists, and there is a clear distinction between their quaint and idyllic style and the high romantic experimentalism and sensibility of Goya, Turner, Delacroix, or Caspar David Friedrich.

God himself changes in depiction and theoretical representation. Thus, for instance, deism had been the common denominator for many of the leading figures of the eighteenth century: a God that was a somewhat cold, technical creator, the famous clockmaker of the universe, high above the ecclesiastical complications and conflicts of benighted earthlings. Not so the deity of the romantics. In a good majority of typical philosophical and literary writing God became deeply involved with the universe itself, with his creation: an involvement that more than once goes all the way to identification. Perhaps under the influence of Shaftesbury and Rousseau we can notice a renewal of neo-Platonism and of pantheism. Mystics of the past and present from Jakob Böhme to Swedenborg and Saint-Martin received considerable attention and admiration. The God imagined by romantic poets was wet, wild, and wooly, speaking to us out of thunderstorms, cascades, and deep dark forests. The "enthusiastic" movements (Christian and Judaic) that had emerged or started spreading already by the middle of the eighteenth century now almost seemed to get the upper hand. They were helped by the widely shared conviction that it is in the Beautiful, rather than in the True and the Good that sacrality expresses itself. This is what Chateaubriand preached with tremendous success, but this is the view held equally by Coleridge, Schelling, or Mörike, preceded by Hamann or Blake. Let us not forget that some of the earliest spokesmen for aesthetic (romantic) religiosity were precisely figures such as Hamann, Klopstock, Wackenroder, and, yes, Rousseau himself.

The question that we can raise in the face of such ambitious growth and inflation is the following: when did it all begin? How did it all develop?

Like all literary or even historical periodization categories, romanticism has its own difficulties and unpleasantries. Sharp borders are impossible to trace, and absolute command and control can never be demonstrated inside a narrative of literary history. Similarities occurring in remote earlier or later periods can be adduced all the time with relative ease. Nevertheless it is clear that throughout the eighteenth century many things that had barely survived at the margins of social and intellectual life tended to grow and to move closer to the center. Moreover such growing trends reached a certain point when they merged, sought alliances with each other, and soon found themselves ready to occupy the center of the scene from which they had been banned until very recently.

The growth of historical interest ("expansion in time") begins early on; taste for popular sagas and ballads, for alternative mythologies, can be noted in the early eighteenth century. Not only Richard Hurd but even Addison and Steele showed how interested they were in ballads and other forms of popular literature. Perrault (or arguably La Fontaine) provided examples of folk creation. Robert Burns was lionized in Enlightenment London as the genuine and spontaneous voice of nature. On the millennia-old pastoral tradition it was not difficult to graft authentically surviving kinds of literary narrative and forms of versification. Each nation tried to discover (sometimes actually invent) its own national epics: the *Niebelungenlied*, *The Song of Igor's Host* (much debated as to authorship and age), *El Cantar del mío Cid*, the imaginatively fabricated manuscript collections of Králové Dvúr and Zelená Hora, the abovementioned Ossianistic fad all had as purpose the validation of the vernaculars and their rise at the level of the *Iliad* and the *Odyssey*.

Travel literature had existed in the seventeenth century (and much earlier), albeit sometimes in standard or predictable forms. In the eighteenth century it swelled mightily: travel inside Europe, at the margins of Europe, outside Europe ("expansion in space"). Fictional studies of the paranormal do not have to await the romantic decades: the Gothic novel, and the *Schauerroman* put in appearances (and gained fans) by the middle of the eighteenth century, growing and growing thereafter. The same can be said about the alterities of culture: if *Rasselas,* the *Lettres persanes,* sundry plays by Racine and Lessing, and the like still evoke non-Western cultures as mere moral, psychological, or political lessons, we also observe how decade after decade Otherness gains more respect and interest in itself, not as mere masks or contrastive backgrounds for Western dilemmas. The literature of the feminine (written by men or women) gains in maturity similarly decade after decade: Jane Austen and Germaine de Staël represent a culmination.

The pure preference for an urban environment was shaken by options in favor of nature or by rejections of the rationalized, civilization-controlled technologies. At the very least we can speak about doubts, debates, and uncertainties with regard to the balance between the natural and the artificial.

The romantic view of sacrality would not have been possible, as mentioned before, without prior preparation by other subterranean mystical trends (from Böhme to Swedenborg, but now renewed by Ballanche, Saint-Martin, Baader, and so many others, men and women alike), or else by the horizontally egalitarian movements of piety and religious enthusiasm of western and eastern Europe: Protestant ("Methodism," "Herrnhuter" movement, Pietism), Catholic (soon thereafter), organization and recognition of Hassidism, but also of Conservative Judaism. These oppositional modes of religiosity were at bottom protest movements against the rationalist structures of religion and against the inclination to adopt deist-moralist principles exclusively or primarily; it is remarkable that they found eloquent and passionate supporters among women at least as much as among men. The flowering of utopian visions (conservative, radical, revolutionary, national, idyllic) can be fully understood only in its connection with shifts in the perception and definition of sacrality. Saint-Simon and Auguste Compte would be prime examples: their theories are "hungry" in as far as they swallow, digest, and thus modify religion (though keeping it still recognizable). Coleridge created the outlines of a whole political sociology based on the symbiosis of church and state. Mme de Krudener, Ballanche, and others who were passionate mystical apologists do not entirely avoid sociopolitical matters. Goethe's *Wilhelm Meister II,* which is often described as a series of approaches to utopia, contains in its imaginative projects rather meticulous indications as to religious behavior and practice. Virtually every east European literature contains one or several attempts at an originary, national (pre-Christian) mythology. Revolutionary figures such as Robespierre and others felt the need to outline an alternative kind of religious ritual once the traditional one was overthrown or forbidden. The popularity of movements such as that of the Freemasons (among the upper classes) is due in my opinion largely to the fact that it provided a utopian/religious substitute to older forms of religious expression.

Criticism threw in its weight by admitting theoretically a multitude of additional discourses that had not been seen as strictly literary until that time. Even more important it created supplementary or adversarial canons that faced the classical and neoclassical traditions. The romantics managed to establish for themselves an impressive pedigree (Shakespeare, Dante, Cervantes, Calderón) that could be placed proudly in the face of the Greco-Roman tradition. The increasing emphasis upon music as the central artistic mode was also much more revolutionary at the time than we think nowadays: in earlier centuries music was generally regarded as mere amusement.

Not least there was the quicksilver movement of substitution, so often encountered in the previous chapters. One field was used to strengthen, replace, or reinvent another. Looking retrospectively we have sometimes the impression of observing a game of musical chairs. In any case, over and beyond combinations, we have the actual daring replacement (or even displacement) of domains. This can be rightly considered a way of unifying and globalizing knowledge. By the same token, however, we can think of it as a response to this universalization, as an attempt to counteract it, and as an effort to preserve or nurture the values of diversity and of singular identities.

While it is true that all these developments—and others yet—cannot be coordinated mechanically, and while it is also true that they found expression most often as contradictions, we can say that a general figure can be distinguished at least as intention and desire. The central human model of romanticism emerged with explosive force in the 1780s and 1790s in England and Germany, and in a different way in France also. Until then all the tendencies listed above were somehow sectional and thereby had a limited impact. Only when enough of these separate changes connected, found some kinship among themselves, does an alternative model of great appeal and energy come to life. At least in its first phase (revolutionary, political, and visionary) romanticism was full of absolute claims and explosive in its purposes. Such a pattern, subsuming the different trends, suggests the hope of a certain regeneration of the human race as a whole, a renewed beginning, a secular salvation. Yes, the progress of the Western world would and did remain central in this general outline, and there was no serious intention to abandon entirely the accumulations, gains, and accomplishments of the past. Nevertheless, enough doubt and anguish about the future advance in the same direction was discernible so that the call for a renewed memorization of the roots, of the earliest origins of humanity could find a sympathetic hearing.

Whether we choose to concentrate upon the unifying elements of the age, or upon its contradictions is less important than their coexistence. Even more decisive is the fact that romanticism as such showed itself incapable of sustained growth and basically unstable. It is its later phases that proved more fertile precisely because of the manner in which they embraced imperfection. I will now try to explain some of the mechanisms of this triumph of imperfection, drawing of course on the separate examinations to be found in the chapters of the present volume.

What soon happened inside the romantic movement was a common realization: namely that a full implementation of the original project (the "cosmic regeneration" mentioned above) was literally and practically an impossibility. Pure romanticism is at best a rarity, but usually, to be fully sincere, an absence, a gap, as an analysis of the work of Chateaubriand, Goethe, Scott, and many others conclusively shows. It remains for most writers a kind of search or nostalgia. Thus for east Europeans or for Americans it is invariably placed in the remote past, or in any case elsewhere, perhaps even in western Europe. For western Europeans it was possibly found in remote parts of the world: the Southern or Eastern hemispheres, the New World. In this particular sense one might argue that romanticism is the glorification of and desperate quest for Otherness, in ways that are very rare in literature, though perhaps more likely and frequent in religion. Judaism certainly, Christianity and Islam also, establish a concept of divinity that is defined precisely by its total difference from the human race and the rest of the created world. It goes without saying that most literature over the ages (realistic or classical, for that matter) tried to deal with the here and now. By contrast the high romantics and at least some of their followers secularized the religious configuration mentioned above (particularly the Judeo-Christian one) and placed the sacred Other in a reality that is nevertheless not quite a reality since it is remote and since we are often uncertain of its claim to doubtless truth.

Once it becomes clear for us that romanticism is a short streak on the horizon, or perhaps even an absence, the next step must be to ask ourselves what exactly replaced it and at such short notice to boot. In other words: how did the romantics deal with their own (now recognized) imperfection? And also: how did they manage to temper the unsatisfied revolutionary ideal that continued to function and to mobilize large human categories? The answers were numerous.

The romantic ideal could be placed in the recent or remote past, it could be placed in the future, it could be placed in the totally elsewhere (a parallel universe, for instance). It could be seen (this was even more frequent and it was even more emphatic on imperfection) as a fragment, as a partial achievement or perception: romanticism was thus downgraded, reduced, bent, tamed, or domesticated. It could be treated ironically as its own eternal opposite or as a kind of enduring tension between opposites: this relativized romanticism, tongue-in-cheek, preserves a paradigmatic vision but treats it with malice, with gentle humor, or else with that pervasive pessimism that was so frequent after 1815 (in Byron, Vigny, Schopenhauer, Leopardi and Foscolo, and scores of others). The surviving echoes and features of romanticism found themselves reduced: the romantic revolutionary potential is captured but reshaped and controlled. Therefore such an explosive potential, instead of being applied to the human race as a whole (or to history as a whole), finds itself channeled toward what was hoped to be some concrete and feasible regeneration and salvation. Social class rebellion might be one of these forms in Spain, in France, in the Russia of the Decembrists or the England of the Chartists and their sympathizers. Likewise national aspiration and revival can be recognized as a consequence among the Czechs, the Hungarians, the Romanians, the Serbs, certainly the Poles, but also the Italians, (combined with the social sometimes) among the Germans, and, naturally, the French before all of them. (For this paragraph and the following section see Sengle 1971–1980; Nemoianu 1985; Bernd 1995; Rinsum 1992, 6:181–310; Nipperdey 1991, 569–87.)

Stepping even farther along the road of reduction and imperfection we discover that romanticism turns from the class or the nation to the contentedness ("perfection") of the family, home, garden, and hearth (Biedermeier in its narrower and more precise sense). Islands of happiness, prosperity, and hope are described and praised. Even more radically, such a diminution might choose to concentrate on the one, the unique, the specific, the individual. The haughty autonomy of selfishness thereby came to be seen as a characteristic mark of romanticism. Subjectivity and the cult of the self, although they had not been unknown a few hundred (or even a few thousand) years earlier became the hallmark of the romantic hero, or narrator.

One other procedure (imperfection par excellence) ought to be mentioned here. It is that of sectionalization: selecting out of the complexity and completeness of an ideal romanticism just one slice and expanding it. This explains for instance the sensationalism or "blood-and-thunder" preferences (or the psychosexual emphases) of some writers after 1815 no less than the increasing reliance on scientific, i.e., philological, historical, anthropological, elements in other writings of the same age. Thus we can probably best understand why the age of Biedermeier is characterized by a peculiar combination of metaphysics and empiricism. What all these cases of relative defeat have in common is the nostalgic regretful abandonment of the universality of romanticism, of its revolutionary claim to achieve something nobody else had or could have accomplished, the abandonment of its world-historical or cosmic grasp, the acceptance of imperfection.

Such a descent from the heights of comprehensiveness is not surprising. In fact we can notice it time and again in the history of Western (and perhaps other) cultures. Does it not remind us of the much-discussed relationship of high modernism to postmodernism? Can we not see something similar at the end of the Middle Ages? Are there not certain parallels here between the process of fragmentation and reduction and all else that happened when the baroque triumphalism moved toward rococo, in the same way in which it moved toward mannerism, neoclassicism, rationalism, Enlightenment? These are all huge and approximate analogies, but they do have some merit, I would argue, at least up to a certain point.

In any case, if we look at the development of events immediately after 1820 or 1830, and sometimes even earlier, the argument tends to become clearer. While this is not yet a widely or unanimously accepted opinion, to me it seems clear that realism in its strongest version and expression, as it emerged in the middle and later nineteenth century would not have been imaginable without the romantic impulses. Jane Austen's novels were also responses to the romantic wave; George Eliot may be said to have begun her career with *Scenes of Clerical Life* and the wealth of realistic material surrounding a sometimes intensely romantic skeleton remained one of the hallmarks of her later novels. Anthony Trollope's *MacDermots of Ballycloran*, much like Balzac's *Les Chouans*, were early dabblings in the romantic style and it took a while for these authors to find their true (realist-style) vocation. In Flaubert, Dickens, Turgenyev, and Tolstoy we find plenty of straight descriptive prose intermingled with romanticism: either in imagery or in the plots. This formula persisted until late in the nineteenth century with Fontane and Raabe, Jókai Mór, and Clarín's *La Regenta*. Similarly it is difficult to say whether we want to consider Manzoni's *I Promessi sposi* as belonging to romanticism or one of the early examples of the realist movement.

While the examples here brought forward are works of fictional prose, it is worth taking into consideration that precisely the paraliterary writings (travel literature, historiography, and the like) played a prominent role in transforming romanticism (or a part of it) into full-fledged realism. Indeed, it stands to reason that works that by their very nature and declared intention aspired to reflect mimetically events of the outside world had to act as connectives between their own (romantic or visionary or ideological) outlines and a realistic discourse. Southey's *History of Brazil* pushed toward realism more than a Gothic novel; Chateaubriand's narration of his travels around the Mediterranean were closer to early realism than his epic/lyrical novel *Les martyrs;* the short pieces of the Spanish *costumbristas* were quasisociological (or so intended); while Pushkin's *Kapitanskaya Dochka* (let alone Scott's novels) had to hold a difficult balance between historically accurate details and their deep roots in romantic thinking and imagination.

At the end of the day we must confirm that romantic prose writing (fictional or not) relied on a closeness to the details of nature and society. This closeness soon proclaimed its independence of any broader outline (fantastic vision for instance) and thus turned into what we generally call realism.

While direct lines of connection between the romantic and the realist must definitely be admitted, quite often a certain intermediate stage can also be noted. This has been called at times "poetic realism," "bourgeois romanticism," or "Biedermeier," and may be regarded simply as a later phase of romanticism, a stage in which the strong ideals and values of the romantic paradigm are softened and toned down while not totally abandoned. Coziness and peaceful intimacy act here as convenient substitutes for broader desires of perfection. We are therefore entitled to speak about a reduction of the romantic paradigm to the size of the family or of the individual. We are entitled to speak about the triumph of imperfection, a conceptual not less than a pragmatic triumph. Mörike, Raabe, Stifter, and dozens of others exercised themselves in the German language in this direction. Němcová in Bohemia and Alecsandri in Moldavia did the same. English literature is rich in productions such as those of Felicia Hemans, Leigh Hunt, or Charles Lamb. Lamartine's *Jocelyn* as well as other of his poetic works may be said to be sentimental variants of *The Prelude* or of *Prometheus Unbound*. Hungarian, Baltic, or Scandinavian literatures are not devoid of similar examples.

However, at least as frequent as this focusing of the search for romantic regeneration and perfection to family or small (personalized, disalienated) circles is another kind of imperfective reduction. I refer to the downsizing from humanity as a whole to the ethnic or national community. This phenomenon was particularly frequent in eastern Europe. There the political and the literary were inextricably combined. Literary genius was considered proof of national revival and credibility. The imagery of the long national somnolence is recurrent; in fact it becomes an obsession, a cliché even, in Czech, Romanian, Hungarian, and South Slavic literatures, and others yet. The act of writing is at the same time a rousing call to awakening and evidence of the act of awakening: many writings by Petőfi, Mickiewicz, and Mácha straddle the line between the imaginary and the nonfictional. The regeneration is concentrated into the world of a single linguistic-historical community, often one that does not enjoy the benefits of independence or other freedoms. However, this separate, limited regeneration is seen as standing symbolically for a change that will be or can be universal.

True, in the overwhelming majority of cases the nationalism of the early nineteenth century is closely linked to liberationist and emancipatory ideals, not only in eastern and central Europe but also in Germany, France, Italy, and this state of things begins to change only well after 1850. (Xenophobic variants of nationalism, exclusionary racism are, strictly regarded, grandchildren of romanticism rather than direct offspring: they are at least two generations away from core romanticism.) That is why I already argued that a number of left-wing discourses ought to be regarded as deriving from romantic goals. There is little disagreement as to the way in which some of these romantic revolutionary ideals were expressed in more purely literary forms, as in the case of Blake, Shelley, sometimes Byron, the early Schiller and Hölderlin, and many others. But more than a few belong to the nonfictional area: the oratory of Saint-Just and other French revolutionists, nondramatic writings by Büchner, the national mysticism of Mickiewicz, Petőfi, or Eminescu can be placed at the same level. To be even more clear: after 1815 it becomes sometimes difficult to separate neatly the purely literary in its national purposes (or in the way in which it is institutionalized and glorified) from the straightforward rhetoric addressed to national awakening. Even more typical are the writings of Robert Owen and of Saint-Simon with their visionary utopianism, which actually and practically suggested modes of transformation of an ageing society into a new world. As romanticism cooled down after 1815, practical as well as cosmic-fantastic structures develop mightily. (Both of these can well be seen as imperfect or incomplete by contrast with the original claims of the movement.) The social and class agitations (in France, in England, in Russia, and elsewhere) translated the romantic paradigm; they prepared it for general and popular consumption. The regeneration of romanticism was supposed to be offered this time not as a universal phenomenon, but as a pragmatic set of gestures intended to heal the wounds, sufferings, and injustices of our body social in place after place. The issue of the split between consciousness and reality could be explained as a split between exploiting upper classes and exploited lower classes. Solving the tensions of the latter (by violent force if necessary) would inevitably lead to a reintegration of consciousness into reality, to a recapturing of a primeval spontaneity. This was held by the left-Hegelians; this was the root of Marxism; this was what many Chartist sympathizers fondly believed. Again, as in the case of national lines of flight more remote consequences can be distinguished: cultural studies and multiculturalism among them.

The popularization of science by the initiation of the great encyclopedic works (Larousse, Brockhaus, Meyer, Chambers), by the felt need to establish almanacs and modern daily journals, the setting up of kindergartens, gymnastic systems, the initiation of museums, and financial sponsorship and patronage by capitalist magnates, hygienic revolutions, and broad-based tourism, all were derived from a popularization of romanticism. The avalanche that threatened to overwhelm Western civilization (at first) was tamed by accepting imperfection.

While there are sometimes hesitations as to the centrifugal lines fleeing from romanticism toward the world of left-wing ideas, it is rarely denied that a whole range of conservative views (whether moderately reformist or hard-line right-wing) sprang from the same romanticism. One may assume that ideologically this link is easier to understand. Indeed romantic writers, as we just agreed, tended to seek a return to the origins, to a primal, happier state of affairs. This search could lead to a more or less imaginary past (as in Arnim's *Kronenwächter* for instance), but it could more specifically zoom in on the Middle Ages not as a kind of vernacular canon but as an actual model to be reconstructed in the contemporary world. Thus romanticism could become open reaction. Joseph de Maistre's acid and pitiless proclamations come to mind. Adam Müller developed an aesthetic politics that strayed far from its purported Burkean roots. Friedrich Schlegel, Coleridge, Wordsworth, and Southey were disliked for their later views, but these views were deeper and more eloquent than their shallow enthusiasms as young people. Chateaubriand was perhaps more constant in his inconstancy throughout his life, but on the whole what his contemporaries decided to choose and maintain out of his writings was stark conservatism. Perhaps the same can be said about Schelling. Let us, as a mere afterthought mention the names of Guizot and Tocqueville, count Széchenyi, Jovellanos and Canovas, Ion Ghica, Sir Robert Peel, and a whole network of moderate (I would call them post-Goethean) thinkers who tried to preserve the acquisitions of the French Revolution but defuse the explosive power of the latter. It was supposed that only the perfectionist claims of the Revolution had to suffer or to be dismissed.

From a sociohistorical point of view (over and beyond the various discourses experimented with) we can confidently speak about strategies of moderation. Societies tried to reestablish a normal and predictable flow, a calm gradualism that should be able to absorb the furies and radical modifications proposed at the end of the eighteenth century, bring back as much as reasonable out of the value traditions of the past, reduce change to a well-controlled rhythm, and make progress orderly. We do more than once wonder about the uniqueness of romantic innovations or projects. In turn we should equally wonder about the adroit manner in which the later (or better, post-) romantic generations captured romanticism and molded it into pragmatic shapes. Objects of every day use were produced in large quantities out of the volcanic material spewed during prior decades. Perfection had been tried and found wanting. It was now the time to turn toward imperfection, toward approximation, toward relativity, as the most desirable modes of dealing with informational processing. Researchers of specific fields such as early-nineteenth-century British fiction cannot but conclude that this particular branch is "the production of social order" (Burgess 2000, 2–4), and the same demonstration can be made by looking at other fields of intellectual and artistic endeavor, including the education of younger generations (Richardson 1994). Domestication of one kind or another is still the closest we have to a common denominator of the literary decades 1820–1850 is the conclusion even of somewhat skeptical examiners (Cronin 2002).

Perhaps more neutral ideologically (though not necessarily always) was another phenomenon: namely the diffusion and specifications of learning and of different branches of science. True this process had begun in the eighteenth century and probably even earlier. In several parts of Europe and to varying extents (quite obviously in central Europe) a model of social advancement and power-gaining emerged in which the central element was not labor directed toward financial increase (as the northern and Protestant methodology depicted by Max Weber claimed) but rather accreditation through cognition, through the acquisition of knowledge. Wider technological and marketing possibilities led to a dramatic increase in the reading public, to the expansion of the kinds of knowledge that were easily available to wider strata, and generally to a broadening of horizons even among classes that had until then been shut off from access to more comprehensive kinds of knowledge. While the dynamics were general we can also point to specific techniques that hastened and facilitated it. I refer to the emergence of systematic sciences that had been until the romantic decades in their infancy or had been vague and subjective. The main point to keep in mind however is that a certain joyful ordering of existing knowledge (whether justified or not) engaged the attention of a wider public and made the raw materials accessible, and even more, exciting for growing categories of the population. The sciences were seen as the salvation of minds and souls, a conviction that was to continue until deep into the twentieth century.

The fact that the science of history had established itself over and above all the others as the queen of sciences, as the valid model to be followed by others and, at bottom, to direct human existence and behavior themselves had deep consequences in the nineteenth century. One of these, as already said several times, was that the other sciences regarded themselves as beholden to history; they felt that they had to begin methodologically by a historical account of themselves and, more powerfully to translate the cause-and-effect relationship into one of continuity. Geology and zoology (Darwinian, Lamarckian, and others) were expansions of history; philology was turned into a form of history and of pedigree generation. Virtually all novels of the time were, at some level, historical novels. Let us not forget that even many of the writings of such a systematic philosopher as Hegel undoubtedly was were very often arranged in a historical manner.

This is not to say that religious salvation found itself suddenly ignored or thrown overboard. On the contrary, whereas many forms of religion (chiefly Catholicism and Anglicanism) had found themselves endangered and belittled during much of the eighteenth century, romanticism proved to be a turning point. It is worth repeating and reemphasizing the points made in an earlier chapter. Chateaubriand in France, Friedrich Schlegel and other romantics in Germany, Coleridge and some of his friends in England, Hannah More on both sides of the Atlantic Ocean, the exiled Mickiewicz for the divided and submerged Poland, all argued in favor of the revival of religion, albeit under modified shapes. The results were seen almost immediately after 1815. Catholicism regained much of its dignity and influence both on a sociopolitical and on an intellectual level. In England with the Tractarians and/or the Oxford Movement, a true renewal of Episcopalianism was set in motion. Jewish and Protestant movements that had begun as popular (and perhaps somewhat suspect or underground manifestations) such as Methodism, Pietism, or Hassidism gained institutional legitimacy. I would go even further and attribute the tension between science and religion that preoccupied so much the Victorian Age to impulses stemming from the romantics. All this is demonstrably true if we think of the obvious romantic tinge that the religious discourses of the nineteenth century gained, and which makes them so different from those of other centuries.

Part of what I just called "romantic tinge" was, of course, the emphasis on the aesthetic. Many romantics foregrounded the Beautiful, rather than the Good and the True, as had been done by earlier theologians, poets, and thinkers. Yes, this was a moderating force, as I argued, but in fact the aesthetic moment was also multidimensional, and its very complexity made it apt to contribute to the explosion and dispersal of romanticism. Although aesthetics became a major branch of philosophy only with Kant, Schiller, Hegel, and Coleridge, it could be seen as an admirable abode for hosting the retreating romantic paradigm as a whole. Indeed if the cosmos or the human species as a whole were not willing or able to undergo a radical change then surely inside the world of ideal beauty, accessible to human minds and emotions such ultimate perfections could be achieved, alluded to, or imagined. Thus in many cases aesthetic activity came to be seen as the equivalent or substitute of prayer and religious engagement. Even when religion remained standing, it was colored or supported by the cult of the Beautiful, deeply combined with it. Nor was religion the only field in which the Beautiful found eager hospitality. History, which I just described as the queen of sciences, tried, particularly in the early nineteenth century but later also, to take as much advantage as it could of all the means of literary aesthetics it could absorb. Politics had to be founded on orotund rhetoric.

Elegance was a symptom of truth in mathematical equations. In fact most human behaviors tried to garb themselves in aesthetic material. The subsequent mockery of nineteenth-century squeamishness or mannerliness is oblivious to the more serious sources of romantic derivation in all such attitudes.

Again, this was not merely the domain of rich and cultivated upper social strata. On the contrary. It may be safely said that the derivations of romantic strategies and subject matters persisted longest and were grafted most solidly in the lower and least cultivated reading public, indeed in popular culture. The ties binding the popular culture of the nineteenth and twentieth centuries with their remote romantic ancestry are rarely studied in depth and in earnest, perhaps because they are too plain to see. Dozens of literary subgenres developed dramatically, spectacularly, and show few signs of being abandoned: the detective novel, science-fiction, the historical novel, horror-prose, romance, fantasy. The same can be said about music and the visual arts, where combinations of theatrical performance, visual spectacle, propaganda, and audio effects grew and grew during the nineteenth and twentieth centuries; one wonders as of this writing whether (given the technological advances in the last few decades) these kinds of combinations could not be considered the chief expression of artistic intention. The "comics" invented in and popular since the mid–nineteenth century are a similar kind of combination of the arts. The birth and lightning-fast spread of cinematography was foreshadowed in the early nineteenth century by the shadow/light games that were so popular, by puppet shows, by the "panoramas" that attracted large audiences, as well as by historical and pseudo-historical huge paintings (or series of paintings) with hundreds or even thousands of characters, the exhibition of which was often accompanied by payment (much as for a play for instance). A history of cinematography indicates clearly that a good part of the early films were the adaptation of movement to already existing forms of visual arts (historical, for instance); the *tableaux vivants* so popular among the upper and middle classes by the end of the nineteenth century were a transitional form.

Later the phenomenon of the 1960s with its youth culture in the West (and soon in planetary proportions) drew clearly and openly from romantic sources: the "revival" of the novels of Hermann Hesse and the circulation of those by J. R. R. Tolkien (with their legion of imitators) are just two possible examples, but it should not be forgotten that such tastes had persisted tenaciously (subterraneously or not) throughout the nineteenth and early twentieth centuries. To offer just a single additional example: the rock group the Doors and its leader, Jim Morrison, claimed to be the continuators of Blake and Nietzsche.

We can also add here a more clearly literary aspect: that of the kinds of criticism and hermeneutic activities practiced in the second half of the twentieth century. Most schools of critical writing active nowadays pride themselves on their use of ambiguity, multiplicity, and dynamic fluidity in the practice of reading, explanation, and interpretation. Whether we talk about poststructuralist movements, deconstruction, diverse variants of critical studies, reader-response, and so many others, they share, despite differences, these features. It is only fair to say that these fluidities and ironic undecidabilities are clearly preceded (and in a number of cases openly admit to harking back to) romantic practices and theories. It is interesting to observe that whereas most of our previous centrifugal lines were predicated upon a search for concreteness and reality (an attempt to achieve at least partially in real life the ideal paradigms of romanticism) here we find the opposite: a mode of discourse that admits without qualms that such paradigmatic achievements are impossible and that the best way to approach them would be simply to look for doubt, uncertainty, implicit contradiction, or mutual suspension of opposite truths. This issue preoccupied poets (such as Coleridge when he talked about the "willing suspension of disbelief" or the recurrent tortured preoccupations of Hölderlin), playwrights such as Tieck, Büchner, Grabbe, or Słowacki, but, even more than these, critics and philosophers. Friedrich Schlegel made out of irony and ambiguity the central element of all his earliest (and most creative work). Before him, Kant effected an almost "Copernican revolution" by codifying the ways in which cognition must remain uncertain. Hegel went perhaps even farther in adroitly adapting Fichte's "thesis-antithesis-synthesis" as the ultimate dynamic on which social reality is founded. These examples and many others act as the appropriate referential background to most critics of the second half of the twentieth century, from Spitzer to de Man. They provide an equally significant background to the speculations of radical skeptics such as Richard Rorty, Jacques Derrida, or Peter Sloterdijk.

In fact every generation of the nineteenth and twentieth centuries had its own neoromanticism, whether strictly literary or more broadly theoretical/ideological. Symbolism, Parnassianism, and "decadence" derive from it. Existentialism borrowed from it the problematic of the individual and of alienation, expressionism the prophetic and frenetic dimension, postmodernism its interest in fragmentariness, irony, parody, and dissipation. And are not after all the diverse neoclassics rooted in the islands of classical enthusiasm of the romantic movement, in Hölderlin and Kleist?

Our conclusion has to be simple but rather clear. Romanticism, under whatever guise and inscribed in whatever discourse, was a relatively short and on the whole elusive apparition. It is difficult to get hold of if we are looking for a solid, clear-cut object with sharply defined limits and shape: as difficult as devising or proclaiming perfection in this sublunary world of ours. On the other hand its forerunners are numerous and widespread, over a whole century. Even more important, its explosion or implosion led in a multitude of directions, covered the whole field of the nineteenth and twentieth centuries, and proved enormously fertile and quite persistent. It is not so much in its declared and central aims that it proved strong and significant, but more in its deformations, modest changes, and multiple practical applications, in a word, in its imperfections. Romanticism becomes fully itself, for better or for worse, only as it ceases to be itself.

Bibiliography

Bernd, Clifford Albrecht. 1995. *Poetic Realism in Scandinavia and Central Europe 1820–1895*. Columbia, S.C.: Camden House.

Bernhard, Marianne. 1983. *Das Biedermeier: Kultur zwischen Wienerkongress und Märzrevolution*. Düsseldorf: Econ.

Böhmer, Gunter. 1968. *Die Welt des Biedermeier*. Munich: Kurt Desch.

Burgess, Miranda. 2000. *British Fiction and the Production of Social Order 1740–1830*. Cambridge: Cambridge University Press.

Cronin, Richard. 2002. *Romantic Victorians: English Literature 1824–1840*. New York: Palgrave.

Farber, Paul Lawrence. 1997. *Discovering Birds: The Emergence of Ornithology as a Scientific Discipline 1760–1850*. Baltimore: Johns Hopkins University Press. (orig. pub. 1982.)

Geismeier, Willi. 1979. *Biedermeier*. Leipzig: Seeman.

Glaser, Horst Albert, ed. 1980–1987. *Deutsche Literatur: Eine Sozialgeschichte*. 10 vols. Hamburg: Rowohlt.

Hobsbawm, Eric. 1962. *The Age of Revolution 1789–1848*. London: Weidenfeld and Nicholson.

Johnson, Paul. 1991. *The Birth of the Modern: World Society 1815–1830*. New York: HarperCollins.

Lankheit, Klaus. 1988. *Revolution und Restauration 1785–1855*. Cologne: DuMont.

Nemoianu, Virgil. 1985. *The Taming of Romanticism: European Literature and the Age of Biedermeier*. Cambridge, Mass.: Harvard University Press.

Nipperdey, Thomas. 1991. *Deutsche Geschichte 1810–1866*. Munich: Beck.

Richardson, Alan. 1994. *Literature, Education, and Romanticism: Reading as Social Practice*. Cambridge: Cambridge University Press.

Rinsum, Annemarie und Wolfgang van. 1992. *Deutsche Literaturgeschichte*. 12 vols. Munich: Beck.

Sauvigny, G. de Bertier de. 1955. *La Restauration*. Paris: Flammarion.

Sengle, Friedrich. 1971–1980. *Biedermeierzeit*. 3 vols. Stuttgart: Metzler.

Ziolkowski, Theodore. 1990. *German Romanticism and Its Institutions*. Princeton, N.J.: Princeton University Press.

INDEX

Acton, John Emerich Dalberg, Lord, 75
Adams, John, 11
Addison, Joseph, 32n20, 162, 216–17, 240
Aeschylus, 203
Aksakov, Sergey Timofeyevich, 98
Alecsandri, Vasile, 206, 245
Alexis, Willibald, 11, 70, 172n56, 238
Althusius, Johannes, 60n3
Apuleius, 222
Arany, János, 117, 206
Aristotle, 65–66, 72
Arnim, Achim von, 69, 154, 238, 247
Arnold, Matthew, 19, 119, 158
Asachi, Gheorghe, 236
Aurevilly, Barbey d', 26
Austen, Jane, 61n17, 70, 126, 241, 244
Austin, Sarah, 168n12

Baader, Franz Xaver, 120, 241
Bachofen, Johann Jakob, 116
Bacon, Francis, 159
Baedeker, Karl, 138
Baker, Houston, 96
Bălcescu, Nicolae, 75, 92, 238
Ballanche, Pierre-Simon, 10, 28–29, 114, 241
Balmes, Jaime, 19, 53, 58, 67, 78, 118, 121–22
Balzac, Honoré de, 11, 39, 61n17, 69, 71, 73, 97, 125, 238, 245
Baraka, Amiri, 96
Barante, Prosper de, 74, 171n51
Barginet, Alexandre Pierre, 69
Barnauskas, Antanas, 117
Baudelaire, Charles-Pierre, 24, 26
Baumgarten, Alexander, 121
Bellay, Joachim du, 204
Belloc, H., 75
Benjamin, Walter, 61n4

Béranger, Pierre-Jean de, 13
Berchtold, Leopold, 162
Bibesco, Martha, 188
Blaga, Lucian, 93–94, 96, 236
Blake, William, 5, 114, 136, 147, 149, 207, 213, 221, 235, 240, 246, 250
Boccacio, Giovanni, 171n44
Bodnărescu, Samson, 206
Böhme, Jakob, 239, 241
Bonald, Louis, Vicomte de, 21, 29, 31n7, 67, 113
Bopp, Franz, 236
Börne, Ludwig, 172n56
Bossuet, Jacques-Bénigne, 67, 71, 87, 115
Brătianu, Ion, 92
Brentano, Clemens, 82n3, 116, 124
Brothers, Richard, 114
Browne, Thomas, 24, 216, 219, 222
Browning, Robert, 76
Brownson, Orestes, 114
Büchner, Georg, 239, 246, 251
Buckle, Henry, 75
Buffon, Georges-Louis Leclerc de, 32n20, 236
Bulwer-Lytton, Edward, 76
Bunyan, John, 167, 171n44
Burckhardt, Jakob, 61n4, 160
Burke, Edmund, 11, 38, 53–54, 69, 72, 78, 81n2, 214–15, 225n8
Burns, Robert, 207–8, 240
Burton, Robert, 24, 216, 219, 222
Byron, George Gordon, Lord, 11, 91, 136, 143, 146–47, 158, 167, 171n45, 178, 207–8, 212, 216, 220, 236, 243, 246

Calderón, Pedro, de la Barca, 208, 242
Campbell, Joseph, 31n13, 105n2, 116
Cánovas del Castillo, Pedro, 247

Cantacuzino, G. M., 188
Carlyle, Thomas, 41; 75, 200n3, 214, 218, 226n13, 236, 238
Carp, Petre, 92
Carrel, Alexis, 13
Castelbajac, Raymond, Vicomte de, 31n7
Castiglione, Baldassare, 222
Cavour, Camillo Benso, Conte di, 116
Cervantes, Miguel de, x, 8, 171n44, 203, 205, 208, 242
Chamfort, Sébastien-Roch Nicolas, 162
Chateaubriand, François-René de, x, 3–4, 9–30, 31n7, 31nn11–12, 32n21, 37, 39–40, 48, 50n14, 53, 56, 58–59, 70, 74–75, 77–78, 80, 87–88, 97–98, 115, 118–19, 121–22, 124, 138–42, 154, 158, 168n5, 170n43, 204, 208, 223, 226n18, 236, 240, 243, 245, 247, 249
Chesterton, G. K., 75, 214
Chomsky, Noam, 212
Ciezkowski, August, 117
Clarín (Leopoldo Alas), 245
Claudel, Paul, 24
Claudius, Matthias, 125
Cobbett, William, 53, 147–57, 169n14, 169n17, 169n19, 169nn21–22, 169nn24–27, 170nn29–32, 170n43, 171n45, 214, 224n5, 224n7, 237
Codru-Drăgușanu, I. G., 146
Coleridge, Samuel Taylor, 5–7, 11, 72, 78, 91, 114–15, 124, 136, 147, 158, 163, 167, 171n45, 198, 207–8, 212–15, 235–36, 240–41, 247, 249, 251
Comte, Auguste, 29, 114, 241
Constant, Benjamin, 9, 16, 29, 31n7, 56, 79, 115–16, 128n2, 162–64, 236
Cooper, James Fenimore, 9, 11, 39, 69, 85, 96–104, 107n16, 108n22, 152, 238
Corneille, Pierre, 64, 203–4
Cortés, Donoso, 78
Cottin, Sophie, 107n18, 170n39
Courier, Paul Louis, 26, 170n29
Courtenay, Baudoin de, 66
Cousin, Victor, 79, 114–15
Cowper, William, 171n45
Creuzer, Friedrich, 115–16, 125, 236
Cruz, San Juan de la, 208
Cuvier, Georges, 66, 236

Dahrendorf, Ralf, 38, 48
Dante, x, 8, 144–45, 158, 203–5, 208, 242
Darwin, Charles, 66, 129n6, 249
Daukantas, Simanas, 238
Davies of Hereford, John, 222
Davis, John, 222
Davison, William, 162

Defoe, Daniel, 149
Delft, Louis van, 171n48
De Quincey, Thomas, 147, 151, 153, 155–56, 170n39, 170n43, 216, 219, 237
Derrida, Jacques, 86, 251
Diaz, Nicomedes Pastór, 78
Dickens, Charles, 61n17, 146, 168n10, 214, 245
Diderot, Denis, 140, 154, 238
Dilthey, Wilhelm, 71, 81
Doderer, Heimito von, 194
Donelaitis, Kristijonas, 239
Dos Passos, John, 70
Dostoyevsky, Fyodor, 61n17, 165
Douglass, Frederick, 96
Drendorf, Heinrich, 198
Drey, Johann Sebastian von, 125
Droste-Hülshoff, Annette Freiin von, 125–26
DuBois, W. E. B., 95–96
Duck, Stephen, 216
Dumas-Père, Alexandre, 69
Dumont, Louis, 48
Dunbar, Paul, 96
Durkheim, Émile, 48, 49n4

Ebert, Karl Egon, 188
Eckermann, Johann Peter, 106n7
Eichendorff, Joseph von, 115
Eliade, Mircea, 31n13, 105n2, 116
Eliot, George, 11, 24, 61n17, 76, 244
Eliot, T. S., 223
Emerson, Ralph Waldo, 236
Eminescu, Mihai, 92–93, 203, 205–6, 208, 246
Engels, Friedrich, 225n8
Eötvös, József, 11, 40
Erasmus, 66
Ernst, Paul, 65

Fallmerayer, Jakob, 167n4
Faulkner, William, 106n12
Fénelon, François de, 12, 24, 42, 119, 122, 214
Ferguson, Adam, 39
Feuerbach, Ludwig, 129n6
Fichte, Johann Gottlieb, 120, 251
Fielding, Henry, 137, 171n48, 217
Filimon, Nicolae, 165
Flaubert, Gustave, 24, 61n17, 245
Földi, János, 236
Fontane, Theodor, 61n17, 245
Foscolo, Ugo, 208, 243
Foucault, Michel, 30n3, 96, 104
Fourier, Charles, 29, 114
Franklin, Benjamin, 169n24, 180
Frazer, James George, 31n13, 88, 116
Froude, James, 73, 75, 114
Fürstenberg, Franz von, 125

INDEX 255

Gallitzin, Amalie von, 125
Garay, János, 178
Garvey, Marcus, 95
Gates, Henry, 96
Gautier, Théophile, 76
Gellius, Aullus, 219
Gellner, Ernst, 38, 48
Gentz, Friedrich von, 55, 72
Ghica, Ion, 11, 247
Gibbon, Edward, 87
Gil y Carrasco, Enrique, 69
Gladstone, Williams, 114
Godwin, Richard, 114
Goethe, Johann Wolfgang von, x, 9, 11, 23, 37–38, 40–49, 50n5, 51nn17–18, 51nn21–23, 53–60, 60n1, 61n10, 61n12, 61n15, 61n17, 62n19, 62n22, 78, 80, 90–91, 97, 106n7, 115, 125, 137, 141, 145, 161, 163, 168n7, 177, 203, 209–10, 223, 236–38, 241, 243
Goga, Octavian, 92–93
Gogol, Nikolay Vasilyevich, 115
Goldsmith, Oliver, 75, 150, 157, 159, 171n45, 213, 216–17
Golescu, Dinicu, 11, 168n13
Görres, Joseph, 116, 125, 236
Goszczynski, Seweryn, 117
Gotthelf, Jeremias, 125–26
Gousset, Thomas, 123
Grabbe, Christian Dietrich, 82n3, 218, 239, 251
Grillparzer, Franz, 125, 145, 168n7
Grimm, Jakob, 74, 116, 236
Grimm, Wilhelm, 116, 236
Gügler, Alois, 58, 118–20, 124
Guizot, François, 11, 16, 27, 29, 53, 56–58, 61n13, 67, 74, 77–80, 115, 121, 171n51, 247
Gundolf, F., 61n4
Günther, Anton, 125
Gusti, Dimitrie, 93–94, 106n10
Gutzkow, Karl, 126

Hadzi, Jovan, 184
Hales, Stephen, 236
Haller, Albrecht von, 158
Hamann, Johann Georg, 125, 222, 240
Hanka, Václav, 205
Harrington, John, 222
Haşdeu, Bogdan P., 117, 205
Hauff, Wilhelm, 69–70
Hayek, Friedrich von, 48
Hazlitt, William, 26, 137, 142, 151, 157–62, 168n10, 171n44, 208, 212, 219, 235, 237
Hebbel, Friedrich, 205
Hecker, Isaac, 114
Hegel, Georg Wilhelm Friedrich, 38, 87, 91, 136, 235–36, 249, 251

Heidegger, Martin, 86
Heine, Heinrich, 145, 168n8, 172n56
Heliade-Rădulescu, Ion, 117, 236
Hemans, Felicia, 125, 245
Herder, Johann Gottfried von, 54, 67, 74, 90–91, 115, 120, 161, 163, 177, 209
Hermes, Georg, 125
Herodotus, 238
Herwegh, Georg, 145, 168n7
Hesiod, 203
Hesse, Hermann, 250
Hobbes, Thomas, 72
Hoene-Wrónski, J. M., 117
Hofbauer, Klement Maria, 19, 58, 113
Hoffmann, E. T. A., 237, 239
Hölderlin, Friedrich, x, 5, 7, 23, 91, 120, 136, 155, 178, 208, 235, 238, 246, 251
Homer, 17–18, 24, 44, 74, 203, 205, 210, 222
Hopkins, Gerard Manley, 225n11
Horvath, Istvan, 117
Hughes, Langston, 95
Hugo, Victor, 29, 39, 69, 74, 76, 81, 82n3, 115–16, 123, 161, 208, 235–36
Humboldt, Wilhelm von, x, 56
Humboldt brothers, 177, 236
Hume, David, 75
Hunt, Leigh, 26, 142–46, 158, 168n10, 212, 216, 219, 237, 245
Hurd, Richard, 240
Hurston, Zora Neale, 96
Hus, Jan, 75

Ibrăileanu, Garabet, 106n9
Imbert-Gourbeyre, Antoine, 123
Immermann, Karl, 70, 72, 147, 152–56, 168n7, 170n38
Iorga, Nicolae, 92–93
Irigaray, Luce, 162
Irínyi, József, 165

James, Henry, 166
János, Andrew, 48
Johnson, Charles, 96
Johnson, Samuel, 87, 137, 235
Jones, John, 216
Jones, William, 236
Jósika, Miklós, 178
Jovellanos, Gaspar Melchor de, 40, 50n11, 78, 247
Joyce, James, 11, 24, 210
Jung-Stilling, Johann Heinrich, 125

Kant, Immanuel, 90–91, 121, 135, 236, 249, 251
Karadžić, Vuk, 117
Karamzin, N. M., 74, 137, 165, 238

Kazinczy, Ferenc, 117
Keats, John, x, 72, 82n3, 147, 171n44, 207, 235
Keble, John, 114
Kerényi, Karl, 105n2, 116
Ketteler, Wilhelm von, 112
Keyserling, Hermann Alexander, 160
Kleist, Heinrich von, 251
Klopstock, Friedrich Gottlieb, 125, 163, 209, 240
Kog lniceanu, Mihail, 92
Kölcsey, Ferenc, 117
Kollár, Jan, 184
Kotzebue, August von, 209
Kovacić, Ante, 178
Krasiński, 206
Kraszewski, Józef Ignacy, 165
Kreutzwald, Reinhold, 118
Kristeva, Julia, 162
Krüdener, Barbara Juliane von, 114, 241

Lafitte, Jacques, 79
La Fontaine, Jean de, 240
La Harpe, Jean-François de, 10
Lamarck, Jean Baptiste, 236, 249
Lamartine, Alphonse de, 23, 74–75, 77, 115, 123, 125, 154, 171n44, 245
Lamb, Charles, 26, 154–55, 162, 216, 219, 237, 245
Lamennais, Félicité de, 13, 29, 31n7, 58, 116, 122, 124, 129n3
Landor, Walter Savage, 76, 237
La Rochefoucauld, François de, 31n7, 162
Larsen, Nella, 95
Lasausse, Jean-Baptiste, 123
Laube, Heinrich, 145, 172n56
Lecky, W. E. H., 75
Lehar, Franz, 196
Leibniz, Gottfried Wilhelm, 56, 154, 163
Leopardi, Giacomo, 208, 243
Lermontov, Mikhail Yuryevich, 98
Lessing, Gotthold Ephraim, 125, 163, 209, 241
Lewis, C. S., 88
Linda, Josef, 205
Linné, Carl, 236
Locke, John, 72
Lockhart, John Gibson, 40
Longus, 24
Lönnrot, Elias, 205
Loury, Glenn, 96
Lovinescu, Eugen, 93
Lukács, György von, 65, 68, 187

Macaulay, Thomas B., 73, 75–76, 225n8
Mácha, Karel Hynek, 246
Macrobius, 219

Madgearu, Virgil, 93
Maiorescu, Titu, 92
Maistre, Joseph de, 77, 123, 247
Maistre, Xavier de, 107n18, 147, 154–56, 162
Malczewski, Antoni, 117
Malebranche, Nicolas de, 12, 119
Maniu, Adrian, 94
Mann, Thomas, 23, 61n4
Manning, Henry Edward, 114
Manzoni, Alessandro, 9, 11, 39, 69, 116, 124, 208, 238, 245
Map, Walter, 219
Martignac, Jean Baptiste, Vicomte de, 79
Marx, Karl, 38, 49nn3–4, 73, 91, 114, 129n6
Maury, Alfred, 123
McKay, Claude, 95
McPherson, James, 205
Meinong, Alexius, 7
Mendelssohn, Moses, 118
Menzel, Wolfgang, 126
Mérimée, Prosper, 76
Michelet, Jules, 74, 114, 123, 209, 238
Mickiewicz, Adam, 69, 115, 117, 178, 203, 206–8, 246, 249
Mignet, François-Auguste-Marie, 73
Mill, John Stuart, 62n19
Milton, John, 13, 17–18, 24, 158, 171n44, 222
Mirabeau, Honoré Gabriel Riqueti, Comte de, 183
Mishima, Yukio, 208
Möhler, Johann Adam, 119
Mommsen, Theodor, 73
Montaigne, Michel Eyquem de, 162, 222
Montalambert, Charles, Comte de, 122
Montesquieu, Charles Louis de Sécondat, Baron de, 15, 42, 87, 91, 106n6, 164
Mór, Jókai, 245
More, Hannah, 58, 112–13, 249
Moreau, Jacques Nicolas, 50n10
Mörike, Eduard Friedrich, 125, 240, 245
Morris, William, 156
Morrison, Toni, 96
Möser, Justus, 51n22, 53–54, 61n8, 151–52, 170n31
Müller, Adam, 72, 77, 247
Mundt, Theodor, 61n4
Murray, John, III, 138
Musil, Robert von, 187
Musset, Alfred de, 76, 123, 161

Nabakov, Vladimir, 28
Nemcová, Boûena, 245
Nerval, Gérard de, 123
Nestroy, Johann, 196
Neumann, John von, 187

Newman, John Henry, Cardinal, 114, 124, 198, 225n11
Ney, Eugène, 17
Niebuhr, Barthold G., 74
Nietzsche, Friedrich Wilhelm, 49, 86, 116, 236, 250
Novalis, x, 5, 72, 91, 120, 125, 154, 198, 237

Owen, Robert, 114, 225n8, 246
Ozanam, Antoine-Frédéric, 122

Palacký, Frantisek, 74–75, 238
Pan, Mallet du, 164
Pater, Walter, 160
Paul, Jean, 120, 198, 218
Peacock, Thomas Love, 153
Péguy, Charles, 208
Peirce, C. S., 86
Percy, Walker, 106n12
Perrault, Charles, 240
Peterson, Kristjan, 118
Petöfi, Sándor, 203, 206, 208, 246
Pindar, 203
Platen, August, 82n3
Plato, 76, 222
Plutarch, 72, 238
Poe, Edgar Allan, 208
Polanyi, Karl, 48, 49n3
Pope, Alexander, 171n44
Popović, Jovan Sterija, 178
Popper, Karl, 48
Posselt, Franz, 171n48
Poteca, Eufrosin, 117
Pratt, Mary Louise, 87, 164–66, 167n2, 171n53
Priestley, Joseph, 236
Proust, Marcel, 11, 22
Pückler-Muskau, Hermann, Prince, 145–47, 168nn7–8, 168n10, 168n12
Pusey, Edward Bouverie, 114
Pushkin, Aleksandr, 11, 39, 69, 98, 208, 238, 245

Quinet, Edgar, 74, 114–16, 123, 209

Raabe, Wilhelm, 61n17, 245
Rabelais, François, 222
Racine, Jean, 64, 203, 241
Radishchev, Aleksandr, 165
Rădulescu-Motru, C., 93, 106n9
Raimund, Friedrich, 196
Ralet, Dimitrie, 139–42
Ranke, Leopold von, 73
Rask, Rasmus, 236
Raumer, Friedrich von, 74, 238
Raupach, Ernst, 74

Renan, Joseph-Ernest, 129n6
Ricci, Matteo, 88, 106n3
Risach, Freiherr von, 198
Rorty, Richard, 86, 251
Rosetti, C. A., 92
Rosmini-Serbati, Antonio, 53, 58, 116–17, 124
Rostow, W. W., 38
Rousseau, Jean-Jacques, 12, 17, 72, 129n6, 137, 140, 158, 163, 183, 239–40
Rubés, F. J., 178
Russell, Bertrand, 212
Russo, Alecu, 117

Said, Edward, 87
Sainte-Beuve, Charles-Augustin, 26, 29, 74, 76
Saint-Hilaire, Geoffroy de, 66
Saint-Just, Louis de, 246
Saint-Martin, Louis-Claude de, 28, 114, 239, 241
Saint-Pierre, Bernardin de, 12
Saint-Simon, Henri de, 29, 51n21, 114, 123, 241, 246
Sand, George, 76
Sartorius, Georg, 51n21
Saussure, Ferdinand de, 66
Schelling, F. W. J. von, 5, 7, 120, 136, 223, 235–36, 240, 247
Scherer, Wilhelm, 61n4
Schiller, Friedrich, x, 11, 75, 163, 177, 203, 209, 236, 246, 249
Schlegel, August Wilhelm, x, 91, 161, 208, 218
Schlegel, Dorothea, 113
Schlegel, Friedrich, x, 11, 49, 72, 113, 115–16, 162, 208, 218, 247, 249, 251
Schleiermacher, Friedrich, 116, 236
Schopenhauer, Arthur, 19, 86, 119, 236, 243
Schumpeter, E. S., 156
Scott, Walter, x, 9, 11, 28, 32n21, 37–41, 48, 50n14, 53, 57, 61n15, 64–65, 68–71, 73–75, 81n2, 82n3, 89–90, 97–98, 104, 123, 141, 158, 168n10, 178, 197, 207–8, 212, 214–15, 218, 238–39, 243, 245
Senancour, Étienne Pivert de, 23
Senoa, August, 178
Seume, Johann Gottfried, 137
Shakespeare, William, x, 8, 17, 78, 169n24, 171n44, 203, 205, 208, 210, 222, 242
Shelley, Mary, 64, 207–8
Shelley, Percy Bysshe, 5, 82n3, 91, 115, 123, 143, 147, 158, 207, 212, 214, 216, 235–36, 238, 246
Sidney, Philip, 65–66
Simmel, Georg, 49n4
Sismondi, Abbé, 161
Skarga, Piotr, 114

Slavici, I., 193
Słowacki, Juliusz, 178, 206, 239, 251
Smith, Adam, 39, 51n21, 53, 69, 150, 214–15
Smollett, Tobias George, 137, 149–50, 168n10, 213, 217
Solger, Karl Wilhelm Ferdinand, 236
Solovyov, Sergey Mikhaylovich, 238
Sonnenfels, Joseph von, 182–84
Sophocles, 203
Southcott, Joanna, 114
Southey, Robert, 11, 53, 75, 78, 82n3, 114, 137, 147, 167, 198, 212–24, 224n3, 224n5, 224n7, 225n8, 225n11, 238, 245, 247
Sowell, Thomas, 96
Spencer, Edmund, 168n12
Spengler, Oswald, 96, 135, 160, 236
Spitteler, Carl, 65
Spranger, Ed, 61n4
Srbik, Heinrich von, 56
Staël, Germaine, Mme de, 9, 16, 27, 29, 53, 56, 58, 90, 97, 115, 157, 160–64, 171n51, 241
Steele, Richard, 32n20, 216–17, 240
Steele, Shelby, 96
Stendhal, 158
Stere, Constantin, 106n9
Sterne, Laurence, 137, 150, 154–55, 158, 171n45, 216–17, 222
Stifter, Adalbert, 29, 70–72, 125, 198, 245
Stolberg, Friedrich Leopold zu, 125
Storm, Theodor, 61n17
Strauss, David, 129n6
Swedenborg, Emanuel, 118, 239, 241
Swift, Jonathan, 150, 204
Széchenyi, István, 11, 40, 247

Taine, Hippolyte-Adolphe, 160
Tasso, Torquato, 24
Taylor, John, 216
Temple, William, 169n24, 204
Thierry, Augustin, 28, 73–74, 115, 238
Thiers, Louis-Adolphe, 79
Thurman, Wallace, 95
Tieck, Ludwig, 115, 154, 208, 218, 239, 251
Tocqueville, Alexis de, 15, 29, 40, 48, 53, 56, 59, 74, 80, 164, 247
Tolkien, J. R. R., 250
Tolstoy, Leo, 61n17, 245
Tönnies, Ferdinand Julius, 49n4
Toomer, Jean, 95
Torgovnick, Marianna, 87

Tracy, Destutt de, 159, 164
Trentowski, Bronislaw, 117
Trollope, Anthony, 245
Turgenyev, Ivan Sergeyevich, 245
Turgot, Anne-Robert-Jacques, 15–16
Tyl, Josef Kajetán, 178

Uhland, Ludwig, 82n3

Vacaresco, Hélène, 188
Valancius, Motiejus, 117
Vega, Lope de, 203, 208
Velitchikovsky, Paissy, 117
Vianu, Tudor, 94
Vico, Giambattista, 74
Vigny, Alfred de, 11, 69, 161, 243
Villemain, Abel, 74
Villeneuve-Bargemont, Alban de, 128n1
Virgil, 203, 210
Vitet, Ludovic, 69, 76–77
Volney, Constantin, Comte de, 91, 106n6, 137, 141, 154, 157
Voltaire, 67, 71, 87, 129n6, 163
Vörösmarty, Mihály, 117, 178, 205–6
Voss, Johann Heinrich, 44

Wackenroder, Wilhelm Heinrich, 240
Wagner, Richard, 205
Washington, Booker T., 95–96, 182
Weber, Karl Julius, 157, 160, 162, 216
Weber, Max, 38, 48, 51n22, 106n4, 150, 176, 180, 248
Welty, Eudora, 106n12
Werner, Zacharias, 163
West, Benjamin, 239
West, Cornel, 96
Wieland, Christoph Martin, 209
Williams, Walter, 96
Winkelmann, Johann Joachim, 163
Wordsworth, William, 5–6, 11, 23, 107n19, 115, 125, 136–37, 147, 150, 155, 158, 168n10, 171n45, 178, 207, 212–13, 235, 247
Wright, Richard, 96

Yearsley, Ann, 216
Yeats, William Butler, 210
Young, Arthur, 151

Zaleski, Jozef Bohdan, 117
Zeletin, C. D., 93